THE TECHNOLOGICAL
TRANSFORMATION
OF JAPAN

THE TECHNOLOGICAL TRANSFORMATION OF JAPAN

From the Seventeenth to
the Twenty-first Century

TESSA MORRIS-SUZUKI

Research School of Pacific and Asian Studies,
Australian National University

CAMBRIDGE
UNIVERSITY PRESS

Published by the Press Syndicate of the University of Cambridge
The Pitt Building, Trumpington Street, Cambridge CB2 1RP, UK
40 West 20th Street, New York, NY 10011-4211, USA
10 Stamford Road, Oakleigh, Melbourne 3166, Australia

© Cambridge University Press 1994
First published 1994

Printed in Hong Kong by Colorcraft

National Library of Australia cataloguing in publication data
Morris-Suzuki, Tessa.
The technological transformation of Japan.
Bibliography.
Includes index.
1. Technological innovations – Japan – History.
2. Technological innovations – Social aspects – Japan.
3. Japan – Social Conditions. 4. Japan – Industries – History. I. Title.
338.00952

Library of Congress cataloguing in publication data
Morris-Suzuki, Tessa.
The technological transformation of Japan: from the seventeenth to
the twenty-first century/Tessa Morris-Suzuki.
Included bibliographical references and index.
1. Technology – Japan – History.
2. Technology – Social aspects – Japan.
3. Technological innovations – Social aspects – Japan. I. Title.
T27.A3M67 1994   94 – 10310
609.52 – dc20   CIP

A catalogue record for this book is available from the British Library.

ISBN 0 521 41463 6 Hardback
ISBN 0 521 42492 5 Paperback

Contents

v

Illustrations

Tables

Acknowledgements

So many people have given help and support to the writing of this book that it would be impossible to name them all. Special thanks are due, however, to Professor Ishii Kanji of Tokyo University, Professor Nakayama Shigeru of Kanagawa University, Professor Fujii Takashi of Niigata University, Professor Yoshioka Hitoshi of Kyûshû University, Mr Suzuki Yukio of the Saga Prefectural Kyûshû Ceramics Museum, and Mr Katsuki Hiroaki of the Ceramics Industrial Research Institute of Sage Prefectural Government.

I am very grateful to my former colleagues at the University of New England, and particularly to Professor Malcolm Falkus, for their encouragement and advice. At the Australian National University, my research has been helped by many colleagues, and my especial thanks go to Professor Gavan McCormack and Professor Mark Elvin. Dr Stephen Large of Cambridge University and Dr Morris Low of Monash University gave invaluable comments on the manuscript, and I am very thankful to Dr Robin Derricourt of Cambridge University Press and Ms Janet Mackenzie for their editorial advice and encouragement.

Mr Shimamoto Shûji of Shôgakukan Publishers and Mr Ogawa Taku of Kodansha International helped me to locate obscure source material and to find illustrations for the book.

The author and publisher would like to thank the following for permission to use illustrations from their copyright material: Kôwa Publishing Company for the pictures reproduced in Figures 2.1, 2.2, 2.3 and 2.4; the Metropolitan Museum of Art, New York, for the cover illustration and Figure 4.1; Iwanami Shoten Publishers for permission to use Figure 4.2, reproduced from *Nihon kindai shisô taikei* (vol. 14, Kagaku to gijutsu, 1989); the United Nations University Press for Figure 4.3; Toshiba Corporation for Figure 5.1; Yûhikaku Publishing Co. for Figure 5.2; the Shitamachi Museum, Ueno for Figure 5.3; Kodansha International for Figures 5.4, 7.3 and 7.4; the editor and publisher of *Bonsai Australia Banzai* (Pluto Press 1991) for Figure 8.1; Gendai Shokan for Figure 8.2; and the National Space Development Agency of Japan (NASDA) for Figure 8.3

Last but not least thanks to Hiroshi and Patrick, for everything else.

Names in this book are given in the normal Japanese order: family name first and given name second, except in quoted references where the Western order is used in the original.

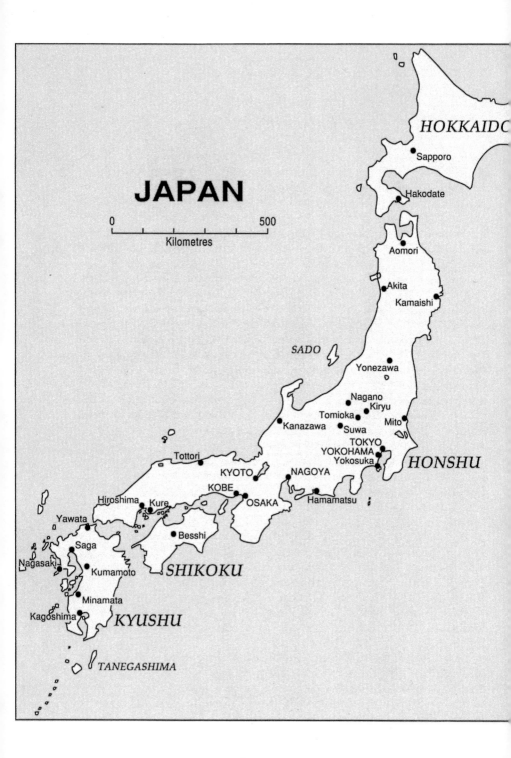

JAPAN

0   500
Kilometres

HOKKAIDO

Sapporo

Hakodate

Aomori

Akita

Kamaishi

SADO

Yonezawa

Nagano
Kiryu
Tomioka
Kanazawa   Suwa   Mito

TOKYO
YOKOHAMA
Yokosuka

Tottori

KYOTO   NAGOYA   *HONSHU*

KOBE

Hiroshima   Kure   OSAKA   Hamamatsu

Yawata

Besshi

Saga   *SHIKOKU*

Nagasaki

Kumamoto

Minamata

Kagoshima   *KYUSHU*

TANEGASHIMA

CHAPTER 1

Introduction

The Japanese Challenge

In the years between 1811 and 1816, the weaving towns of central England experienced a new and (from the factory owners' point of view) alarming form of social unrest. Groups of handloom weavers, whose livelihood was threatened by the introduction of automatic looms, descended upon the factories at night, attacking and smashing the hated looms. The protesters invented for themselves a mythical leader whom they named Ned Ludd. In folk memory, therefore, they became known as the Luddites, and the name itself came to be extended to all uncompromising opponents of technological 'progress'.

In the mid-1980s, scenes very like those of the Luddite riots were re-enacted in the US cities of Detroit and Washington DC as American workers turned their hammers on Japanese cars and television sets. The US machine-smashing, of course, took place in daylight and in the full view of the nation's television cameras. But the emotions which underlay the public drama were essentially the same as those which had fuelled the riots of the British industrial revolution. Like the original Luddites, the US machine-smashers had picked out a tangible symbol of profound economic and social change. Just as the automatic loom was the visible representation of the industrial revolution itself, so, in the late twentieth century, Japanese cars and televisions represented a shift, both in the nature of technology and in the balance of world economic power. It was Japan's ability to master the latest technological advances in certain key areas of technology (such as electronics and the automobile industry) which had stimulated the nation's rapid ascent to the status of industrial superpower[1] and created growing trade surpluses with older industrial regions, including the United States; and it was that shift of economic dynamism which (in the eyes of the new US

1

Luddites) undermined their livelihoods, their skills and their sense of place in the order of things.

The western reaction to Japan's growing technological dominance has not always been one of fear and rejection. In many quarters it has involved curiosity, admiration and efforts at emulation. The curiosity, however, has almost inevitably been tinged with a strong sense of bemusement that this small, overcrowded, resource-poor nation should have become such a force in the world industrial system. Until the last quarter of the twentieth century it may still have been possible to see Japan's technological strength simply as the result of successful foreign borrowing, and to dismiss the Japanese capacity for original research. From the late 1970s, however, such complacency has become increasingly untenable. By the end of the 1980s Japanese companies were leading the race to produce superconducting microchips and to commercialise high-definition television. Japan's research spending now exceeds that of all other OECD countries except the United States,[2] and Japan was also the largest exporter of technology to the newly industrialising East Asian countries, which are in turn among the most rapidly growing economies in the world.[3]

But the 'Japanese challenge' is not just an economic one; it is also a challenge to our intellectual preconceptions about the nature and causes of technological change. When historians have tried to devise explanations for long-term technological dynamism, they have often focused on the achievements of Western Europe and North America. The division of Europe into small competing nation-states, the rise of a powerful bourgeoisie, the overthrow of the stultifying power of the church, the liberating intellectual climate of the Enlightenment: all these, it has been argued, provided the impetus for the rise of modern western science and technology. Once begun, the wave of progress spread across the Atlantic to the United States, where the unrestricted social space of a pioneer society enabled it to extend to new and unimagined frontiers. In this reading of history, Japan's experience is a mere postscript to a European (or, at most, a North Atlantic) narrative. As Joel Mokyr puts it in his celebration of the triumph of modern technology,

> Nations such as Korea and Japan clearly are capable of creating new technologies, and not just copying them. But the inventions that are being made today in research laboratories in the Far East are quintessentially western in nature. Although some of these societies have preserved much of their own culture and traditions, in the field of technology the Western heritage is unchallenged.[4]

Recently there have been encouraging signs of a more global approach to the history of technology.[5] The development of this approach, though, is hampered by the scarcity of comprehensive English-language studies on the technological history of Japan (and indeed of other recent non-western industrialisers). Without an understanding of the complex processes of technological change in these societies, many of the most intriguing questions in the study of technology—questions about the impact of culture and social structure on technology, and about the determining force of technology in social development—will remain difficult, if not impossible, to answer.

Explaining the Challenge: Culture, Institutions and History

If it is important to include Japan in the study of technological history, it is just as important to include history in the study of Japan's contemporary technological might. Many writers, it is true, have explained Japan's receptivity to new technologies in terms of cultural tradition. Japan is said to be a nation which lacks that adventurous individualism, that mistrust of authority, fostered in Europe by the puritan revolution. Japan's philosophical and religious heritage—above all Confucianism—is believed to have prized the subordination of self to the interests of the group, and could readily be used to evoke loyalty both to the corporation and to the nation. Whether these cultural characteristics are interpreted in a positive light—as promoting diligence and social harmony—or more critically—as creating a nation of uncomplaining drudges—is very much a matter of personal choice. In either case, however, culture is seen as a source of technological strength. The Confucian ethos, it is argued, may discourage individual scientific genius, but it creates a loyal workforce who are swift to acquire the skills needed for international competitiveness.[6]

Others have pointed to the role of the traditional Japanese household in Japan's industrial and technological development. The family hierarchy is seen as the wellspring of Japanese social values.[7] By drawing on the enduring ideals of family membership, it is claimed, Japanese companies succeeded in creating a form of management which secured the lifelong commitment of employers, nurtured their skills, and enabled them to adapt to the constantly changing technological demands of the modern world.[8] In this version of events, though, 'culture' tends to be presented as something created in remote antiquity, and somehow handed down intact to the present day. The sense of history as an ongoing process of human conflicts and human choices is often lost, and therefore theories which seek to explain and elucidate serve, in the end, only to intensify the aura of mystery surrounding Japanese society.

A second set of analyses concentrates less on abstract notions of culture than on more clearly defined institutional peculiarities: particularly on the role of the state as prime mover in Japan's technological development. Here the historical focus is sharper. A number of scholars, for example, have looked in detail at the early years of Japan's industrialisation, arguing that it was the Meiji government which played the leading part in selecting and importing foreign technology.[9] Chalmers Johnson's famous study of the Ministry of International Trade and Industry (MITI) has documented the guiding role of the state in industrial development from the Second World War,[10] and Daniel Okimoto has taken up the same story from the early 1970s onwards. Okimoto's argument is that the state does not control Japan's technological development through a rigid system of planning, but rather provides a set of long-term industrial goals, encouraging Japanese industry to meet those goals by delicate adjustment of the market mechanism. He likens the process to the skill of Japanese gardeners, who 'bend trees into all sorts of exquisite shapes, and produce a work of art that is consciously designed but still completely natural'.[11]

Efforts to unravel the causes of the Japanese challenge, of course, seldom rely on a single all-encompassing explanation. The more common approach is to emphasise some combination of cultural and institutional factors, often encompassing the pre-industrial development of the Japanese market economy, high standards of education, the skill and adaptability of Japanese technicians, the high levels of savings, and the cohesive strength of Japan's business groups (*keiretsu*), as well as the legacy of cultural tradition and the power of the state.[12] This list of factors certainly goes some way towards explaining the speed of Japan's technological development since the late nineteenth century—and yet it is hard to escape the feeling that something is missing. For one thing, most of the institutional studies concentrate on a small segment of Japanese history: the first decades of industrialisation, for example, or the postwar 'economic miracle'.[13] This makes it difficult to gain an overall vision of the dynamics of Japan's modern technological development, and of the continuities and contrasts between one historical period and another. Emphasis on the role of central government and big business groupings also tends to obscure other parts of the story which may be less readily visible but are just as important.

Imitation and Innovation

In the pages which follow we shall take an approach to Japan's technological history which is somewhat different from the perspectives outlined earlier. This approach is based on three main themes. The first concerns the relationship between *imitation and innovation*. Traditional stereotype depicts the Japanese as a nation of imitators, who have only recently, as they reached economic maturity, begun to participate in the process of creative invention. Even those who are keen to emphasise the inventiveness of contemporary Japanese technology often seem to accept that this creativity is a new phenomenon. But a close look at the processes of technological diffusion in Japan makes it clear that 'invention' and 'imitation' are not radically opposed alternatives, but are really two ends of a spectrum along which outside inspiration and innate creativity are combined in many complex ways. Japan's ability to react swiftly and constructively to the nineteenth-century challenge of western technology was based on a heritage of technological innovation within Japan. The two centuries leading up to Japan's opening to the west had been a period of quite rapid development and diffusion of techniques within Japan's main craft industries. Most importantly, many Japanese people—commoner and intellectual elite alike—had discovered the process of invention itself. In other words, they had come to recognise the importance of new productive techniques in enhancing their own or their region's wealth and power.

The enthusiastic adoption of western technology from the mid-nineteenth century onwards did not diminish the importance of indigenous innovation. Importing foreign ideas was seldom a simple matter of unreflective copying, but almost always involved a degree of selection and adaptation. Western techniques could rarely be put to work in Japan without some modification to suit local raw materials and local skills. This process of modification, however, forced Japanese companies to develop their own research capacity, and this in turn created the basis for more fundamental adaptations to imported ideas. But technological change in modern Japan has not only been a process of refining borrowed technologies: it has also involved the application of science to existing indigenous techniques in industries like silk weaving, ceramics and brewing. Here too the foreign and the local, imitation and invention, have worked together to create the distinctive pattern of Japan's modern technological system.

Technology and the Japanese Periphery

In exploring Japan's discovery of innovation, therefore, the chapters which follow will try to encompass both the *centre*—that is, the large-scale, sophisticated technological projects of central government and major corporations—and the technological role of the *periphery*—the activities of small firms and local communities. They will examine the way in which the social institutions both of centre and of periphery supported the process of rapid technological change in modern Japan, and will also consider the consequences of that technological change for Japan's social development itself. In many ways, as we shall see, it is from the periphery that the most intriguing questions arise, for it is here that conventional emphases on government guidance and social harmony have least explanatory power.

Consider an example. When you travel from the sprawling commercial centre of Fukuoka in Kyûshû to the port city of Sasebo, the first part of your journey takes you through a stretch of flat, undistinguished farmland dotted here and there with roadworks and cement factories. After passing the small city of Saga, the line begins to climb into the mountains and the landscape changes. The villages here have a character of their own. They are densely clustered at the bottom of narrow valleys, and are not set in that patchwork of rice fields which surrounds most rural settlements in Japan. Still more strikingly, in each village a few red-brick smokestacks rise above the familiar pattern of low grey-tiled roofs.

If you leave the train at the small town of Arita, the reason for all this soon becomes apparent. The region is one of the major centres of Japanese ceramics production. In Arita itself, the importance of the potteries can hardly be missed. Every street is lined with shopfronts displaying the blue-and-white crockery and the huge, gilded urns for which the town is famous. Even the bridges spanning the narrow river which winds through the centre of town are decorated with grotesquely ornate ceramic jars, while the gravel in the river itself is coloured by the fragments of countless pieces of porcelain discarded over the past three hundred years.

What is interesting about the Arita district is not just that its potteries have survived the transition from pre-industrial to industrial society, but that they have continued to play their part in the technological changes of the late twentieth century. The cluster of rather unprepossessing buildings just down the hill from Arita's porcelain museum, for example, houses a prefectural research laboratory, where potters experimenting with new variants of traditional designs work side by side with scientists engaged in analysing the intricate structures of new ceramic materials. A number of local potteries have also moved into the production of fine ceramics, developing new materials and moulding techniques for complex industrial components—from filters for bioreactors to blades for rotary turbines.

Arita may be unusual in the length and continuity of its industrial history, but in other respects it is only one of thousands of little agglomerations of local manufacturing which exist all over Japan.

When we look at places like these, the familiar explanations for Japan's technological strength seem to leave much unexplained. The enterprises here are mostly small, and offer neither lifetime employment nor sophisticated training programs. Local firms have from time to time benefited from central government grants or commissions, but in general their technological development has received little imprint from the remote, and often mistrusted, guiding hand of the Tokyo bureaucracy. Concepts of social harmony and group consciousness, too, seem out of place, for the history of technological change in a small community like Arita is fraught with instances of friction, rivalry and power play between local interest groups.

The development of small regional factories forms a crucial part of Japan's modern technological history. It is a well-known fact that Japan, even today, is a country of small firms: about 58 per cent of Japan's factory workers are employed by enterprises with less than one hundred workers, and 46 per cent by enterprises with less than fifty.[14] But the significance of these small-scale enterprises is more than just numerical. As David Friedman emphasises in his study of the machine tool industry, they create a flexible network of suppliers and customers which, in a very real sense, underpins the entire edifice of contemporary high-tech Japan.[15]

The most important thing from our point of view, though, is that small regional factories are the parts of industry which are furthest removed from the centres of leading-edge technological research and least susceptible to the influence of new ideas. Looking at the diffusion of technological know-how to these remote and unglamorous corners of the economy, therefore, can tell us things about the technological system which we would never learn by focusing purely on the achievements of giant corporations and major government-funded laboratories.

Social Networks and Innovation

Thirdly, and most importantly, the book will try to analyse the relationship between centre and periphery in Japan's technological history by outlining the development of Japan's *social network of innovation*: that is, the network of communications which linked research and production centres in Japanese society. When we study Japan's technological development, it becomes clear that the social institutions which supported that development have a rather distinctive structure. Technological research and development in Japan tends to be dispersed amongst a large number of small institutions which are linked together in a way that allows information to flow easily between one institution and another. This network structure, which is evident at least from the late Meiji period onwards, can be contrasted with the institutional structure of research and development in other industrialised countries like Britain and France, where technological know-how has been more strongly concentrated in a few elite institutions. One of the main arguments of this book is that the structure of Japan's social network of innovation has helped Japan to become a world leader in certain branches of technological development, but has proved poorly adapted to other types of technological advance.

The historian of technology Iida Kenichi likens technological history to the relationship between rivers and the sea. The individual histories of technology in different countries are like rivers, shaped by local geography, which flow into the ocean of global technological knowledge. The rising tide of the sea as it pushes its waters back into the mouth of a river is like the inflow of technology from the international community into the national technological system.[16]

If we borrow this analogy, then the differing social networks of technology in different countries are like variations in the geology of river mouths. The same tide can have drastically different effects, depending upon whether the river estuary is broad or narrow, sandy or rocky, twisted or straight. Similarly the institutional structures of the social network of innovation influence both the speed and the nature of a country's reception of technological ideas. A particularly important role is played by the structure of the research system, which often acts as a filter for the entry of new technological ideas. The way in which private and government research institutions import technological ideas depends not only on their structure and their international connections (whether, for example, they are particularly closely linked to counterparts in certain foreign countries) but also their strategy and ideology: on the way in which their members perceive the international technological environment and interpret their own mission. By looking closely at the structure and the internal politics of the Japanese research system, then, we can (to a degree) understand why some technologies were more readily absorbed and applied than others. The same filtering process is repeated as ideas are transferred from the research system to production. The structure of the social network of innovation helps to determine which ideas are most readily communicated, and where they are communicated to.

Focus on the evolving structure of the social network of innovation helps to emphasise the importance of historical continuities. The argument here is that Japan's social network of innovation is not the product of some immutable cultural essence, but rather of ongoing processes of conflict and compromise in modern Japanese development. Each generation, in dealing with new technological challenges, made use of an existing repertoire of ideas and social institutions. These ideas and institutions did not rigidly determine the way in which new challenges were confronted, but provided the framework within which various social groups struggled to promote their own visions of the future. A particularly important force, as we shall see, has been the continuing interplay of tensions between periphery and centre in Japanese history. Again and again in the course of Japanese industrialisation small firms and little local interest groups have banded together, creating institutions which, they hope, will harness the might of modern technology to their own particular objectives. And again and again the central authorities have attempted to draw together and standardise these diverse initiatives, imposing on them an official, nation-centred vision of development.

The first part of this book looks at the historical background to Japan's modern technological development, and explores the surprising wealth of pre-industrial inventiveness which laid the foundations for the development of Japan's social network of innovation in the industrial age. Part II takes up the story from the beginning of Japanese industrialisation in the Meiji Era (1868–1912), and offers a reinterpretation of Japan's rapid adoption of industrial technology during that turning-point in the nation's history. The period from the First World War to the end of the Pacific War has been relatively neglected by English-language studies of Japanese technology but, as we shall see in Chapters 5 and 6, this period is crucial to an understanding of Japan's modern technological might. On the one hand, this was the time when large Japanese companies began to create their own research capacity, and to develop their own rather distinctive methods of dealing with the challenges of mass production. On the other, the 1930s and early 1940s were a period when the government experimented with new ways to force the pace of technological change, in the process developing some ideas which were to reappear in Japan's postwar technology policy.

The processes of industrial development in the late nineteenth and early twentieth centuries created an innovation network which has helped to sustain Japan's remarkably rapid technological transformation in the past four decades. The final section of the book shows how the institutional framework not only encouraged the rapid spread of new technologies but also influenced the nature and directions of technological change in Japan in the late twentieth century. This issue of the social shaping of Japanese technology becomes particularly important when we look at the developments of the past twenty years. Japanese innovations in areas like semiconductors and robotics are now influencing industrialised and industrialising countries throughout the world. The social forces which fashion these technologies therefore affect not only Japan's own future but the future of other societies as well. As Japan becomes a technological leader, where is it going to lead us? It is to this question that we shall turn in the final chapter.

No study of this size could hope to cover every aspect of Japan's modern technological development. In writing this book, indeed, I have combated repeated temptations to pursue all sorts of intriguing alleyways through the history of Japanese technology: narratives of considerable intrinsic interest and importance, but whose inclusion would have made the book unmanageably vast. What I have tried to do is to include examples of technological change which help to clarify the relationship between society and technology in modern Japanese history. The emphasis is largely on industrial rather than agricultural technology, not because agriculture is unimportant, but because the development of Japanese agricultural techniques has already been the subject of some excellent English-language studies.[17] By providing an overview of technological change in Japan from the seventeenth century onwards, I hope that this book may provide a fresh historical dimension to the understanding of Japan's contemporary industrial power, and may also offer some new thoughts on the broader question of the relationship between technology and society in the modern world.

PART I

The Tokugawa Heritage, 1603–1867

CHAPTER 2

Society and Technology in Tokugawa Japan

When Japan opened its doors to western influence in the mid-nineteenth century, the word 'technology' was a relatively new intruder into the English language.[1] Popularised in the 1820s, 'technology' was commonly understood as being 'the science of industrial and mechanical arts'. It was identified, in other words, with such emblems of western industrial might as the steam engine, the blast furnace and the spinning mule.

It is not surprising, then, that few western visitors were impressed by Japan's domestically developed technologies. On the eve of the Meiji Restoration of 1868, Japan was a country of dirt roads and slow-moving ox-carts, where the only indigenous pieces of power-driven machinery were occasional waterwheels used for tasks like irrigation, pounding rice and crushing ore. The houses were low and wooden, often with roughly thatched roofs, and most of the population eked out a living working long hours in the rice fields. Hunger was common and famine not unknown. The official guidebook to the Paris International Exhibition of 1878, in which Japan was a participant, noted that the country was blessed with natural riches, but went on to observe:

> Unfortunately, for the Japanese to exploit their potential wealth themselves, they would need accumulated capital, which they lack, and also a sustained energy and enthusiasm for work, which they scarcely display at all.[2]

In the past century and a half, however, we have come to interpret the term 'technology' in a much broader way, as incorporating all those ideas and practices which people use to maintain and enrich their material existence. This rethinking of the meaning of technology has encouraged a reassessment of Japan's early technological history, and a recognition that Japan's twentieth-century technological might has roots which go back to pre-industrial times, and particularly to the

13

Tokugawa period (1603-1868). One of Japan's contemporary technological leaders even argues that

> in present day Japan, whether we think of the production of LSI microchips
> or whatever, we can say that the same production system and the same
> workplace atmosphere was already fully developed in the Tokugawa period.[3]

This may be pushing the point too far. There can be little doubt,
though, that industrial Japan was heir to a technological tradition
which in some areas of production had reached high levels of
sophistication. Unlike the Western European tradition, however, it was
one based upon invisible technology, carried in the heads of human
workers rather than embodied in the visible might of large, labour-
saving machines. 'Tradition' in this context is not meant to imply
something handed down intact from great antiquity. On the contrary,
many of the techniques used by craftspeople and farmers in the mid-
nineteenth century were relatively recent innovations. During the two
and a half centuries of Tokugawa rule more productive seed varieties
had been developed and better methods of planting and fertilising
crops introduced. Silk and cotton production had expanded, and new
forms of spinning and weaving equipment had been developed.
Japanese artisans had adapted a knowledge of mechanics (derived from
imported western clocks) to create complex clockwork automata
(*karakuri ningyō*). In handicraft industries such as lacquer-working,
pottery and paper-making, too, there had been an extraordinary variety
of regional experimentation and innovation. Most of the traditional
local crafts whose products fill the souvenir shops of Japan today,
indeed, have their origins in the Tokugawa age.

This restless technological activity involved little in the way of
revolutionary new ideas. To use Joel Mokyr's term, there were few
'macroinventions'.[4] But the steady flow of 'microinventions'—small-
scale improvements in existing techniques—points to a crucially
important feature of Tokugawa society: a growing recognition of the
value of *innovation* itself. The search for new techniques, which was
sometimes carried out in a systematic and experimental way, implies an
attitude to inventiveness which was fundamental to Japan's later ability
to absorb and adapt imported industrial technology.

There was, of course, nothing natural or spontaneous in this desire to
improve methods of production. In agrarian societies where humans
live on the margins of subsistence, it is much more common to
minimise risk by following tried and tested methods as closely as
possible. What was there, then, in Tokugawa society that encouraged
some farmers, artisans and merchants to look beyond established
custom to the development of new products and techniques? What was

the impetus for the microinventions which flourished in silk production and other crafts? How, in short, did Tokugawa society discover innovation?

Foreign Influences in a 'Closed Country'

There are four aspects of the Tokugawa system which seem to offer answers to this question. The first relates to the foreign influences, from Europe as well as from the Asian mainland, to which Japan was exposed before the beginning of the Tokugawa period. Secondly, the separation of the ruling warrior class from the land created a crucial economic role for the merchants, and at the same time produced a stratum of educated, underemployed samurai, some of whom turned their energies to scientific and technological matters. Thirdly (and most importantly) the peculiar political structure of Tokugawa Japan stimulated economic competition between different parts of the country, so promoting the development of new products and techniques. Lastly, peace and social order produced a favourable environment for the growth of markets and so for the nationwide flow, not only of goods, but also of technical know-how. Together, these developments opened up new channels for the communication of technological knowledge, and slowly but surely eroded the natural conservatism of a society where secrecy was the principal means of converting that knowledge into wealth.

At the beginning of the seventeenth century, when the Tokugawa family gained control of Japan after decades of civil warfare, relations between Japan and the outside world were at a critical turning-point. European missionaries, who had first arrived in Japan some sixty years earlier, were vying for the ransom of Japanese souls, and their political manoeuvrings threatened to undermine the stability of the state. The new weapons of war which the westerners had introduced into Japan were also a disturbing element in the delicate balance of domestic political power. Worse still, the Portuguese and Dutch treasure ships, which arrived in Japanese ports laden with Chinese silks, sailed away laden with Japanese gold and silver, gradually draining the country of its limited supplies of precious metals.[5]

In response to these problems, the third Tokugawa Shogun— Tokugawa Iemitsu—expelled all westerners apart from the Dutch, and imposed a policy of strict controls on Japan's trade and communications with the outside world: controls which were to be maintained until the arrival of Commodore Perry's US fleet more than two hundred years later. Because this has become known as the 'closed country' (*sakoku*) policy, it is easy to imagine that Tokugawa Japan was an utterly isolated and inward-looking country, but such an assumption is highly misleading.

In the first place we need to remember that, for almost a hundred years before the introduction of the 'closed country' policy in 1639, Japan had been exposed to a greater variety of foreign influences than ever before in its history. From the 1540s onwards, Japan had been visited first by Portuguese and Spanish missionaries, and later also by Dutch and British merchants. Richard Storry may have been correct when he observed that

> the European race, the Portuguese, with whom the Japanese had the longest contact up to 1639 was perhaps the one least likely to pass on to them the revolutionary discoveries in astronomy and natural science, and indeed the experimental method generally, that laid the foundations of modern western technology.[6]

Nevertheless, the arrival of the Europeans certainly opened a window to some important new technological ideas.

For one thing, the very shock of exposure to unfamiliar cultures stimulated a questioning of the familiar and the traditional within Japanese society itself. In more practical terms, the western intruders also brought with them a knowledge of clocks, telescopes, glass-working, velvet, and sugar-sweetened cakes, as well as of those staples of modern European culture, tobacco and firearms.[7] Europe may also have had an influence on mining and metal-refining techniques, which experienced rapid development in Japan around this time. One of the new techniques, a method for separating the silver which was often combined in copper ores, was known as *namban buki*: *namban* or 'southern barbarians' being the common contemporary Japanese term for Europeans. According to the family history of the famous mining house of Sumitomo, their ancestors learnt this technique from European traders in the early seventeenth century, though there is evidence that other Japanese miners had acquired the same piece of know-how from China in the previous century.[8]

During the long years of relative seclusion from the west the imported knowledge remained, as it were, quietly fermenting away within the confines of craft workshops all over Japan. Even the knowledge of guns, whose use was controlled by the Shogunate, was not lost. For many decades it was contained and preserved in government-controlled armories in the port of Sakai and the mountain village of Kunitomo. Gradually, however, the secrets of firearms spread to other regions, and by the early nineteenth century gunsmiths in many parts of the country were producing slightly modified replicas of seventeenth-century European matchlocks.[9] In other fields of invention, as we shall see, Tokugawa Japan's interaction with western ideas was to be much more creative.

From the point of view of Tokugawa technology, however, Japan's initial contacts with Europe were probably less important than contacts with its Asian neighbours, China and Korea. During the 1590s Japan's ruler Toyotomi Hideyoshi had launched the country's first attempt at foreign conquest, dispatching his armies on an abortive mission to invade the Korean peninsula. In terms of human suffering, and of the legacy of bitterness which it bequeathed to Japan's relations with Korea, the campaign was a disaster. Japan's culture, however, was undoubtedly enriched by this violent encounter with continental Asia. Like the Mongol armies who harried China's northern borders during the Song Dynasty, Japan's warriors plundered, not only material goods, but also knowledge. Military leaders competed with one another to bring home shiploads of Korean craftworkers, doctors and Confucian scholars.[10]

Korea was a gateway to the knowledge of the Chinese empire, the most significant of all Japan's sources of foreign technology. Despite the 'closed country' policy, the first century of Tokugawa rule was in fact a period of enthusiastic borrowing of Chinese ideas and culture. Although China's influence on the intelligentsia may have declined in later years, imported knowledge continued to percolate through Japanese society, gradually undergoing a process of transformation and assimilation as it did so.

The Chinese publications imported into Japan in the early Tokugawa period included not only books of Confucian philosophy, but also a wide range of scientific and technical works. Chinese medical and mathematical texts were in particular demand, and the latter, together with the newly introduced Chinese abacus (*soroban*) encouraged great advances in mathematical knowledge amongst the expanding Japanese merchant class.[11] Many of these books were published in *kanbun*, that is, a modified form of the original Chinese, and this awkward literary style meant that they could be read only by the highly educated. Gradually, however, Chinese books began to be translated into more colloquial styles, or to be quoted by other Japanese writers, so allowing their content to reach a wider audience. One of the most influential was the *Tian Gong Kai Wu* or *Development of the Works of Nature*, a richly illustrated encyclopedia of Chinese agricultural, mining and manufacturing techniques composed in the late Ming Dynasty. This study was published in two separate Japanese editions during the Tokugawa period, and its influence on Japanese writers is evident from the enthusiasm with which they borrowed and improved on its illustrations.[12]

Knowledge of Chinese technology did not come only from the written word. In the period immediately preceding the imposition of the 'closed country' policy, some important techniques were transferred directly from the Asian mainland by craftworkers who visited or settled in Japan. The treadle-operated tall loom (*takabata*), for example, which enabled weavers to create complex patterns in the fabric, was brought to the port city of Sakai by Chinese silkworkers in the late sixteenth century. From there it spread to the Nishijin district of Kyoto, where it led to great advances in the manufacture of silk cloth, and stimulated the development of even more sophisticated draw looms (*karabikibata*) in the second half of the Tokugawa period.[13] Even when tight restrictions were imposed on foreign commerce, and all westerners but the Dutch were expelled from Japan, Chinese merchants were allowed to maintain a trading post at Nagasaki, and Chinese ships continued to sail, not only between Japan and China itself, but also between Japan and Southeast Asian kingdoms including Siam, Tongking and Cochinchina. In the late seventeenth century Nagasaki had more than a thousand Chinese residents, their presence providing a small but important channel for the inflow of scientific and technological ideas.[14]

There is a curious historical symmetry in the fact that, at the same time but on the other side of the world, Western Europe was also imitating and adapting the same pieces of borrowed Chinese technology. The wave of commercial expansion which had brought European merchants to the doors of Japan had also created a European market hungry for the products of the Chinese empire. The political chaos surrounding the collapse of the Ming Dynasty, however, disrupted trade between China and Europe for much of the seventeenth century. European inventors, like Japanese artisans, therefore began to experiment with techniques which might replicate the splendours of Chinese craft products like the porcelains of Jingdezhen. By the end of the century, both Japan and Europe had developed their own imitations of Chinese glazes, and both were shamelessly exporting ceramics marked with phony Chinese inscriptions.[15] Transplanted to the different environments of Europe and Japan, however, the ideas pilfered from the Chinese seedbed of technology germinated and developed in distinctly different ways.

Heredity and Hierarchy

In the European context, technological change in the seventeenth and eighteenth centuries was promoted by the opening of markets overseas and by increasing social mobility at home. In Japan, the social forces behind technological change, and therefore also the trajectory of technological development itself, were very different. Foreign trade, as we have seen, was tightly restricted, and even domestic commerce faced considerable impediments. Japan was divided into a mosaic of small fiefdoms, with the Shogun himself exercising direct control over the wealthiest and most strategically important parts of the country. (The Emperors, who were the theoretical rulers of Japan, were relegated to a purely ceremonial role, which in practice consisted of performing a few traditional rituals, bestowing titles on the nobility and living a life of rather elegant idleness in the imperial city of Kyoto.) As a result, the transport of goods was hampered by repeated crossings of political boundaries, often accompanied by the levying of tolls and duties.

Social status was, at least in theory, hereditary and immutable. Society was divided into distinct strata: samurai warriors (*shi*), peasants (*nô*), artisans (*kô*) and merchants (*shô*). The merchants, who were regarded as speculators rather than producers, were deliberately placed at the bottom of the pile, superior only to the outcastes who were excluded from full membership of society altogether. The Tokugawa passion for hierarchy was duplicated within the major social classes. There were, for example, numerous different grades of warrior (their titles varying from one part of the country to another), each with their own appropriate level of income, mode of dress and style of housing. Repeated sumptuary laws were introduced to reinforce the visible distinctions of status, and by the eighteenth century, even hairstyles had developed into a multiplicity of forms, with each style indicating a particular social rank or profession.[16]

In this hierarchical world, the main channel for the transmission of technological knowledge was the family. Farming, which occupied the great majority of the Japanese population, was a family activity, carried out on a small plot of land which was generally passed on intact from one generation to the next. Success in farming depended upon experience and family traditions accumulated by previous generations and, where possible, kept secret from strangers.

The role of the family in Japanese technology extended far beyond the confines of the village. Even scientific knowledge tended, at least until the early Tokugawa period, to be the preserve of a few scholarly families who transmitted their 'house learning' from father to son.[17] The patriarchal family structure, incidentally, restricted the access of women to technology. Daughters, though important members of the household as an economic unit, were potential 'spies in the camp', liable to transfer precious knowledge to potential competitors when they married into another family. It made little sense, therefore, to lavish care on their training, and in some cases it was necessary to conceal from them the technological secrets which would be passed on to the male heir alone.

In the expanding towns, craft skills like carpentry, lacquer-working and lantern-making were transmitted, not only through the family, but also through the simulated family ties of the apprenticeship system. This operated in Japan very much as it did in many other pre-industrial societies, including those of Western Europe. Boys in their early teens would be apprenticed to a master craftsman, usually for a period of ten years. During those years the apprentice lived in the master's household, obeyed his instructions and was expected, not only to learn the secrets of the craft, but also to fetch water, prepare meals, and generally make himself useful about the house.[18]

Apprenticeships in Tokugawa Japan, as in mediaeval Europe, were commonly supervised by craft guilds who jealously protected their members' privileges, often refusing membership to 'strangers' from other towns.[19] In this sense, the existence of guilds was a powerful barrier to the diffusion of skills. On the other hand, though, the requirement of many guilds that young artisans should undertake a period of travel, before settling down as master craftsmen in their own right, may have stimulated the exchange of ideas between different parts of the country.[20]

Within the apparently rigid structures of Tokugawa society, however, important forces of change were at work. The great irony of Tokugawa history, indeed, was that a system designed to ensure unending political stability ultimately promoted social, economic and political change.

Soroban and Sword

Consider, for example, the consequences of the strict status divisions of Tokugawa society, which removed the warrior class from agricultural society and encouraged them to move into castle towns, where they lived divorced from productive labour and sustained largely by heavy rice-taxes imposed on the farmers. This deliberate separation of producers from consumers had an unintended but predictable consequence: the rise of the merchant class. However much Confucian traditionalists might scorn the role of the merchant, the reality was that Japan's rulers could not live by rice alone, but needed middlemen to convert their rice-taxes, first into gold or silver, and then into all the other necessities of survival. Great urban merchant families like the houses of Mitsui and the Ono were soon engaged both in commercial transactions and in the production of commodities like soy sauce and saké (rice wine). As their businesses grew, so did their managerial and accounting skills. A working knowledge of arithmetic (including the use of the *soroban* or Japanese abacus) came to be a necessary part of a merchant's education, and double-entry book-keeping became established practice in larger firms.[21]

By the eighteenth century, the demands of the urban population—both samurai and commoner—were transforming the economy of rural Japan. In villages close to the major cities, farmers were turning their attention to the production of cash crops like silk, cotton and indigo or, in the slack seasons, to the making of handicrafts for sale on the urban market. These little family-based rural enterprises came to be organised by a new breed of merchant, often drawn from the ranks of the peasantry itself. Much of the silk cloth of the late Tokugawa period, for example, was made, not in the workshops of urban artisans, but in farmhouses where peasants supplemented their meagre earnings by weaving fabrics with machinery and materials supplied by local wholesale merchants (*tonya*).

The machines on which they wove their silk were, at least in the more advanced areas, likely to be the tall looms first introduced to Japan at the beginning of the Tokugawa period, and this is significant because it reflects the impact of rural industry on the spread of technology. Until the first half of the eighteenth century, knowledge of the tall looms had been a secret jealously guarded by a few urban weavers' guilds: above all by the powerful weaving guilds of Nishijin, the silkmaking district of the imperial capital Kyoto. During the eighteenth century, however, a few Kyoto weavers transplanted their knowledge to newly emerging textile centres in eastern Japan, such as the small town of Kiryû. Once it had escaped the bounds of the urban guild system, the new knowledge travelled quickly. Local records from Kiryû describe how use of the new looms spread from one village to the next, little by little displacing the simpler and slower backstrap loom (*izaribata*) (see Figure 2.1).[22]

In other crafts like cotton-weaving, lacquer-working and paper-making, too, rural production, free from the constraints of the guilds, encouraged the diffusion of technology and skills. Rural putting-out merchants thus became one part of the social network through which ideas were communicated between small family workshops. At the same time, the power of the urban guilds themselves was gradually eroded. Attempts to restrict membership meant that the master craftsmen became increasingly a privileged elite, some of whose 'apprentices' would remain with them for life as wage workers.[23]

These rural developments had a further, crucially important effect: they led to the emergence of a well-to-do class of farmer, often with a substantial interest in craft industry, who had both the time and the capital to try out new techniques. A classic example is the case of wealthy silkfarming families like the Tajimas from Shimamura in

Backstrap loom
(izaribata), c. 1695

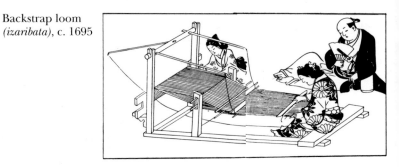

Tall loom
(takabata)

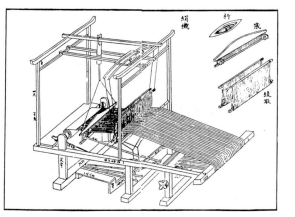

Draw loom
(karabikibata)
c. 1770

Figure 2.1 Weaving looms
Source: Kikuchi, T., Zufu Edo jidai no gijutsu, vol. 2, pp. 404, 409 and 415

modern Gumma Prefecture, who maintained meticulous records of their experiments in cross-breeding silkworms, as well as keeping a collection of samples of cocoons from each hybrid variety which they raised.[24]

Science and the Samurai

On the other side of the equation, separation from the land also had profound implications for the samurai themselves. Because they had neither estates to run nor (under *Pax Tokugawa*) battles to fight, the samurai became little more than a class of bureaucrats, collecting taxes, maintaining law and order, and assisting in the administration of their domains. The number of samurai, however, always exceeded the number of official posts to be filled, and, since the best posts tended to go to those of high rank, many more lowly members of the warrior class found that they had little hope of advancement within their own domains. One outlet for the energies of these well-educated but underemployed samurai was the pursuit of learning. Many set themselves up as independent scholars, often concentrating upon the study and teaching of aspects of Confucian philosophy. During the eighteenth century, however, a growing number turned their attention to scientific studies, including the acquisition of those fragments of western learning which filtered into Japan through the Dutch trading post on Deshima.

Paradoxically, indeed, Japan's hierarchical and class-bound administrative system may have served, in some ways, to encourage the spread of new ideas. In China, the existence of a single, meritocratic bureaucracy meant that the most able members of the social elite were constantly being drawn into the service of the state; in Japan, by contrast, gifted but low-ranking samurai often found themselves on the periphery of the political establishment, and so free (within well-defined limits) to pursue ideas which diverged from Tokugawa orthodoxy. While China's elite was unified, Japan's tended to be fragmented, characterised by the continual appearance and disappearance of little groups surrounding some particularly respected teacher.[25] The unusual and ambivalent status of the lower-ranking samurai, in other words, created a group of people who had the leisure to pursue new ideas, and in some cases had the knowledge and incentive to apply these ideas to practical production.

If we wanted to choose a single individual whose life exposed, in the most colourful way possible, the effects of the Tokugawa system on a poor but ambitious samurai, we could hardly do better than consider the story of Hiraga Gennai (1728–80): playwright, satirist, scientist, inventor and monumental egotist. Hiraga was certainly not a typical eighteenth-century intellectual, but his biography is an intriguing illustration of the forces which moulded Tokugawa innovation, and his ideas—in some ways far ahead of their time—indicate intellectual currents which were to become increasingly important as the era drew to its close.

Hiraga's career began conventionally enough. He was born into a low-ranking samurai household in the Domain of Takamatsu and was trained in *honzôgaku*—the science of natural history (focusing in particular on medicinal plants), which, in Japan, was strongly influenced by Chinese traditions. While in his twenties, however, Hiraga was sent to study at that source of all foreign knowledge, Nagasaki, and from then on his destiny began to diverge from the predictable career path of the minor domain official.[26]

By 1752, when Hiraga first visited Nagasaki, the revolutionary stirrings of European scientific thought and economic power were beginning to raise a faint echo even in remote Japan. The eighth Tokugawa Shogun, Yoshimune (who ruled from 1716 to 1745), although as suspicious of the Europeans as any of his predecessors, recognised that the Dutchmen who came to conduct trade in Deshima possessed formidable skills of navigation and an extraordinary ability to predict the position of the stars in the sky. Yoshimune, who had an enquiring mind and an interest in the practical sciences, began to encourage the study of European astronomy, cartography, medicine and military science, and even ordered two of his samurai retainers to study Dutch so that they could learn from the Deshima traders.[27] Official encouragement was short-lived, but 'Dutch learning' (as the imported western sciences were called) acquired a dynamic of its own. The handful of scholars who had direct contact with the Dutch passed their knowledge on to disciples; the disciples in turn set up as teachers, often in the great cities of Osaka and Edo; and so the small and uncertain trickle of western learning percolated slowly from one part of Japanese society to another.[28]

Hiraga himself, although he never learned the Dutch language, was soon enthusiastically engaged in the study of 'Dutch learning', perusing the illustrations in European texts on botany and zoology, and even making his own replicas of odometers, thermometers and other western scientific instruments.[29] It was this contact with the Dutch, indeed, which was eventually to provide Hiraga with his greatest claim to fame: his part in introducing the knowledge of electricity to Japan. In the mid-eighteenth century, it should be remembered, electricity was still a scientific novelty in Europe, where machines for generating static electricity attracted large crowds at fairs and exhibitions, and were proclaimed as miracle cures for everything from headaches to infertility. One such machine was presented to the Shogun by a Dutch merchant in 1774, but attracted little interest in official circles. Hiraga, however, had earlier obtained a broken generator from an interpreter who worked with the Dutch community in Nagasaki. After lengthy experimentation, and with the help of other scholars of western learning, he finally succeeded not only in restoring the original, but also in producing his own copies of the *erekuteru* (as he called it), which he then unblushingly claimed as his own invention.[30]

Hiraga's scientific approach to electricity was a traditional one, for he interpreted its properties in terms of the Chinese doctrine of the five elements, but his technological approach was distinctly modern: he saw his *erekuteru* as a useful means of making money. In order to do this, he established a salon which well-to-do residents of the capital could attend, either to receive medical treatment or simply to marvel at the wonders of the new machine.[31] His insatiable technological curiosity, however, was driven not only by self-interest but also by a philosophy which was to become increasingly powerful as the Tokugawa period progressed: the doctrine of economic mercantilism. Hiraga recognised, much more quickly than most of his fellow samurai, that the only way for Japan to reverse the perpetual outflow of wealth into the hands of foreign traders was to use both indigenous and imported knowledge in order to develop Japan's own resources into products both for export and domestic use, and it was the very shortage of those resources which made the application of knowledge all the more urgent.[32]

Hiraga's attempts to put this philosophy into practice were quite extraordinarily diverse, and almost invariably unsuccessful. He experimented with sheepfarming in the hope of setting up a Japanese woollen industry; he prospected for domestic sources of asbestos, which he used in an attempt to devise a fire-resistant fabric; with the support of wealthy merchants, he opened an iron ore mine in the Chichibu region of eastern Japan, and also endeavoured to develop the large-scale production of charcoal for use in smelting iron.[33] His more fruitful ventures included the establishment of a pottery producing a new style of ceramics (which, with typical lack of modesty, he named 'Gennai ware'), and a survey of mines in present-day Akita prefecture, which seems to have resulted in the transfer of techniques for separating silver from copper.[34] In between these technological enterprises, Hiraga also gained a name for himself as a scholar of Japanese botany and geology, an author of popular (and sometimes pornographic) literature, and as a pioneer of the use of of western oil-painting techniques. One of his most interesting contributions to scientific knowledge in Japan was his role in organising 'exhibitions of products' (*bussankai*), the public displays of mineral ores, medicinal plants and other strange or useful natural resources which enjoyed immense popularity in mid-eighteenth-century Japan. Hiraga's death, appropriately, was as dramatic as his life: at the age of fifty-one, after killing an acquaintance in a drunken brawl, he attempted suicide and died in prison of his self-inflicted wounds.[35]

Hiraga Gennai was, of course, an outsider, whose exploits often attracted the derision of his contemporaries, but his enthusiasm for exotic ideas was not unique. Other low-ranking samurai, like Takamori Kankô, took up the investigation of electricity where Hiraga had left off,[36] while men like Hosokawa Yorinao, from a similar social background, experimented with the making of clocks and automata.[37] More importantly, perhaps, the mercantilist vision of a Japanese economy strengthened by western scientific and technological knowledge gained increasing currency in the final decades of the Tokugawa period.

By the early nineteenth century, teachers of 'Dutch learning' were no longer isolated eccentrics, but were attracting growing numbers of disciples. The most significant example was probably Ogata Kôan (1810–63), an official from the small domain of Ashimori, whose interest in western medicine was aroused by his own history of chronic ill-health. Ogata's private academy—the Tekitekisai Juku, established in Osaka in 1838—was ostensibly a medical school, but in fact taught a wide range of western scientific knowledge including chemistry, botany and ballistics. At its peak, the school had over 600 regular students and perhaps as many as 2000 loosely associated 'disciples', most of them drawn from the samurai class. The student registers, which still survive, bear the names of several men who were to become standard-bearers of Japan's opening to the west in the 1850s and 1860s.[38] According to one of the school's most eminent alumni, life at the Tekitekisai Juku consisted of long periods of intense study, interspersed with bouts of drunkenness and juvenile practical joking of the sort beloved by students everywhere. Although the formal teaching methods were conventional, involving much copying and memorising of Dutch texts, the natural high spirits and curiosity of the students led to a good deal of practical scientific experimentation. Dormitories were often turned into makeshift laboratories as students attempted to replicate experiments described in their text books, or concocted malodorous brews of iodine, ammonium chloride and other chemicals.[39]

The most interesting thing about the intellectual world of men like Hiraga and Ogata is the way in which it transcended the supposedly rigid Tokugawa order. In schools such as the Tekitekisai Juku, sons[40] of samurai might rub shoulders with the children of merchants or farmers, and people from the most humble of origins could sometimes be picked out for special patronage and training. The social fluidity which characterised Dutch learning was possible because many of its practitioners were doctors, who enjoyed a peculiar position in Tokugawa society. The four-class system drawn up by the Tokugawa shoguns had never been able to find an appropriate niche for professions like medicine.[41] Physicians employed by the Shogun or domain lords might receive substantial stipends, but had to wear special robes to distinguish them from normal samurai retainers;[42] at the other end of the scale, village doctors might simply be farmers' sons who had done a little learning and set themselves up in general practice. Medicine, then, was a fairly respectable alternative to boredom and poverty for the low-ranking member of the ruling class, and a possible path to upward mobility for the commoner: Ogata Kôan the samurai could derive part of his medical knowledge from Hashimoto Sôkichi (1763–1836)—doctor, botanist and enthusiastic experimenter with electricity—who had begun his career as a penniless craftsman painting designs on umbrellas.[43]

'Develop Products, Promote Enterprise'

While the vertical flow of ideas—from class to class—was encouraged by the urbanisation of the samurai, the horizontal flow—from region to region—was encouraged by the division of the country into competing economic units. The political map of Tokugawa Japan was extraordinarily complex. The central and most strategically important areas of the country were under the direct control of the Shogun, but the rest of the nation was divided up into a patchwork of domains, more than 250 in all, each ruled by a lord (daimyo). All daimyo owed nominal loyalty to the Shogun's government, and could be deprived of their fiefs at its pleasure, but within his own domain the lord possessed virtually unrestricted powers over law, society and economy.

In a sense, therefore, Japan—with its multiple centres of political power—was more similar to mediaeval and early modern Europe than to the centralised Chinese empire; and this is significant, for it is precisely political decentralisation which has been singled out by some scholars as a key element in the European scientific and technological revolution.[44] Tokugawa Japan, obviously, did not experience anything like the great intellectual upheavals of seventeenth- and eighteenth-century Europe, but the fragmented political structure does seem to have allowed the mildly unorthodox (like Hiraga Gennai) to escape the intellectual confines of their own domain and sell their skills in other parts of the country. Most importantly, economic rivalry between the domains was a powerful stimulus to the diffusion of technological ideas.

This rivalry was intensified, rather than restrained, by Tokugawa attempts to preserve stability and order. Having won power on the battlefield, the Tokugawas always ruled with a nervous eye on the rival lords who had once been their equals and enemies. One mechanism for maintaining power over the daimyo was the famous 'alternate residence' system, whereby every daimyo was required to divide his time equally between his own domain and attendance at the shogunal court in Edo, and when absent from Edo, was forced to leave his family behind as virtual hostages of the Shogun. This was not only a means of preventing political conspiracies: it was also intended to produce a constant drain of wealth from the domains into the Shogun's capital, so weakening the daimyos' economic basis for resistance to the shogunate. A substantial share of each lord's resources was absorbed by the cost of maintaining a large establishment in Edo and of travelling regularly to and fro between the capital and his domain. In the case of poorer areas, as much as 80 per cent of the daimyo's budget might be spent in Edo. Further stresses were placed upon domain budgets by repeated requests from the Shogun for contributions to the cost of public works, including the rebuilding and expansion of his numerous castles: requests which could not politely be refused.[45]

The alternate residence system may have been political in inspiration, but it had a very important economic effect. Just as integration with the world market had caused an outflow of wealth at the beginning of the Tokugawa period, so integration with the national market was now causing an outflow of wealth from the domains; and just as scholars like Hiraga Gennai were proposing mercantilism as a means of strengthening the nation as a whole, so daimyo sought to protect their own local economies by developing cash crops and handicrafts for 'export' to the consumer centres of Edo and Osaka. In short, the constant danger of falling behind other regions in terms of economic power provided the spur which forced the ruling elite to overcome their instinctive conservatism. The result was the introduction, in one domain after another, of schemes to 'develop products and promote enterprise' (the so-called *shokusan kōgyō* policies).

Like similar policies in early modern Europe, these schemes involved efforts to encourage the import, and prevent the export, of new technological ideas. Consider, for example, the case of Yonezawa Domain in northern Japan. The daimyo of Yonezawa had made the error of opposing Tokugawa Ieyasu in the period before his overwhelming victory at the Battle of Sekigahara in 1600, and in revenge his domain was reduced to one-eighth of its original size. Attempts by domain officials to restrain expenditure proved unsuccessful, and by the middle of the eighteenth century the region was facing famine and civil unrest. The response to this crisis, however, was a bold and imaginative one: the government of Yonezawa borrowed money from wealthy Edo merchants, and used this to expand local agricultural and craft production.[46]

Experts were brought in from other parts of the country to establish indigo plantations for the production of dyestuffs, and to teach local farmers the art of weaving crepe cloth. The most important element in Yonezawa's policies for promoting industries, though, was the improvement of silk technology. The imposition of tight import restrictions on Chinese silk in the 1680s had created new market openings for Japanese silkfarmers, and Yonezawa was one of the first domains to take advantage of the opportunity. In the 1780s and 1790s silk producers from neighbouring fiefs were invited by the daimyo to tour his domain and advise on the establishment of a silk industry. The government offered loans to any farmer who would establish mulberry plantations for the raising of silkworms, set up twelve domain nurseries for propagating mulberry seedlings, and also published its own handbook, the *Guide to Silk Farming* (*Yōsan Tebiki*), to teach families the secrets of sericulture.[47]

The motives behind this import of technology were simple, and were clearly expressed in the literature of the day: the aim was to turn the limited natural resources of the domain into gold. As an early-nineteenth-century manual on silk farming explains:

> The immediate benefit which silk farming brings to society is that it enables unused land along river banks, in the mountains and by the edge of the sea to be planted with mulberries, and silk spinning and weaving to flourish. Needless to say, when the products of the region are exported to other areas, the domain will become rich and its people prosperous. This is called 'enriching the country'... It is a natural consequence that states which sell their produce to other domains, and so bring in gold and silver, should become rich, while the people of countries with little produce, which thus allow gold and silver to flow out of their lands, become poor. By increasing the production of commodities one enhances the flow of precious metals into the country while suppressing their outflow.[48]

Similar policies for the import of silk technology were introduced during the eighteenth century in domains from Tsugaru in the far north to Kumamoto on the southern island of Kyūshū. Mineral resources, too, could provide a basis for 'developing products and promoting enterprise'. In the northern region of Akita the daimyo and his advisers confronted the economic crisis of the eighteenth century by recruiting experts (including Hiraga Gennai) to survey the domain's extensive copper and silver mines, and to advise on better methods of refining ores. Efforts were also made to impose closer supervision over the powerful 'mine masters' (*yamashi*), who controlled the day-to-day running of the mines.[49] Further south, Matsue Domain set up its own iron foundry, while lords of Hiroshima encouraged the processing of locally produced iron by providing loans for the establishment of blacksmiths' forges. The desire to make use of local skills and raw materials often led to high levels of specialisation. Tottori, for example, had long been famous for its swordsmiths, but during the peace of the Tokugawa era the domain encouraged its smiths to beat their swords, not into ploughshares, but into threshing-forks. Financial incentives were given to encourage the spread of this new metal-working technique, which had been introduced to the domain from the port of Sakai in the mid-seventeenth century, and soon Tottori was selling its farm tools to villages all over the country.[50]

Mercantilist competition involved, of course, not only policies to acquire technology from other parts of the country, but also measures (sometimes of a draconian nature) to prevent others from borrowing or stealing the technical secrets of one's own domain: measures which are vividly illustrated by the story of the Arita porcelain industry. Around the beginning of the Tokugawa period craftsmen brought over from Korea had discovered and developed a rich source of kaolin clay (the raw material for porcelain) in the mountainous region around the village of Arita in the domain of Saga. At first, the Arita potters lacked the know-how to produce sophisticated multicoloured porcelains like those of Ming China, but during the seventeenth century painstaking experimentation by local artisans created glazes which rivalled the exuberant decorations of Chinese polychrome ware.

By the second half of the century, Arita porcelain had become one of Japan's few significant export items, and in a matter of three or four decades some two million pieces of pottery had been shipped by Dutch merchants to the ports of Southeast Asia and the capitals of Europe.[51] Although exports later declined as the kilns of Meissen and Sèvres began to produce their own imitations of Chinese and Japanese wares, growing demand from Japan's own expanding merchant class maintained the prosperity of the potteries, and during the early nineteenth century several hundred thousand bales of porcelain were sold each year to other parts of Japan.[52] Not surprisingly, by this time a large share of domain revenue was derived from levies on the production and sale of ceramics.[53]

The attitude of the domain to this moneyspinner was both protective and possessive. Loans (many of them never repaid) were provided to encourage the setting up of kilns and to help the Arita potteries through times of hardship.[54] At the same time, officials were appointed to supervise the running of the potteries, and a strict division of labour was encouraged: by the late seventeenth century production was divided into at least nineteen separate processes, each performed by different groups of workers.[55] This specialisation may incidentally have enhanced the skill and productivity of workers, but its logic was far removed from that of Adam Smith's classical celebration of the division of labour. Rather than encouraging productivity, the aim was to ensure that no artisan possessed the full range of skills needed to make finished works, and thus that no-one would be able to sell the secrets of Arita porcelain to other domains.[56]

The most vital of all technical secrets was the knowledge possessed by the 'colour painters' or *akaeshi*, who were responsible for preparing the materials for coloured glazes. This skill was restricted to a limited number of households, who were gathered into a special village—the *akaemachi*—where they lived under the watchful gaze of the daimyo's guards, posted at strategic points both to keep strangers out and to keep the colour painters in.[57] During the late eighteenth century, as part of a series of financial reforms, the separation of tasks was intensified, and the colour painters were persuaded to sign an agreement guaranteeing that their secret knowledge would be passed on only to the eldest son, so avoiding the risk of technology passing into unauthorised hands.[58]

Japanese mercantilism, like its European counterpart, then, had a repressive as well as an expansionist side to it. On balance, though, there can be little doubt that the dynamics of economic competition helped to promote the nationwide diffusion of skills and know-how. For all the efforts to preserve local secrets, rivalry between the domains meant that the gains to be made from technical piracy ultimately outweighed the risks. The records of domain officials in Arita note the fines and loss of privileges imposed on potters who travelled outside the region without permission, and by the beginning of the nineteenth century rival ceramics districts (like the town of Seto) had managed to acquire many of the secrets of the Arita porcelain industry.[59]

The politics of Tokugawa Japan, in other words, left Japan with a distinctive economic and technological structure. Instead of being concentrated in a few major cities, craft know-how came to be distributed in many small centres throughout the country. When the first modern economic surveys of Japan were undertaken in the first decade after the fall of the Tokugawa Shogunate, it was found that the distribution of craft manufacturing throughout the country was surprisingly even. Out of sixty-four regions of Japan, fifty derived between 20 and 40 per cent of their wealth from 'manufacturing' (which, in the context of the day, meant the craft production of goods like soy sauce, saké, silk and cotton cloth, paper and pottery).[60]

Precisely because they were linked to the national market, however, each centre tended to specialise in the production of one or two particular items: here porcelain, there lacquerware, elsewhere again silk brocades. Even imported crafts like the making of spectacles came to be concentrated in a particular small region of western Japan. As an early nineteenth-century writer commented:

> Where there are people with an understanding of the economy, there we find the skilful production of local specialities. Some of the first examples were silk in the Ôshû district and silkworm eggs in the Ôshû Honba district, paper in Suwa and Ishimi, sugar in Kii and so forth. Besides these, in recent times so many districts have developed their own special products that it is impossible to list them all. Products which did not exist at all fifty or a hundred years ago have now begun to be produced in large quantities by various domains.[61]

Peace and the Printed Word

The growth and survival of specialised craft communities in Japan depended on the existence of channels for the nationwide flow of goods and ideas; and the development of transport and communications, in turn, was helped by the urban growth which accompanied two and a half centuries of *Pax Tokugawa*. With the end of civil warfare, regular markets revived, and castle towns became thriving centres of commercial activity. In the east, the Shogun's capital, Edo, grew to be one of the biggest cities, not just in Japan but in the world: a sprawling metropolis of over one million people, insatiably sucking in goods of all types from all parts of the country. In the west, Osaka (with a population of almost half a million in the late eighteenth century) was the focal point from which the produce of Japan's richest agricultural districts was traded with other regions. Between 1724 and 1730, for example, average annual shipments of goods from Osaka to Edo included 1.3 million rolls of cotton cloth, 9.8 million litres of soy sauce and 15 million litres of saké.[62]

The transport of such enormous quantities of merchandise was seriously hampered by aspects of shogunal policy. As part of the 'closed country' strategy, the Tokugawas restricted the building of ships above a certain size, and banned the use of ribbed hulls and multiple sails. The predictable result was a growing number of maritime disasters, as more and more sailors braved the seas in heavily laden and inadequately constructed vessels.[63] On the other hand, the alternate residence system and the growth of commerce undoubtedly encouraged better land transport. Inns and relay posts were set up along the main highways, and, although letters took at least four days to travel the 500 kilometres from Osaka to Edo, some ingenious merchants devised systems of flags or beacons, so that information about prices on the Osaka and Edo markets could be communicated to surrounding towns and villages in a matter of hours. (This, it should be said, was frowned on by the authorities, who were well aware of the subversive potential of effective communications.)[64]

By the late eighteenth century the cities, and particularly the metropolises of Edo and Osaka, were nodes in a network through which new ideas flowed from one part of the country to another. The private colleges in the cities provided a forum for the exchange of ideas between samurai and educated townspeople; markets, like the great silk markets of Kyoto and Fukushima, brought local merchants together to compare and exchange the products of their own regions; domain policies, meanwhile, encouraged a small but significant direct flow of skilled workers from one district to another. Opportunities to observe crafts and techniques from other parts of the country gave producers greater confidence to try out new methods for themselves. The cities, too, were emerging as the centres for the development of another and increasingly important channel for the dissemination of technical ideas: the printed word.

Printing had long been known in Japan, but until the late sixteenth century was confined to religious uses and the reproduction of Chinese classics. The new wealth of the merchant classes, however, created a flourishing market for secular texts of all sorts: from romantic novels to satire, and from poetry to encyclopedias. Although movable type was sometimes used, woodblock printing was generally preferred (in part because it was covered by a form of copyright protection).[65] Specialist secondhand bookstores and shops selling imported Chinese works (*karahonya*) appeared in the big cities, but the greatest commercial success of all was the development of commercial libraries (*kashihonya*), which lent out their works to those whose enthusiasm for reading outstripped their incomes. By the first decade of the nineteenth century Osaka had about three hundred commercial libraries and Edo more than six hundred.[66] As well as catering to urban demand, a growing number of booksellers were also setting up mobile libraries which travelled through the countryside, selling or lending books to the growing numbers of literate farmers (a few of whom were beginning themselves to write texts on agricultural techniques). Printed texts provided an important new vehicle for the spread of technological ideas, and one which gradually but surely eroded the power of the urban guilds to maintain their monopolies on knowledge.[67]

Relatively high levels of basic literacy (perhaps around 40 per cent for males) are often put forward as a reason for Japan's successful

adaptation to the economic and political challenges which it confronted from the late nineteenth century onwards. But, as historian
Harvey Graff observes, 'writing alone is not an "agent of change"; its
impact is determined by the manner in which human agency exploits it
in a human setting'.[68] What was significant was not simply the fact that
some Japanese farmers and artisans could read and write, but that they
had access to books, and, even more importantly, had ideas which they
were eager to exchange with one another.

So too, with technology itself, it was not so much the complexity or
sophistication of techniques of production themselves that mattered,
but rather the way in which those techniques were used in everyday life.
In terms of their splendour or ingenuity, Japan's handicraft techniques
may have been no more impressive that those of the Chinese Empire or
the Turkish Sultanate. But the diffusion of those skills through a
network of dispersed but interconnected productive centres gave the
Japanese system a particular dynamism and flexibility, and was therefore to hold the key to Japanese society's response to its encounter with
the industrial and technological might of the west.

The Nature of Tokugawa Technology

Under the smooth surface of the Tokugawa order, then, forces were at
work which stimulated technological change. But the *type* of change
which they encouraged was very different from the transformations
occurring simultaneously in the western hemisphere, as Europe
entered the age of industrial revolution. Tokugawa Japan, in fact, is a
nice illustration of the fact that technological 'progress' is not unilinear,
but can move in many different possible directions. Although, in eight-
eenth- and nineteenth-century Japan, we can find some examples of
the sort of labour-saving mechanisation which had occurred in
mediaeval and early modern Europe, the diffusion of these new
techniques was slow and uncertain. Many Tokugawa innovations, in
fact, demanded *more* rather than *less* labour: in the words of the
economic historian Hayami Akira, they were part, not so much of an
'industrial revolution' as of an 'industrious revolution'.[69] Instead of
involving the application of inanimate energy to large machines, they
involved increasingly painstaking observation and precise regulation of
the processes of nature: in short, they required *jutsu*, that specialised
human skill which enables human beings to perform remarkable feats.
(The term *jutsu* is the root both of the modern word *gijutsu* or
technology, and of the older word *majutsu* or magic).

These characteristics of Tokugawa technology were partly (as in traditional economic theory) a reflection of Japan's natural endowments—

its shortage of most raw materials and its abundance of underused farm labour. As Francesca Bray points out, Japanese rice-farming demanded enormous inputs of labour at certain times of the year, but during the slack seasons of the year left workers underemployed, creating an ideal climate for the growth of seasonal, labour-intensive cottage industries.[70]

But Tokugawa technology was shaped by politics as much as by economics. Labour-saving innovation, in the eighteenth-century context, meant standardisation, economies of scale and the introduction of more productive machinery. These strategies, however, made little sense in a country where restrictions on overseas trade and a stable population size limited the growth of markets, and where a complex status system fragmented the domestic market into a mosaic of small niches. Rather than attempting large-scale production of standardised goods, it was more profitable to pursue what would now be called product differentiation: creating distinctive local specialities, often using a particular local raw material, and aimed at a specific segment of the social order.

For the purposes of this technological strategy, quality tended to be more important than quantity, and emphasis was placed less on increasing the productivity of the workers than on ensuring that they performed to minutely specified standards. Japan's technological development, therefore, took the form of a sort of involution. Rather than generating large-scale breakthroughs to radically new forms of production, it created a proliferation of small variations on existing themes. Crafts like lacquer-work diversified into literally hundreds of distinct local techniques: some used gold, silver, mother-of-pearl or even egg-shell inlays; others involved the mixing of lacquer with various mineral pigments, the engraving of patterns in the varnish, or the use of special techniques to buff and polish the finished vessel.[71]

There was a further factor which channelled Tokugawa inventiveness towards small-scale, labour-intensive innovation rather than labour-saving mechanisation. The introduction of substantial mechanisation into craft industries would have required large changes to social organisation and, although economic necessity had persuaded Japan's rulers of the need for innovation, anything which caused major disruptions to existing social relationships was still looked on with suspicion. Even in areas like saké-brewing where (as we shall see) relatively large-scale production did develop, entrepreneurs had to work within the bounds of shogunal and domain regulations, all designed to ensure that the 'development of products' did not seriously disrupt the established patterns of village life. It was not until the fall of the Shogunate burst apart the confines of the social order that the fully fledged development of mechanised factories was possible.

The distinctive character of Tokugawa innovation also implied a distinctive impact on society and on the natural environment. The labour-intensive character of many innovations placed a heavy burden on the human workforce. Innovation may have brought wealth to enterprising farmers and merchant families and increased the skills of many craft producers, but it also (as the following examples show) led to long working hours, increased intensity of labour and minute regulation of the working lives of many ordinary Japanese producers.

On the other hand, Tokugawa technology has, in recent years, often been held up as a model of environmental sustainability. Agricultural and craft manufacture techniques were commonly developed in a village setting, where the local community had considerable control over the way in which new ideas were put to work. From the point of view of the village as a whole, the most important consideration was the need to maintain the long-term health of the land, and many Tokugawa technological practices show a great sensitivity to the complex inter-connections of the natural environment. Silkfarming, for example, was often incorporated into a self-sustaining ecological cycle, where detritus from silkworms was used as a fertiliser on the rice fields, and mulberry trees helped to prevent erosion of the banks of irrigation channels. Even the straw sandals which farm families wove in the winter would, after months of wear, be returned as mulch to the soil.

At the same time, though, there were currents within Tokugawa technological development which pointed in another, more exploitative direction. Mining, for example, often involved considerable environmental destruction, and particular problems seem to have been generated by the miners of iron sand, who formed an itinerant group, moving from one area to another as sources of iron ore were depleted. As we shall see, their approach to natural resources often came into conflict with the perspectives of the more settled agrarian community.

Silk and Cotton

The silk industry provides a most vivid illustration of the characteristics of Tokugawa innovation. Silk production involves a number of distinct steps. First, silkworms must be hatched and reared to produce cocoons (sericulture). Next, the gossamer-thin strands of silk are unreeled from the cocoon and, at the same time, two or more strands are wound together to form the basic silk thread (reeling). The thread is then wound off onto convenient sized reels or bobbins (winding), and finally may be treated in a variety of different ways to produce the raw material for different types of silk cloth. For example the thread is often given a strong twist, and several threads are sometimes twisted together. (These final processes are known as 'throwing'.) The silk thread is now ready to be dyed and woven into the finished fabric.

In Europe, it was the later processes—throwing and weaving—which were the main focuses of innovation. As early as the fourteenth century, the silkmakers of Luca in Italy were using water-power to drive their throwing-machines, whose construction was a closely guarded secret. One of the best-known stories of the British industrial revolution tells how, in the early eighteenth century, Thomas Lombe and his half-brother John succeeded in stealing the techniques of the Italian silk mills and establishing their own silk factory in Derbyshire. Meanwhile, the draw looms used for weaving complex patterned silk were also gradually being made more efficient, and by the beginning of the nineteenth century the French inventor Joseph-Marie de Jacquard had perfected his famous automatic loom, where the pattern of the fabric was encoded onto punched cards which were then used to control the raising and lowering of the warp threads.[72]

There are some interesting parallels between these developments and innovations in Tokugawa silk processing. Perhaps the most striking is the introduction of water-powered silk-throwing machines, which occurred in Japan about sixty years after the Lombe brothers had set up their first mill in England. In the Japanese case it was a wheelwright from Kiryû, one Iwase Kichibei, who first thought of applying water-power to the large multi-spindled wheels (*hacchô guruma*) used to throw silk, and his invention resulted in a substantial growth of silk production in the Kiryû region.[73] But it is equally significant that, while the Lombes' enterprise marked the beginning of the rapid spread of water-powered (and later steam-powered) factories throughout Britain, Iwase's invention was not widely taken up by producers in other parts of the country.

The same caution about adopting labour-saving technologies is even more obvious in the case of silk reeling. Until the nineteenth century, Japanese silk producers used extremely simple reeling equipment, where the silk filaments were twisted together by hand and then wound around a wooden roller or frame (see figure 2.2). From the middle of the eighteenth century, however, new reeling devices (*zaguri*), using gears or drive belts, began to appear in various parts of the country, and in the early nineteenth century there are even some reports of these machines being water-powered rather than turned by hand.[74] Although they greatly increased productivity, however, these new techniques were only slowly and tentatively adopted during the Tokugawa period. Part of the reluctance stemmed, of course, from the eternal human fear that newfangled gadgetry would put people out of work: a fear which was particularly understandable in Tokugawa Japan, with its small and

Simple forms of silk-reeling equipment.

The more complex silk-reeling machine *(zaguri)*
of a type used in modern Japan.

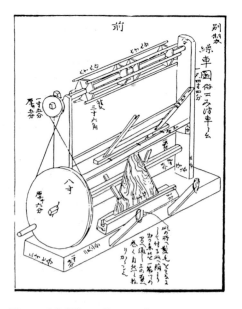

Figure 2.2 Silk-reeling equipment
Source: Edo kagaku koten sôsho, vol. 13, pp. 225 and 226, and vol. 15, p. 45.

limited markets. A contemporary account of the Nishijin silkmaking district noted that, since the *zaguri* 'can finish five days' work of manual spinning in a day, spinners no longer have the yarn to spin and therefore have little to do'.[75] But a more important problem was probably the issue of quality. The new reeling frames, although they increased output, produced silk thread which was coarser and more uneven than the silk made by skilled workers using the old-fashioned reeling-frames. A number of domains even banned or restricted use of the new machines because, in the words of one official decree, they 'bring disgrace to one of our famous products and damage the interests of the state'.[76]

In a world where markets were restricted and deeply divided by status, wealth came, not from large increases in output, but from developing a wide range of products to specialised, exacting standards. As a result, the most striking developments in Tokugawa silkmaking occurred, not in the processing of the raw material, but in the production of the cocoons themselves (an area which was relatively neglected by European innovation).

Silkworms are very sensitive creatures, vulnerable to disease and to sudden changes of temperature. The production of raw silk was therefore a delicate and time-consuming task, in which the slightest lack of care could make the difference between success and failure. As European silkfarmers were to realise when disaster struck, the key to a good crop of silk lay in the careful selection of silkworm eggs. In Europe, silk producers generally raised worms from eggs laid by their own moths, but by the early eighteenth century Japan had developed a specialised trade in silkworm eggs, with many farmers buying eggs from professional breeders. Eggs from the best districts, particularly from the region around Fukushima in northern Japan, could command particularly high prices, and merchants from Fukushima, in return for the payment of an annual levy, acquired the right to have their cards of silkworm eggs stamped with an official seal of quality.[77]

But market dominance was not easy to maintain. Producers in other regions competed vigorously with Fukushima egg merchants, and in reply, Fukushima producers were forced to engage in a continuous process of selective breeding in order to improve the quality of their stock. By the second half of the seventeenth century, for example, the successful silkfarmer and merchant Satô Tomonobu had adopted the technique of keeping samples of a number of different varieties of silk moth, which he would breed with local stock in order to produce hybrids whose silk had the right hue and texture to meet current fashions.[78] The first Japanese manual on silkfarming, published in 1702, listed five varieties of silkworm, but by the middle of the 1860s an encyclopedia for silkfarmers was able to describe about two hundred. Even though the later list undoubtedly involves some double counting (because the same type of silkworm was often given different names in different parts of the country), these figures provide an impressive picture of the variety produced by selective breeding in the Japanese silk industry during the Tokugawa period.[79] Even the nineteenth-century French expert Natalis Rondot, who was reluctant to admit that Japanese silks could rival the best products of his own country, was moved to exclaim, 'but what diversity of quality we find in the land of the rising sun!'[80]

Successful silkfarming depended, not only upon the use of good, healthy eggs, but also upon meticulous control of temperature, feeding and hygiene. Here again, Tokugawa producers gained technical knowledge through a process of trial and error and sometimes conscious experimentation. Narita Jûbei, the unusually erudite farmer who wrote one of the most popular Tokugawa texts on silkfarming, revealed a widespread practical approach to technology when he observed that

> if you have blind faith in everything that is written in books, and do not think
> for yourself, it is just as bad as having no books at all: you will never learn
> anything.[81]

The same mixture of observation and trial and error was used by another nineteenth-century farmer, Nakamura Zen'emon, to solve one of the most perplexing problems of sericulture: the accurate measurement and control of temperature. During the 1830s, Nakamura suffered from a serious illness, and was treated by a doctor trained in Dutch medical techniques. Nakamura was quick to realise that the thermometer with which the doctor measured his temperature (and which, of course, had been introduced to Japan by Hiraga Gennai) could hold the key to solving the problems of temperature control in silkfarming. After making his own thermometers (in itself no easy task), Nakamura set about testing them in his silk sheds, and devised a schedule of ideal temperatures, which varied slightly according to the stage of the silkworms' development and the type of silk which was being produced. These discoveries were compiled into a short handbook for silkfarmers which was published in 1849: four years before the arrival of Commodore Matthew Perry opened the floodgates to the inflow of western technology into Japan.[82]

By the nineteenth century, the careful, piecemeal process of experimentation in silkfarming had produced considerable results. Silkfarmers like Satô Tomonobu, Narita Jûbei and Nakamura Zen'emon were part of that emerging group of wealthy farmers who often rose to become substantial landowners with an important role to play in village affairs, and this meant that the techniques they developed were spread by personal influence, as well as by the handbooks which some of the more highly educated amongst them composed. At least one hundred texts on silk farming were written during the Tokugawa period, of which more than a quarter are known to have been composed by silk producers or merchants themselves.[83] By comparing the information in successive contemporary texts, we can tell that, from the early to late eighteenth century, the length of time between the hatching of the silkworm and the spinning of the cocoon was reduced by about fifteen days, and that the amount of silk on each cocoon increased, in the more advanced districts, by some 25 per cent.[84]

This increase in output, however, did not necessarily mean a reduction in the hours of labour devoted to silkfarming. Instead, as the season of the silkworms grew shorter, so the intensity of labour (carried out by the women of farm families) within the season increased. Improved methods of feeding, for example, meant that the silkworms' food had to be chopped to precise sizes, sieved and winnowed as many as eight times a day. The worms had to be moved frequently from one part of the house to another to protect them from heat and cold, and the most stringent levels of hygiene were demanded of silkworkers. Not only were farm women required to change their clothes frequently and to wash their hands before touching any silkfarming implement, they were even expected to speak in hushed voices so as not to disturb the sensibilities of the worms.[85] One silk manual recommended that from the seventh or eighth to the fifteenth or sixteenth day of the silkworms' life their 'guardians' or 'mothers' (i.e. the silkworkers) should not leave their charges untended for a single moment.[86]

The development of this minutely regulated technology of silkfarming was to prove vital to Japan's industrial future. When Japan began to open its doors to the west in the mid-nineteenth century, it was the export of raw silk which would provide most of the foreign exchange needed to import western industrial know-how and machinery. Japan was able to export silk on such a large scale because, during the 1850s and 1860s, European silk production was devastated by an epidemic silkworm disease known as the *pébrine*. Careful research by the French scientist Louis Pasteur, however, revealed that this disease was in fact endemic to Japan as well as to Europe: it was Japanese sericultural techniques which had prevented it from wreaking havoc in the Japanese industry.[87] As one French study written in the 1860s observed, the techniques of Japanese silk farmers ... can be of real assistance to us. They seem far removed from all the refinements of our sericultural art; but that is precisely their strength ... The real teacher is not Japan but nature; however, Japan has had the wisdom to follow nature, while we have made the mistake of trying to force it.[88]

Silk, of course, was the fabric worn by the upper classes. Although, with economic changes, more and more merchants and wealthy farmers were able to afford silk clothes, sumptuary laws restricted the wearing of the finest silk fabrics by commoners, and some rich merchants were able to wear their richest robes only in the privacy of their own homes.[89] At the other end of the social scale, however, cotton—the material worn by ordinary people—underwent a process of technological change which closely paralleled the changes in silk production. Cotton production, even more than sericulture, was a Tokugawa innovation. Cotton plants are thought to have been brought to Japan from China in the eighth century AD, but the variety introduced was unsuitable to the Japanese climate and soon died out.[90] It was not until the closing years of the sixteenth century that cotton was reintroduced as a consequence of Toyotomi Hideyoshi's pillaging of Korean culture, but by the late eighteenth century the plant was being grown throughout large areas of western Japan and had become the most popular material for the clothes of farmers and craftspeople.

The processing of cotton, like the processing of raw silk, underwent a gradual process of technical improvement. Spinning wheels (a Chinese invention) were introduced in the early eighteenth century, replacing simple devices which allowed the cotton to be twisted together between the fingers, and by the beginning of the nineteenth century the tall loom was beginning to be used for the weaving of finer grades of cotton cloth.[91] The most striking changes, however, were not related to mechanisation but rather to the development of an enormous diversity of types of cotton fabric. At one end of the process, selective breeding of cotton plants increased the number of varieties recorded in Japan from six in the seventeenth century to about fifty by the 1830s.[92] At the other end, developments in techniques of weaving and dyeing produced an extraordinary range of colours, designs and textures, many of them specialities of particular regions.

Tie-dyeing, starch-resist dyeing, twill weaves, figured weaves and combinations of these techniques were used to create products appropriate to a wide range of different markets. With typical Tokugawa frugality, even the weaving of fabrics made from discarded rags was developed into an art form in itself. Most striking of all was the development of *kasuri* weaving, in which a pattern is produced by dyeing parts of the unwoven thread. This technique reached Japan via Okinawa from

Southeast Asia (where it is generally known as *ikat*). During the eighteenth and early nineteenth centuries it was diffused and developed to a level of considerable sophistication by Japan's women weavers. Many of them were anonymous, but some, like Inoue Den (1783–1867) in Kyûshû and Kagiya Kana (1782–1864) in Shikoku, are still remembered for their contribution to local craft industries.[93] Within less than two centuries, such polymorphism had occurred that, according to a recent study of the subject, 'there is no other country in the world where so many different methods are used and so many different designs created'.[94]

Gold, Silver and Iron

We are so accustomed to thinking of modern Japan as a resource-poor country that it comes as something of a shock to discover that, at the beginning of the Tokugawa age, Japan was one of the largest exporters of precious metals in the Old World. In the 1580s, for example, Portuguese galleons alone shipped out of Japan an annual trophy of about 20,000 kilograms of silver.[95] The German physician and traveller Engelbert Kaempfer, writing at the beginning of the eighteenth century, expressed the view that

> had the Portuguese enjoyed the trade to Japan but twenty years longer, upon the same footing as they did for some time, such riches would have been transported out of this Ophir to Macao, and there would have been such a plenty and flow of gold and silver in that town, as sacred writ mentions there was at Jerusalem in the time of Solomon.[96]

The wealth of Japan's gold and silver mines was the result of a minor technological revolution which had taken place during the sixteenth century. The expansion of trade with China and of the use of money at home had stimulated a new interest in finding and recovering precious metals, and contact with the Chinese and Europeans had provided new means of doing so. Between 1540 and 1700 fourteen major gold, silver and copper mines were opened in Japan, among them the copper mines of Ashio and Besshi, and silver mines at Ikuno and on the desolate island of Sado off the west coast of Japan.[97] While earlier mines had been little more than trenches in the earth or burrows which attempted to follow a seam of ore into a hillside, the new mines were surveyed with care and contained complex networks of underground tunnels.[98]

As they dug deeper into the heart of the earth, Japanese miners encountered terrors familiar to the miners of early modern Europe. Temperatures rose to intolerable levels; mineshafts flooded; poisonous gases caused suffocation or explosions. In Europe, attempts to overcome these problems of underground mining inspired some of the most vital technological innovations of the seventeenth and eighteenth century—above all, the development of the steam engine, first used to pump water from the tin mines of Cornwall—but in Japan responses to the challenges of mining were hesitant. Hand-turned fans provided some ventilation to deep shafts, and bamboo torches were gradually replaced by oil lamps for illumination.[99] Although a number of relatively complex pumping devices were known in Japan, their use in the mines was at best sporadic. In the Sado mines, for example, a type of Archimedian screw and later a system of scoop-wheels was used to raise water from some shafts, but, as a remarkable scroll-painting of the mines shows, in the latter half of the Tokugawa period most of the work was still being done by the labourers themselves: hunch-backed figures clad in loin-cloths, carting water by hand in simple wooden buckets.[1]

The cheapness of labour was a major barrier to change. Most miners worked on contracts which bound them to the mine for long periods of time, and in areas like Sado many of the workers were convicts.[2] Labour was expendable and relatively unskilled. In any case, what with accidents and lung disease, few miners lived long enough to pass on skills to descendants.[3] But change was also inhibited by the complex system which governed the control of mines. From the early seventeenth century onwards Japan's mines were divided into two groups: the richest and most important belonged to the Shogun, while lesser mines belonged to the local domain lord. Neither Shogun nor lords, however, had much direct interest in the running of the mines. Some were contracted out to powerful private entrepreneurs called *yamashi* (literally 'mountain masters'), while others were placed under the supervision of samurai administrators, who in turn subcontracted the digging of individual tunnels to families of miners.[4] This fragmented system of management made it difficult for large-scale innovations to be introduced in a coordinated way.

Despite their resistance to mechanisation, the mines reflected the Tokugawa passion for extracting the maximum value from resources. This is most clearly evident in the techniques which were applied to metal refining. The main methods of refining in use during the Tokugawa period had been introduced during the sixteenth or early seventeenth century, and technical innovation from then on took the form of applying these techniques more thoroughly and systematically so that, as the richer seams were slowly exhausted, every last drop of precious metal could be wrung from the poorer remaining ores.

The result was a complex, painstaking and closely supervised process of refining, involving a sophisticated division of labour. An early-nineteenth-century illustrated guide to the copper mines of Besshi, run by the Sumitomo family, shows how the mined rock was first crushed by hand, and the fragments of ore carefully selected.[5] A few mines used water-powered crushing hammers, but here, as in most places, this part of the work was performed by women, who were believed to be particularly skilled at sorting the precious metal from the dross (see Figure 2.3). The ore was then smelted in two stages, the second stage involving the blowing of air through the molten metal to remove sulphate impurities. This procedure was in essence a forerunner of the famous Bessemer process, which was to revolutionise European steel-making in the second half of the nineteenth century, and some historians have even suggested that the Japanese technique may have provided the seeds of the idea from which Bessemer developed his famous technique.[6]

The smelting of the copper, however, was not the end of the story. The next step was to separate the small quantities of silver which were contained in much of the Besshi ore. To do this, the copper was first mixed with lead and hardened. The mixture was then reheated to a carefully controlled temperature, and the silver-and-lead alloy (which had a lower melting temperature) was allowed to run off. This alloy was smelted again in an ash furnace which separated the silver from the lead, which was then cast into rods to be recycled for future use. Meanwhile the very earth from the floors of the furnaces where the copper had been smelted was being dug up, pulverised and panned in running water to recover any minute traces of copper which might have been lost in the smelting process. It is hardly surprising that, at their peak of production, major mines like Besshi employed many thousands of workers.

The story of Tokugawa iron technology is a rather different one. Iron production was privately controlled, and catered for a large and growing market. With the spread of cash crops and the commercialisation of farming, iron tools became almost an essential part of agricultural life. By the middle of the eighteenth century the philosopher Miura Baien was describing iron as the most truly valuable of all the metals, because 'it is vital to the daily life of the people'.[7] Although the ironworkers, like gold and silver miners, were an impoverished and despised group, tied to their masters by long contracts, the growing demand for iron outstripped the traditional supplies of labour, and often forced the iron masters to recruit temporary labour from local farm villages.[8]

The popular use of iron, in the form of ploughshares, threshing forks, kitchen knives and carpenters' tools, stimulated a wave of interconnected innovations which greatly increased the output of Japan's foundries. One development, which begins to be recorded

Figure 2.3 Ore selectors at Besshi copper mines c. 1800
Source: Edo kagaku koten sôsho, vol. 1, p. 234

around the beginning of the seventeenth century, was an improved method of selecting the alluvial iron sands which provided the raw material for most Japanese iron- and steelmaking. Rather than simply digging the sands out of pits in the earth, the iron masters began to divert water from streams to wash the iron sands into large settling ponds (a process which often played havoc with local agriculture, and caused some of the earliest recorded cases of environmental conflict in Japan).[9] Meanwhile, the smelting of the iron itself was being shifted from open-air hearths into furnaces enclosed in high-roofed thatched buildings (called *takadono tatara*) which protected production from the vagaries of the climate.[10] Temperature control—so essential to iron-making—was greatly enhanced by improvements in the construction of bellows: first from simple, hand-pumped box bellows to foot-operated pumps, and then, by the early eighteenth century, to complex, hinged balance bellows (*tenbin fuigo*) which were four times as efficient as their predecessors (see Figure 2.4).[11]

The ironmakers may have been regarded as a wild and dangerous bunch, living in the mountains and shifting from place to place as iron sands and timber were exhausted, but they were also the possessors of a rich store of knowledge and experience. The production of iron, in an age before the introduction of accurate temperature measurement, required extraordinary judgement and vigilance. Great care was taken in the construction of the furnace itself, with particular efforts being made to create a smooth rock-hard foundation at the base of each clay furnace. During the firing of the *tatara*, which might last as long as five days, a constant watch had to be kept on the colour of the fire and the height of the flames to ensure that the correct heat was maintained, and the ironworkers were forced to live for days on end in the enclosed heat of the ironmaking shed, catching what moments of sleep they could, curled up in a corner between the bellows and the roaring furnace.

As in so many other areas of Japanese technology, it is the quality and diversity of the product which astonishes. Iron sands were carefully assessed for colour, weight and texture, so that the very best sand could be selected for the making of high-grade steel. The furnace, moreover, was destroyed and rebuilt after each firing, because its clay walls absorbed the dross and impurities from the iron. Not only were different raw materials and techniques used to produce cast iron, pig-iron or steel, but the processing of the metal after it left the furnace created a wide range of different irons suitable for different purposes. Steel which, in areas with high-quality iron sand, could be produced in a single firing, might be cooled in air, tempered in water or further forged and purified to produce varied qualities of colour and hardness; pig-iron, which was sent to cities like Tottori to be treated in the

Separating silver from copper at Besshi mines
(the figure at the back is using a box bellows)

Balance bellows *(tenbin fuigo)* in use in iron smelting

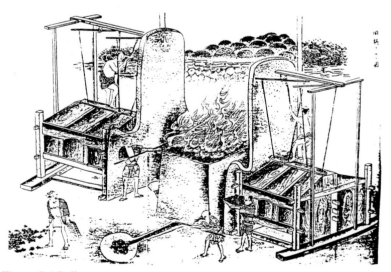

Figure 2.4 Bellows
Sources: Edo kagaku koten sôsho, vol. 1, p. 243; Kikuchi T., *Zufu Edo jidai no gijutsu,* vol. 2,
p. 487.

blacksmith's forge, might be heated and hammered to produce differing degrees of hardness or malleability, and then fused with thin layers of steel to create the perfect material for anything from scissors to carpenters' saws.

Although most iron in use during the Tokugawa period was produced from iron sand, the Nambu region in the northeast (part of modern Iwate Prefecture) possessed rich sources of highly magnetic iron-bearing rock, which was smelted with a special local technique involving the use of a charcoal ash flux. This technology may have emerged from the combination of old ironworking traditions with western metallurgical know-how introduced through the Spanish and Portuguese.[12] Whatever its somewhat hazy origins, the special local know-how of the Nambu region was to prove of particular importance when Japan began to adopt western methods of iron-smelting in the mid-nineteenth century.

Saké-brewing

If you wished to find Japanese parallels to the European development of mechanisation and factory production, the best place to look would probably be the saké breweries. Already by the late seventeenth century the prodigious thirst of Japan's growing urban population had encouraged the establishment of relatively large breweries, where dozens of workers, each with their own clearly specified tasks, toiled away amid the huge vats of steaming rice. Saké-brewers often figure in the fiction of the period as archetypes of the *nouveau riche* merchant class, and their wealth enabled them to invest in relatively complex forms of mechanisation.

During the century-and-a-half which followed, several important changes altered both the organisation and the technology of brewing. The first change was a gradual shift of the breweries out of cities and into rural areas where they could take advantage of local supplies of seasonal labour. The main area to benefit from this movement was the Nada region to the west of Osaka which, by the early nineteenth century, had emerged as the leading saké-brewing district.[13] The Nada breweries prospered, not just because of their geographical position, but also because they were quick to adopt and develop new techniques which increased the output and the quality of their product. The power of the rivers which flowed from the surrounding mountains into the Sea of Japan was harnessed to drive mechanised hammers for polishing rice; the scale of production was expanded so that, by the first half of the nineteenth century, some breweries were processing around 1800 litres of rice a day; careful attention was given to the layout and design of breweries, to ensure the smooth flow of raw materials from one stage of production to the next; deliberate experimentation helped to determine the ideal mix of rice, water, yeast and other ingredients.[14] One of the most famous stories in the history of saké concerns the Nada merchant Yamamura Tazaemon, who discovered that one of his two breweries consistently produced a better wine than the other. He therefore systematically exchanged, first the raw materials used in the breweries, and then the workforce, until at last he determined that the difference resulted from the quality of well-water in the better brew. (Some eight decades later, the results of this trial-and-error experimentation were confirmed by scientific proof that the water in Yamamura's better brewery contained trace elements which enhanced the brewing process).[15]

The inventive dynamism of the saké industry, however, was driven by a rather unusual set of technological and social constraints. Unlike grapes, which ferment naturally if given the right conditions, rice needs very careful treatment before it can become the raw material for wine. First, a mould called *kôji* must be allowed to grow over the surface of the rice, creating a chemical compound suitable for fermentation. Next a small amount of the treated rice is mixed with water and yeast to form the basis of the brew. This is then mixed with larger quantities of rice and water and left for several weeks, before being ready for consumption. The final stage of the brewing process involved exposing the saké to heat for a short period of time in order to improve its shelf-life. (The procedure, which we know as pasteurisation, seems to have originated in China, and had been practised in Japan at least since the seventeenth century.)[16]

From the point of view of quality, the ideal time for making saké was midwinter, when the cold would inhibit the growth of any stray moulds which might compete with the all-important *kôji*. The problem was that cold also slowed fermentation, and so prolonged the production process.[17] The choice between slower winter fermentation and faster autumn or spring fermentation, however, was not left to the brewers themselves. Saké, because it used that measure of all wealth, rice, was a profoundly political product. From the middle of the seventeenth century onwards the Shogunate and domains repeatedly imposed restrictions on saké-making, both to prevent too much rice from being diverted into saké production, and to prevent labour from being attracted out of the rice fields and into the breweries. By the eighteenth century the making of 'new' or autumn saké had been banned in many places.[18]

The brewers' response to these technical and political challenges was to develop ways of compressing as much production as possible into the short winter saké season. Hence the importance of increasing the scale of production and of introducing labour-saving devices like the waterwheel. Happily for the Nada brewers, who adopted these methods most successfully, mechanisation in this case resulted in improved, rather than lowered, quality. Water-driven crushing hammers could polish rice far more effectively than human feet (which had been used before mechanisation), and the saké of progressive districts like Nada rapidly acquired a reputation for its taste as well as its low cost.

Carpentry and Instrument-making

European innovation, at least by the closing stages of the British industrial revolution, was starting to acquire that intellectual coherence which is characteristic of modern technology. New techniques, in other words, were beginning to be fitted into the framework of a set of sup-posedly universal scientific laws, whose findings could be used to illuminate the production processes of any branch of industry. Invention in Tokugawa Japan lacked that underlying conceptual unity. Although individual ideas might sometimes be transferred from one area of production to another—as the thermometer was transferred from medicine to silkfarming—there was no sense that the secret arts (*jutsu*) of, for example, brewing and metal-refining might be governed by the same natural principle—the laws of chemistry.

Intellectually, then, Tokugawa innovation was not a single broad river but rather a series of small, roughly parallel, streams. Economically, however, the innovations which we have looked at were closely interconnected. Silk production, for example, allowed some families to accumulate the wealth to buy new and better iron tools for farming; the use of iron tools reduced the time taken to grow staple crops, and so provided greater opportunities for farmers to seek by-employment in industries like saké-brewing; the expansion of new cash crops and industries, including ironmaking and brewing, increased the com-mercialisation of the economy, and thus the demand for money and the need for the mining of precious metals.

Every innovation, in other words, created ripples which were felt in many other parts of the economy; and one of the most important points of confluence for the impact of innovation was the world of the Japanese carpenter. Carpenters in Japan were the men who built, not only houses (including, of course, specialised buildings like breweries) but also reeling frames, weaving looms, waterwheels and bellows. Other closely related groups of artisans specialised in the production of equally important implements of production: coopers (*okeya*), for example, were responsible for making wooden buckets, including the enormous vats required by the saké-makers of Nada. Technological change, therefore, placed new demands on the carpenter and gave birth to specialised branches of the trade: groups of loom carpenters and waterwheel carpenters, for example, began to appear in various parts of the country.[19] At the same time, the growing precision required for the making of complex equipment encouraged further development of the already sophisticated skills of the Japanese carpenter. Tools like the carpenter's plane proliferated into a variety of forms— convex gouging planes, concave gouging planes, side-shaving planes and so forth—and the making of carpenters' tools in itself became a specialised trade in which the most exacting standards of accuracy were expected.[20] Carpenters' tools had traditionally been made by blacksmiths, but during the eighteenth century, just as certain districts of Japan acquired a reputation for the making of iron agricultural implements, so some (like the towns of Wakamatsu and Suwa) became famous for the quality of their saws, planes and chisels.[21]

Other forms of Tokugawa instrument-making also achieved remarkable levels of precision. The mechanical clock is believed to have been introduced to Japan by Francis Xavier in 1551, but it was Tokugawa artisans who succeeded in adapting the imported mechanism so that it moved according to the Japanese system of time. This was no mean feat. In Tokugawa Japan the period which we regard as lasting twenty-four hours was divided into two distinct parts: night and day, each consisting of six hours. Regardless of the season, the counting of the day-time hours began approximately at sunrise and ended approximately at sunset. The hours themselves were numbered, with a delightful leap of logic, six o'clock, five o'clock, four o'clock, nine o'clock, eight o'clock and seven o'clock. By sunset, therefore, the counting of the night-time hours could begin again at six. This meant, of course, that day-time hours were longer than night-time hours in summer, and shorter in winter: a difficulty which Japanese clockmakers addressed with considerably ingenuity. Some clocks had several interchangeable face plates with different spaces between the markings for the hours. On others there were sliding weights which had to be adjusted manually at sunrise and sunset to slow down or speed up the working of the mechanism. Others again had a double verge-and-foliot system which adjusted automatically to speed or slow the hands as they marked and measured the elusive flow of time.[22]

It was the clock which gave rise to that other most intriguing of all Tokugawa innovations: the automaton. In Japan, with its long tradition of puppetry, the idea of dolls which mimicked human behaviour had long exerted a particular fascination on artists and artisans, but it was the introduction of clockwork which provided the opportunity for new and far more realistic ventures into the mechanical representation of the human form. The designing of automata (*karakuri ningyô*) became a pastime which in particular attracted some of those low-ranking samurai whose interests tended towards science and Dutch studies. Among the most talented was Hosokawa Yorinao (d. 1796), the designer of a cavalcade of wonderful creations including a tea-serving doll who began a series of delicate movements as soon as a tea-cup was placed on the tray which she held in her hands.[23]

The technological significance of Japanese automata is a matter of debate. Historians such as Okumura Shôji emphasise that most were designed for pleasure by members of the upper classes.[24] Unlike the automata of Jacques Vaucanson and other European inventors—which provided the inspiration for practical mechanical devices—Japan's *karakuri ningyô*, it is argued, remained nothing more than elegant and ingenious playthings.[25] On the other hand, there were exceptional cases like that of Benkichi (d. 1870), the brilliant craftsman from Kaga Domain, whose interest in automata was combined with wide-ranging experimentation with static electricity, firearms, survey instruments and later cameras;[26] or, more famous still, the story of Tanaka Hisashige (1799–1881).

Tanaka was a craftsman from Kurume in Kyûshû whose skill in making astronomical instruments was so impressive that he was taken on as a pupil by one of the leading scholars of Tokugawa astronomy and later by a prominent teacher of Dutch studies.[27] Like his more illustrious predecessor Hiraga Gennai, he dabbled in a wide range of enterprises, amongst other things inventing a portable lamp and a fire extinguisher and, in 1852, establishing a shop called the Hall of Automata (*karakuri dô*) in Kyoto. By the time that Tanaka's shop opened for business, however, Commodore Matthew Perry's fleet of black ships was already setting sail for Japan, bearing with it ideas and assumptions which would shatter the imposed serenity of the Tokugawa state.

Soon after Perry's arrival, Tanaka, who had been summoned by Saga Domain to advise on technological modernisation, was set to work unravelling the secrets of western technology: within a year, he had built Japan's first working model of a steam locomotive, and by the 1870s he had established a machine-making firm which was to form part of the twentieth-century manufacturing giant Toshiba. Tokugawa innovation, as Tanaka Hisashige's career shows, generated knowledge and ideas which could be harnessed to the far more dramatic technological changes of the late nineteenth century.

Understanding the history of the Tokugawa period can help us to understand, not only reasons for Japan's rapid industrialisation, but also some of the characteristics of the industrialisation process. The developments of the seventeenth and eighteenth century left Japan with a deep stratum of skilled, and increasingly specialised, craft-workers. The striking feature of this skilled workforce was that it was not exclusively concentrated in a few metropolitan areas, but was widely dispersed amongst many regional communities, each with its own particular technical strengths and creative style.

The most important legacy of the Tokugawa period, however, was perhaps its influence on ideas about innovation. At the grassroots, well-to-do farmers and successful artisans were acquiring an appreciation of the value of technical knowledge as a source of wealth, and in some cases were even developing a systematic approach to experimentation with new techniques. At the level of domain and shogunal adminis-tration, efforts to 'develop products and promote enterprise' had made the borrowing of techniques from other regions an accepted part of government strategy. Mercantilist competition between the regions, as well as the spread of the printed word, were undermining the traditional technological secrecy imposed by the guild system. Mean-while, a number of low-ranking samurai were developing an interest in studying and disseminating new scientific and technological ideas. By the late eighteenth century, even the social philosophies of Japanese scholars were beginning to incorporate notions of technological and economic change. Where early Tokugawa thinkers had tended to emphasise harmony and stasis, some of their successors in the second half of the Tokugawa period were starting to speak of the need for the benign ruler to increase prosperity by encouraging the improvement of agriculture and craft manufacturing.[28]

The growing receptiveness to innovation, however, inevitably ran up against limits imposed by the nature of the Tokugawa social order. Tokugawa society had no officially recognised means of accommo-dating large-scale social change, and could therefore absorb new technologies only if their social consequences did not undermine the broad framework of the status system. The efforts of the political authorities to control the growth of saké-brewing and restrict the spread of the silk-reeling *zaguri* are illustrations of this continuing tension between innovation and social order. Tokugawa society helped to lay the foundations for Japan's later large-scale import of foreign technology, but the radical innovations of the industrial west could be accepted only after the Tokugawa order itself had been overthrown.

CHAPTER 3

Opening the Doors

Of Cannons, Iron Furnaces and the Outer Domains

It is a golden day in early summer. The wind is just strong enough to tilt the smoke which rises from a row of four tall chimneys, but not enough to ruffle the rice plants growing in the surrounding fields. The rice crop promises to be a healthy one, but the farmers on the hillside have, for a moment, been distracted from their perpetual concerns about pests, weeds and the weather, and are hurrying down to gaze at the extraordinary spectacle taking place below them. There, in a large open courtyard, a gaggle of dignitaries are gathered in a circle. The more important of them have removed their sandals, and are sitting on the straw mats spread on the ground for their comfort. All are craning forward to watch in wonder as a model steam train, built by Tanaka Hisashige and others on the basis of a Russian original, circles and circles on its miniature railway.

The year is 1855, and the scene has been recorded for us with that loving attention to detail so characteristic of Tokugawa paintings. But there is more to this picture than immediately meets the eye. In the buildings at the back of the courtyard we can see pottery being shaped and fired and metal being smelted. The workers engaged in these activities scarcely seem to have interrupted the rhythm of their labour, as though they feel no special awe at technical novelties like the steam train; and this is perhaps not surprising, for they are, in fact, part of a team of craftsmen and scholars brought together by Saga Domain just before the arrival of Perry to experiment with western military and industrial techniques.

The story of Saga's interest in western technology really goes back to the beginning of the nineteenth century. The Domain of Saga was not only situated next to the port of Nagasaki, Japan's window on the outside world, but was also one of a number of domains charged with the responsibility of defending Nagasaki from foreign incursions. The defence of Nagasaki was undertaken by the neighbouring domains in turn on a rotating basis, and it was Nabeshima Narinao, the Lord of Saga, who had the misfortune to be officially responsible for the city in October 1808, when the British ship *Phaeton* sailed into Nagasaki harbour. The British were at that time at war with the Netherlands, and the *Phaeton* had been engaged in harrying Dutch merchant shipping. As he approached land, however, Captain Pellew, master of the *Phaeton*, impudently raised the Dutch flag, in the hope that he might be allowed to enter port and buy provisions from the Japanese. The arrival of this mysterious ship threw both the Japanese authorities and the legitimate Dutch traders into a state of total confusion. By the time they had established that the vessel was indeed British, and had drawn up plans to detain it, the *Phaeton* had taken advantage of a favourable tide and sailed off unscathed in the direction from which it had come.[1]

The episode was a stark reminder to the Japan of the ease with which westerners could breach the official policy of isolation. More immediately, it was a personal disaster for Nabeshima Narinao, who had been hundreds of kilometres away in Edo at the time, and was sentenced to house arrest for his negligence. (Several of his retainers were forced to commit suicide.) The *Phaeton* affair was only one of a series of incidents which recurred with growing frequency as the frontiers of expanding western colonialism encroached upon the sea margins of the 'closed country'. In 1811, the crew of the Russian ship *Diana* were arrested as they surveyed the Kurile Islands to the north of Hokkaidô; in 1813 the British, who had obtained temporary control of Java, tried unsuccessfully to open trade with Japan; in 1837 an American vessel, the *Morrison*, visited Japan in a vain attempt to return a group of Japanese fishermen who had been picked up in the Pacific after being blown off course in a storm; in 1846 a US mission consisting of naval vessels *Columbus* and *Vincennes* was rebuffed in its attempt to open negotiations with the Shogunate, and in 1849 the captain of the British warship *Mariner* encountered a similar reception.[2] Knowledge of the west's growing military might, and particularly of the defeat of China in the Opium War of 1840–42, persuaded the more thoughtful members of the Japanese elite that the status quo could not continue indefinitely. The Shogunate, conscious of the foreign threat, not only began to strengthen coastal fortifications but even relaxed its restrictions on the domains, allowing them, amongst other things, to experiment with western-style military technology. The unfortunate experience of Nabeshima Narinao, however, left a particularly profound impression upon his son Naomasa, who succeeded him as daimyo of Saga in 1830.

Naomasa, anxious to avoid a repetition of the *Phaeton* incident, made frequent personal visits to Nagasaki and became deeply convinced of the need to study western armaments.

The quickening interest in foreign techniques which is evident in domains like Saga from the 1830s onwards was only partly a response to external threats. Another stimulus was the growing crisis of domain finances: a crisis which reflected the underlying inability of the Tokugawa political order to adapt to the circumstances of an increasingly commercialised economy. Financial problems were unusually acute in Saga, where Nabeshima Narinao's handling of money seems to have been no more competent than his defence of Nagasaki. The situation was so dire, indeed, that his son Naomasa, when summoned back from Edo to assume power on Narinao's death, was forced to set out on his journey at night to avoid the Edo merchants who were clamouring for the repayment of loans to the domain.[3] The younger Nabeshima therefore inherited not only a fear and respect for the westerners but also an economic predicament which he tackled, energetically though traditionally enough, by a policy of 'developing products and promoting enterprise'.

The reforms introduced by Nabeshima Naomasa included a system of bureaucratic appointments based on merit not rank, a radical redistribution of farm land, and the licensing of a trading venture in Nagasaki to sell Arita porcelain directly to the Dutch. The most innovative aspect of his policy, however, was the encouragement which he gave to the domain's expanding circle of 'Dutch scholars'. Naomasa's desire to develop defensive weaponry capable of resisting European incursions into Japanese waters led him to focus particularly on the production of western-style cannon. Here, however, Japan faced one major technical difficulty. The traditional Japanese *tatara* method of ironmaking was perfectly adequate for producing small cast-iron objects like pots and pans, but was incapable of producing the large volumes of homogeneous molten iron needed to cast a cannon. A small group of scholars and artisans, including a mathematician, several traditional ironworkers and the samurai scholar Sugitani Yōsuke (1820–66), was therefore commissioned to learn and emulate the secrets of western iron-casting.[4]

The task was a daunting one. The main source of information available to them was a single volume describing the state-owned ironworks in the Dutch city of Leiden, which had been translated into Japanese by Sugitani. Indeed, the contemporary Japanese eagerness for information on military-related technologies is revealed by the fact that this same Dutch document was rendered into at least three separate Japanese translations in the closing years of the Tokugawa era.[5]

Remarkably, with the help of Sugitani's translation and a process of trial and error, the Saga team actually succeeded in building Japan's first reverberatory iron furnace by 1850, three years before the arrival of Perry, and by 1853 the domain was producing cast-iron cannon both for its own use and to meet orders from the Shogunate.

Meanwhile in November 1852, the very month when Commodore Matthew Perry was setting sail on his mission to Japan, Saga's ventures into western technology took a further step with the establishment of the Seirenkata, an experimental centre designed to test and apply western techniques not only in military-related areas such as metal-smelting, shipbuilding and armaments manufacture, but also in fields like the manufacture of textiles, paper, ceramics and dyestuffs.[6] It was here in 1855 that Tanaka Hisashige's model steam train was developed and displayed to its admiring audience. The Seirenkata also acquired a substantial library of western technical texts, which were catalogued, translated and studied by the institute's Dutch scholars.

Now that one domain had begun to acquire western military and metallurgical techniques, the dynamics of the Tokugawa system created a predictable chain reaction. Saga's newly obtained knowledge was a disturbing element in the delicate balance of power between domains and Shogunate, and provoked a swift competitive response. The first to take up the challenge was the influential southern domain of Satsuma which, like Saga, had an energetic ruler with an interest in Dutch studies. By 1851 the daimyo of Satsuma, too, had ordered a local group of scholars and artisans to build a reverberatory furnace, memorably observing that, after all 'the westerners and the people of Saga are human, just like us' (*seiyôjin mo hito nari, Sagajin mo hito nari, Satsumajin mo onajiku hito nari*).[7] In the north, the domain of Mito—a focus for Japan's emerging nationalist ideology—hired the brilliant 'Dutch scholar' Ôshima Takatô (1826–1901) to help construct a western-style ironworks, while officials of the Shogunate dispatched a technician to study in Saga and, in 1854, established their own reverberatory furnace at Nirayama on the Izu Peninsula.[8] By 1868, there were eleven Japanese reverberatory furnaces in existence or in construction, and a further three in the planning stage.[9]

The setting up of the very first western-style furnaces, planned and built entirely by Japanese technicians, was a very considerable achievement. It is true that the reverberatory furnace, which had been in use in Europe since the seventeenth century, was not a very complex piece of technology: the main innovation lay in the fact that the iron to be smelted was not piled directly on top of the fuel in the furnace, but was placed in a separate chamber, and flames from the fire were forced back onto it by the arched roof of the furnace, so that impurities from the fuel were less likely to contaminate the smelted metal. The difficulties involved in applying this technology from a single foreign handbook, however, are illustrated by Ôshima Takatô's succinct and rather touching account of the construction of the Mito furnace.

Ôshima Takatô was the son of a doctor, and had studied Dutch medicine first in Edo and later in Nagasaki.[10] His chief claim to expertise in iron-smelting was the fact that he had produced one of the alternative translations of the Leiden text which had also provided the know-how for Saga's reverberatory furnace, and it was on this basis that he was approached by a leading official in the Mito administration and invited to work for the domain. His first step was to design a scale model of the furnace, which he made with the help of a local artisan. Then, with a small group of associates, he moved to Mito and began work on the site which had been selected for the furnace. Before constructing the ironworks, however, it was necessary to find a suitable source of clay for brickmaking, and to experiment with the firing of bricks (which were not, of course, a familiar form of construction material in Japan). Next, Ôshima and his team had to locate a source of fuel, and to establish which varieties of fuel might be suitable for firing the furnace. Meanwhile, skilled metal-workers had to be instructed in the art of making the various pieces of metal equipment for use in the ironworks. In the midst of all this, construction was temporarily halted by a severe earthquake, but, almost two years after starting work on the project, Ôshima was able to test the firing of his first furnace.[11]

It quickly became obvious that there was a major problem. Although the furnace was correctly designed, the ingots of iron which were placed into the furnace did not become fully liquid, and lumps of unmelted metal remained. This was because Ôshima was using ingots produced by the traditional *tatara* method, which were unevenly carbonised, so that some parts of the iron had a much higher smelting temperature than others.[12] Undaunted, Ôshima returned to his home domain of Nambu and, with financial support from local wealthy merchants, opened up an iron mine to provide a source of raw materials which more closely approximated to those used in the west. In order to smelt the iron ore (which was very different from the iron sand traditionally used in *tatara* ironmaking) it was necessary to construct a western-style blast furnace—the famous Kamaishi blast furnace which, after decades of destruction, reconstruction and changes of ownership, was eventually to provide the basis for Japan's modern iron and steel industry.[13] Using the iron ingots produced at Kamaishi, Ôshima was finally able to put the Mito furnace into successful operation, and the domain's first cannon were cast. In 1858 a major celebration was held to mark the triumph of the Mito ironmaking enterprise, but, in the middle of the merry-making, a messenger arrived to say that the daimyo of Mito had fallen into disgrace as a result of a conflict with shogunal advisers. The party broke up, and the reverberatory furnace was forced to close. Ôshima concludes his account with the words: 'later, during fighting [at the time of the Meiji Restoration], it was completely destroyed by fire'.[14]

Given the problems involved, it is hardly surprising that several of the early furnaces were total failures. The significant point, though, is that some (including the Saga and Satsuma furnaces) *did* succeed, and that their success had far-reaching effects upon Japan's economic development. For one thing, as we have seen, the introduction of this single piece of western technology set in motion a chain reaction of change which engulfed many other areas of industry. In order to operate reverberatory furnaces, it was necessary to develop new methods of construction, find new ways of making construction materials like bricks, introduce new techniques for treating iron ore, and improve methods of transporting raw materials to feed the voracious maws of the western-style ironworks. As a result, technicians and domain bureaucrats, who had begun by focusing narrowly on western military techniques as a means of national defence, were gradually forced to widen their perspectives, and to recognise the value of western technology in areas far removed from the building of warships and the casting of cannon.[15]

The new ironworks were also important, not only in developing the technological hardware of buildings and machinery, but also in developing the 'software' of modern factory-style systems of employment and labour relations. Indeed, historian Erich Pauer identifies the reverberatory furnaces as containing 'the roots of Japan's factory system', and thus as representing the 'starting point of a new period in the economic development of Japan'.[16] When we recall the developments which had already occurred in areas like saké-brewing, this view seems questionable, but it is certainly true that the furnaces, with their relatively complex division of tasks and their reliance on day-labour for less skilled employees, helped to hasten the transformation of Japanese employment structures.

A close look at the early ironworks also helps us to glimpse some possible explanations for Japan's dynamic response to imported technology. One explanation lies in the relatively narrow gap between imported technologies and endogenous know-how. Japanese technicians were well aware that their scientific knowledge was far behind that of their western counterparts. However, both they and the craftsmen with whom they worked had a rich store of empirical knowledge which could be of use when applying relatively mature western

technologies like the reverberatory and blast furnaces. Several historians have suggested that Ôshima Takatô's Kamaishi blast furnace
(which continued to supply iron to other furnaces long after the
closure of the Mito foundry) survived in part because it could draw
upon the traditional skills of local ironworkers and other artisans.[17] It
may be remembered that the Nambu region, where the blast furnace
was situated, was one of the few where Japanese metal-workers had
traditionally extracted iron from ore-bearing rock, rather than from
sand (see p. 49). Ôshima relied, however, not only on the traditional
know-how of the region's iron masters, but also on the specialised skills
of other craftspeople, such as the carpenters who constructed the
furnace's water-powered bellows.[18] In this sense, the technological
developments of the Tokugawa era provided a crucial foundation for
Japan's first faltering steps towards the introduction of western-style
industrial techniques.

But it is the organisational, as well as the technological, legacy of the
Tokugawa system which helps to explain the absorption of western
ideas. The dynamics of rivalry between domains and Shogunate
ensured that, rather than a single furnace being constructed to a single
model, a host of rival ventures were set up in different parts of the
country, each using the particular natural and human resources
available to that region. This dispersal and diversity of effort may well
have been a crucial factor in success. Just as, in nature, diversity helps to
ensure survival, so in the case of human technology, experimentation
with a number of slightly different models helped to ensure that at least
some would come up with that particular mixture of human skills and
natural resources which allowed this imported technique to flourish in
the unfamiliar environment of mid-nineteenth-century Japan. This
pattern of regional rivalry was repeated in many other areas of early
technological borrowing from the west. Saga Domain's Seirenkata, for
example, competed for status and prestige with Satsuma's Shûseikan,
which included not only the domain's ironworks but also experimental
factories producing glass, porcelain, paper, agricultural implements
and carpenters' tools, and employing in all some 1200 workers. The
development of these domain institutions in turn provoked a response
from the Shogunate which, in 1855, expanded its translation bureau
into a centre for research into western techniques, known as the
Bansho Shirabesho, or Institute for the Study of Barbarian Documents.

Japan and the Black Ships

By the time that this institute was established, however, circumstances
had been profoundly altered by the arrival of Commodore Matthew

Perry with a message from the US President demanding the opening of Japan to western commerce. Perry's arrival has often been depicted as a dramatic and epoch-making intrusion, awakening Japan from the prolonged slumber of its feudal age. But, as we have seen, some sections of Japanese society were very much awake already. The main impact of Perry's arrival, then, was to intensify and accelerate processes of change which had already, in a rather tentative way, begun to take shape in Tokugawa society.

Above all, Perry's flotilla of warships, which included the first steamships ever seen in Japanese waters, focused the mind of Japan's rulers on the virtually non-existent state of Japan's naval defences. The Shogunate now found it necessary to balance the desire for domestic control against a growing fear of foreign aggression, and within three months of Perry's arrival, the prohibition on the building of large ships had been abolished. The import of foreign ships, however, remained a shogunal monopoly until 1862.[19] So, while the Shogunate devoted much of its energies to buying naval vessels from the Dutch, training Japanese seamen to sail them, and developing dry docks for ship repair, the domains immediately turned their attention to building their own warships. Like the building of reverberatory furnaces, the construction of western-style ships became a competition among the domains for power and prestige. Even remote, impoverished fiefs such as Uwajima in Shikoku joined in.

It was Satsuma, however, with its strong leadership and tradition of interest in Dutch studies, which won the race to build the first Japanese steamship. In 1855, technicians working at the domain lord's Edo residence completed a 15-horsepower steam engine, which was then fitted to a 21-metre boat constructed in Satsuma, and used to drive an external paddle wheel.[20] It seems almost inconceivable that Japanese scholars and artisans were able, only two years after their first encounter with a steamship, to build a working model of a paddle-steamer. The secret, of course, lies in the fact that Japan's Dutch scholars were already quite familiar with the *idea* of steam power, which they knew from technical texts acquired from the Dutch. Scholars like Ogata Kôan had translated illustrated Dutch studies of steam engines, and it was a translation of a Dutch book—G. J. Verdam's 1837 *Volledige Verhandeling over de Stoomwerktuigen* (*Complete Treatise on Steam Engines*)—which provided much of the technical know-how for the construction of the Satsuma vessel.[21]

The Shogunate, meanwhile, had also turned to the Dutch for assistance in constructing its first naval dockyard. The Nagasaki dockyard, completed in 1861, was a relatively complex and sophisticated affair, incorporating its own ironworks, and containing imported equipment such as a steam hammer.[22] It was quickly followed by the construction of the Yokosuka and Yokohama dockyards, completed with French technical assistance.[23] As well as setting up its own dockyards, the Shogunate also commissioned some wealthy domains to develop their shipbuilding capacity. The Ishikawajima dockyards in Edo, for example, were built by the Domain of Mito on the orders of the Shogunate, and were used to construct ships for shogunal use.[24]

The enthusiasm with which every scrap of available western knowledge was seized and utilised is nicely illustrated by the story of Admiral Putiatin and the tsunami. In 1854 a Russian naval vessel commanded by Putiatin, following hard on the heels of Perry, put into the Japanese port of Shimoda to demand trading rights in Japan. While he was in harbour, a major earthquake struck and the resulting tsunami destroyed the Russian vessel. To avoid being marooned in Japan, Putiatin reached an agreement with the Shogunate whereby Japanese shipwrights would construct a large western-style sailing vessel under the technical guidance of his Russian crew. The ship—a 100-ton wooden schooner—was completed in 1855, and Putiatin was able to pilot it safely home to Russia. As part of the agreement, however, he left behind the construction plans of the ship, and within a few years the shogunal navy had acquired six Japanese-built copies of the original Russian design.[25] When Perry arrived in Japan, the country had no naval vessels at all: by the time of the Meiji Restoration in 1868, the Shogunate had a fleet of forty-five ships and the domains a total of ninety-four.[26]

Hired Foreigners and Japanese Abroad

As so often in the history of technology, it was an external threat which forced the political authorities to accept the risks of change. The power of the west left the Shogunate little choice but to open the doors to military techniques which would change the balance of domestic power; the daimyo in turn were forced to recognise the need for innovations which would disrupt the social stability of their domains. But, because Japan was not colonised, nor even economically dominated by the west, it was able to call upon existing political and intellectual resources to face the challenge. Indeed, a vital instrument in confronting the technological threat from the west was an expanded and revised version of the well-established policy of 'developing products and promoting industry'.

The fear which drove this policy was not an irrational one. The western powers preferred, if possible, to obtain access to Japanese ports and trade by peaceful means, but they were quite prepared to use military force where necessary. This was clearly demonstrated in 1863 and again in 1864 when Britain, in retaliation for anti-foreign incidents, bombarded the sea defences of Satsuma and Chôshû. Meanwhile, by 1858, the reluctant Shogunate had been forced to sign treaties allowing first the United States and then the other major western powers the right to trade within the bounds of certain specified treaty ports.

Once the doors had been opened, however, it became increasingly difficult for the Shogunate to maintain its theoretical monopoly on foreign trade, and—just as importantly—to limit the access of its political rivals to western knowledge. The treaty ports, at first restricted to the remote towns of Shimoda and Hakodate, were soon expanded to include Nagasaki and Yokohama (opened to foreigners in 1859), Niigata (1860) and Kobe (1863), and from the early 1860s foreigners were also admitted to Osaka and Edo.[27] The exact size of Japan's foreign population in the final years of the Shogunate is impossible to determine, but by the early Meiji period there were already more than 250 western trading companies operating in Japan, and probably an even larger number of Chinese merchant ventures.[28]

The growing foreign communities offered a precious new source of information on western technologies, and one which both the Shogunate and the domains were quick to tap. A small number of foreigners (like the Dutch instructor who was sent over to run the Shogunate's new naval training centre at Nagasaki)[29] were brought to Japan specifically because of their technical expertise, but many were people who simply happened to be in the right place at the right time. Some of these early advisers, indeed, had no real technical expertise at all. What they did have, however, was that crucial ability to find out information: to read western books, consult other western specialists and, where necessary, to hire their own expert assistants. As steam engines increased the demand for coal, for example, the Domain of Saga hired a young Scottish merchant, Thomas Glover (1838–1911), to help in the expansion of the small and rather primitive coalmine on the island of Takashima, off Nagasaki. Glover had no technical training and no experience of coalmining, but despite these disadvantages was still able to supervise the sinking of the first European-style coalmining shaft in Japan.[30]

For both domains and Shogunate, the hiring of foreigners was in many ways an extension of the familiar mercantilist practice of borrowing or stealing technical know-how from other regions. Now, however, local crafts could be strengthened by the import of technology, not only from neighbouring domains, but also from much more distant sources. The official in charge of the Arita potteries, for example, was really just giving a new twist to an old story when he invited Gottfried Wagener, a German chemist in the employ of a Nagasaki trading venture, to teach local potters the secrets of western chemical glazes.[31] Likewise, Maebashi Domain was merely extending the long history of technical borrowing in the silk industry when it brought in a Swiss technician in an attempt to set up a western-style silk-reeling mill.[32] (Both of these ventures in technical borrowing, which occurred in the troubled years between the fall of the Shogunate in 1867 and the abolition of the domains in 1872, encountered considerable local resistance, but both paved the way for later successful imports of western technology.)

The assistance of foreign technicians was sought both to develop products for export (as in the case of Arita and Maebashi), and to protect local industries from the onslaught of imported manufactured goods. Some of Japan's more farsighted political leaders clearly recognised that the threat from the west was not simply a military one, but also a threat of economic domination. To respond, Japan needed industrial machinery as much as it needed guns and warships. This philosophy was pursued most explicitly and most successfully in the Domain of Satsuma, whose industrial complex, the Shûseikan, became the basis for an ambitious policy of self-strengthening through westernisation. In 1866 the domain completed an agreement with Platt Brothers of Oldham in England for the purchase of machinery to establish a western-style cotton mill. Platt provided, not only the cotton spinning mules, but also a team of seven technical experts to help establish the factory. The cotton mill, housed in an impressive stone building and containing 3648 steam-driven spindles, was opened in 1867, and three years later a second western-style cotton mill was also set up under the control of Satsuma in the port city of Sakai.[33]

The ideology which drove this process of westernisation was very clearly set out in a memorandum written in 1868 by the domain official responsible for the planning of Satsuma's cotton mill projects. This document not only points out that mechanised spinning could increase productivity twentyfold, but also emphasises the connection between western mechanised technology, wealth and national power:

> it is becoming everywhere more and more evident that machinery is the basis of wealth. There is belief that the reason why Britain is now able to flaunt its might to the world is because it possesses machinery. Some might think that this is a mistaken belief arising from [British] pride, but in my humble opinion it is nothing less than the truth.[34]

Though powerful outer domains like Satsuma were the first to employ these developmentalist ideologies, by the second half of the 1860s the Shogunate, too, was beginning to accept the need for radical change. The last Shogun, Tokugawa Yoshinobu, was particularly conscious that the survival of the regime depended upon rapid adoption of western technology, and initiated a number of schemes, including an unfulfilled plan to build Japan's first railways with the help of US engineers.

It is easy to assume that 'foreign borrowing' was inevitably borrowing from the west, but the opening of the ports also meant an important revival of contacts between Japan and other parts of Asia, particularly China. The westernisers of the late Tokugawa period tended to view China with some scorn: its failure to stand up to western incursion presented a case study of the fate which Japan's modernisers sought to avoid. In practice, however, China, with its greater experience of international trade, possessed valuable know-how in various areas of technology, particularly those connected with agriculture and the processing of agricultural goods. For example, new techniques for firing tea, which was one of Japan's three main export items in the 1860s, were introduced with the help of Chinese technicians and merchants. Of some 160 foreigners employed by local governments just after the Meiji Restoration, forty-three were Chinese.[35]

The use of hired foreigners as sources of technical know-how was, of course, to be continued and greatly expanded under the Meiji regime from 1868 onwards, but it is important to realise that, in its employment of foreign advisers as in so much else, Meiji Japan was building upon foundations laid in the Tokugawa age. The same is true of another Meiji policy: the sending of Japanese students overseas for technical training. During the 1860s a small number of talented individuals were selected for overseas study by the Shogunate and (illegally) by the powerful outer domains of Satsuma and Chôshû.[36] Although some concentrated on the study of languages and social sciences, others received university training in engineering and science subjects. All were young, highly educated and intensely nationalistic samurai, and many were to play central roles in Japan's later industrialisation. Diplomatic missions by the Shogunate to America (1860) and Europe (1862 and 1864) also gave some members of the Japanese elite a chance, if not for overseas study, at least to experience life in the west at first hand.

The most interesting opportunity to observe western technology was probably the Paris International Exhibition of 1867. Japan, officially participating in an event of this kind for the first time,[37] sent displays organised by the Shogunate and by the domains of Saga and Satsuma, and accompanied, not only by samurai officials, but also by a select group of merchants and artisans.[38] The exhibition, as it turned out, provided the forum for a genuine exchange of ideas: Japan's silk, lacquerware and porcelain attracted intense curiosity, and helped to inspire the fashion for *Japonisme* which swept Europe in the ensuing decades; the Japanese delegation, on the other hand, took the opportunity to visit French workshops and factories, and many returned to become instant experts and educators in various fields of western technology.[39]

For Japanese travellers of the late Tokugawa period, the experience of the west must have been astonishing and bemusing. Some, like Shibusawa Eiichi, who attended the Paris Exhibition and was later to become one of Japan's most famous industrial entrepreneurs, spoke of the great western industrial cities with their huge factories and their thousands of industrial workers.[40] Many returned to their own country impatient with its limitations and conservatism, and fired with a missionary zeal for change. But their comments also shed a sometimes surprising light upon the relationship and contrasts between Japanese and western science and technology on the eve of Japan's industrial revolution.

Amongst the members of Japan's first official delegation to the United States in 1860 was a young man by the name of Fukuzawa Yukichi. A Dutch scholar who had studied at Ogata Kôan's Osaka academy, he would come to be known as one of Meiji Japan's leading proponents of westernisation. For Fukuzawa, this first encounter with the west was both fascinating and stimulating. But although he found much to surprise him in the United States, his reaction to American industrial technology was somewhat restrained. Fukuzawa and his fellow delegates were introduced to the San Fransisco telegraph system and taken on a tour of a sugar refinery, and, as he later recorded in his memoirs,

> I am sure that our hosts thought that they were showing us something entirely new, naturally looking for our surprise at each new device of modern engineering. But on the contrary, there was nothing really new, at least to me. I knew the principle of telegraphy even if I had not seen the actual machine before; I knew that sugar was bleached by straining the solution with bone-black, and that in boiling down the solution, the vacuum was used to better effect than heat. I had been studying nothing else but such scientific principles ever since I had entered Ogata's school.

No, what really amazed Fukuzawa about US technology was not its scientific sophistication but its remarkable profligacy with raw materials:

> there seemed to be an enormous waste of iron everywhere. In garbage piles, on the seashores—everywhere—I found lying old oil tins, empty cans and broken tools. This was remarkable to us, for in Edo, after a fire, there would appear a swarm of people looking for nails in the ashes.[41]

PART II

Technology in Industrialising Japan, 1868–1945

CHAPTER 4

Technology and the Meiji State, 1868-1912

'Under Reconstruction'

A story written in 1910 by the famous Meiji physician and novelist Mori Ôgai begins with a description of the main character, Watanabe, walking along a street full of people in western dress and entering a western-style restaurant.

> The front of the building facing the canal was covered with scaffolding ... Inside he found a wide passage. By the door was a pile of little Japanese cloths for wiping one's shoes and next to these a large western doormat ... Apparently in this restaurant one was supposed to observe the Western custom and wear one's shoes indoors. There was no sign of life in the passage, but from the distance came a great sound of hammering and sawing. The place was under reconstruction, thought Watanabe.[1]

The restaurant is, of course, a metaphor. As the story unfolds it becomes obvious that it is Japan itself—noisy, shrouded in scaffolding and full of disconcerting novelties—which was being reconstructed.

Mori Ôgai's imagery suggests the enormously unsettling effect which the changes of the Meiji Era (1868-1912) had upon many people in Japan. The revolution of 1867-68 which swept away the Tokugawa Shogunate had itself been surprisingly swift. Attempts at modernisation by the last Shogun, Tokugawa Yoshinobu, were too little and too late to win over the increasingly restless and assertive outer lords. By 1866 the powerful domains of Satsuma and Chôshû had formed a secret anti-shogunal alliance, and even when, in 1867, Tokugawa Yoshinobu agreed to surrender his powers to the Emperor and form a ruling council of lords, his opponents were not appeased. Seizing their opportunity, they attacked the Shogun's army, which was quickly routed. They then marched on Edo (soon to be renamed 'Tokyo' or 'Eastern Capital') and took control of the Shogun's castle, in which

71

they installed the young and politically inexperienced Emperor Meiji. The official justification for this revolution was that it represented a 'restoration' of power to that symbolic figurehead, the Emperor. In practice, however, political control was concentrated in the hands of a few young, energetic samurai, most of them drawn from the leading rebel domains of Satsuma and Chôshû.

The period from the revolution of 1868 to the death of the Emperor Meiji in 1912 was one of the most remarkable epochs of change in Japanese history. During these years Japan became a centralised state with a cabinet and parliament; a nationwide railway and telegraph network was established; a large merchant marine was developed, and Japan acquired the most modern and powerful military force in Asia. By the end of the Meiji Era Japan had more than 32,000 factories employing over 800,000 workers. Many of these were no more than simple workshops using craft techniques inherited from the Tokugawa age, but a number used modern techniques borrowed or adapted from the west: between them they contained some 5400 steam engines and over 2700 electrically powered machines.[2] From 1885 to 1915, while agriculture grew at the respectable but moderate rate of around 1.8 per cent a year, manufacturing and mining surged ahead at a rate of over 5 per cent a year.[3] By 1910 therefore, the industrial sector's share in Japan's GDP, which had amounted to just under 13 per cent in 1888, had expanded to almost 20 per cent.[4] Japan, in short, was firmly on the road to industrialisation.

This economic and technological dynamism is a source of fascination to many historians, for the events of the Meiji age are not only fundamental to the entire course of modern Japanese development, but may also have a wider relevance to present-day industrialising countries. Many scholars have turned their attention to Meiji Japan in search of lessons to guide contemporary less-developed countries in their pursuit of modern technology.[5] The Meiji period has consequently become one of the best-ploughed fields of Japanese economic and technological history. As is so often the case, however, repeated study has resulted, not in consensus but in deepening controversy about the nature and causes of change. As a result Meiji Japan has become the focus for some heated debates on the nature and causes of technological change.

The State-centred Approach

The more conventional, and still probably the more influential, view of technological change in Meiji Japan can be described as the 'state-centred' approach. Looked at from this perspective, the story goes roughly as follows.

The State and Industrial Infrastructure

Freed from the constraints of Tokugawa feudalism, the new leaders of Meiji Japan were able to embark upon a radical program of reform and westernisation. The Meiji oligarchs themselves were a remarkably able and farsighted band of men who pursued the goals of military and industrial might with single-minded determination. Within a matter of years they had abolished the feudal domains and swept away the status divisions of Tokugawa society, creating the basis for a more fluid and dynamic social order.

Because Japan was a latecomer to industrialisation, forced by outside pressure to leap from the feudal into the modern age, there was no time to develop the intellectual and social structures which had sustained innovation in the west. Instead, the state was obliged to fill the gap, acting as a go-between in the import of foreign techniques. Japanese industrialisation therefore became 'industrialisation from above'.[6]

The lynchpin of this program of forced modernisation was the Kôbushô (variously translated as 'Ministry of Industry', 'Ministry of Engineering' or 'Ministry of Construction'), which during its brief existence from 1870 to 1885 embarked on an ambitious program of importing relatively advanced western technology. The aim, in the words of Itô Hirobumi (the famous Meiji politician who headed the Ministry from 1873), was to

> make good Japan's deficiencies by swiftly seizing upon the strengths of the western industrial arts; to construct within Japan all kinds of mechanical equipment on the western model, including shipbuilding, railways, telegraph, mines and buildings; and thus with one great leap to introduce to Japan the concepts of enlightenment.[7]

The Ministry's achievements included the construction of Japan's first railway lines—linking Tokyo to Yokohama, and Kobe to Osaka and Kyoto, as well as a rail and boat link from Kyoto to Tsuruga on the Japan Sea coast—and the creation of a nationwide telegraph network, completed by the 1880s. Both of these projects were carried out in the face of considerable criticism. Sceptics pointed out that the improvement of roads for horse carts would be as useful as the building of railways and would cost a fraction of the price,[8] while the telegraph system became the target of attacks by conservative samurai and other dissidents. In 1873 more than hundred telegraph poles were demolished by protesters in one region of Japan alone.[9] For the Ministry, however, the new infrastructure was not merely an economic necessity, it was also a visible representation of the centralised state, capable of conveying the government's writ to remote parts of the country, and (if necessary) of conveying soldiers to ensure that the writ was enforced.

In both these projects, the government made use of the best available foreign technology. At the peak of its railway construction program in 1876, the Kôbushô was employing more than one hundred British engineers and technicians. At the same time, though, the Ministry was always conscious of the dangers of technological dependence on the west, and was determined to ensure that the hired foreigners imparted their knowledge to their Japanese counterparts and went home as quickly as possible.[10] For this reason, it set up a training centre for Japanese railway engineers in Osaka, and, at the other end of the technological spectrum, adapted traditional Japanese tunnelling and masonry techniques to the more mundane aspects of railway-building.[11] In telegraph construction, too, the state resisted attempts by foreign enterprises to obtain control of Japan's lucrative communications business. State control of the telegraph system was not only important for strategic reasons, but also enabled the government to encourage the local production of simple pieces of communications equipment. As early as 1870, for example, the Ministry commissioned a leading Arita potter to produce a porcelain insulator for the telegraph system, so laying the basis for the development of industrial ceramics in Japan and of one of Arita's largest present-day enterprises.[12]

The same combination of nationalism and ambitious western borrowing characterised the Ministry's ventures in mining. During the early Meiji period Japan's mining industry was divided between state and private ownership, with the Kôbushô controlling several major enterprises while others remained in the hands of traditional mine-owning families. There were, however, distinct differences between state-owned and private mines in terms of their approach to technology. The private concerns of the early Meiji period tended to be cost-conscious and cautious in their approach to western techniques. By contrast, the Kôbushô mines were enthusiastic, not to say profligate, in their use of imported ideas and expertise.

Foreign mine technicians and Japanese experts were employed to advise on improved methods of tunnelling and refining. Steam engines were brought in to pump water from the mines, and explosives were introduced for blasting tunnels. Amalgamation and precipitation techniques for separating precious metals were adopted, water-powered stamp mills were constructed, and imported jigger machines used for ore separation.[13]

The Kôbushô's management of the Kamaishi ironworks was symbolic of the government's general technological approach. At Kamaishi, a new integrated ironworks was constructed, complete with blast furnace, wrought-iron furnace, and a railway linking the ironworks to the nearby mines and harbour. Machinery and expertise were imported from

Britain, and the Ministry had visions of Kamaishi works' not only supplying local demand but also exporting its products to the Asian mainland. In the end, however, the Ministry's insistence on large-scale production and imported techniques proved its downfall. The Kamaishi works was plagued by shortages of ore and fuel, transport problems and high costs, and in 1883, just three years after it had started production and with a loss of more than ¥2 million, the new ironworks was closed. It was only after the iron foundry was sold to private interests in the late 1880s that it began to operate on a profitable basis.[14] In this context it is worth noting that the shift from small-scale traditional *tatara* ironmaking to large modern ironworks— as well as the development of huge privately owned copper refineries at Ashio and Besshi—would lead to severe problems of air and water pollution, provoking conflicts with local farmers and fishermen on a far larger scale than those caused by Tokugawa iron-mining techniques.[15]

The Ministry's industrial empire also included the state-owned Nagasaki and Hyôgo shipyards, and the Akabane machine works, established in 1871 to produce western-style equipment such as steam engines, sugar mills, cotton spinning mules, and silk-reeling machinery.[16] All of this, however, constituted only a part of the Meiji government's drive towards industrialisation. The Kôbushô's ventures in transport, communications, mining and heavy industry were paralleled by the activities of the Ministry of the Interior which, under the leadership of the powerful Meiji oligarch Ôkubo Toshimichi, focused on the development of Japanese agricultural and textile technology, running experimental farms, sending agricultural delegations to China and India as well as to the west,[17] and operating its own model factories. Like the Kôbushô, the Ministry of the Interior made extensive use of imported techniques, often with unfortunate results. In 1879 for example, it imported a number of 2000-spindle English spinning mules, which it sold cheaply to local governments and private entrepreneurs. As it turned out, the equipment was too small-scale for modern factory production, Japanese technicians had difficulty installing and maintaining the mules, the quality of the spun thread proved to be poor, and many of the enterprises which acquired the mules went bankrupt within a few years.[18]

The same predilection for imported techniques was evident in the Tomioka silk-reeling works, perhaps the most famous of all Meiji model factories, which had been set up in 1872 by Itô Hirobumi and the westernising entrepreneur Shibusawa Eiichi, but was taken over by the Ministry of the Interior a few years later. The contrast is particularly vivid when we compare the Tomioka works with Japan's first large-scale private silk factory, established by the Ono merchant firm at Tsukiji in

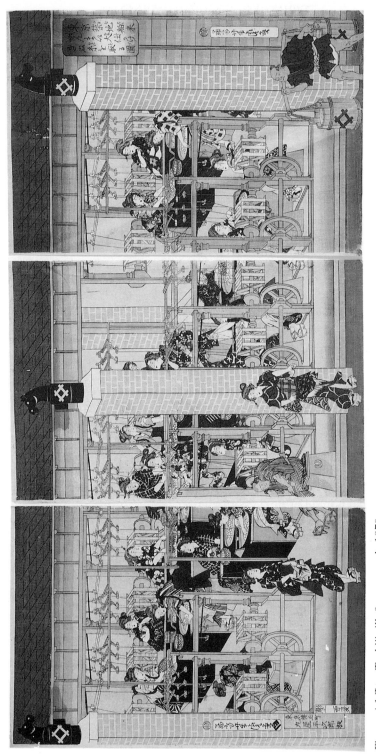

Figure 4.1 The Tsukiji silk factory, early 1870s
Source: Metropolitan Museum of Art, New York.

Tokyo. The Tsukiji works were designed with advice from the Swiss technician who had earlier served as adviser to the Domain of Maebashi (see p. 65), but, although Tsukiji was foreign in inspiration, its technology was drastically modified to suit Japanese conditions. The machinery was wooden, built in Japan, and driven, not by steam or water power, but by the labour of human beings who spent their working days tied to the endlessly turning rows of drive-wheels (see Figure 4.1).[19] Tomioka, on the other hand was steam-powered, furnished with imported French reeling equipment and run with the help of eight French advisers (four of them skilled women workers brought in to train their Japanese counterparts). Its brick and concrete factory compound included workers' dormitories, a school and a hospital.[20] Wada Ei, a young woman who went to work in the factory in 1873, later wrote:

> neither picture nor words could convey the surprise I felt when I saw the appearance of that factory. The first thing that struck me was that at each reeling bench, everything from the bench to the ladles and spoons were all of pure brass, shining with an unclouded golden sheen ...[21]

(As would soon become evident, it was only in these moments of first encounter that modern factory technology appeared to glow with such untarnished splendour.)

Militarisation and Assistance to Private Industry

One of the few points on which historians generally agree is that the Meiji government's initial policies were heavily biased towards imported and relatively sophisticated technologies. There is also widespread consensus that most of the state enterprises based on these techniques were failures in a commercial sense, running up large losses in the early years of their operation.[22] In spite of this, advocates of the state-centred approach suggest that these government initiatives were crucial to Japan's technological development. In the context of early Meiji Japan, there were no private entrepreneurs who had the capacity or confidence to enter fields like railway and telegraph construction. Without direct state intervention, therefore, the development of Japanese infrastructure would have been a slower and more uncertain process. Other state enterprises too, although they may have been financial failures, provided an all-important demonstration effect, familiarising Japanese entrepreneurs and workers with the concepts of modern western technology. They also acted as centres for experimentation, in which the inevitable early problems of imported techniques could be ironed out at public (rather than private) expense.

The main achievement of the Japanese government, then, was to overcome the sense of risk which forms a powerful barrier to innovation. In so doing, it laid the basis for the rapid adoption of western techniques by a handful of enterprises which would later evolve into giant industrial combines (*zaibatsu*). The mechanism by which technology was transferred to these firms was a straightforward one: from 1881 the government-run enterprises were sold to a select band of private buyers at bargain-basement prices. The explicit motive for the sell-off of state enterprises was parsimony. By the early 1880s the costs of industrial investment were imposing immense strains on the budget and fuelling the fires of spiralling inflation. The sale of most state-owned enterprises (excluding strategically significant concerns like the railways and telegraphs) was seen as a means of restoring some order to government finances. On another level, however, it also offered a direct incentive to a handful of Japanese entrepreneurs: all of them powerful, wealthy and with close personal and ideological links to the Meiji political elite. The main beneficiaries included the Mitsui merchant house, the Furukawa mining family, and Iwasaki Yatarô (the founder of the enterprise which was to evolve into the Mitsubishi business empire). Iwasaki, for example, paid ¥459,000 over twenty-five years for the Nagasaki shipyards, in which the Meiji government had invested more than ¥620,000, and ¥1.7 million for the Sado and Ikuno gold and silver mines, which had cost the state an investment of some ¥2.8 million. Assets for which there were few potential buyers went particularly cheaply: after spending ¥2.2 million on the ill-fated Kamaishi iron-works, the government eventually sold the works to a local merchant, Tanaka Chôbei, for just ¥12,600.[23]

The entrepreneurs who bought mines or factories from the state gained something more than cheap machinery and equipment. They obtained a ready trained source of technical expertise, and, equally importantly, inherited established technical links with western firms. From this point on the state's central role in the acquisition of foreign technology began to be supplanted, as large Japanese enterprises embarked upon their own schemes for importing and adapting western techniques. While the number of foreign technical experts employed by the state fell sharply after 1880, the number employed by private firms remained high throughout the last decades of the nineteenth century (see Table 4.1)

In 1885 the Kôbushô was abolished and its powers, together with the industrial and agricultural functions of the Ministry of the Interior, were transferred to the recently created Ministry of Agriculture and Commerce (Nôshômushô). Despite changes in government organisation and policy, however, many scholars argue that the central govern-

Table 4.1   *Foreign technicians employed by government and private enterprise,*
1870s–1890s

	Government	Private Enterprise
1870s	1,294	916
1880s	513	2,100
1890s	140	1,930

Source: N. Umetani, *Oyatoi Gaikokujin 1: Gaisetsu*, p. 54.

ment continued to play a vital role in the promotion of technological change during the last decades of the Meiji era.

An important vehicle for the promotion of innovation in this period was military policy. Japan's first steps towards the creation of an overseas empire, culminating in the Sino-Japanese War of 1894–95 and the Russo-Japanese War of 1904–05, were accompanied by a surge in military spending. Military arsenals and the navy's dockyards, which between them employed over 50,000 workers in 1903, used relatively sophisticated imported techniques, sending their leading technicians for training with major western armaments firms, including Vickers and Krupps.[24]

As historian Yamamura Kôzô points out, military expansion had important spin-offs for civilian industry. Strategic considerations persuaded the government to offer special assistance to private dockyards and to the merchant marine. From the mid-1890s onwards subsidies were given both to shipbuilding firms and to shipping lines which used Japanese-made vessels.[25] Government arsenals, moreover, produced a wide range of industrial machinery (including steam engines, lathes and gears) which were sold to private enterprise. Workers trained in these arsenals often moved on to employment in civilian industries, taking their knowledge of imported production techniques with them. Besides, military demand provided a vital market for many of Japan's more technically advanced industries in the first faltering stages of their development.[26] One of numerous Meiji enterprises to benefit from the government's pursuit of military might was the Tanaka Machine Works, established by Tanaka Hisashige, the designer of automata who had made Japan's first model steam engine. After the abolition of the domains, Tanaka had set up a small machine shop in central Tokyo, producing telegraphic equipment and electric lights. In 1892, the year after Hisashige's death, his son succeeded in obtaining a naval order for the production of torpedoes, and it was from this basis that the company (renamed the Shibaura Machine Works in 1893) emerged as one of Japan's leading producers of industrial machinery, and as the progenitor of the twentieth-century electrical machinery giant Toshiba.[27]

Strategic needs also provided the motive behind the one major government-run enterprise to be established after 1880: the Yawata steelworks. Until the end of the nineteenth century, Japan's only means of domestic steel production was the traditional *tatara* method: suitable for crafting a few high-quality samurai swords, but totally incapable of meeting the needs of modern industry or satisfying the ravenous demand of the expanding state arsenals. To overcome this problem, the Yawata steelworks, financed by the spoils of victory in the Sino-Japanese War, was opened with great fanfare in 1901. In the event, it proved to suffer from all the problems of the earlier Meiji state-run enterprises. The works relied almost entirely on imported German know-how, and the technology used turned out to be unsuitable to local coal and iron resources. The designers had neglected the coordination between the various elements (blast furnaces, converter and open-hearth furnaces), so vital to the success of any integrated steel plant. Steel production was also hampered by shortages of skilled technicians and uncertain supply of raw materials.[28] The costs, originally estimated at around ¥5 million, blew out to ¥25 million, and less than a year after its official opening the steelworks was temporarily closed while the design faults in its furnaces were rectified.[29] It was not until 1910 that Yawata steel began to make a profit.[30] By the eve of the First World War however, a mixture of determination, perseverance and a fine bureaucratic disregard for commercial considerations had enabled the government to take Japan's first step into the technologies of the 'second industrial revolution'.

Laying the Intellectual Foundations

Some writers who take a state-centred approach to Japan's technological development concentrate on the government's role in creating the physical infrastructure of industrialisation: laying railway lines, importing machinery, constructing steelworks.[31] Others, however, also acknowledge the vital role of the state as a propagator of the ideology of technological change itself.[32]

The new system of compulsory primary education, introduced from 1871 onwards, placed considerable emphasis on the spirit of scientific enquiry. Lessons in *kyūri*—'mastery of the principles of things' (as physics was called in early Meiji Japan)—introduced children to phenomena such as vacuums, electricity and magnetism and to instruments like the thermometer and barometer.[33] A favourite text was

Fukuzawa Yukichi's *Illustrated Course in Physics* (*Kunmô Kyûri Zukai*), published in 1868 and adopted as a primary school text by the Ministry of Education in 1872.[34] Fukuzawa's book was closely modelled on western science texts, but was couched in readily comprehensible Japanese terms, and included delightful illustrations which placed scientific experiments firmly in the context of recognisable everyday life (see Figure. 4.2).

At the other end of the scale the Meiji state actively cultivated the corps of Japanese engineers and technicians who could take over the running of its factories, mines and railways from western advisers. This technical elite was drawn largely from the ranks of the ex-samurai and was trained in the prestigious new educational institutions established by the Meiji government: the most important, in the early stages, being the Imperial College of Engineering (Kôgakuryô Daigaku, later known as the Kôbu Daigakukô), set up by the Kôbushô in 1873. Despite the social status of its students, the Imperial College of Engineering placed great emphasis on practical skills as well as academic training, an approach undoubtedly influenced by its down-to-earth Scottish director,

Figure 4.2 Illustration from Fukuzawa Yukichi's science text (showing the use of lenses)
Source: Iida K., ed., *Nihon kindai shisô taikei 14: Kagaku to gijutsu*, pp. 101-2.

Henry Dyer (1848–1918), who believed in 'good practical training and sound common sense, two faculties which are not possessed in marked degree by those who have spent an undue proportion of their time at schools or colleges'.[35]

One of the great strengths of the Imperial College was its electrical engineering faculty, headed by another talented 'hired foreigner', William Edward Ayrton, who appears to have been the first Professor of Electrical Engineering to be appointed anywhere in the world. A number of Ayrton's students went on to become pioneering entrepreneurs in Japan's fledgeling electrical machinery industry, and one, Asano Ôsuke, was later responsible for creating the government-run Electrical Research Industry (Denki Shikenjo), set up under the auspices of the Ministry of Telegraphs in 1891.[36]

In 1885, the Imperial College of Engineering was merged with Tokyo University (which had itself grown out of the Tokugawa Shogunate's Institute for the Study of Barbarian Writings), and by the end of the Meiji Era, Japan had four Imperial Universities—Tokyo, Kyoto, Tôhoku and Kyûshû—all of which included engineering faculties. Military training centres like the Naval Academy, established in 1870, also played an important role in teaching engineering and the natural sciences, while selected students continued to be sent overseas to study at prestigious institutions such as the Universities of Edinburgh, Glasgow, Leipzig and Freiburg and the newly established Massachusetts Institute of Technology.

In its zeal to preach the message of enlightenment and industrial progress, however, the government was too impatient to rely solely on the slow process of educating future generations. It needed a more immediate means to influence the minds of the population, and, as Ôkubo Toshimichi observed,

> the old adage tells us that seeing is worth a hundred explanations: the only quick and easy way to enhance human knowledge and promote the industrial arts is to teach people by showing them.[37]

Hence the Meiji mania for industrial exhibitions.

The second half of the nineteenth century was, of course, the age of exhibitions. The Great Exhibitions of London (1851 and 1862), Paris (1855, 1867, 1878 and 1889), Vienna (1873) and Philadelphia (1876) were vast, self-indulgent celebrations of the triumph of industrial technology and the nation-state: occasions which combined the nationalistic fervour later associated with Olympic games and a technological hubris reminiscent of the 1960s space race. For Japanese participants, these international exhibitions were both a forceful reminder of their own country's industrial backwardness, and an excellent opportunity to study the best in foreign technology. Japan's contributions to the exhibitions were therefore planned with care.

The Japanese presence at the 1873 Vienna Exhibition, for example, included not only examples of Japanese porcelains, silks, lacquerware and so forth but also a team of twenty-four merchants and artisans, among them experts in sericulture, ceramics, shipbuilding, and instrument-making. Most received from the Kôbushô a grant to spend six months in Europe, and used the occasion to conduct extensive investigations of factories and workshops throughout Austria and beyond.[38]

The success of the international exhibition encouraged the Meiji government to sponsor its own national industrial displays: the first, organised by the Ministry of the Interior in 1877, was held in Tokyo's Ueno Park in 1877, and was seen by some 450,000 visitors. It is true that most of the items put forward for display were the products of traditional agricultural and craft techniques: the dyestuffs, for example, included no chemical dyes, but only selectively bred species of indigo and other dye plants; the exhibits in the machinery section were all made of wood, and were powered by nothing more sophisticated than waterwheels.[39] Little by little, however, the reality of the industrial exhibitions came closer to the government's ideal of modernisation and enlightenment. At the third national exhibition of 1890, visitors could ride around the site in an electric tram (albeit one imported from America); at the fifth and last exhibition of 1903 they were able to view the displays at night under the artificial brilliance of over three hundred electric lights.[40]

In a sense, perhaps, the quality which distinguished the Kôbushô, the Ministry of the Interior, and all the other Meiji organs of government from their Tokugawa predecessors is best symbolised, not by the railways, the mines or the state-run steelworks, but by the history of the Japanese clock. Tokugawa scholars, bureaucrats and skilled artisans had (as we have seen) been aware of various pieces of western science and technology, including the mechanical clock. The reaction to this foreign knowledge, however, had been an attempt to incorporate it into the existing Japanese social and intellectual framework. In the case of the clock, this meant using immense mechanical ingenuity to adapt the western mechanism to the complexities of the Japanese time system, with its hours of varying lengths. The imported technique, in other words, became part of the indigenous technological system.

In Meiji Japan, however, this approach to foreign knowledge was no longer possible. Now Japan was not simply importing a few exotic western gadgets, but was attempting to acquire an entire system of interrelated industrial technologies. Some Meiji intellectuals, it is true, proclaimed the need to maintain a 'Japanese spirit' (*wakon*) while borrowing 'western science' (*yôsai*); but in practice, the new techno-logical system demanded fundamental changes in attitudes and social institutions, as well as in methods of production. The most important change of all was the acceptance of the underlying assumptions of modern western science: the notion of universal natural laws which could be revealed by human reasoning and experimentation, and the notion of the measurability of all things. The Meiji state, therefore, dealt with the problem of time, not by adapting the western clock to suit the Japanese time system, but by abandoning the Japanese time system in exchange for the unvarying regularity of western hours. How else could railway timetables be scheduled and factory shifts be planned? In 1873, the year in which Japan's first railway line was completed, the government issued a decree revising the calendar and establishing the standardised 24-hour day.

This passion for regularisation and standardisation was soon ex-tended to other areas of Japanese life. In 1886 Japan joined the inter-national metric convention, and, under a law introduced in the first session of the newly established Japanese parliament in 1890, became *de jure* the first Asian nation to accept the nationwide use of the metric system.[41] The new systems of time, weights and measures were not welcomed by all Japanese people. The old measures of length, the *sun* and the *shaku*, may have been cumbersome, varying as they did both from region to region and from one craft to another, but they had a comfortable familiarity about them, and indeed it was not until the middle of the twentieth century that the metric system came into widespread general use. The new calendar, too, was seen as an un-natural imposition, and was ignored by many country people until well into the twentieth century. 'We have come along thus far with the traditional calendar, and it has caused no trouble to anyone. Why has the government suddenly decided to abolish it?' ran the popular complaint. 'The old system corresponded to the seasons, the weather, and the movement of the tides ... [Now] nothing is the way it should be.'[42] From the point of view of the government, however, the new systems of time, length and weight represented, not only the rationality of the new industrial era, but also the unity of the nation and the power of the state to impose its rules even upon the most basic human con-cepts of space and time.[43]

The Revisionist Approach

The state-centred version of Japan's technological development has been retold in detail because it is essential to our understanding of modern Japan. There can be no doubt that the Meiji government's pursuit of westernisation, its political reforms, its building of railways, mines and factories, its military ambitions and (above all, perhaps) its educational and cultural policies were vital factors in Japan's acquisition of western industrial techniques.

There are, however, a few points which need to be made about the state-centred approach to the technological history of Japan. The first is that the Meiji government did not (as sometimes implied) possess preternatural foresight and vision in its pursuit of technological modernisation: as the US historian T. C. Smith once observed, Meiji Japan's rulers were not like homing pigeons, who 'rise in unison and unerringly fly to the one possible goal'.[44] Confused organisational structures (such as the overlapping jurisdictions of the Kôbushô and Ministry of the Interior) and sharp changes in policy direction (such as the sell-off of government enterprises) attest to the fact that the Japanese government, like Japan's engineers and technicians, was 'learning by doing'. One of the great strengths of the Meiji leaders, in fact, was the fact that, as a group who had seized power without a prolonged revolution, they had little commitment to any defined philosophy and were, in many respects, free to make up their own ideology as they went along.

The second point to observe is that, in devising this ideology, the government often relied less on radically new ideas than on reinterpretations of old concepts to suit new circumstances. The modernisation programs of the domains like Satsuma clearly provided the model for Meiji schemes to apply western technology to the task of 'promoting enterprise and developing products'. Even the most famous of Meiji slogans—'enrich the country, strengthen the army' (*fukoku kyôhei*)—was not original, but based on ideas from the classical Chinese Rites of Zhou which had been taken up and popularised by Tokugawa philosophers. It was, indeed, symptomatic that the militantly westernising Kôbushô derived its name, not from western counterparts like the British Board of Works, but from the ancient Chinese bureau responsible for the supervision of state-owned craft workshops.[45]

The most important point to make about the state-centred approach, however, is that it is not the whole story. Technological change in Meiji Japan was not confined to state-owned enterprises, nor to the handful of embryonic *zaibatsu* who possessed close links to the government. Instead, the really significant feature of Meiji innovation is that it was quite widely spread through many companies and craft workshops in many parts of the country. The innovation which was occurring in these enterprises, however, had little in common with the advanced western techniques embodied in the railways, the telegraph or the Yawata steelworks. Much of it, indeed, was not imported technology at all, but incremental improvement of techniques developed in the Tokugawa period. Interpreting the causes of this bottom-up, as opposed to top-down, process of technological change obviously requires something more than the state-centred narrative which we have just outlined.

The need to explain the innovative activities of small private enterprises has given rise to an alternative, 'revisionist' interpretation of Japan's technological history: one which places much less emphasis on government policy, and much more on the workings of the market and the initiatives of private entrepreneurs. In recent years perhaps the most influential exponent of this revisionist analysis has been Japanese historian Nakaoka Tetsurô. Although he accepts that the government provided strong support for the development of certain (particularly military-related) industries,[46] Nakaoka also emphasises the limitations of Meiji technology policy. During the second half of the twentieth century, after all, many governments in less developed countries have tried to emulate Meiji Japan by establishing large industrial projects based on imported technology, and many of these have ended in failure. 'Transplanted technology' as Nakaoka points out, 'can only operate when it harmonises with local domestic factors which, in their turn, change under the influence of the transplanted foreign technology.'[47] Technological modernisation was possible in Japan not just because of wholesale borrowing from the west, but because Japanese entrepreneurs and artisans developed intermediate technologies which fitted the existing economic structure. A case in point is the Kamaishi ironworks, where government efforts to introduce the latest western technology failed. After the works were sold to private enterprise, the new management reverted to simpler techniques, similar to those used by Ôshima Takatô before the Meiji Restoration. These became the basis for a gradual upgrading of indigenous technological skills.[48]

These intermediate techniques, then, were not the products of government technological policy, but were rational responses to market conditions in Japan, spurred on by exposure to competition from imported manufactured goods. Most importantly, they were supported by the high level of craft skills in pre-industrial Japan, which enabled Japan's modernising entrepreneurs to make use of existing technical know-how and to graft new factories into existing networks of production and trade.[49]

The same emphasis on private initiative and careful selection of techniques emerges from Gary Saxonhouse's studies of the Meiji cotton industry. The early state-run cotton factories used mule spinning equipment imported from Britain, and were without exception financial failures. When Japan's first major private spinning factory,

Yamanobe Takeo's Osaka Spinning Mill, opened in 1883, it followed the government's lead in using the spinning mules common in British factories. Within a few years, however, it had switched over to the use of the more recently developed ring-spinning technique, which rapidly spread to other Japanese spinning firms as they were established during the 1880s and 1890s. This choice of techniques was driven by sound commercial considerations. Ring spinning was ideally suited to producing strong, thick cotton thread which matched the demands of the local cotton-weaving industry.[50] Furthermore, while mule spinning involved heavy labour better suited to male workers, ring spinning allowed companies to make use of Japan's abundance of cheap, manually dexterous female workers.[51]

As they brought in the new ring technology, Japanese entrepreneurs made organisational and technical adaptations which fitted the imported technique to Japanese conditions. One of these adaptations involved mixing higher-quality long-staple cotton with cheaper short-staple cotton to create a raw material which was both affordable and suitable to ring-spinning technology.[52] This 'technological adaptation', however, also had its darker side. To make the most of low labour costs, Japanese companies operated their factories day and night and worked their women employees for immensely long hours, often in appalling conditions. As social historian Patricia Tsurumi notes:

> eleven hours of daily work was the 'official' time worked ... [but] for two or three hours after the shift ended, operatives could be kept busy at cleaning and machine maintenance or in preparing materials to be used during their next shift ... Factory rules authorising two fifteen-minute rest breaks and one thirty-minute meal break were often ignored. Machines were run during official rest periods, so all or some of those who worked them were unable to rest. Operatives often had to eat while their machines were running.[53]

The conclusions to be drawn from Saxonhouse's studies are virtually the reverse of those implied by the state-centred approach to Meiji development. Rather than suggesting the need for large-scale government intervention to encourage technological change, Saxonhouse and his colleagues argue:

> an important lesson to be learned from the historical experience of Japan is that the relative absence of deliberate market intervention policies ... helped both to ensure the efficient choice of imported technology and to have it adapted in appropriate directions both during and after the labour surplus phase had come to an end.[54]

There are problems, however, about accepting this lesson too literally, and these are not only related to the heavy social and environmental costs of Japan's industrialisation. Saxonhouse's own work demonstrated that the spread of 'appropriate' technology in Japan was

not simply a rational response to market signals, but was also helped by
some rather unusual social institutions. In the case of cotton spinning,
the most important was the All-Japan Cotton Spinners' Federation (Zen
Nihon Bôseki Renmei), a cartel of large private companies which,
amongst other things, published a technical journal, sponsored overseas study missions, and encouraged the exchange of technical ideas
between its member companies.[55]

Institutions of this sort, I would argue, are quite critical to understanding technological change, not only in cotton spinning but also in a
wide range of Japanese industries. To pursue this point, though, we
need to turn to a third version of Japan's technological development in
the Meiji period—a version which might be described as the 'social
network approach'—and to relate the history of technological change
in Meiji Japan, beginning from a quite different starting point.

The Social Network Approach

The state-centred approach to Japan's technological history begins at
the centre, with the oligarchs and ministries; it begins in the capital
with its frock-coated dignitaries and its emerging red-brick facades. The
social network approach starts at the opposite end, with the outer edges
of society: the region and the village.

The Meiji government was, of course, a militantly centralising institution. It saw the creation of a united economy and polity, and of a
single national identity, as vital to Japan's survival in the modern world.
To forge this unity, the Meiji revolutionaries moved swiftly to abolish
the feudal domains, which in 1871 'returned' their powers to the
central administration and were replaced by seventy-two prefectures
(later reduced to forty-three).[56] This dismantling of the feudal system
allowed the new regime to absorb much of the talent and technical
know-how accumulated by the old domains in the final decades of
Tokugawa rule. Technical experts, both Japanese and foreign, were
brought to Tokyo from modernising regions like Satsuma, Saga and
Mito: even the industrial machinery installed in Saga's Seirenkata was
shifted to the capital, where it was put to use in the Kôbushô's new
Akabane machine works.

The speed and vigour with which the Meiji regime stamped its
authority on the nation makes it easy to take its ideology at face value:
to assume that ordinary Japanese citizens overnight shed their old
regional loyalties and rivalries, and identified themselves whole-
heartedly with the new state. But human sentiments and identities are
not so easily manipulated. Although the most able domain leaders were
absorbed into the new central government, a broad layer of lower-level

officials, village heads and local notables remained outside the charmed circle of the Meiji elite. For them, as well as for the mass of farmers and craftspeople, a sense of place—of local identity—was the most powerful bulwark against the disturbing and sometimes threatening intrusion of the stream of decrees which emanated from the new government in Tokyo.[57]

The Prefectures and Innovation

Local reactions to the policies of the Meiji regime took many forms. At times they erupted into overt opposition, expressed either in brief violent protests against such things as conscription and compulsory education, or in more complex and organised political movements like the Freedom and Popular Rights movement of the 1880s.[58] At an economic level, though, the most common response was the creation of a mass of local institutions and projects designed to ensure that, whatever the intentions of the central government, 'our' region should not miss out on the fruits of modernisation.

These assertions of regional self-interest occasionally took the form of large, sophisticated modernisation projects mirroring those of the central government, the outstanding example being the massive Lake Biwa project, initiated by Kyoto City in 1881. Originally intended as a scheme to improve the city's water supply and provide motive power for waterwheels, by 1891 the project had expanded to include Japan's first hydroelectric power station.[59] But most local technological initiatives were more modest. Few prefectural governments possessed the financial or intellectual resources for large complex projects: the main concern was to preserve local craft industries from the impact of foreign manufactured imports and to encourage local producers to seek out nationwide and international markets. In practice this involved, not the massive import of foreign industrial techniques, but a more gradual upgrading of indigenous skill and know-how.

To appreciate the importance of local organisations in Japan's technological development, we might consider one of the most famous examples of indigenous innovation in nineteenth-century Japan: the 'rattling spindle' (garabô). This was a simple mechanised spinning device in which cotton was packed into bamboo or tin tubes and then drawn out and twisted onto a series of rollers (see Figure 4.3). The rattling spindle appears to have begun as one of those labour-saving innovations which Tokugawa producers chose to ignore. Its inventor, Gaun Tokimune (1842–1900) was the son of a farmer who had developed a thriving business weaving soles for cotton socks.[60] By the 1850s the family was putting out cotton for spinning to neighbouring farm

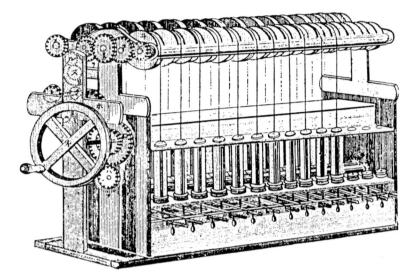

Figure 4.3 The rattling spindle *(garabô)*
Source: Nakamura T., et al., *Kindai Nihon no gijutsu to gijutsu seisaku*, p. 78.

households, and Gaun, then in his teens, began to experiment with the design of a more productive spinning machine. Gaun's mechanical devices, however, did not impress the rest of his family, who dismissed them as distractions from his proper duties and packed him off to the local Buddhist monastry, where he remained until the age of thirty.[61]

By the time Gaun returned to the outside world, the Tokugawa Shogunate had fallen and Japan's domestic cotton industry was weathering the full force of the influx of imported machine-made textiles. Gaun revived and improved his invention, which was then quickly copied and developed by others (Japan having no system of patent protection until 1885). By the late 1880s, 500-spindle, water-powered versions of his machine were in operation, and the rattling spindle was being used by hundreds of manufacturers in many parts of Japan. In the Mikawa region of Aichi Prefecture alone there were 483 such cotton mills by 1887.[62] The invention, in other words, helped to create a stepping stone between traditional craft production and the imported western spinning techniques which gradually displaced the rattling spindle from the 1890s onwards.

As Nakaoka Tetsurô points out, the invention succeeded partly because it was simple and could easily be reproduced by local carpenters throughout the country, and partly because of market conditions in early Meiji Japan. The coarse cotton thread produced by the rattling spindle resembled the handspun thread with which Japanese customers were familiar, and which many preferred to fine-spun imported yarn.[63] But this still leaves some important questions unanswered. How did Gaun Tokimune—who, like so many inventors, had little capital and less business acumen—turn his invention from design into marketable reality, and how did knowledge of the machine spread to so many small-scale producers in so many parts of Japan?

The answer to the first question lies in the policies of Gaun's local prefecture, Chikuma (later incorporated into Nagano prefecture), which in the early Meiji period had suffered severe economic disruption and distress. The prefectural officials responded to these problems in the established manner of the old domains, by introducing policies to encourage local crafts. In 1873 they set up an association, funded partly by the local administration and partly by donations, to 'provide work for the destitute and unemployed'.[64] Two years later, under the new name of the Association for Developing Production (Kaisan Sha), the organisation was remodelled into something more in keeping with the mood of the Meiji Era, and its duties were expanded to include investigations of the production techniques used in local industries, and the general promotion of 'skills for a prosperous country' (fukoku no jutsu).[65] It was to this body that Gaun Tokimune turned for help in launching his rattling spindle onto the market. In 1876 the Association for Developing Production not only agreed to provide public demonstrations of the machine, but also lent a part of its premises to Gaun who, with the support of a small group of financial backers, set up a factory there to manufacture the spindle on a commercial basis.[66]

Chikuma's Association for Developing Production was far from being unique. Similar bodies were appearing all over Japan in the first decade of the Meiji period, and were to play an equally vital part in other branches of Japan's technological development. Like the domains before them, the new prefectures tended to focus upon the encourage-ment of specific local crops and crafts: Hamamatsu, with its mild moist climate, set up tea plantations and processing factories to provide employment for ex-samurai and training in the techniques of tea-farming;[67] Iwate Prefecture created an Industrial Guidance Centre (Kôgyô Shidôsho, founded in 1872) to develop local skills like metal-casting and woodworking.[68] Meanwhile, the techniques used in Japan's small-scale silk- and cotton-weaving workshops were being revolution-ised, largely as a result of measures taken by Kyoto City government to protect the region's famous Nishijin silk weaving industry.

Kyoto, indeed, was particularly enterprising, with good reason. The city had suffered a double blow, first from losing its status of imperial capital, and second from the development of Japan's silk trade with the west. As foreign merchants moved in to purchase the best of Japan's raw silk output, the Nishijin weavers, who had traditionally had access to the finest silks, faced a crisis which stimulated a bold response. In 1872 the mayor of Kyoto dispatched a well-to-do silk merchant, Sakura Tsuneshichi, and a talented weaver, Inoue Ihei, to France to 'acquire a knowledge of [French] woven textiles and buy weaving machinery'.[69] They were joined by a second weaver, Yoshida Tadashichi, whose interest in foreign techniques was so great that he had specially petitioned the local authorities for the opportunity to take part in the expedition.

Although none of the three spoke a word of any European language, they managed to reach Lyon safely and in 1873 Sakura and Inoue returned with a basic knowledge of French weaving techniques and a mountain of luggage containing, amongst other things, a Jacquard loom and a sample of Kaye's flying shuttle, the invention which, 140 years earlier, had initiated the revolution in British textile manufacture. The third member of the party, Yoshida Tadashichi, anxious to make the most of his overseas experience, chose to stay in France until the following year. It was a fatal choice. On his return journey the ship in which he was travelling was wrecked in a storm, sending him and his laboriously acquired trove of technical knowledge to the bottom of the ocean.[70]

Despite this disaster, the expedition had profound consequences for the Japanese weaving industry in Nishijin and beyond. Local loom carpenters studied and reproduced the Jacquard loom, and the flying shuttle (*battan* as it was called in Japan) was soon incorporated into existing draw looms for use in the region's workshops. Knowledge of new techniques was disseminated by the Hall of Weaving, an experimental workshop set up by the mayor of Kyoto in 1877, and by the Hall of Dyeing, established in 1880 under the supervision of a local craftsman who had been dispatched to Europe to study chemical dyestuffs.[71] From these centres, ideas spread, not only within the local weaving community but also much further afield. In 1876, for example, Iwate Prefecture's Industrial Guidance Centre hired a graduate of Kyoto's Hall of Weaving to teach the secrets of the flying shuttle, so initiating a chain reaction which resulted in the spread of this new technique throughout the northeast of Japan.[72] Other craft industries like ceramics were encouraged by the Kyoto government's Bureau of Chemistry (Seimikyoku), set up in 1871 to act as a experimental centre and training school for new techniques. The bureau hired the German chemist Gottfried Wagener (who had earlier advised the Arita potteries on the use of improved technologies), and later sent its director overseas to study ceramics technology in the Chinese pottery centre of Jingdezhen, as well as in Germany and Austria.[73]

Knowledge of new techniques like the rattling spindle and flying shuttle was also spread by another quintessentially Meiji institution, the industrial exhibition. Here, as in other fields, it was local rather than national government which took the lead. Kyoto's successful series of industrial exhibitions was inaugurated six years before the Interior Ministry organised the first national exhibition. Local displays and prize competitions (*kyōshinkai*), inspired partly by the great international exhibitions and partly by the Tokugawa tradition of 'exhibitions of products', were held in every region of Japan during the first decades of the Meiji Era, and served both to diffuse know-how and stimulate intense technological competition between different areas. The quality and educational value of the displays inevitably varied: an exhibition organised by Nagano Prefecture in 1877 'to dispel the ignorance and open up the intelligence of the people', included items such as 'eleven prints showing English physics and botany' and 'a photograph of an American oil refinery' alongside exhibits like 'one piece of black coral', 'an American doll' and an assortment of stuffed birds.[74] At their best, however, regional exhibitions could play a vital role in the spread of knowledge. Prize exhibitions of cotton thread and textiles, organised by Aichi Prefecture in the 1880s, encouraged the rapid local spread of the rattling spindle, while Kyoto's third city exhibition held in 1874 provided the first opportunity for entrepreneurs from other parts of Japan to see the Jacquard loom and flying shuttle in operation.[75]

Some local authorities went even further. In the city of Kanazawa in Ishikawa Prefecture, which had been a thriving centre of Dutch studies in the Tokugawa period, a local merchant proposed the creation of a permanent industrial museum to spread knowledge of the latest innovations. Opened in 1876, the museum offered displays of craft products and equipment, as well as special exhibitions and prize competitions for industries such as ceramics, metal-working and làcquerware. From 1880 onwards it also employed travelling teachers of agricultural and craft techniques, who were sent out to bring the museum's accumulated store of knowledge to the remoter corners of the prefecture.[76] The museum library's catalogue in itself provides an insight into the extent of local government involvement in industry and technology. Of 159 periodicals listed, 93 were yearly or monthly prefectural reports on the promotion of industry.[77]

All these activities, of course, allowed a convenient blurring between the logic of localism and the ideology of Meiji nationalism. Ventures like Kanazawa's industrial museum could easily be justified in terms of the Meiji rhetoric of 'enlightenment', even though it is clear that its establishment was part of a pattern of regional rivalries: Kyoto had snatched the lead as an organiser of industrial exhibitions; Kanazawa was determined to go one better.[78]

Trade Associations and the Diffusion of Ideas

The activities of local government shaded at the edges into those of a mass of local organisations established by small-scale private producers and merchants. The private individuals who set up model factories, technological training centres and producer associations generally came from the same social background as local officials—they were medium-sized merchants, successful 'improving' farmers, or lower-ranking ex-samurai—and they shared with their official counterparts a distinctive mixture of fierce local pride and a slightly patronising sense of social obligation.

The technological initiatives of the public and private sectors, too, were often confusingly intertwined. Kyoto's Hall of Weaving, for example, was briefly transferred to private control before being handed back to the city administration,[79] and, as in the case of Gaun Tokimune's rattling spindle, local government institutions often lent land (and sometimes also equipment) to private entrepreneurs. The most important of the private technological initiatives was the establishment of trade associations (*dôgyô kumiai*) or producer groups which, as well as helping with the marketing of products, checked their quality and offered technical advice to members. Trade associations began as replacements for the abandoned guilds and regulations of the Tokugawa period, and as a sort of mutual protection against the influx of foreign goods. The story of the Iyo cotton-weavers in the city of Matsuyama, to whom Kagiya Kana had introduced the techniques of *kasuri* weaving earlier in the century (see p. 43), is typical of a pattern repeated in hundreds of towns and villages throughout Japan.

During the early Meiji period, the Iyo weaving industry experienced a severe depression—partly caused, perhaps, by the growth of foreign competition. In 1886, after much local debate, a meeting of merchants, weavers and dyers was held, at which they agreed to form a joint association, the Iyo Woven Textiles Improvement Association (Iyo Orimono Kairyô Kumiai). The association was given the right to inspect the products of members and reject poor-quality cloth. It also provided a forum for the exchange of ideas on new techniques, and a channel for the inflow of technological knowledge from other parts of the country. In 1898 it set up a panel to investigate the uses of imported dyestuffs, and dispatched representatives to consult with experts in other parts of Japan; in 1902 it acquired (on behalf of its members) a licence for the use of a patent improved loom. Its regular meetings, moreover, offered members an opportunity to hear lectures on new techniques and on 'industrial morality' (kôgyô dôtoku).[80] In other words, the Association played an educational role in some ways reminiscent of the part played by local scientific societies in the British industrial revolution, while at the same time giving its members the financial and bargaining power which they needed to acquire improved technologies. It also provided the basis for widening circles of industrial cooperation. By the end of the Meiji Era it had joined with four other associations to form the Ehime Prefecture Federation of Weaving Trade Associations.[81]

Similar associations fulfilled similar functions all over Japan. In the silkweaving districts organisations like the Kiryû Company (Kiryû Kaisha, a trade association set up by prominent weaving families in 1878) oversaw what would now be called 'quality control', while the producer association of the Nishijin weavers (Nishijin Orimono Dôgyô Kumiai) set up a textile research laboratory (the Kyoto Senshoku Kenkyûjo, opened in 1907), which flourishes to the present day.[82] In the rapidly growing silk regions of Nagano Prefecture, numerous groups of silk-reelers created small cooperative associations (sangyô kessha) to inspect the thread produced in their members' workshops, and some even invested in jointly owned water-powered silk-throwing factories. By forming associations, the small-scale silk-reelers were able to put pressure on local sericulturalists to supply them with standardised, high-quality cocoons.[83] This helped them to compete with the larger mechanised silk factories, which, in parts of Japan, were beginning to organise silk farmers into something approaching a subcontracting system, distributing particular types of silkworm eggs to them in order to ensure that their cocoons met the demanding standards of the modern silk factory.[84]

In Nagano and in other silk-producing districts like Gumma Prefecture these cooperative associations also played a vital role in the spread and improvement of the zaguri silk reeling frames which had begun to appear during the Tokugawa period (see p. 37).[85] By the early 1870s, zaguri were beginning to be driven by foot pedals, allowing the user to reel two or more threads at once, and a simple device borrowed from western silk-reeling machinery was being incorporated into the frames to ensure that the silk fibres cohered firmly as they were reeled.

The story of Gaun Tokimune's rattling spindle, too, is inseparable from the story of the local educational initiatives and trade associations. The real success of the spindle was due, not just to Gaun's own efforts, but to the enthusiasm of a small group of cotton producers in Mikawa district of Aichi Prefecture, who grasped the possibilities of attaching Gaun's machine to the water-power supplied in abundance by the region's rivers. Under the leadership of one Kammura Rôsaburô, the Mikawa spinners expounded the virtues of the rattling spindle to local craft producers and in 1884 formed a trade association with a membership of more than two hundred.[86] As well as providing a limited degree of quality control, the association generated the stimulus for further refinements to the design of the rattling spindle. In 1888 it invited Gaun to work with its members on an improved version of the water-powered spindle, for which Gaun, Kammura and a business associate were finally awarded a patent in 1889.[87]

Local Organisations and Grassroots Innovation

The purpose of this journey through the local affairs of Meiji Japan is to emphasise that the initiative for technological change did not all come from the top, nor was it wholly reliant on the import of modern western technology. Instead, there was a very widely dispersed process of grassroots innovation, only a fraction of which has been described here, and much of which involved the incremental improvement of existing techniques. The rattling spindle, the improved *zaguri* and the various modified weaving looms were just part of a widespread pattern of very simple but economically important improvements to indigenous techniques. From 1899 (when Japan's patent law was extended to cover inventions by foreigners as well as Japanese nationals) to 1905, 73 per cent of the 4708 patents granted went to Japanese inventors, most of them for new developments in traditional areas such as better weaving looms and improved farm tools.[88]

   This grassroots innovation, however, was not just a matter of individual entrepreneurship. In fact, the more closely we look at local innovation, the more obvious it becomes that the conventional, bipolar division between 'the state' (equated with central government) and 'the private sector' is a misleading and artificial one. Between central government and private citizen stood an immensely complex layer of intermediate social institutions—local government, trade associations etc.—which were vital to the spread of technological knowledge in the Meiji Era and beyond.

   The local institutions captured in microcosm the balance of continuity and change in Meiji Japan. Their enthusiasm for novelty reflected the stimulation of Japan's opening to the outside world—a stimulation which came not only from the direct import of foreign know-how, but also from what Arnold Pacey calls 'the mere rumour of … unfamiliar technique[s]'.[89] The new, more flexible social order of the Meiji age made it possible for prefectural authorities to push the boundaries of innovation much further than their domain predecessors had done, encouraging ex-samurai to enter industry and farmers to take up factory work. At the same time, though, many of the underlying structures of local society remained intact. The leading figures in prefectural governments and trade associations were generally the lower-ranking ex-samurai, wealthy farmers or successful merchants who had established their position in local society before the Restoration, and who were able to draw on the Tokugawa experience of 'developing products and promoting enterprise'.

The most important contribution of these grassroots institutions was their role as channels for the transmission of new ideas and as instruments in overcoming the innate human fear of the unfamiliar. It was one thing for a small-scale entrepreneur to read an account of an innovation like Kaye's flying shuttle, the Jacquard loom or the rattling spindle, but quite another to be able to see the machine in action, try it out and if necessary borrow it from a body like Kyoto's Hall of Weaving, Kanazawa's industrial museum or Iwate's industrial guidance centre. Local trade associations took this process one step further, not only providing a trusted source of information on new techniques, but also serving as a means of sharing the risks of innovation amongst many producers.

Another crucially important function of the local bodies was their role in overcoming organisational barriers to innovation. Both prefectural technology centres and trade associations tested and modified new techniques so that they could easily be fitted into existing production systems. The rattling spindle is an excellent example of the process. Small, simple, hand-turned spindles slotted comfortably into the familiar structure of the family-based craft workshop. As capital was accumulated and the scale of production grew, the number of spindles could be increased and machines could be harnessed to water-power, thus becoming a basis for small-scale factory production.

An even more striking example of this process of adaptation was that immensely successful but oddly neglected Japanese innovation, the rikisha (rickshaw).[90] It could be argued, indeed, that the rikisha was just as important to Japan's modern economic development as the railway: while the railway provided the means of transportation between the emerging cities, the rikisha provided the means of transportation within the commercial and industrial heartlands. By 1888 there were some 38,000 rikishas in use in Tokyo alone.[91] Rikishas were typical Japanese intermediate technologies in that they were simple, adaptable and remorseless in their demands on human labour. In terms of Japan's economic development, however, the rikisha had two particularly significant functions. It was the first Japanese transport vehicle to be exported, opening up markets which would later be more thoroughly cultivated by exporters of Japanese bicycles and motor vehicles, and it also played a crucial role in the emergence of the subcontracting system. By the 1870s rikisha-makers were already beginning to purchase parts such as seats, wheels etc. from small-scale specialist producers, so creating subcontracting chains which would survive and be replicated throughout the history of Japanese vehicle manufacturing.[92]

The rikisha proliferated rapidly because it fitted in so easily to the existing organisational structures of Japanese society. It could be operated by small-scale, family enterprises, built and repaired by local carpenters or blacksmiths, and it could run on narrow, poorly paved urban alleyways. Even here, however, local governments and associations had their part to play. In 1872, for example, Nagano Prefecture instituted a hire-purchase system to encourage local inns to acquire and operate rikishas, while the following year Tottori Prefecture established an agency to assist local entrepreneurs to buy and operate rikishas.[93]

The strength of local organisations, in short, lay in the immediacy of their contact with enterprise. They understood how local industry operated, and could convey new ideas in terms which small-scale producers understood. Their weakness, on the other hand, was that they themselves had only limited access to modern scientific and technological information. Very few prefectural governments or trade associations had the financial capacity or the knowledge to develop direct contacts with the outside world in the way that Kyoto City had done. Most had to rely on the uncertain trickle of technical knowledge which reached them through personal contacts, published information or national exhibitions, and the innovations which they promoted were therefore generally of the intuitive type which could be understood through practical experience with little knowledge of scientific principles.

Periphery and Centre

The problems at the local level, in other words, were the converse of the problems of central government. The Meiji leaders, as we have seen, had little difficulty in acquiring or importing advanced western technology, but seemed to have much greater difficulty in understanding the realities of agriculture and craft industry in their own country. This gap in understanding might have persisted throughout the Meiji Era but for a gradual shift in official thinking which began to be evident in the early 1880s. By this time, the Meiji leadership was reluctantly abandoning its belief that it could, through a few large-scale projects, transform Japan overnight into an industrialised nation. Its new approach involved a greater willingness to provide legal and financial assistance to regional technological projects, but at the same time can be seen as an attempt to draw those projects into nationwide, centrally controlled systems which conformed to its own vision of development.

An early sign of the changing direction was a massive, thirty-volume report on the economy compiled for the government between 1882 and 1884 by a prominent official, Maeda Masana (1850–1921). This report, the *Kôgyô iken* (*Opinions on the Promotion of Industry*) was a sombre and sobering reflection on the effects of a decade and a half of Meiji westernisation.[94] Wherever he turned, Maeda found evidence of traditional craft industries struggling to survive the impact of western manufactured goods. In major export industries such as sericulture, opportunities for profit had encouraged inexperienced producers to enter the market, lowering the quality and reputation of Japanese goods.[95] The report concluded with an appeal for a strengthening of the technological foundations of traditional industries: an appeal, in other words, less for the large-scale importation of technology than for the encouragement of indigenous innovation.[96]

Maeda's *Opinions on the Promotion of Industry* reflected a growing acceptance of the fact that Japan's industrial future was founded on the skills of the silkfarmer, the potter and the saké-brewer as much as it was on the technologies of the railway and the telegraph. In economic terms, after all, small-scale craft industries were responsible for by far the largest share of Japan's industrial employment and output (indeed, as late as 1920, only one-fifth of Japan's non-agricultural workforce could be described as working in 'modern' industry).[97] In political terms, too, a small group of successful local entrepreneurs were beginning to make their voices heard in the corridors of the Tokyo ministries. A good example was the Katakura silk firm, which had begun with a backyard workshop and ten *zaguri* reeling frames, but by 1894 owned the largest silk factory in Japan.[98] The Meiji Constitution of 1889 gave such entrepreneurs (provided their assets exceeded a certain size) a voice in parliament, while nationwide producer groups like the Greater Japan Silk Association (Dai Nippon Sanshigyô Kai) and the All-Japan Cotton Spinners' Federation acted as lobby groups for their interests.

One outcome of these shifting political currents was a closer relationship between central government and groups of dominant local industrialists, accompanied by an increasing official interest in the initiatives of the regions. An early step in this direction was taken in 1881, when the Ministry of Agriculture and Commerce convened the first of a series of national Industrial Promotion Congresses

(Kangyôkai), attended by representatives of all the prefectures. The discussions at the congress foreshadowed the finding of Maeda's report: there was much talk of foreign competition, of declining consumer confidence and of 'rough and careless production' (*sosei ranzô*), but also much praise for the local trade associations and their role in improving the quality of production.[99]

In response to these deliberations, the government decided both to encourage and to standardise the activities of local producer associations. The initial measure of 1884 was a cautious one. A set of uniform rules for trade associations were drawn up, and associations were allowed, with the approval of two-thirds of the producers in their industry and area, to impose compulsory membership on local enterprises. The creation of trade associations, however, remained a matter for local initiative, and the enforcement of regulations was entrusted to local authorities. Besides, the regulations prescribed no punishments for those who failed to join trade associations, so the matter of compulsion remained somewhat academic. This first tentative measure, however, gave considerable impetus to the spread of local associations, and during the 1890s a growing number of prefectures began to devise their own policies to support the creation of trade associations and penalise those who failed to join them. By the late 1890s some associations were actively lobbying for a tightening of the trade association laws, and in 1900 and 1903 the government introduced two new measures (the Major Export Products Trade Association Law and the Major Products Trade Association Law) which allowed associations to fine local producers for failing to join or for failure to abide by their regulations.[1]

By the beginning of the twentieth century, too, intervention by central government was beginning to draw the diverse technological efforts of local government into a national system of industrial research. During the 1880s the Ministry of Agriculture and Commerce began to send out its own technical advisers to assist the various technology centres set up by local authorities, and in 1903 the government introduced a law to encourage and regulate the establishment of technical colleges. This worked much like the earlier regulations on trade associations: in other words, it provided a standardised national framework, but left the actual initiative for the creation of the colleges to local government and local entrepreneurs, who responded with enthusiasm.[2]

Unlike the state-run universities, which trained a small elite for employment in ministries and public enterprises, the technical colleges taught middle-level technicians who would find employment in private firms.[3] They served, in other words, as a replacement for the declining apprenticeship system, and often as a source of innovation and experimentation with new ideas. A good example was the Arita technical college, founded in 1895. Here, as well as training students in the techniques of ceramics, the staff installed and ran the town's first working coal-fired kiln and experimented with new designs in porcelain ware.[4]

The promotion of local research activities had been a major theme of the Maeda report, which had called for the development of a nationwide network of prefectural laboratories linked to a national laboratory, with its headquarters in Tokyo and regional branches in other major cities. This would make it possible to link craft knowledge to modern science, creating a basis for innovation in areas like chemical dyestuffs, where intuitive know-how and straightforward reverse engineering were insufficient. Official reaction to this proposal was not immediate, for the wheels of Meiji bureaucracy could grind very slowly, and more pressing issues like the war with China intervened. In 1901, however, the Ministry of Agriculture and Commerce finally issued an ordinance defining national standards and regulations for prefectural research laboratories and technical education centres, and in 1905 it introduced a modest financial support scheme for local laboratories which received the Ministry's seal of approval. The first year's funding amounted to just 15,000 yen, distributed to eleven local research centres (including textiles research laboratories in Ehime, Fukui, Yamanashi and Kyoto, and Kyoto City's ceramics laboratory), but by the end of the Meiji era the sum had more than doubled, and the number of recipients had risen to fourteen.[5]

At the apex of the emerging research system stood the Ministry of Agriculture and Commerce's own Tokyo Industrial Research Laboratory, established in 1900. By 1909 the laboratory, housed in a substantial brick building and equipped with the 'best and latest appliances for investigation', had a professional staff of thirty-seven, a support staff of seventy, and a library of some 1000 foreign and 200 Japanese technical texts.[6] The Tokyo laboratory, with its relatively generous funding, thus became a source of reference and advice for its poorer provincial cousins: its director, for example, was frequently called on to serve as chief judge at local technical exhibitions. A network of personal connections linking the research system also began to appear, with a number of researchers from the Tokyo laboratory going on to prominent positions in local research laboratories.

The heavy hand of government guidance and largesse was not welcomed by everybody. Nationwide standardisation in silkfarming was opposed by the leading entrepreneurs of western Japan, who had already established their own systems of quality control, and were afraid of losing the advantages which they had obtained from their own earlier initiatives.[7] Proposals to fund local research stations, too, were opposed by some parliamentarians who argued (in the words of one sceptic) that 'when the government exerts itself to help in such matters, it almost always creates unendurable interference'.[8]

The critics were right, of course. Government encouragement and funding was intended precisely to channel local energies towards the central government's own encompassing vision of technological modernisation. Still, it is hard to deny that the systems put together by government legislation helped to provide the resources for indigenous inventions: not large and dramatic inventions, but many small, incremental adaptations of existing techniques.

A key element in all of these endeavours was the translation of Tokugawa techniques into the language and methods of modern science. At the Ôji sericultural station (established by the government in 1886), for example, knowledge of physics and biochemistry was applied to improving the design of the traditional Japanese silk-raising house, while microscopes (of which over 2000 were in use in Japanese silkfarming by the mid-1890s) were added to the existing armoury of protection from the spread of disease.[9] The Tokyo Industrial Research Laboratory, too, despite its trappings of modern 'high technology', concentrated mainly upon recasting existing craft knowledge into the forms of modern science. Of the five departments established by 1909, only one (the electro-chemical department) concentrated on modern imported techniques. The remaining four worked mainly on the analysis of Japanese mineral resources and of traditional techniques such as lacquer-making, ceramics, paper-making and textile dyeing, producing research papers with titles like *Report on Chrysalis Oil in Gumma and Nagano Prefectures, New Colours in Lacquers* and *The Bleaching of Shell Buttons*.[10] An important part of the Laboratory's responsibilities, in fact, consisted of examining existing craft products to determine their chemical and physical properties, for which it charged (inter alia)

> one yen for each testing of clays or fire bricks for refractive power, absorption or contraction … One yen for each testing of paper for folding, strength, elongation and sizing … Two yen for each determination of fibres, yarns or textile fabrics for loss on scouring.[11]

A similar function was fulfilled by the Fermentation Laboratory (Jôzô Shikenjô), set up in 1903 by the Ministry of Finance (for whom the liquor tax was an all-important source of revenue). Here, trained biochemists analysed the nature and workings of the mysterious *kôji* mould which constituted a vital part of the saké-brewing process.[12] The laboratory also undertook detailed surveys of the brewing industry in various parts of the country, looking at issues such as labour relations and wages, as well as at techniques of production.[13] On the basis of this research it was possible to devise methods of improving the quality of saké and of prolonging its shelf-life, to develop new brewing equipment, and to reduce costs by increasing the scale of production.

This process of converting the accumulated wealth of craft knowledge into scientific know-how is often overlooked by historians of technology, who tend to focus on the more visible and dramatic import of modern western techniques. Yet it was absolutely vital to Japan's modern technological development. It is true that some of the individuality and poetry of traditional crafts was lost when, for example, lacquer ceased to be seen as the resin of a special tree and became (in the words of the Tokyo Research Laboratory's chemist) 'a monobasic acid of the formula $C_{14}H_{18}O_2$ [which] is oxidised to oxyurushic acid $C_{14}H_{18}O_3$ on drying'.[14] But it was this translation of existing knowledge into scientific forms which allowed the world of the craft workshop and the local trade association to be linked to that of the factory and the modern research laboratory. It was this, in other words, which linked the local economy to the modernising vision of the central state, so initiating a tremendous acceleration of the process of indigenous innovation already evident in Tokugawa Japan.

The Social Network of Innovation in Meiji Japan

This chapter has presented three differing and yet partly complementary versions of the development of technology in Meiji Japan. The central government provided the gateway for the entry of advanced western technology; market factors encouraged the development of simple, intermediate techniques by small firms. The connecting factor, which helps to make sense of the relationship between these two extremes, is the social network of innovation.

The upheavals which accompanied the transition from the Tokugawa political order to the centralised Meiji state resulted in the reshaping of this network. The new system bore traces of its pre-Meiji heritage, but was at the same time distinctively different both in its structure and in its implicit objectives. In the first years of the Meiji era, the technological initiatives of local, grassroots groups were relatively far removed from the ambitious modernisation schemes of the central state. While central government laid the foundations of a modern industrial infrastructure, with railways, telegraph and imported mining, factory and military technologies, regional institutions encouraged incremental innovation and the incorporation of simple foreign techniques into existing production systems. By the end of the century, however, centre and periphery were beginning to be woven together into a multi-layered hierarchy of connected institutions which proved an effective means of spreading technological information.

At the level of the village or the local region, trade associations and similar organisations provided a forum for the exchange of technical ideas and experience, as well as acting as an entry point for the inflow of technological information from 'above'. Local research laboratories and technical high schools (with which the trade associations were closely connected) created an intermediate layer between the grass-roots organisations and the educational and research institutes of the capital. Prefectural bodies were in turn linked together by structures like the Industrial Promotion Congresses, and by the controlling hand of the central ministries which provided a growing share of their funding.

The effect was a system in which new and imported ideas were not simply concentrated in a few elite institutions run by the state or large private enterprises, but rather dispersed throughout a wide range of bodies, varying in size, structure and geographical location, but all involved to some extent in the processes of importing, modifying or developing new technologies. These bodies did not work in isolation from one another, but were linked by many and varied channels of communication. The dreams and hopes which inspired their search for new techniques varied. Large state projects like Yawata steel were driven by visions of national glory, and developed with little regard to the disruption which they inflicted on local society. The projects of pre-fectural institutes and local trade associations tended to be more sen-sitive to the complex and conflicting interests of regional society, but even they, in their desire to create employment and increase wealth, encouraged the use of technologies (like rikisha transport) whose burden on the human worker were heavy. In this sense, the Meiji social network of innovation not only promoted rapid innovation, but also began to define a distinctive pattern of innovation, which would influ-ence the course of Japan's technological history into the middle of the twentieth century and beyond.

CHAPTER 5

Systems-building and Science-based Industry, 1912–1937

In 1915, three years after the death of the Emperor Meiji, the recently established Hitachi machinery firm was commissioned to produce a 10,000-horsepower turbine for a new hydroelectric power station. The order was placed with Hitachi because the outbreak of war in 1914 had prevented the delivery of equipment ordered from Germany. Since the largest turbine previously produced by Hitachi had a capacity of just 100 horsepower, the assignment was, to say the least, a challenging one. To design the equipment, Hitachi's chief engineer, a Tokyo University graduate, began by extracting all the useful information he could find from his university notes on electrical engineering, and then made careful sketches of the exterior of a large-scale turbine in use at another major power station. Not surprisingly, the venture suffered numerous setbacks, the most important occurring when the turbine's penstock (pressure pipe) ruptured because of structural weaknesses in the cast steel used in its production.

Meanwhile, Hitachi was also involved in producing equipment for Japan's largest and most ambitious electricity scheme, the massive Inawashiro hydroelectric power plant in Fukushima Prefecture. Like other power stations, Inawashiro had relied on imported equipment until supplies were disrupted by the outbreak of war in Europe. The component ordered from Hitachi was a circuit-breaker, but the product which Hitachi supplied proved quite inadequate to deal with the high voltage of the station's power lines; the day after delivery it exploded, causing serious damage.

The following year a generator installed by Hitachi in its own mines fell apart during operation because of a failure of the governor designed to control the rotation speed of the turbine, and in 1917 an electric induction machine being tested in Hitachi's workshops blew up, severing the leg of the supervising engineer. Investigation revealed

105

that the explosion occurred because Hitachi, unable to obtain the cupro-nickel from which crucial parts of the machine were normally made, had substituted an inferior alloy.[1]

This litany of misadventures serves to illustrate the point that, even after the rapid changes of the Meiji Era, there was nothing simple or inevitable about Japan's continuing acquisition of industrial technology. Like many industrialising countries today, Japan faced the problem of pursuing a moving target. No sooner had one area of foreign scientific and technological know-how been conquered, than whole new regions of knowledge, pioneered by researchers in the leading industrial nations, appeared on the horizon.

The aim of this chapter is to examine the ways in which Japanese industry confronted the challenges of the rapidly changing technological system. The object, however, is to present something a little more complex than a simple 'how-done-it' story of triumph over adversity. For most of the problems posed by the new technologies, there was a variety of possible organisational solutions. The solutions which Japanese enterprises chose were strongly influenced by the Meiji legacy of know-how, industrial skills and economic structures. But the solutions themselves also shaped the evolution of Japan's social network of innovation. Out of the challenges, the achievements and the disasters of the interwar and war years emerged systems of research and production which would provide the basis for the explosion of technological energy in Japan after the Pacific War.

Corporate Research and the Social Network of Innovation

For much of the Meiji Era central and local government, as well as bodies like trade associations, had acted as crucial intermediaries between private firms and the outside world, channelling new technological knowledge to individual enterprises. By the early twentieth century, however, Japanese companies themselves were creating links to the international technological community, and a growing number were becoming importers of industrial know-how in their own right.

The way in which they did this was powerfully influenced by two aspects of the economic and technological environment. Firstly, the emergence of Japanese corporations as major independent importers of technology coincided with that wave of innovation which is often called 'the second industrial revolution'. Between the 1880s and the 1920s, industrial production in Western Europe and the United States was transformed by new metallurgical and chemical technologies, the widespread diffusion of electrical power, the introduction of the automobile and the aeroplane, and the elaboration of the techniques of mass production. The quickening pace of technological change posed special problems for a newly industrialising country like Japan. While the imported techniques of the early Meiji period, such as the flying shuttle and the Jacquard loom, had generally been 'visible' techniques which could be understood by a skilled artisan with little formal education, the technologies of electricity generation, the combustion engine, or the production of chemical fertilisers could be grasped only by someone with a firm grounding in the principles of modern science. To understand, absorb and make use of these technologies, companies needed to develop their own scientific expertise. The corporate import of technology was therefore closely associated with the emergence of the corporate research laboratory.

A second influence on the nascent technology strategy of Japanese companies was their position in the world economy. Here the Japanese story is very different from that of the contemporary industrialising countries of Southeast Asia, where new industrial companies are often subsidiaries of foreign multinationals, producing components which may be assembled on the other side of the globe. Although (as we shall see) a number of Japanese firms had tie-ups with large foreign companies, they did not become links in a complex international production system of the sort which exists today in industries like electronics. Instead, most foreign-affiliated firms produced finished goods for the Japanese market. Although Japan's reliance on exports grew rapidly in the first decades of the twentieth century, Japan never became as export-dependent as present-day industrialising countries like Taiwan and Malaysia. A large share of the manufactured goods which it *did* export, moreover, went to less industrialised regions of East and Southeast Asia. For all of these reasons it was possible, and sensible, for many Japanese firms to modify imported technology, producing goods which were cheaper and simpler than their western prototypes.

The scientists and technicians employed by Japanese companies in the first half of the twentieth century, then, were not simply involved in studying and copying western technology, but also in adapting it to local needs. They, like their employers, were for the most part firm believers in the gospel of industrial progress, and rarely questioned the fundamental assumptions of western technological knowledge. They were well aware, however, that the details of productive processes could be altered to reduce costs and increase corporate profit.

The historical context helps to explain the organisational response of Japanese companies to the challenge of the 'second industrial revolution'. A large number of firms set up their own research laboratories, but most of these were relatively small in size—appropriate to the tasks of importing and modifying technologies rather than of conducting large-scale fundamental research. So a network of many small private laboratories came to be imposed on the network of small public laboratories which had begun to take shape in the Meiji period. The private research system was closely integrated with its public counterpart. University and other government-funded research laboratories provided advice to private firms, and some of Japan's most important twentieth-century industries developed under the powerful technological tutelage of military arsenals and research establishments. At the other end of the scale, large private firms themselves exerted great influence over the technological development of Japan's small firms. For a variety of reasons which we shall explore, subcontracting became a very important feature of industry in interwar Japan, and subcontracting networks became a means by which large companies at once encouraged the modernisation of small firms and imposed their own version of technological progress upon them.

With the onset of the world depression in 1929 and Japan's deepening military involvement in China during the 1930s, state policies towards science and technology underwent a gradual change. There were increased efforts to intervene in, plan and centralise control of technological change. These attempts, though, were only partly successful. The most important overall outcome of developments in the Taishô (1912–26) and early Shôwa periods (from 1926) was an extension and reinforcement of the dispersed network of many small research institutions which had begun to appear in the Meiji Era.

Science and Business: Company Research and the Acquisition of Technology

In 1900, according to one estimate, there were fewer than 700 Japanese trained technicians (i.e. graduates of universities or technical colleges) employed in private enterprises. Even the most modern mines and factories commonly employed just one graduate engineer who was expected to supervise all technical aspects of the enterprise's operations. By 1910, however, the number of graduate technicians in private firms had risen to about 2500, and a handful of pioneers were beginning to organise their technical staff into distinct research divisions.[2] (A company like Hitachi, however, which hired five Tokyo University graduates in the two-year period from 1911 to 1912, was still regarded as exceptional if not eccentric.)[3]

The development of corporate research was usually gradual: from lone technician to research or technology section, and only later to fully fledged corporate research laboratory. The story of Shibaura Electric, the company which had grown out of the ventures of that master of automata Tanaka Hisashige, provides a good illustration of the process. In 1893 the company, lacking the capital to sustain its technological ambitions, had come under the control of the Mitsui business empire, which proceeded to rationalise its management and convert it into a limited company. At this stage the company's only full-time researcher was its Testing Supervisor, Koganei Harumasa, who from 1906 onwards conducted experiments in a converted judô shed at the back of the factory compound (see Figure 5.1). As is often the case in Japan, however, the contents of the research room were rather more sophisticated than one might have guessed from its unimposing exterior. By 1909 Koganei had obtained Japan's first oscillograph, purchased from the Cambridge Instrument Company at a cost of 10,000 yen, and installed it in the judô shed with firm instructions that it was to be touched by no-one but himself. Four years later Koganei's research activities were rehoused in new purpose-built premises, and in 1921 a specialised research division was established, with three subsections specialising in electrical engineering, materials and chemistry. Each subsection in turn employed three or four principal researchers, who were allocated specific research topics. Research, in short, had

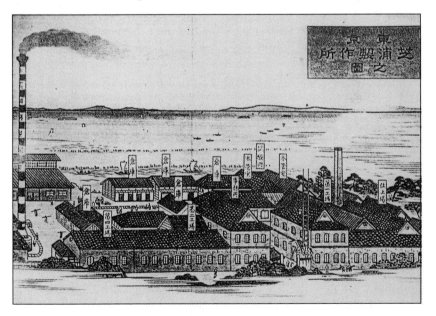

Figure 5.1 The Shibaura electric factory (Koganei Harumasa's research laboratory is in the rear left-hand corner)
Source: Tokyo Shibaura Denki KK, *Tokyo Shibaura Denki Kabushiki Kaisha hachijû gonen shi,* p. 48.

been transformed from the marginalised activity of a single individual to an organised part of the company's strategy. Even the massive earthquake of 1923, which destroyed Shibaura's research section along with its factory, was unable to check the trend towards systematised research and development. The company's new factory, built in the industrial zone of Tsurumi on the shores of Tokyo Bay, contained a greatly expanded area for research, and by 1933 the Research Division (now renamed the Shibaura Electric Tsurumi Research Laboratory) had a total staff of sixty-four.[4]

Many Japanese companies went through the same process in the years from the late Meiji period to the 1930s. The very first company research centres, including the Onoda Cement laboratories and Tokyo Electric's Mazda Lamp laboratory, were established in the 1890s, but within forty years their number had grown to about three hundred.[5] Most, however, operated on a very modest scale. While the Bell Laboratories in the US employed more than 3600 people by 1925, and Du Pont's chemical department employed more than 1200 research scientists, Tokyo Electric, which boasted one of Japan's largest private laboratories in the 1920s, had a research staff of about one hundred.[6] But the small size of these research centres was not just a consequence of the 'backwardness' of Japanese industry: rather, it reflected the very specific function of the research laboratory in interwar Japanese industry.

Prewar Japanese firms regarded their research arms, not as potential sources of an unending stream of fundamental technological breakthroughs, but as windows on the technical knowledge of the outside world, and as channels through which that knowledge could be transferred to the factory floor. As a 1923 report by Shibaura's Research Division put it,

> At present it is hoped that [the laboratory] will deal as far as possible with practical problems. This is not to say that it has ignored practical problems in the past, but we feel that in future we would wish to further advance our work on actual problems. For this reason, our intention is to maintain close links with the Planning and Factory Divisions, and to devote the efforts of the entire research staff to solving, as quickly and effectively as possible, problems presented to us by those divisions.[7]

Research sections provided, as it were, a watchtower from which the company could scan the horizon for promising new technologies. Research divisions like Shibaura's maintained libraries of western technical texts, subscriptions to the leading journals in their field, and indexed card files of scientific abstracts.[8] Some went considerably further than this: by the 1930s Hitachi had established a specialised patents division which devoted considerable time and effort to collecting all the available information on every patent granted in Japan since 1889.[9] By accumulating this infrastructure of technical knowledge, Japanese companies improved their ability to select and bargain for the technologies which they needed to acquire from others.

Once a firm had identified technologies which it wished to acquire, there were four main ways in which it could go about obtaining them. Firstly, it could establish a direct tie-up with a western firm, exchanging a portion of its financial independence for the benefits of access to western know-how; secondly, it could purchase a licence to use foreign patented knowledge; thirdly, it could try independently to 'reverse engineer' existing technologies; or, lastly, it could embark on the relatively arduous process of developing an entirely original method of creating a particular product. These four steps, of course, mark an ascending scale of originality and inventiveness. Even firms which chose to rely on foreign tie-ups, however, were not merely passive receptors of ready-made foreign ideas.

Tie-Ups with Foreign Firms

Direct affiliation with emerging foreign (mostly US) multinational companies was particularly common in areas like the electrical goods industry. Japan had the good fortune to embark on its industrial revolution at a time when electrical power was beginning to be put to practical use in industry and the household. This meant that many Japanese firms (including small-scale enterprises) were able to move straight from manual craft production to the use of electrical equipment, bypassing, as it were, the age of steam.[10] Geographical circumstances also favoured Japan. Its mountainous topography with fast-flowing rivers was ideally suited to the development of hydroelectric power. Between 1914 and 1925 power consumption in Japan rose from just under 300,000 kilowatt hours to over 1.5 million annually, and by 1936 Japan was the third-largest consumer of electricity in the world.[11] The spread of electricity brought with it a rapid increase in demand, not only for power-generating equipment but also for electrically driven machines, but the technologies involved in manufacturing this equipment involved a level of scientific knowledge far beyond that of the ordinary skilled craftworker.

Foreign firms, meanwhile, were often willing to purchase shares in Japanese electrical goods companies because they recognised that, without the sales and service support of a local firm, the expanding Japanese market would be hard to penetrate. In the first decade of the twentieth century both Tokyo Electric and Shibaura Electric formed tie-ups with the US giant General Electric (GE), Tokyo Electric selling

51 per cent of its shares to GE, while Shibaura exchanged 24 per cent of its capital for patent licences, factory blueprints, research information, and staff training by its US mentor.[12] Mitsubishi Electric, a latecomer to the field established in 1921, also sought out a US partner, offering 10 per cent of its stock to Westinghouse in return for access to technical data.[13] In a few instances, the impetus came, not from the Japanese but from the western side. The Nippon Electric Company (NEC), established in 1899, began life as sales and service subsidiary of Western Electric, before eventually acquiring its own capacity to produce equipment under licence from its US parent company; Fuji Electric (which would later become the electronic giant Fujitsu) was set up by the German company Siemens in cooperation with the Japanese Furukawa concern, and also graduated from sales of imported products to manufacturing in its own right. Western capital, in short, played a very active part in making the rod which, in the late twentieth century, would beat its own back.

For foreign-affiliated firms, the research or technical division acted as a bridge between themselves and their western partner. Mitsubishi Electric's technical division, for example, was responsible for supervising a carefully-designed program of technical exchange with Westinghouse. Managerial and organisational methods as well as production techniques were eagerly imported from the US firm. From 1924 to 1940 more than sixty Mitsubishi Electric technicians were sent for short periods of work and study at Westinghouse, during which each was expected to concentrate on a particular area of technology: anything from the production of electric fans to the use of control mechanisms in the engines of warships.[14]

Other companies pursued a more independent line towards their foreign partners. In fact, Japanese companies seem to have enjoyed extraordinary latitude in their technical relationship with western companies, largely, no doubt, because Europeans and Americans were still quite unable to conceive of Japan as a serious competitor in technologically advanced industries. Tokyo Electric, for example, relied less on the training of its technicians in the US, and more on the import of ideas and industrial machinery from its partner General Electric. A major benefit of the tie-up with GE was that it gave Tokyo Electric access to the technique of producing gas-filled tungsten light-bulbs, which were far more efficient than their carbon filament predecessors, and so helped the company to obtain a virtual monopoly of the lucrative and rapidly growing Japanese electric lighting market. In the 1930s, a further agreement with General Electric's affiliate RCA (the Radio Corporation of America) allowed Tokyo Electric to import the essence of US know-how on radio production, as well as much of the embryonic technology of television.[15]

The close relationship with GE (which was, after all, Tokyo Electric's controlling shareholder) did not inhibit the Japanese company from pursuing its own innovation strategy. Lighting techniques imported from GE were studied and improved in Tokyo Electric's laboratories, which succeeded in reducing costs by using cheaper production materials and even in improving the quality of the finished products: developing, for example, a longer-lasting double-coil lamp and devising its own techniques for frosting the inside of light bulbs.[16]

The remarkable ability of Tokyo Electric to go its own way is suggested by the events which followed the destruction of the company's research laboratory in the great Kantô earthquake of 1923. It was decided that a new laboratory should be constructed as quickly as possible, but, according to the company's official history,

> H. U. Pierce and O. Pruessman, the directors who at that time represented GE on the company's board, insisted that research should be conducted by GE, and the later post-development stages by Tokyo Electric, and so emphasised that effort should be directed towards building a [new] factory to increase production. However, Yamaguchi Kisaburô, who was then the company president, and Factory Director Niizeki Kôsaku felt that innovation was in the interests of Japan, and therefore went ahead independently with the construction of a research laboratory.[17]

One of the projects enthusiastically taken up by the new laboratory was research on the technology of television, a topic which aroused the interest of a number of the more adventurous research scientists in prewar Japan. On the very last day of the Taishô Era (25 December 1926) a researcher at Hamamatsu Technical College (using techniques derived in part from reports on the work of Logie Baird and others) had succeeded in transmitting a single written character to a receiver set up in his laboratory.[18] By the late 1930s the national broadcasting company NHK was developing plans for a television service to be inaugurated at the Tokyo Olympics, planned for 1940, and Toshiba became involved in the technical groundwork for this ambitious project. In the event, both the introduction of television and the Tokyo Olympics themselves were delayed by unforeseen political cataclysms. The first foundations, however, had already been laid for the resurgence of the postwar Japanese television industry.[19]

Licensing Patented Know-How

In other industries such as chemicals production, western firms had less interest in acquiring a Japanese partner. Many of the largest western chemical companies belonged to powerful international cartels, which gave them supreme confidence in their ability to dominate overseas markets. As a result, it was more often Japanese chemical companies which had to take the initiative in importing foreign technology, and these imports of know-how tended to take the form of single patent-licensing arrangements, as opposed to the packages of patent licences, technical assistance and investment which characterised the electrical machinery industry.

Without the ongoing technical support of a foreign partner, however, patent licensees often encountered great difficulties in putting imported knowledge into practice and, to overcome these problems, were forced to expand their own technical and research capacity. A case in point is the story of the calcium cyanamide process, invented by the German scientists Frank and Caro in 1906, which involved combining calcium carbide and nitrogen at high temperatures to form a valuable source of synthetic fertiliser. The process consumed enormous amounts of electrical power but, ironically, this was precisely one of the features which made it attractive to Japanese entrepreneurs. The large hydro-electric schemes built in the early part of the century tended to suffer from problems of excess capacity in periods of low consumer demand, and therefore offered surplus power at very cheap rates to corporate customers. By stimulating the rise of energy-consuming industries, this gave the Japanese economy an 'addiction' to power consumption which was to cause enormous problems in later years.

In the early twentieth century, however, the combination of cheap electricity and new chemical technology offered enticing prospects for profit, and in 1908 two Japanese entrepreneurs, Noguchi Jun and Fujiyama Shôichi, travelled to Europe to negotiate a licence for the use of the Frank–Caro patent. Noguchi and Fujiyama were able to grasp the significance of the technology because of their own technical back-grounds. Both were electrical engineering graduates from Tokyo Imperial University, and both had conducted their own research on synthetic fertilisers after graduation.[20] Noguchi also had extensive experience in electrical power generation, and from the first, planned the cyanamide venture as part of a scheme to use excess power from a hydroelectric plant in southern Kyûshû.[21] However, their factory, con-structed in the small fishing port of Minamata in 1909, proved to have substantial technical problems. The output from the patented process was much lower than anticipated, and extensive work on the design of the factory's chemical furnaces was necessary to raise it to the expected level.[22] Fujiyama, meanwhile, had quarrelled with Noguchi and left to join the Mitsui mines, whose extensive and well-established research facilities he used to develop an improved continuous-flow version of the

Frank–Caro process. This innovation was granted a Japanese patent in 1914, and provoked a battle over patent rights between Noguchi and Fujiyama which lasted until the mid-1920s.[23]

Noguchi's company, Nippon Chisso, was one of a number of prewar Japanese firms which developed a considerable research capability without establishing a formal research and development laboratory (its first laboratory was not opened until the early 1940s).[24] During the 1920s the firm expanded into the production of synthetic ammonia using the imported Casale process, and in the 1930s, Noguchi's technicians worked on a range of polymers such as vinyl chloride and acetaldehyde. As their experience grew, so they were able to reduce their dependence on licensed technology, and to create their own productive technologies, drawing inspiration from published information on the latest developments in the chemical industry worldwide. This growing independence allowed Chisso to modify techniques to their own specific needs.

The 'appropriate technologies' which they developed, however, were appropriate solely in the sense of being designed to maximise profit in the environment of interwar Japan. They provided a starting point for the phenomenal growth of the chemicals industry in interwar and postwar Japan, but Chisso's home-grown process for acetaldehyde production was also to cause one of the worst environmental disasters of the twentieth century (see p. 207).[25]

Reverse Engineering

If the use of licensed know-how meant something more than following a prescribed technological recipe, reverse engineering meant something more than simple copying. There were, of course, some instances where foreign machines were taken apart and replicated piece by piece. But reverse engineering, which almost certainly remained the most common method of acquiring technology in the interwar years, increasingly involved an understanding of underlying scientific principles, and an ability to adapt foreign models to the needs of the domestic market.

Enterprises like Hitachi, which deliberately avoided formal links with foreign firms, were particularly reliant on this path of technological development. Most of Hitachi's early technology was derived from two sources: published information in technical journals and sketches of imported machinery. From 1918, however, the establishment of a Research Division enabled the firm to test and 'debug' its imported techniques, and to devise improved designs: among them, more efficient hydroelectric generators and highly sensitive electric equipment to prevent interference in those places (common in Japan's mountainous territory) where electric cables and telephone lines ran side by side.[26]

In the intangible world of the chemical industry, straightforward reverse engineering of the finished product was impossible, and companies which were unable to acquire patented know-how were forced to go through the slow process of attempting to replicate experiments which they found described in technical publications. Often these publications, to avoid revealing commercial secrets, were written in deliberately broad and general terms, making life extremely difficult for the would-be Japanese imitators. Tokyo University graduates Kumura Seita and Hata Itsuzô, for example, were commissioned by the powerful Suzuki trading house to produce the recently discovered substance viscose for use in synthetic textiles. After long and painful experience, they discovered that the western published material on viscose production omitted details of the crucial ageing process, which was necessary to allow the viscose thread to form. Several years of trial and error elapsed before they were able to develop a reliable technique for artificial silk production which, from 1918 onwards, was put to use in the newly formed Imperial Artificial Silk Company (Teikoku Jinken, usually known as Teijin for short).[27]

The First World War was crucial to the success of all these ventures. During the war, Japan was temporarily cut off from large-scale imports of western goods, and new companies like Hitachi and Teijin were therefore able to establish a foothold in the market at a time when there was virtually no foreign competition. This allowed them a breathing space to overcome the numerous technical problems involved in entering complex new industries. Because the First World War coincided precisely with the diffusion of electrical and chemical technologies in Japan, companies which relied on trial and error in the acquisition of these technologies were able to make their errors at a time when the market was unusually forgiving. This helps to explain why, in the long run, independent companies like Hitachi developed just as successfully as foreign-affiliated rivals like Tokyo Electric and Shibaura Electric.

Original Invention

Writing in the 1930s, the prominent Japanese technologist Ôkôchi Masatoshi (of whom more hereafter) made the surprising claim that Japanese researchers were skilled and original inventors, but that Japan's weakness lay in an inability to commercialise radically new ideas. In the first place, he argued, many companies were unprepared for the lengthy period of developmental work necessary to take the invention from the laboratory bench to full-scale production. More importantly perhaps, few private firms were prepared to take the risks involved in radical innovation: they were willing to spend time and money refining imported technologies because they knew that there was a marketable product at the end of the development process, but were reluctant to make a similar investment where the final outcome was uncertain.[28] As we shall see shortly, an ambitious government-supported scheme was initiated to try to overcome this problem. There were, however, some independent private companies whose research, contrary to Ôkôchi's strictures, did take them beyond the modification of imported ideas into realms which involved a high degree of originality.

The classic example of Japanese innovation is the case of the Toyoda Loom Works, established by Toyoda Sakichi in 1906. Toyoda Sakichi was a carpenter who, although he was born in the last year of the Tokugawa Era, was in many ways typical of the inventive genius which characterised some of the best of Tokugawa artisans. His home region of Nagoya was one of the main centres of Japanese cotton-weaving, and Toyoda developed a particular interest in improved weaving looms, which he studied on visits to government exhibitions of industry in Tokyo. On the basis of observation and experimentation, Toyoda came up with a series of patented textile machines, from a slightly more complex version of the traditional draw loom, through several designs of power loom, to an automatic loom which he patented in 1916.[29] In the process he obtained financial backing from the Mitsui conglomerate, extended his business interests into cotton-spinning in Japan and China, and made a fortune which enabled him to send his eldest son Toyoda Kiichirô to study engineering at Tokyo University.

By the 1920s Toyoda's inventive activities, which had begun as back-yard tinkering, had developed into relatively large-scale research. An experimental factory, set up near Nagoya in 1924, was used as a basis for refining the Toyoda loom. Here the younger Toyoda demonstrated a systematic approach to research which was far removed from the craft know-how of the carpenter's workshop. To test an improved version of the power loom, for example, he made thirty prototypes which were put to work for two years. Experience from these prototypes was used to iron out initial flaws in the design, and then a further large-scale test was carried out on two hundred of the new looms.[30] The large-scale test, as Toyoda Kiichirô later recalled, revealed numerous failures, both mechanical and human, which would otherwise have been overlooked.

Any invention [he wrote] has many valuable aspects, but at the same time, before these can be put to use, it also has all sorts of faults. If you can find the faults and fix them there and then, you can exhibit the strong points of your invention to their best advantage, but I became very aware of the fact that identifying the faults at an early stage was something which could well take longer, and cost more, than the original invention itself.[31]

Toyoda's research techniques, in other words, had taken the first step on the road from craft ingenuity to the technology of mass production, where standardised, reliable quality would be all important. It was, of course, this experience in large-scale machine production which would ease the company's entry, ten years later, into the mass production of automobiles.

Other inventions, rather than evolving from craft tradition, sprang directly from the modern research laboratory. Among Japan's genuinely original contributions to prewar technology was the development of a technique for the production of the chemical monosodium glutamate (an achievement which some might regard as a mixed blessing). MSG was synthesised from gluten by the prominent Tokyo University professor Ikeda Kikunae, who then combined with the industrialist Suzuki Saburôsuke to commercialise the product. But, just as imported technology needed refinement and adaptation to the conditions of the workplace, so Ikeda's invention too needed extensive developmental work before it could be introduced into the factory. In the case of MSG, the main problem was the shift from small-scale laboratory production to large-scale manufacture, and for much of 1908 and 1909 Ikeda virtually abandoned his university work to concentrate on research in the laboratory of Ajinomoto, the firm which he and Suzuki had established.[32]

The initial reaction to this local innovation was cautious: the Ajinomoto management found itself forced to counter public rumours that its product was made from snakes (see Figure 5.2). Within a matter of years, though, Ajinomoto had become an immense commercial success. Meanwhile the use of untried technology produced entirely unexpected problems. Developmental work in Ajinomoto's laboratory had focused strictly on devising a viable and profitable production process, and this process turned out to entail the large-scale emission of hydrochloric acid and the dumping of waste starch products into the neighbouring Kawasaki River. As in the case of Nippon Chisso, commercially 'appropriate' technology proved to be highly inappropriate in environmental terms. Ajinomoto thus became the target of one of Japan's earliest protest movements against industrial pollution, and in the early 1920s had the dubious distinction of being one of the first Japanese manufacturing companies to be persuaded to pay compensation for environmental damage.[33]

Worker Training and the Invention of Corporate Culture

The Japanese companies which began to make rikishas in the 1870s and 1880s had to assemble some twenty to thirty different component parts in order to produce a finished vehicle. By contrast, when the first large-scale Japanese production of cars began in the 1930s, manufacturers found that the production of a small range of trucks and passenger cars involved the assembly of between 5500 and 6000 components.[34] Each component, besides, had to be made to standards many times more exacting than those required in rikisha production.

The development of complex, science-based industries like the car industry, in other words, depended on something more than the import of technology and the establishment of research laboratories. Corporate research could absorb new technology and adapt it to the needs of the Japanese production system, but that alone was not

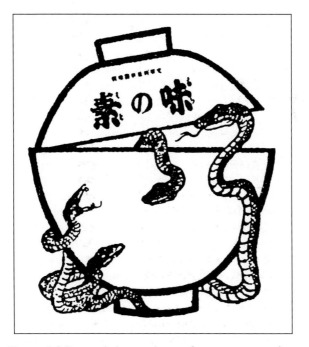

Figure 5.2 Domestic innovation and consumer reaction. This contemporary cartoon illustrates rumours that Ajinomoto's new food flavouring was made from snakes.
Source: Uchida H., ed., *Gijutsu no shakai shi,* vol. 5, p. 69.

enough. The growing complexity and interdependence of industry demanded that the production side, too, be transformed. New forms of organisation, new skills, attitudes and labour relationships were necessary. The human material of technology had to be moulded to the needs of the integrated network of modern industry.

Traditional craft skills like those of the the silkweaver, the carpenter and the blacksmith were plentiful in interwar Japan, but were inappropriate to the needs of the modern electrical machinery, chemical or heavy industrial factory. The arts of the craft workshop were deeply individual and were acquired through decades of observation and practice. What was needed in the newly emerging industries, on the other hand, was a basic standardised knowledge of mechanics and physical processes, to be obtained through formal education as much as through practical experience.

The local technical colleges set up in the late Meiji period provided one source of skilled labour, but they had an inherent drawback. Workers who were trained through the public education system gained ownership of their own skills: their qualifications were a valuable asset which enabled them to sell their labour to the highest bidder. In times of rapid industrial growth like the period of the First World War, when skilled labour was particularly scarce, large companies found themselves plagued by a continual haemorrhaging of skills as trained workers were tempted away by the promise of higher wages elsewhere. To fill the gaps and stem the flow, it was important to develop systems of training which would transfer to the company the notions of loyalty and duty implicit in the rapidly vanishing apprenticeship system. The solution, in other words, was to set up technical education systems inside the company.

The first company training schools, such as the Mitsubishi shipyards' technical school in Nagasaki, appeared as early as the 1890s, but the shift towards corporate technical training gathered particular momentum from about 1910 onwards as the Hitachi Machine Works (1910), Nippon Kôkan (1913), the Ashio copper mines (1913), Shibaura Electric (1914), Sumitomo (1915) and other large companies developed their own training systems.[35] At Hitachi the process began just two years after the company was founded, when thirty-six apprentices were accepted for training in foundry work, electrical mechanics and the use of machine tools. In 1921, company education was extended with the establishment of the Hitachi Mechanical School, which gave more advanced training to graduates of the apprenticeship course. The school buildings were all situated inside the factory compound, and classes were combined with practical experience on the shop floor. As well as technical education, apprenticeships and courses in the

Mechanical School contained heavy doses of initiation in the corporate ethos. Food and uniforms were provided by the company, and classes included physical education, ethics and (from 1926 onwards) military training. Hitachi trainees enjoyed privileges such as their own library, baseball field and tennis courts, but were required to repay their obligations to the company by staying with Hitachi for at least three years after graduation.[36]

This alone, however, was not enough to ensure that workers resisted the lure of better wages elsewhere. According to the company's training supervisor, 'so many people left to work with other firms that there were loud complaints from the factory'.[37] During the interwar years, therefore, a growing number of companies began to offer other incentives to loyalty: retirement benefits, for example, health insurance schemes, or attendance bonuses which rose after so many years' service to the firm. These examples of corporate 'benevolence' were not just responses to the need to foster a stable and educated workforce, but were also intended as a counterweight to the attractions of the trade union movement, which experienced an upsurge of militance in the 1920s before being repressed in the 1930s. As Andrew Gordon observes, the corporate welfare schemes were neither comprehensive nor entirely effective:

> Listed in a sentence or two, the total range of company 'benevolence' appears impressive, and the workers appreciated, indeed expected, these non-wage benefits, but company welfare programs in heavy industry did not simply generate the long-term commitment or the good will often credited to them. They frequently lacked substance, were cut back or abandoned when business needs dictated, and could exacerbate rather than reduce tension within the enterprise. When employers changed a provision of an important benefit, workers often protested at this denial of their 'just' reward.[38]

The demands of profit-making and the traditions of autocratic management made it difficult for companies in interwar Japan to find adequate answers to the problems of skilled labour turnover. Their efforts, however, did suggest possible solutions which would be more fully implemented in the wave of social change which followed the Second World War.

An alternative approach to the distressing disloyalty of skilled workers might have been to subdivide skilled work into small, repetitive components which could easily be performed by untrained workers. This was, of course, the essence of the Taylorite notion of scientific management which dominated US managerial thought in the early twentieth century. Taylor's ideas were in fact introduced into a number of Japanese firms in the decade from 1910 to 1920. (Mitsubishi Electric, with its close ties to Westinghouse, was a particularly enthusiastic disciple of scientific management.)[39] Most Japanese firms, however, were not only smaller and less mechanised than their US counterparts, but were also in a state of greater technological flux. Products and techniques were changing rapidly, and the limited size of the Japanese market left no room for truly gargantuan mass-production systems like that of Ford's River Rouge plant in Detroit. In this environment, it was difficult to find a place for the narrow, static specialism of scientific management, and Taylorite ideas, when they were put to use, tended to be given a curious, distinctively Japanese twist (as we shall see in our discussion of the Institute for Physical and Chemical Research).

The State and Corporate Research

The Research Network: Public Education and Private Innovation

Corporate research and training was, for the most part, developed through the independent initiatives of private firms. But it is important to recognise that these corporate initiatives could succeed because their roots were nourished by the existing network of government education and research institutions. The close connections which developed between corporate and state research bodies enabled technical information to flow rapidly through the Japanese innovation network, but also influenced the content and aims of private research.

State-funded universities and technical colleges, of course, provided the graduates who filled most positions in corporate laboratories or research divisions. They also offered a very important continuing source of advice and support to private industry. Sometimes (as in the case of Ajinomoto) this might involve a university professor's active participation in the establishment of a new enterprise. More often, however, the relationship was a more casual one, where university facilities were borrowed for research purposes or faculty consulted on particular technical problems. Hitachi, for example, used the old-boy network to obtain access to an experimental electrical transformer at Kyoto University, on which it based its early commercial designs,[40] while Toyoda Kiichirô cultivated an impressive stable of technical consultants (including three professors of engineering and two professors of physics from Tokyo University) whose advice enabled Toyoda to overcome the initial problems of entry into the automobile industry in the late 1930s.[41]

Elite educational institutions like Tokyo Imperial University, indeed, nurtured powerful old-boy networks, which have played a remarkably important part in the diffusion of technical know-how from the Meiji period to the present day. Influential university professors like Ikeda Kikunae would often train large cohorts of students who later entered private industry, and whose common discipleship provided a link which lasted throughout their lives. Even today, many leading Japanese technicians belong to intellectual coteries whose 'family trees' can be traced back to the 1920s or 1930s.[42] These informal networks were probably as important as more formal institutions like the Japan Association of Civil Engineers (set up in the 1890s) in creating channels for cooperation and the flow of ideas between Japan's industrial researchers.

Government research institutes such as Tokyo Industrial Laboratory also offered increasingly valuable support to the innovative efforts of private industry. Between 1916 and 1925 the laboratory's work was extended to include research on industrial chemicals, electrochemicals, synthetic textiles and alumina, enabling it to become an important consultant to relatively advanced, science-based enterprises as well as to traditional industries like ceramics and lacquer-making.[43] One of its most striking contributions to prewar technological development was its work on the technology of ammonia production. During the First World War the Japanese government had appropriated German companies' right to a number of strategic patents, including Fritz Haber's Nobel Prize-winning process for ammonia manufacture. The technical data were handed over to a hastily established Temporary Research Institute for Nitrogen Fixation, later incorporated into Tokyo Industrial Laboratory, which conducted development work on the Haber process and designed appropriate machinery for commercial production: a task which took ten years. The resulting technology was eventually presented free of charge to a newly created private company, Shôwa Fertiliser, who also acquired one of the laboratory's leading chemists as its chief technician.[44]

Prefectural research laboratories and technical colleges continued to concentrate mainly on the needs of local small firms, but even they occasionally offered valuable contributions to the rise of modern industries. Much of the basic research on artificial silk, for example, was undertaken by Hata Itsuzô, who was a professor of chemistry at Yonezawa Technical College before joining the newly formed Teijin company in 1917. Hata's position at the college gave him access to the wealth of know-how on the reeling of natural silk which had accumulated in the Yonezawa region since the introduction of sericulture in the seventeenth century (see p. 29), and so helped him to solve some of the technical problems involved in the spinning of the new artificial thread.[45]

The Military and Technological Development

In supporting technological change, however, the state also imposed its own concerns and visions on the path of progress. To the Japanese government, the technologies of the 'second industrial revolution' appeared less as a source of growth and profit than as a challenge to Japan's security. The horrors of the First World War had revealed the profound military implications of technological change. Survival in the total wars of the twentieth century would require the capacity to produce—at high speed and in vast quantities—a wide range of complex machines of destruction: tanks and aeroplanes, for example, as well as the more conventional guns and warships.

Total war, in fact, implied a blurring of the distinction between military and non-military industries. The entire productive capacity of the nation had to be capable of mobilisation in times of crisis, and for this reason it was, in the government's eyes, necessary to nurture the development of industries which would have had little hope of surviving the harsh winds of the market.

The most important case in point is the automobile industry. Through technical tie-ups and reverse engineering, Japanese companies had little difficulty in acquiring the basic techniques of car production. But, with a domestic market circumscribed by poverty and a lack of experience in the techniques of mass production, Japanese firms could not hope to compete with Ford or General Motors. When Ishikawajima Shipyards attempted to launch a passenger car (based on the British Wolseley) onto the market immediately after the First World War, they discovered that, without the benefits of mass production, their vehicle would cost ¥10,000, while imported US competitors cost only ¥6000–7000. From the government's point of view, however, a domestic capacity to build trucks and tanks was essential to national security. The Military Automobiles Assistance Law was therefore passed in 1918, offering large subsidies towards the production of vehicles which met specified military standards.[46] The new law came just in time to rescue Ishikawajima's venture from failure. The company converted its car factory to truck production, and became one of three firms contracted to produce motor vehicles for the military (the other two being Jitsuyô Jidôsha and Tokyo Gasuden).[47]

The development of Japanese aircraft technology was equally dependent upon military support. Japan's interest in aerial warfare goes back to the days of the Russo-Japanese War, when army officers had attempted (unsuccessfully) to conduct reconnaissance using fixed balloons.[48] In 1909 the Army and Navy Ministries, together with the Ministry of Education, set up a Temporary Council on Aeronautics which supported the earliest experiments in aircraft technology, and the following year the Army succeeded in producing Japan's first aircraft. As in the case of electrical goods, so too in aircraft production, Japan's rapid advance was helped by the remarkable readiness of western firms to part with their technological secrets. After the First World War, when private companies like Nakajima and Mitsubishi emerged as aircraft contractors for the military, their designs were closely modelled on western prototypes. Nakajima's early military aircraft, for example, were based on Gloster planes, while the first Japanese-made planes to be used by the Navy were copies of the British SE5, made by Mitsubishi with the help of a team of ten engineers borrowed from the Sopwith aircraft company.[49]

The basis for more original developments, however, had already been laid by the establishment in 1918 of an Institute for Aeronautics, which was set up as a research institute attached to Tokyo University, but maintained close links with the military and counted several military officers amongst its research staff.[50] In 1932, immediately after the Japanese take-over in Manchuria, this research infrastructure was greatly strengthened by the establishment of a Naval Aircraft Arsenal at Yokosuka, where huge sums of money were invested in developing and testing new aircraft designs.[51] The typical pattern, during the 1920s and 30s, was for the Army or Navy to invite competitive tenders from the handful of Japanese aircraft producers for planes which could meet a fairly detailed list of specifications. The winning company would then receive help from the military in refining and developing its basic design. This strategy was used to help Japanese aircraft producers outgrow their reliance on foreign advice. Under a 'three-year plan' (1932–34) to promote Japan's technological independence in aircraft production, Nakajima and Mitsubishi worked with the Navy on the building and testing of five major prototypes, in the process refining the skills which were eventually to produce distinctively Japanese designs like the famous Zero fighter (see below, p. 152).[52]

The technologies of peace and war were, above all else, *interrelated*. Truck and aircraft factories could not stand alone, but needed the support of a wide range of other industries producing materials, components and machinery. So the military's central research laboratories (the Navy's set up in 1923 and the Army's in 1925) soon found themselves cooperating with private firms on projects far removed from armaments production in its conventional sense. During the 1930s, for example, the Navy worked with Sumitomo Metals on the development of a specially strong form of duralumin, known as ESD alloy, which was to be a key to the Japanese aircraft technologies of the Pacific War.

The interrelatedness of modern technologies meant that military needs exerted an influence, not only on the rise of new industries, but also on the selection of techniques in existing industries. In the production of steel, for example, Japan faced a choice between three main paths of technological advance. The Bessemer and Thomas steel processes, developed in Europe in the 1850s and 1860s, were relatively cost-effective, but needed specific types of pig-iron as raw materials (high in silicon and phosphorus respectively). On the other hand, the more expensive open hearth process, developed by Siemens and Martin in 1864, could handle a wider range of raw materials (including scrap iron), and produce a wider range of types of finished steel.

The military favoured the open-hearth process because it was capable of creating a high-quality product suited to their increasingly sophisticated weaponry. The problem with the technique, however, was that to be economically viable, it relied on substantial use of scrap metal, most of which had to be imported from the United States or western Europe. One of Japan's most brilliant prewar technicians, Imaizumi Kaichirô (1867-1941), aware of the dangers of this reliance, encouraged the introduction of the Thomas process, and used his senior position in the private steel firm Nippon Kôkan to develop suitable mixtures of phosphorus-rich raw materials for the company's Thomas furnaces. But the state-owned Yawata steelworks (which in 1934 merged with six other firms to become Japan Steel) persisted in the construction of larger and larger open-hearth furnaces—a choice which was to cause immense problems when Japan confronted foreign trade embargoes after the outbreak of war in China.[53]

The Institute for Physical and Chemical Research and the Emergence of 'Scientism'

The coming together of commercial and strategic concerns was most vividly illustrated in the Taishô government's major technological initiative: the creation of the Institute for Physical and Chemical Research (Rikagaku Kenkyûjo, normally abbreviated to Riken). The story of Riken is also particularly intriguing because it shows how foreign institutional models, transplanted to Japanese soil, often evolved into something very different from their western archetypes. The establishment of Riken in 1917 was a response to the increasingly complex scientific basis of industry, and particularly to the events of the First World War, which had highlighted the strategic importance of science and technology. A growing number of businessmen, academics and bureaucrats became convinced that Japan needed a large, centralised research establishment on the lines of Germany's Kaiser

Wilhelm Association (established six years earlier). Like the Kaiser Wilhelm Association, Japan's research institute was to be a joint initiative of government and private industry, its initial endowment of over ¥2 million coming mainly from corporate donors, while the government provided the major share of its early running costs.[54] The Japanese institute also followed the German model in being divided into a number of separate research laboratories concentrating on specific research themes, both pure and applied, and in attracting to its ranks many of the nation's most outstanding scientists.

The notion of the institute as a single, state-funded centre for advanced research was a compelling one, but practical realities gradually modified the original vision of the institute's objectives. In the first place, the financial demands of Riken soon outstripped the capacities of government funding, and it was forced to look for other sources of income. Besides, the institute quickly discovered that, although its scientists were capable of original innovation, Japanese companies seemed unwilling or unable to put their inventions into practice. The solution to these problems, devised by Riken's dynamic director Ôkôchi Masatoshi, was for the institute itself to commercialise its own inventions, thus earning revenue to support future research activities. In 1928 Ôkôchi established the Physical and Chemistry Industrial Promotion Company (Rikagaku Kôgyô KK), with the research institute as major shareholder but with contributions from a number of other large investors, including the Mitsui, Mitsubishi and Sumitomo zaibatsu.[55] The institute's corporate arm acted as a holding company, providing what would now be called 'venture capital' to a mass of industrial firms created to apply the fruits of Riken research projects. Within twelve years Rikagaku Kôgyô had become the centre of a web of over sixty enterprises, extending throughout Manchuria and the Korean peninsula as well as the Japanese archipelago itself.[56] What had begun as a scientific research institute had grown into an industrial conglomerate.

As a national body supported by government fund Riken continued to interpret its mission in nationalistic and strategic terms. Ôkôchi himself enthusiastically expounded a philosophy which he called 'scientism' (kagakushugi)—as opposed to 'capitalism' (shihonshugi) —according to which financial profit would become the servant of science and technology, rather than vice versa. Science and technology themselves, however, were seen above all as sources of national prestige and power. As Ôkôchi wrote in 1937, 'in the final analysis future wars will not be wars of military might versus military might. They will be wars involving the entire nation's scientific knowledge and industrial capacity.'[57] To fight large-scale wars, it would be necessary to have the capacity to produce and maintain massive amounts of industrial equipment. Thus, concluded Ôkôchi, 'we can say in a sense that wars are ultimately determined by the productive capacity of the machinery industry'.[58]

In keeping with this philosophy, Riken focused particularly on the development of the industrial machinery and machine tool industry, which accounted for thirty-six of the seventy-one industrial enterprises set up by Rikagaku Kôgyô between 1932 and 1940.[59] Many of its other ventures were in areas like rubber and metal alloys, which provided vital inputs to machinery manufacture. Riken's inventive record is impressive: by 1939 it held 542 Japanese and 136 overseas patents.[60] Amongst its successes were its work on magnesium metal and its design of an innovative piston ring for automobile and aircraft engines. But the institute's expansion from research into manufacturing forced it (like other Japanese corporations) to focus more and more closely, not just on technological innovation itself, but also on the production systems necessary to put innovation into practice—in other words, on the human side of technology.

By the 1930s Riken was involved in a lively debate on appropriate forms of skill training for Japanese industry. While Ôkôchi, using the slogan 'one factory, one product',[61] advocated high levels of specialisation, other leading figures, including those associated with the quasi-governmental Industrial Harmony Association (Kyôchôkai), suggested that the most important task was for Japan to expand its core of multi-skilled technical workers.[62] Ôkôchi's emphasis on specialisation was inspired by Taylorite ideas of scientific management. At the same time, though, he recognised that the rigid separation of manual labour from decision-making (an important feature of Taylorism in the US) was impossible in Japan's rapidly changing technological environment. The introduction of new technologies, he observed, was not just a matter of matching machinery to the skills of the workforce, but also of encouraging workers to contribute to continual technological change. One scheme which particularly appealed to Ôkôchi was the 'suggestion' system, whereby workers were invited to submit written proposals for improving productivity, and received rewards for particularly useful suggestions.

The suggestion system, it should be noted, was an idea which Ôkôchi had borrowed from US firms such as National Cash Register. As Ôkôchi sternly observed in the 1930s,

> there are some places in Japan where the suggestion system has been introduced, but it has not been very effective. The reasons for this seem to be 1. lack of a serious approach to the matter; 2. shyness; 3. lack of group consciousness [*kyôdôshin ga sukunai koto*]. People in our country have a

strong group consciousness in time of war, but have a bad tendency to lack enthusiasm for the battles of peacetime.[63]

The Japanese worker's lack of group consciousness was, however, perhaps compensated for by the energetic propaganda activities of organisations like Riken, which produced broadsheets, books and numerous films to spread the news, both of its latest innovations and of its industrial and managerial philosophy.

Subcontracting and Small Firms

The Changing Face of Traditional Industry

Government-funded research centres—whether they were older-established bodies like the Tokyo Industrial Laboratory or more recent ventures like Riken and the military research institutes—acted as nodes in the innovation network, through which new ideas were passed on to selected corporate recipients. The ideas which they transmitted, however, were not value-free, but were imbued with a particular vision of the relationship between technology and the 'national interest'.

In the same way, during the interwar years both central government and large corporations came to act as increasingly important channels of technology to small companies. As this happened, the speed of technological change in small firms increased, but at the same time its character changed. The incremental improvement of traditional techniques which had been common in the Meiji period was gradually replaced by a process in which new ideas were imposed from above to suit the needs of the expanding system of modern industry.

To understand this process we need for a moment to shift our gaze away from the cement and glass of the modern factories and laboratories, and into the side streets with their rows of rickety wooden workshops (see Figure 5.3). Small-scale manufacturing, rather than disappearing before the advancing tide of new technologies, had proliferated during the early years of the twentieth century. In 1921 some 87 per cent of Japan's manufacturing establishments employed fewer than ten people, and many of these very small firms were still making traditional craft products such as farm tools, straw matting, crockery, pots, pans and kitchen knives.[64]

The political upheavals of the Meiji era, it should be remembered, had not involved any radical redistribution of wealth towards the poor, and Meiji legal reforms had actually served to shore up the structures of the pre-industrial family. As a result, while new technologies drastically altered the world of large-scale industry, changes in household technology were slow and uncertain. Japan, it is true, was a world leader in

Figure 5.3 Backstreet workshops. A typical row of small houses and workshops from around the early 1920s. Note the electric light on the gable of the end house.
Source: Shitamachi Museum, Ueno, Tokyo.

household electrification: in 1935 89 per cent of Japanese households had access to electric lighting, as compared to 85 per cent in Germany, 68 per cent in the United States, and about 44 per cent in Britain.[65] With low average incomes and relatively high electricity charges for private users, however, few families could afford many electrical gadgets, and items like refrigerators and washing machines remained a rarity. In 1937 less than 1 per cent of Japan's 12.9 million households owned an electric refrigerator and only about 0.2 per cent owned an electric washing machine. By comparison, at the beginning of the 1940s just over 50 per cent of the 35 million households in the United States had mechanical—mostly electric—refrigerators, and a similar percentage had mechanical washing machines.[66]

A few consumer novelties like radios, gas stoves and electric fans were beginning to be a common sight in urban areas, but in country areas the household environment had changed little since the Tokugawa period, as US researcher Ella Lurie Wiswell discovered when she went to live in a Kyûshû village in 1935:

> Our house was on the main road to Kakui. It was not a typical farmer's house, for it had been a country inn at one time. Thus the toilet and bath were attached to the house instead of being outdoors away from the building. Still, it was rustic. The kitchen was a lean-to with a dirt floor and a built-in wood burning stove. There was no running water and no heat. Water had to be brought from the nearby well in buckets suspended from a yoke over the shoulder ... It required many trips to and from the well to fill the wooden bath-tub, and the water was heated by a wood stove built into the bath tub itself.[67]

Although the survival of small firms was partly a result of poverty and consumer conservatism, the techniques used by these firms were far from static. The spread of electrification and the application of scientific knowledge to craft production brought significant changes to traditional industries. In pottery towns like Arita and Seto, coal-fired kilns and mechanical wheels were common by the 1920s.[68] In saké-brewing, the new technique of adding small amounts of alkali to counteract the acids produced by the kôji moulds reduced fermentation time by more than a week. By the mid-1930s, many blacksmiths' shops were substituting power hammers or belt hammers for traditional handcrafting techniques.[69]

These developments were strongly supported by local research laboratories. Indeed, the period from the First World War to the beginning of the Pacific War was in some ways the golden age of the local laboratory. At least fifty were established between 1914 and 1941, including textile research laboratories in Ibaraki, Tochigi and the Mikawa district, ceramic laboratories in Nagasaki and Arita, and brewing laboratories in Akita and Niigata.[70] Until the 1920s, these laboratories, working closely with local craftspeople, devoted most of their energies to applying the fruits of science to traditional production techniques. From the late Taishô period onwards, however, a new element began to alter their relationship to regional industry. This element was the spread of subcontracting.

Industrial Associations, Local Laboratories and Subcontracting

Subcontracting exists to a greater or lesser extent in every industrialised country. It seems clear, however, that prewar Japanese firms in modern industries were particularly likely to subcontract part of their work to small enterprises, rather than concentrating production in large integrated enterprises. There were exceptions, of course: when Noguchi

Jun's Nippon Chisso corporation expanded into Korea, for example, it created a huge integrated industrial complex (*kombinâto*, as it is called in Japanese) combining mines, power generation, chemicals manufacturing and port facilities. Like other aspects of Japan's colonial administration, this industrial experiment provided a testing ground for organisational ideas which would be more widely applied within Japan itself after the Second World War.

All the same, it is true of interwar, as of postwar, Japan that firms tended to be 'narrowly specialised, engaged in one line of business or perhaps a few closely allied ventures',[71] and therefore that a relatively large share of their inputs were purchased from other enterprises. Figures from a sample survey of the machinery industry conducted by the government in 1934 show that 42 per cent of companies with 30–100 workers, and 76 per cent of companies with more than 100 workers, relied to a greater or lesser degree on outside suppliers of parts and components.[72] Certain industries, such as machine tools, automobiles and textile machinery producers, were particularly dependent on outside sourcing.[73] In 1937, when the Toyoda family firm gave birth to its better-known offspring the Toyota Motor Company, the enterprise proceeded to build for itself a huge integrated production complex at Koromo near Nagoya. The factory site contained seventeen different workshops, including a metal-casting works, machine shop, panel pressing, welding and painting sections.[74] In spite of this, the company continued to put out work to outside suppliers, a number of which (following a strategy similar to Ôkôchi's concept of 'one factory, one product') had been specially established as independent firms by Toyota itself.[75] On the eve of the Pacific War, Toyota was buying parts from some four hundred different companies, about one-third of which were in the local Nagoya region, while the others were in metropolitan Tokyo and Osaka.[76]

There seem to have been several reasons why the expanding firms of interwar Japan relied so heavily on subcontracting. Perhaps the most important was the current of instability and uncertainty which ran below the surface of Japan's rapid prewar growth. Economic expansion between 1912 and 1937 was marked by sharp fluctuations: from the First World War boom to severe postwar recession, and from the crisis which followed the Wall Street crash to the industrial resurgence which accompanied Japan's seizure of Manchuria and the subsequent rise in military spending (see Table 5.1). In these unpredictable conditions, many firms were reluctant to invest in large integrated ventures, and preferred to hedge their risks in times of expansion by subcontracting work to outsiders. Besides, in a country where poverty limited the size of the market for complex manufactured goods, the economies of scale

Table 5.1   *Economic and population growth in Japan, 1911–1938*

Period	Average annual growth rate of GNP (real)	Average annual growth rate of population	Average per capita growth rate of GNP
1911–15	3.35	1.36	1.99
1916–20	4.77	1.11	3.66
1921–25	1.93	1.26	0.67
1926–30	2.53	1.50	1.03
1931–35	4.98	1.36	3.62
1936–38	5.07	0.95	4.12

Source: R. Minami, *The Economic Development of Japan*, p. 43.

necessary to justify large-scale integration were often lacking. Small volumes of production discouraged the introduction of capital-intensive mass-production methods, and encouraged firms to rely on the more flexible arrangements offered by the subcontracting system.

Whatever its motives, subcontracting had a vital formative influence on the development of Japan's social network of innovation. Large firms, at least in the early stages, seem to have regarded subcontractors simply as convenient sources of cheap components, and to have made relatively little effort to help their smaller partners adopt and develop new technologies. But their sheer power to impose technological standards, and to reject components which fell short of those standards, forced many small firms to pull themselves up by their own technological bootstraps.

As Shibaura Electric developed the production of high-voltage electrical equipment, for example, it turned to the Arita pottery company of Kôransha, which was already producing simple electrical insulators, in its search for a supply of good-quality, high-voltage insulators. Results from experimental studies at Tokyo Industrial College were supplied to Kôransha, who then produced a sample of 3000 insulators. These were put through a rigorous testing procedure at Shibaura's Tokyo factory, and rejected as unsuitable. Many months of further trial and error were needed before Kôransha eventually developed a product which met Shibaura's exacting standards, but by the end of the First World War Kôransha had emerged as one of a handful of Japanese ceramics companies which were able to compete in the lucrative electrical components market.[77]

By the 1920s and 1930s, the increasing importance of subcontracting to Japanese industry was forcing the government as well as business to pay closer attention to the needs of small firms. Japan, in short, was beginning to discover the 'small firm problem' (chûshô kigyô mondai). This issue began to become evident during the economic boom of the First World War, when not only private enterprise but also military arsenals started to make extensive use of subcontractors. The sharp growth in demand for equipment forced state enterprises like the Tokyo and Osaka Arsenals, which had until now generally manufactured their own machine tools, to turn to small private metal-working firms for purchases of tools and spare parts. Since the small companies involved rarely possessed the know-how to meet the arsenals' technological standards, the military themselves began to provide technical assistance. During the First World War, for example, the Tokyo Arsenal lent metal-working machinery to its subcontractors, and gave them training in the use of precision measuring equipment and quality control.[78] One consequence was the emergence of a mass of very small companies producing machines and machine tools, many of them working as subcontractors: by 1924 Japan had 2202 machine manufacturers, of whom 84 per cent employed fewer than thirty workers.[79]

A particularly important impetus to change, however, came from the evolving role of local business associations and research laboratories. During the economic recession which followed the First World War, the growing salience of the 'small firm problem' persuaded the Japanese government to strengthen the basis of cooperation amongst local groups of small enterprises (particularly those producing goods for export). From 1925 onwards the existing system of trade associations (dôgyô kumiai) was reinforced by a new set of measures to promote the creation of so-called 'industrial associations' (kôgyô kumiai), whose powers reached much further. Industrial associations did not simply act as a source of mutual aid and advice, but were in effect cartels, with authority to control prices and production, to set up joint factories financed by member firms, and to engage in the joint marketing of members' products.[80]

In terms of technological diffusion, the new industrial associations at first played a role very similar to that filled by their Meiji predecessors. They continued to act as monitors of production standards and as channels of technical information from the outside world, cooperating closely with the prefectural research laboratories which proliferated throughout the country during the interwar years, and sometimes contributing money or equipment towards the expansion of the laboratories.[81] With the gradual militarisation of the economy and the growth of government controls, however, the power of industrial associations increased, and their nature underwent a subtle metamorphosis. From the early 1930s onwards, as military demand expanded, prefectural-level industrial associations started to act as intermediaries in the subcontracting process, actively seeking out orders from Army and Navy arsenals and then distributing the orders amongst local small firms.[82] In the process, the associations acquired new power to influence the development of member firms, and to impose upon them the forms of technological change demanded by central government policy.

The activities of the prefectural laboratory, too, were changing, as illustrated by the case of the Yamagata Industrial Research Laboratory, established in 1919. During its early years the laboratory, limited by poor funding, concentrated mostly on handicrafts such as wood-working, lacquerware and pottery. In 1933, however, the laboratory appointed a new head with a background in metallurgy, and from then on paid increasing attention to the introduction of metal-casting and metal-working technologies. An important part of this strategy involved developing close links with local subcontractors. Surveys of sub-contracting firms were carried out, and the companies were given advice and training in the use of metal-working machines such as multi-purpose lathes, grinders and milling machines.[83] In 1936 the government itself began to provide financial assistance towards schemes which would improve the technological level of subcontractors, and the Yamagata laboratory spent its share of the bounty on analytical equip-ment, which it used to test the quality of metals used by local small firms.[84]

The results of these efforts were limited. Even when they had the know-how, small companies often lacked the capital to buy up-to-date equipment. As the pressures of military demand intensified in the second half of the 1930s, quality was often sacrificed to quantity. Figures from the Ministry of Commerce and Industry suggest that only 60–70 per cent of the parts supplied to the military by subcontractors met the necessary standards, and only 30–40 per cent were delivered on time.[85] All the same, the efforts of industrial associations and local research laboratories, as well as the pressures of central government and corporations, helped to create a web of connections which slowly but surely drew traditional small producers into the expanding production system of modern industry.

The implications of this process are particularly evident when we look at declining industries of interwar Japan. The most desperate case of all was that of the silk industry, once the vanguard of Japan's industrial revolution. During the 1920s and 1930s silk producers, already battered by the effects of the world recession, were confronted with growing competition from the new technology of artificial silk. In Nagano Prefecture, the heartland of Japan's silk-reeling industry, employment in the silk mills fell from 121,000 in 1930 to 54,000 in

1940.[86] Most of those who lost their jobs were young women from farm families, and their loss of income added to the sufferings of local silk-farming families, already impoverished by the collapse in the market for raw silk. In some areas farmers, deprived of cash earning, were reduced to bringing bags of rice or charcoal to the local shops in the hope of bartering them for goods like tobacco.[87]

The collapse of the silk industry devalued the centuries of mental and manual skill accumulated by the region's silk farming families. Farm women, who had been the traditional repositories of much of that knowledge, were transformed in the process into 'unskilled' labour. By 1937 the local authorities had accepted that the decline of the silk industry was irreversible, and began to look for alternative industries to create local employment. A prefectural committee, set up to examine the problem, pointed to the potential of the precision machinery industry: precision machinery, after all, was one of those areas of industry whose growth was fuelled by the expansion of military demand, and its production required an abundance of cheap and manually dexterous labour. To encourage the transition to this new industrial base the prefecture created a Mechanical Training Centre in the silk town of Okaya, added departments of mechanical engineering, electrical engineering and applied chemistry to the three local technical schools, and in 1939 established an Industrial Research Laboratory.[88] In the short term the policies were only partly successful. The rising employment in the machinery industry (from 1800 in 1930 to 6300 in 1940)[89] was much too small to offset the collapse of the silk industry. In the longer term, however, they contributed to an extraordinary transformation in the industrial structure of the region, and to the conversion of the silk women of Suwa and Okaya into the assembly-line workers of the postwar era (see below, p. 181).

Government Planning and the Rise of Technology Policy

In 1929 the Wall Street crash and subsequent contraction of world trade plunged the Japanese economy into deep recession. Two years later, Japanese troops seized control of Manchuria, marking the beginning of a new phase of escalating Japanese aggression on the Asian continent. The resulting expansion of military spending induced a rapid economic recovery, strongly focused on the growth of military-related heavy industries (see Table 5.2), but the increase in international tensions which followed the 'Manchurian incident' also intensified government concerns about Japan's technological ability to fight a prolonged war.

Table 5.2   *Indices of industrial production 1940*
(1930 = 100)

Industry	Index
Iron and steel	344.7
Non-ferrous metals	211.5
Machinery	263.2
Ceramics	173.5
Chemicals	336.0
Oil and coal products	307.1
Paper and pulp	151.1
Textiles	139.7
Wood products	169.4
Foodstuffs	108.2
All manufacturing	207.9

Source: Andô Yoshio, *Kindai Nihon keizai yôran*, p. 10.

Economic and political crisis, combined with the growing power of the military, led to the emergence of a new approach to industrial policy, and with it increased government efforts to control Japan's technological destiny. Industrial policy itself was nothing new. As early as 1910 the Ministry of Agriculture and Commerce had set up a Committee to Investigate Production (Seisan Chôsakai), made up of bureaucrats, businessmen and academics, whose brief was to examine the state of various industries and propose policies to increase production. This was followed in 1918 by the Military Industries Mobilisation Law, which created a government agency to collect information on industrial capacity and its potential for conversion to military uses in time of war.[90]

The knowledge accumulated in this way enabled the government to identify certain 'key industries' (*kiso kôgyô*), to which promotion measures were targeted.[91] The policy measures introduced, however, were piecemeal. In 1913 the government brought in tax exemptions to encourage the expansion of a range of industries including aluminium production and the manufacture of steam-powered and electrical machinery (as well as some less technologically advanced products like condensed milk); from 1915 onwards it established generous government subsidies for the synthetic dyestuffs industry, and in 1924 added an import licence system to protect this industry from foreign competition.[92]

Signs of more comprehensive government intervention, however, began to appear in the late 1920s. Some historians trace the beginning of the shift to 1927, when the government established the Bureau of

Resources (Shigen Kyoku).[93] This small body, staffed by civilian bureau-crats and representatives of the military, was empowered to compile and assess data on the output and financial status of all enterprises. It was, in this sense, a logical development of the earlier government efforts to determine Japan's productive capacity. One of its initiatives, however, was to produce a comprehensive survey of research projects under way in both state and private laboratories.[94] In its first years the activities of the bureau were limited, and the actual inspection of mines and factories was left to the newly created Ministry of Commerce and Industry, formed from sections of the old Ministry of Agriculture and

Figure 5.4 Japan prepares for war. The German-Japanese Alliance celebrated in the improbable setting of a caramel advertisement
Source: Yamazaki H., ed., Shôwa Kôkoku 60-nenshi, p. 77.

Commerce in 1925.[95] The information collected by the bureau would, however, provide the essential foundations for the growth of government planning as Japan slid towards total war in the 1930s.

A second step towards a planned economy was taken in April 1931, at the nadir of the depression following the Wall Street crash, when the Japanese Parliament passed the Major Industries Control Law (Jûyô Sangyô Tôseihô). This extended to large companies the principles embodied in the Industrial Associations Law of the mid-1920s (see above p. 134). Large firms in key industrial areas were encouraged to form cartels in order to regulate production and prices, and were required to report their activities to government.[96] The Major Industries Control Law had been intended as a short-term measure to deal with the crisis of the world depression, but it survived and was reinforced as the militarisation of the economy intensified.

The forward march of industrial policy was accompanied by a more coherent approach to technology policy. From 1917 onwards a regular system of awards for inventors was established,[97] and in 1926 the government began to provide grants to support the work of private industrial research laboratories.[98] Though the sums involved in both these schemes were small (see Table 5.3), they did reflect an emerging official awareness of the value of private research. Financial incentives were reinforced by a system of national conferences, which brought together representatives of industrial research laboratories from all over the country to exchange information and ideas on the latest

Table 5.3 *Grants to inventors and private research laboratories 1926–1937*
(¥ thousand)

Year	Industrial Research Assistance Scheme	Encouragement of Inventions Scheme
1926	250	46
1927	250	77
1928	250	77
1929	200	77
1930	200	62
1931	100	53
1932	100	73
1933	150	93
1934	180	103
1935	150	113
1936	150	123
1937	150	143

Source: Kôgyô Gijutsu Chô, *Kenkyû hakusho,* 1951, p. 181.

technological initiatives.[99] More important, perhaps, was the growing state attention paid to academic research in science and technology. It is fair to say that, until the 1920s the government had perceived universities mainly as teaching institutions rather than as centres for original research. Funds were allocated to each university chair, without distinction between teaching and research funding, and this tended to entrench the power of professors and lead to a certain rigidity in university activities.[1] It was only in 1918 that the Ministry of Education had introduced the first system of government grants for research, and these were small in scale and number (between 120 and 130 grants of ¥200–500 were awarded each year), and confined to the natural sciences.[2]

In 1932, however, after extensive lobbying by the academic community, the Japanese government followed other industrialised countries in setting up a more comprehensive system of financial encouragement for research. The Japan Committee for the Promotion of Science (Nihon Gakujutsu Shinkô Kaigi), established with funding from the Imperial Household and the Ministry of Education, provided somewhere between ¥250,000 and ¥500,000 worth of finance for academic research each year during the 1930s, and offered grants for work in the social sciences and humanities as well as the natural sciences. The provision of funding, of course, had the advantage of enabling the government to exert some influence over the nature of academic research. As time went on, it is noticeable that grants to team (as opposed to individual) research projects increased, and that areas like engineering consumed a larger and larger share of the research budget.[3] The scene was being set, not only for future Japanese successes in the development of industrial technology, but also for fierce debates about the relationship between academia and the state in postwar Japan.

One of the crucial technological issues targeted by the state was the development of substitutes for scarce raw materials. The emergence of new technologies for war and peace—including the development of the aircraft, automobile and chemical industries—had created a demand for resources which Japan lacked, the most important of these being oil. As the world economy splintered into increasingly autarchic trading blocks in the 1930s, the Japanese authorities became more and more concerned about the likely exclusion of their country from access to these vital raw materials. In these troubled circumstances, an idea which gained increasing currency was the notion of technology as a substitute for resources. With scientific knowledge and inventive creativity, it was argued, researchers could develop alternatives to scarce resources and so match demand for raw materials with the geological wealth available within the Japanese empire.[4]

In 1926, for example, a technician from the naval fuel depot at Tokuyama had been sent to Europe to study techniques of coal lique-faction. Work on this technology, which would enable the relatively rich coal resources of Korea and Manchuria to be converted into oil, was later taken up by several companies, including the state-owned South Manchurian Railway Company and a Korean subsidiary of Nippon Chisso.[5] More conventionally, in 1934 the government also introduced a Petroleum Industry Law by which the state would license and subsidise the importing and refining of petroleum. This in effect debarred foreign companies from access to the Japanese petroleum market, and created a sheltered environment in which Japanese firms could expand their technological capabilities and their scale of production. The Petroleum Industry Law was to become the model for a series of subsequent measures which, in the late 1930s, extended a similar mixture of government control and encouragement to the automobile, machine-tool and other strategic industries.[6] As a Japanese observer remarked in the early 1940s, 'the wars of the past have been wars of resources, but the wars of tomorrow will be wars of science and technology'.[7]

Between the end of the Meiji Era and the outbreak of war in China, Japanese business and government, like their counterparts in the west, faced the problems of absorbing and adapting to the new technologies of the 'second industrial revolution'. Throughout most of this period, the philosophy of private enterprise and state alike was dominated, as it had been in the Meiji period, by the notion of pursuing the technological trajectory of more advanced industrialised countries towards the ultimate goal of 'a prosperous country and a strong army'. To achieve this aim, it was necessary to develop an infrastructure of scientific knowledge and to devise new organisational structures suited to the complexity and interdependence of the technologies of the twentieth century.

The approach which Japanese enterprises took to these problems was influenced both by the institutional legacies of the Meiji Era and by the particular economic circumstances of interwar Japan. Technological research was seen, not so much as a means of generating radically original inventions, but rather as a bridge between foreign technology and the local workplace. Many of Japan's larger companies therefore began to develop their own research laboratories, but these remained relatively small in size and funding. Efforts by the government to centralise scientific and technological research in the Institute for Physical and Chemical Research led instead to the emergence of a new industrial conglomerate whose energies were dispersed among a large number of research and industrial activities spread throughout the empire. The development of more technologically advanced industries, moreover, did not lead to the disappearance of Japan's small traditional firms, but rather to the transformation of many of those firms into subcontractors for modern industry. This transformation was strongly supported by the network of local laboratories and local trade associations which had developed from the processes of Meiji industrialisation. At the same time, the local institutions themselves were forced to change: the trade associations giving way to more coercive industrial associations and the local laboratories increasingly turning their attention from traditional industry to modern science-based technologies.

Although the speed of technological change in interwar Japan was in many ways remarkable, the processes of change were fraught with problems and tensions. The poverty of the local market restricted the potential for introducing the techniques of mass production, and encouraged large firms to rely on small-scale subcontractors. The limited technological know-how and organisational skills of small firms in turn made it hard for Japanese enterprises to compete with imports in advanced technological areas. Increasingly, government protection was seen as being the only way to ensure the growth of the new industries whose existence was seen as vital to national security.

These dilemmas of Japanese development were to come to a head in the crisis of the Second World War. As industrial leaders like Ôkôchi Masatoshi had foreseen, the fortunes of war, by the 1940s, depended far more on industrial and technological capacity than they did on military tactics. Japan's invasion of China ultimately brought Japan into direct conflict with the United States: the most powerful industrial economy in the world. The Japanese government responded to this crisis, as we shall see, both by developing emergency measures to increase Japan's technological independence and by attempting to define a distinctively Japanese path of technological progress—a short cut which would somehow bypass the long and arduous process of catching up with the western powers. Both attempts ended in disaster, but the war years are worth closer examination, for they were to have a deep and pervasive influence on the course of Japan's technological development in the second half of the twentieth century.

CHAPTER 6

A War of Science and Technology, 1937–1945

Just as the Meiji Restoration is commonly seen as the great divide between 'pre-modern' and 'modern' Japan, so the Pacific War has come to be regarded as the dividing-point between a militarised, imperialistic, semi-modern Japan and the re-constructed Japan of the high-growth era. This dichotomous perspective has had some unfortunate results. Many studies of Japan's economic or industrial history either begin or end at the Pacific War, leaving the war itself, and its connections to past and future, to fall into a sort of historical black hole. Other histories, though adopting a broader chronological framework, skim over the war as though it were a temporary aberration with little bearing on what followed. From the point of view of Japan's technological history, however, this approach is hard to justify.

Historians of technology recognise the powerful influence which the Second World War exerted on the development of technology in Europe and the United States. In particular, the experience of large, government-funded endeavours like the Manhattan Project (which developed the atomic bomb) encouraged a much more active and interventionist approach to technology policy in the postwar period. In Japan, of course, the influence of the war was an ambivalent one. On the one hand, as in the west, the wartime crisis stimulated greater government interest in promoting technological innovation, and many of the policies pursued during the war left lasting legacies for the postwar period. On the other, the bitter experience of defeat meant that important aspects of wartime ideology and policy came to be seen above all as lessons in what to avoid.

A New Order for Science and Technology

In July 1937, after a skirmish between Chinese forces and Japanese troops stationed near Beijing, the Japanese military launched a wholesale invasion of Chinese territory. From that moment on Japan was involved in a widening circle of military conflict which would end only with the surrender of August 1945. The Japanese invasion of China provoked a spiral of diplomatic conflict with the United States and its allies, and this in turn pushed Japan into a closer relationship with Germany and Italy, with whom the Japanese government signed the Tripartite Pact in 1940. The outbreak of war in Europe opened the way for further Japanese expansion on the Asian mainland: by the middle of 1941, through agreement with the puppet Vichy government in France, Japan gained *de facto* control of the French colony of Indo-China, and in response the allied powers imposed embargoes on the export of a range of strategic materials (including oil) to Japan. So the cycle of conflict moved with remorseless momentum towards Japan's attack on Pearl Harbor and its invasion of the resource-rich countries of Southeast Asia.

The slide into total war did not mark any sharp turning point in government policy towards technological development, but rather intensified and speeded up trends which had been evident since the early 1930s. Growing hostility towards the west and its allies, and the emerging Japanese vision of a 'Greater East Asia Co-Prosperity Sphere', involved an inescapable questioning of the west as a model for Japan's technological development. This questioning was inextricably bound up with the worsening shortages of raw materials which plagued Japan as military production expanded and western embargoes began to bite. Amid the political convulsions which accompanied the rise of Japanese militarism, technology became, for the first time since the early Meiji period, a topic of widespread intellectual and political debate.

The underlying paradox was that Japan, while attempting to turn its back on the western (particularly British and US) model of modernisation, was at the same time becoming more and more in need of western technology in order to build up its military strength. One approach to the problem was to draw a distinction between a 'US path' and a 'German path' of technological development, and to present the second alone as an appropriate model for Japanese emulation. A study published in 1942, for example, argued that

> US technological rationalisation promotes the most highly specialised mechanisation in order to reduce wage costs to their lowest possible level, and therefore it does not hesitate to make profligate use of raw materials, in terms both of quantity and quality. On the other hand, German technological rationalisation aims to limit the quantitative use of raw materials to the minimum and, qualitatively, to promote the use of substitutes. It therefore encourages the use of skilled labour even if this means that wage costs become comparatively high.[1]

The obvious conclusion was that Japan, with its shortage of resources and abundance of labour, would do best to abandon US technology and turn exclusively to Germany in search of scientific and technological inspiration. This approach, however, soon came up against a large practical stumbling block, for despite the rhetoric of the Axis alliance, the German government proved singularly reluctant to allow Japan access to advanced German know-how.[2] Even when formal agreements on technology transfer were reached, the cooperation offered by German firms often proved half-hearted. One history of Japan's modern technology recounts the story of a research scientist from the South Manchurian Railway Company who was sent to Germany to study the Uhde Company's relatively advanced coal liquefaction technology. When he arrived at Uhde's offices, the scientist discovered that the agreement on 'technology transfer' enabled him only to examine fourteen pages of complex blueprints within the company's own premises. He was allowed neither to remove nor to copy any part of the documents. The Japanese scientist eventually resorted to sketching the plans from memory when he returned to his hotel at night, and smuggling these rough copies out of Germany concealed in his wife's underwear.[3]

Faced with these obstacles, a number of Japanese academics and bureaucrats began to argue that imitation of the west should be rejected altogether, and replaced by the search for a specifically Japanese path of technological development. As one commentator observed:

> our country's industries have been developed on the basis of so-called 'imported technologies', developed in Europe and America and mainly designed to use resources available within the European and American great powers.[4]

Reliance on imported technology, in other words, was the main reason for Japan's dependence upon imported (particularly western-controlled) resources, and the solution lay in devising new technologies which matched the mineral wealth of Japan and its expanding empire.

> The resources of the Greater East Asia Co-Prosperity Sphere are awaiting the creation of the new technologies which will make most effective use of them. It is only then that these resources will acquire value. The existence of scientific research which may give birth to this new technological creativity will provide a firm basis for the cultivation of the Co-Prosperity Sphere, and for this reason the promotion of such research is currently an urgent necessity.[5]

In practical policy terms, however, it made little difference whether the aim was to emulate Germany or to develop a distinctively East Asian technological system: either approach implied large-scale government intervention to force the pace of technological change. Like every

other sphere of economy and society, technology was to be mobilised
for war. At the level of individual industries, a series of measures
modelled on the 1934 Petroleum Industry Law were passed in the late
1930s: the Automobile Manufacturing Industry Law in 1936, the Artificial Petroleum Law and Steel Industry Laws in 1937, the Machine Tool
Industry Law and the Aircraft Manufacturing Law in 1938, the Shipbuilding Industry Law and the Light Metals Manufacturing Industry
Law in 1939, and the Important Machines Manufacturing Law in 1941.[6]
All of these gave the government the power to control entry to the
industries involved (through a licensing system) while also offering
generous incentives towards investment. Their aim was to drive out
foreign investors (such as Ford and General Motors) and increase the
size and efficiency of domestic Japanese manufacturers. In many cases,
licences were withheld from firms unless they exceeded a certain size.
In this way, Japanese companies were forced to 'rationalise' their
activities through mergers or takeovers, and in the process, it was
hoped, achieve greater economies of scale.

The success of these industry promotion laws is controversial. David
Friedman, assessing the Machine Tool Industry Law, observes that 'the
rush to qualify for state-sponsored benefits motivated many firms to
make uneconomical investments or to merge incompatible, often phys-
ically separate assembly operations under a single operational banner'.[7]
There can be little doubt, though, that the laws provided some firms
(such as Nissan and Toyota) with the protection which they needed to
gain a foothold in technologically advanced industries. Between 1937
(when the company received a government licence) and 1940, Toyota's
annual production of vehicles rose from 4013 to 14,787.[8] The government's enthusiasm for 'rationalisation' also encouraged some mergers
which would have lasting effects on the evolution of Japanese industry:
among them, the 1939 merger of Tokyo Electric and Shibaura Electric
to form the electrical machinery giant Toshiba, and the empire-
building of Hitachi, which merged with Kokusan Kôgyô in 1937 and,
two years later, swallowed up a further five major machinery
manufacturers.

Industry policies could help to reduce Japan's dependence on
foreign capital, and to build up domestically owned firms, but they did
little to reduce the country's dependence on foreign technology. The
protection and nurturing of particular industries, therefore, needed to
be accompanied by the expansion of Japan's research capabilities. In
fact, the early years of the war saw a sharp expansion in research
spending, both state and private, and the establishment of many of the
technological institutions which were to play a key role in Japan's
postwar expansion. By 1942, total expenditure on scientific research

had reached a level of some ¥350 million, more than twice the level of expenditure in 1935.[9] This reflected both relatively generous funding for existing universities and research laboratories, and the profusion of new technological institutions which appeared, as the Japanese phrase has it, like bamboo shoots after rain: university-based institutes like Tokyo University's General Research Laboratory (1939) and Osaka University's Industrial Science Laboratory (1939), as well as independent government-funded institutes like the Machine Research Laboratory (1937) and Central Aeronautics Research Laboratory (1939).[10]

A particularly important role was played by the National Mobilisation Law of 1938, passed in response to the outbreak of war in China. Under this law the government acquired enormously increased powers to control the deployment of capital and workers throughout the economy. It also assumed new powers to direct and encourage technological research: one section of the law empowered the newly created government Planning Agency (Kikaku In) to issue ordinances on research in technological areas of key national importance. The research, which might be entrusted to government laboratories or to private firms, was supported by grants both from the military and from the relevant government departments. The first ordinance, on aluminium technology, was issued in April 1940 and within the next three years more than 500 technology projects were initiated by the agency.[11] The result was not just a rapid growth of research and development activities, but also a focusing of research on areas like chemicals and machinery technology, which had strong military links (see Table 6.1). Another aspect of military mobilisation was its impact on the training of workers. As conscription depleted the ranks of the skilled workforce, the government was forced to pay closer attention to the problems of training, and in 1939, under the powers of the National Mobilisation Law, it issued the Factory Technicians Education Ordinance of 1939, which obliged all large companies to introduce in-house skill training schemes.[12]

For the enthusiasts of Japan's new role as the leader of an Asian Co-Prosperity Sphere, however, these piecemeal measures were not enough. Emboldened by the rise of centralised economic planning, they envisaged the development of a technological plan under which the state would be free to mobilise and deploy the forces of scientific and technical knowledge to meet national needs. A leading advocate of this approach was Miyamoto Takenosuke, a trained engineer who supervised the technological side of Japan's economic plans for North China. Miyamoto recognised that there were two 'quite different ideologies: one which uses the application of technology as a basis for the pursuit of liberal [jiyûshugiteki] objectives, and one which uses it as the

Table 6.1   *Research projects of industrial laboratories, by topic, 1942*

Research Topic	Public Laboratories	Private Laboratories
Machinery	444	1,404
Electrical equipment	451	1,428
Metals	263	1,092
Chemicals	1,264	3,205
Textiles	282	107
Mining	126	487
Construction	130	16
Total	2,960	7,739

Note: excludes military research. Figures are for number of projects.
Source: Kôgyô Gijutsu Chô, *Kenkyû hakusho 1951*, Tokyo, Kôgyô Gijutsu Chô, 1951, p.46.

basis for the pursuit of totalitarian, state-centred objectives'. At present, he argued, it was inevitable that

> the application of technology, which is one of the most important resources of any nation, should follow the latter course. In this sense, the state control of technology ... will become an important aspect of technological activity.[13]

Ever since the 1920s, Miyamoto had been active in organising forums where state-employed engineers and technicians could expound their visions of Japan's future, and the Japan Technology Association (Nihon Gijutsu Kyôkai), which he had helped create, played a leading role in lobbying for a state-planned technological system. By 1939 the government had already introduced a system of registration for all research laboratories, thus acquiring the information needed to draw up an overall plan for technological development, and in 1941 the Planning Agency published a grandly titled *Outline Plan for the Founding of a New Order for Science and Technology* (*Kagaku Gijutsu Shintaisei Kakuritsu Yôkô*), in which it called for the 'establishment of a Japanese type [*Nihonteki seikaku*] of science and technology based on the autonomous resources of the Greater East Asia Co-Prosperity Sphere'.[14] This objective was to be achieved by setting up a Technology Agency (Gijutsu In), which would unite the government's various fragmented technology policies under one roof. The Technology Agency would have direct control over the funding and development plans of all Japan's research laboratories, private as well as public, and would be responsible for ensuring that their activities served the needs of the state.[15]

At this point it should be said that not all those involved in the development of Japanese technology supported the views of Miyamoto and the planning bureaucrats. Many academic scientists bitterly resented government interference in their research activities, and argued that heavy-handed government planning would stifle rather than encourage creativity.[16] In fact, despite the differences in political context, there were certain similarities between the debates which appeared in the pages of the Japanese press and debates which were occurring simultaneously in Britain. In Britain, however, it was the political left, represented by figures like J. D. Bernal and J. B. S. Haldane, who called for greater government planning of science and technology, while the right, represented by Karl Popper and others, argued that intellectual enquiry should be pursued in an atmosphere unpolluted by political concerns.[17]

From the point of view of the new Technology Agency, however, the most powerful threat came, not from the principled resistance of scientists, but from the more Machiavellian opposition of other government bodies like the Ministry of Education and Ministry of Commerce and Industry. These well-established departments had no intention of allowing their technological activities to be absorbed by the upstart Technology Agency. Besides, military research, which remained under the control of the Army and Navy, absorbed a larger and larger proportion of the nation's total research expenditure, leaving the Technology Agency to squabble with other ministries over a dwindling share of the pie.[18] As the war situation worsened and shortages increased, long-range planning tended to give way to a stream of ad hoc measures designed to shore up the collapsing economy. In 1943, for example, the Research Mobilisation Council (Kenkyû Dôin Kaigi) was set up to focus funding on priority areas of research, and in 1944 the government began to coopt science students into war-related research.[19] During its brief life, therefore, the wartime Technology Agency had little opportunity to attempt the grandiose centralised plans dreamed of by its progenitors.

The failure of technology planning, however, did not mean that wartime policy had no long-term effects. When we shift our attention from the bureaucracy to corporate and government research laboratories, it soon becomes obvious that the impact of war was significant indeed.

The War and Corporate Research

The most obvious consequence of the war was a sharp rise in the number of private, as well as state-controlled, research establishments.

Between 1935 and 1942 the number of technological research laboratories in Japan is estimated to have doubled to about 1150, of which roughly half were corporate laboratories, while the number of researchers increased from around 28,000 to over 49,000. This growth was undoubtedly nourished by the research funding available under the National Mobilisation Law, but may also have been a response to the disruptions of the war economy, which forced companies to switch to the manufacture of military products or to economise on the use of scarce resources.

It is interesting to look at these figures in international context. Kamatani Chikayoshi's studies suggest that, in terms of the number of its research establishments, Japan was rapidly catching up with the United States and Germany by the early 1940s. The number of researchers in Japan was also not far behind the figure for the US. In terms of funding, however, Japanese research laboratories were still far more poorly endowed than their US, and particularly their German, counterparts (see Table 6.2).

The wartime development of corporate research in Japan was, however, qualitative as well as quantitative. The merger wave of the late 1930s created a number of large companies which had not one but several research laboratories, and which therefore needed to devise overall strategies for the management of research. In the case of Toshiba, the old Tokyo Electric and Shibaura Electric laboratories were placed under the organisational umbrella of a new General Research Laboratory, which in turn was subdivided into a number of branch laboratories: for electric lighting, metals, chemicals, electronics industry, and so forth. In

Table 6.2 *Research institutions: An international comparison*

	Japan (1942)	USA (1938)	Germany (1938)	USSR (1938)
No. of research institutions	1,154	2,000	1,000	2,300
Annual research expenditure (¥m)	352	4,000	8,000	1,600
No. of researchers (thousand)	49	50	100	80

Source: Kamatani Chikayoshi, "Kigyô o chûshin to shite kenkyû taisei no suii", in Hiroshige Tetsu, ed., *Nihon shihonshugi to kagaku gijutsu*, Tokyo, Sanichi Shobô, 1962, p. 119; Kôgyô Gijutsu Chô, *Kenkyû hakusho 1951*, Tokyo, Kagaku Gijutsu Chô, 1951, p. 46.

practice, each of these branch laboratories had considerable autonomy, and the electronics industry laboratory, which was seen as having special strategic significance, was eventually hived off and placed under the direct control of the company president.[20] Hitachi, whose size was similarly swollen by mergers, took a more centralised approach, setting up a large brand-new Central Research Laboratory (opened in 1940) whose brief was to pursue basic as well as applied scientific and technological research.[21]

This emphasis on basic research is significant. Just as the First World War had brought home to many Japanese companies the need to develop their own research capacity, so the Second World War made them aware of a need to move from modifying imported technologies to developing more original productive techniques. The search for a distinctively 'Japanese path' of technological development could not succeed without a deeper understanding of the scientific bases of modern technology. In the words of the proclamation issued by the Toyota Motor Company in 1940, when it established its own Toyota Institute for Physical and Chemical Research:

> Now that we are facing a second Great War in Europe it has become extremely difficult to import western knowledge, and as the Allies have closed their research sections to outsiders it has become very hard to gain information on their research successes. In such a climate it is more and more urgent that we ourselves should conduct independent and self-directed research and should establish research institutions to open up our own path to progress.[22]

In practice, plans for long-term basic research were constantly subverted by the demands of the military, which dictated that companies should use their research laboratories to solve technological problems of immediate strategic importance. The work done in the new wartime laboratories, however, did have some long-lasting effects on Japan's technological development. A particularly important area of investigation was electronics, which was recognised by the military as holding the key to the secrets of radar, a vital piece of wartime technology which Japan lacked. Toshiba's electronics industry laboratory was one of several corporate research centres which performed work for the military in this area, in the process developing the 12G-R6 vacuum tube, which was to form the basis of Toshiba's radio technology in the immediate postwar years.[23]

Work on radar and military communications also stimulated research into new polymer materials which could be used as insulation for electronic equipment. Research into polyethelene, for example, was helped by the capture of Allied radar equipment which used polyethelene insulation. The equipment was handed over to Sumitomo

Electric, who worked with Sumitomo Chemicals and with staff of Kyoto and Osaka Universities to unlock the secrets of its chemical structure.[24]

Two points about this research project catch the eye. The first is that it was a project which crossed institutional boundaries, involving universities as well as corporations. This was typical of wartime research. In order to focus the best minds on the task of solving urgent technological problems, the government had, since 1942, encouraged the setting-up of so-called 'research neighbourhood groups' (*kenkyū tonarigumi*), named after the neighbourhood groups which were a major instrument of social control in wartime Japan. The groups (of which there were over 200 by 1945) were in effect small research teams drawn from a variety of public and private institutions and brought together to work on a particular research topic of military significance.[25] Many of these provided the basis for connections between industry and academia which lasted long after the end of the war.

The second point of interest about the polyethelene project is its ironic outcome. The results of the research work came too late to be of any use to the military: by the time that laboratory experiments were complete and Sumitomo was preparing to move to commercial production of polyethelene, the war was already over. The basic knowledge of this and other petrochemicals, however, was to prove vital to the emergence of the peacetime petrochemical industry in postwar Japan.

There was indeed, a certain irony about the whole wartime project of creating a distinctively 'Japanese form' of technology. In practical terms, the scope for a radical departure from the western path of technological progress was limited. Japan's existing technological system—its transport network, electricity grid, weapons systems and so forth—was by now largely based on western models. From the Meiji period onwards, many of the most truly original elements in Japanese technology had involved local efforts to combine imported knowledge with indigenous craft skill. This form of bottom-up indigenous development, however, was totally antithetical to the ideals of the wartime leadership, who envisaged 'Japanese-style' technology in terms of large-scale, centrally controlled projects dedicated to the greater glory and military might of the state. There was no scope here for encouraging the innate creativity of ordinary craft workers or of village and prefectural organisations. The forging of Japan's new technological role was to be entrusted instead to a scientific elite, who were themselves deeply imbued with western concepts of science and technology. As a result, the identifiable differences between Japanese and western wartime technology were differences of style and emphasis rather than of substance.

A good symbol of the characteristics of Japanese innovation in these years was the Mitsubishi Zero fighter. During the 1930s Mitsubishi

Aircraft, under the guidance of an energetic young technician named Horikoshi Jirô, had begun to move from reliance on foreign technology to the independent design of its own aircraft. Horikoshi insisted on devising a radically new design of all-metal monoplane, which he hoped would be able to exceed the speed achieved by more conventional biplanes, and his enthusiasm for novelty led to numerous difficulties and failures in the early stages of development. The Mitsubishi technicians, however, were quick to learn from their mistakes, and by 1935 had produced a fighter plane which was capable of reaching speeds of more than 400 kilometres an hour.

The Navy then raised the stakes by asking Mitsubishi to produce a fighter with a speed of more than 500 kilometres an hour at 4000 metres—a level of performance unequalled by any existing aircraft. This task was a particularly difficult one because the quality of Japanese aircraft engines was far below that of western rivals like the United States. Horikoshi and his fellow engineers chose to tackle the problem, not by increasing the power of the engine, but by reducing the weight of the aircraft. The advantage of this approach was that it did not involve highly advanced technological know-how, but instead required straightforward but immensely painstaking attention to detail. Every part of the aircraft, down to each individual bolt and screw, was examined and pared down to the minimum. The Zero fighter, which was Mitsubishi's answer to the Navy's challenge, was as a result very economical in its use of scarce resources, but operated within the narrowest of margins in terms of the safety of its pilots.

'Japanese-style' technology as embodied in the Zero fighter, in other words, did not represent a fundamental departure from the paradigms of western technology: like its western rivals it aimed to fly higher and faster and achieve ever greater destructive power. It achieved these aims, however, in slightly different ways: less by the massive mobilisation of advanced science than by extreme precision, obsessive parsimony with resources, and a noticeable disregard for the safety of the human operator who would fly the finished machine.

Subcontracting and the 'Just-in-time' System

The Zero fighter is an appropriate symbol of wartime Japanese technology in one other important respect. The design was so successful that the Navy ordered the plane to be produced not only by Mitsubishi itself but also by its main competitor, the Nakajima Aircraft Company. As wartime recruitment cut deeper into the industrial workforce, however, it became harder for large companies to keep up with the military's unending demand, and more work was farmed out to

subcontractors. By the later stages of the war over 40 per cent of Nakajima's total production and over 30 per cent of Mitsubishi's was being
carried out by subcontractors, some of it by 'home factories': literally
individual households where one room had been converted into a tiny
workshop for the production of aircraft components.[26] When these components were finished, a member of the family would carry them to the
nearest railway station where they were collected by a man with strong
muscles and a large backpack. He in turn, having made his calls at
several stops along the line, would convey the components by train and
foot to the Nakajima or Mitsubishi factory to be assembled into Japan's
most formidable and feared weapon of war.[27] Not surprisingly, this
system created enormous problems in terms of quality and reliability,
and added to the already considerable risks of piloting a Zero fighter.

The exigencies of war, in other words, focused the minds of Japan's
business leaders on the problems of coordinating the supply of parts,
and on the need to impose tighter technical control on the activities of
small subcontracting firms. The Navy itself attempted to tackle the issue
by appointing an officer to examine the production systems of armaments and aircraft factories. The results of the study were compiled into
a manual of mass-production techniques for distribution to subcontractors, both large and small, though there is little evidence that
managers or workers paid much attention to the Navy's technical
advice.[28] A more important role seems to have been played by the
Nihon Nôritsu Kyôkai (known in English as the Japan Management
Association, though a more literal translation would be Japan
Association for Efficiency). This body, set up in 1942, played an active
part as a consultant to military industries during the war and was later
to become a pioneer of new methods to promote technological coordination between large and small firms.

Private companies too were devising their own methods to keep up
with the demands of wartime production. At Toyota's Koromo factory,
completed in 1938, company president Toyoda Kiichirô devised a
radically new production system whereby parts would not be stored in
warehouses, but would be produced and delivered just in time for the
day's production. This meant that scarce resources would not be left
lying idle, but would be used in the most efficient way possible. It also
helped the company to adapt its production rapidly to changing
military demands, and to reduce the amount of capital tied up in
unsold stock. The introduction of the system, however, required complex coordination and considerable adaptation by the workers, who
were required to work late into the night when extra parts were needed,
but allowed home early on quiet days. Kiichirô's nephew Toyoda Eiji,
who helped to put the system into operation, later recalled:

To get people to accept [the system], we had to rid them entirely of their notions of the old way of doing things. It was, in a sense, a brainwashing operation. Kiichirô's manual was impressive. A full four inches thick, it described in meticulous detail the flow production system we were to set up. This is the text that I and the other instructors used to teach the new system to the workers. That marked the beginning of the Toyota production system.[29]

So the wartime passion for avoiding the waste of resources laid the foundations of one of postwar Japan's most successful managerial techniques: the famous 'just-in-time' system, which in the 1970s and 1980s would be seen as a panacea for the problems of industrial enterprises throughout the developed world.

None of these developments, however, could enable Japan to catch up with the productive capacity of the United States in the space of a few years. As Ôkôchi Masatoshi and others had foreseen, Japan's lack of the mechanical infrastructure of mass production meant that, as the war progressed, shortages of the most basic manufactured goods became widespread. By pouring money into technological research, the government was able to encourage the design of relatively sophisticated weapons of war, but all too often found that it was impossible to turn the designs into reality. A classic example was the case of the Navy's Comet fighter, designed in 1938. This light and high-speed plane compared favourably with US aircraft like the Buccaneer, but problems in setting up production lines to manufacture the Comet meant that it was not ready for use until late 1943, by which time the tide of war was already turning against Japan.[30]

Scientists and Social Responsibility

The most important legacy of war was a human rather than an organisational one. The war years saw an enormous increase in the number of trained scientific and technological researchers, and a particularly sharp rise in the number of very able students attracted to science subjects. There were several reasons for this. The relatively generous funding of the natural sciences increased their prestige in the eyes of the younger generation, and many young people undoubtedly chose scientific careers in the genuine belief that they offered the best means of contributing to Japan's victory. But another unmistakable attraction of the natural sciences was the fact that science students were exempt from conscription until the very closing stages of the Pacific War. It was not until February 1945 that military recruitment was extended to include students of science and engineering: in the meantime, the number of students graduating in science subjects had risen from

14,952 in 1940 to 31,028 in 1945.[31] A very small but rapidly growing number of these were women. As in other countries, war removed some of the taboos which excluded women from modern technology, and the number of women studying science at tertiary level rose from less than fifty in 1935 to over a thousand in the year of Japan's surrender.[32]

At the same time, though, the harnessing of scientific knowledge to military ends raised moral questions which were to haunt the scientific community in the postwar period. Just as the atomic bomb became, for many western scientists, a symbol of the destructive potential of their own quest for knowledge, so Japan's wartime research exposed the deadly possibilities of modern technology when harnessed to the pursuit of national glory. Japan itself was already working on atomic research in the closing phases of the war, although its atomic projects, organised by the Institute for Physical and Chemical Research and the Navy's Fleet Administration Centre, were still some way from producing results.[33] Work on other weapons of mass destruction, however, was much more advanced. The Army's research laboratory had been experimenting with chemical warfare since the early 1920s, and from 1929 onwards chemical weapons had been manufactured, in great secrecy, on the island of Okunojima in the Seto Inland Sea. After the outbreak of war in China the Okunojima factory grew to employ some 5000 workers. Not only were its products used with deadly results during fighting in China; the pressures of wartime production created also appalling working conditions in which many workers themselves suffered long-term injury through exposure to chemicals.[34] The ultimate consequences of the total subordination of science to the goals of military might were most grotesquely revealed by the case of Unit 731 in Manchuria, in which military doctors used prisoners (mostly Chinese) in human experiments to test the effects of biological weapons.[35]

Although the details of these stories did not become generally known until some years after the end of the war (important documents on Unit 731 were still being published in the 1990s), a general awareness of the wartime uses and abuses of science coloured postwar debates on the social meaning of science and technology.[36] One consequence was that academic science became the subject of fierce political debate, with a variety of different scientific organisations representing different perceptions of the social and political role of science. Another was a shift in public perceptions of technology. The reaction against the horrors of war created a widespread consensus that human knowledge should be harnessed to peaceful production rather than to the pursuit of military glory. At the same time, the experience of atomic bombing and the vision of huge US B-29 bombers in the skies above Tokyo convinced many people that Japan had indeed lost the war because their technology was inferior to that of the west. 'Japanese-style' technology had been put to the test, and had failed. What remained was a faith in a vision of western technology somehow purged of its destructive elements and dedicated to the improvement of human life: the sort of aspiration that, in the immediate postwar years, would be captured by Tezuka Osamu's comic-book figure Astroboy (known in Japanese as 'Mighty Atom'), the invincible 'child of science' whose limitless powers would be used only to protect humankind.[37]

The period of the Second World War marked the high tide of Japanese government efforts to centralise and control the development of technology. In almost all respects these efforts were a failure. The dream of a centrally-planned 'New Order for Science and Technology' foundered on the obstacles of bureaucratic rivalry; the effort to force the pace of technological changed failed to keep up with the insatiable demands of total war; the search for a uniquely Japanese form of technological progress revealed no shortcut to international industrial and military supremacy. But the developments of the war years had one profoundly paradoxical consequence: the unsuccessful attempt to win the 'war of science and technology' left Japanese institutions, human skills and public attitudes remarkably well prepared for the massive import of western technology in the years which followed the surrender to the Allied powers in 1945.

PART III

The Making of a Technological Superpower, Since 1945

CHAPTER 7

Technology and the 'Economic Miracle', 1945–1973

Democracy, Technology and the New Japan

At midday on 15 August 1945 the Japanese people heard the wavering voice of Emperor Hirohito, broadcast on the radio for the first time, announcing Japan's surrender to the Allies. A few hours later the Prime Minister, Suzuki Kantarô, made his government's first postwar broadcast. In it, he spoke of the way in which the enemy had unleashed the revolutionary scientific powers of atomic weaponry on the citizens of Hiroshima and Nagasaki, and called on his listeners to cooperate in the task of protecting and developing the eternal existence of the Japanese people in our land.

> ... It is essential [he went on] that the people should cultivate a new life spirit of self reliance, creativity and diligence in order to begin the building of a new Japan, and in particular should strive for the progress of science and technology, which were our greatest deficiency in this war.[1]

So, without hiatus or compunction, the vision of technology as the basis of the Greater East Asia Co-Prosperity Sphere was transformed into a vision of technology as the basis of the new Japan.

The birth of that new Japan, however, proved to be a complex and painful process. During the final stages of the war Allied bombing had inflicted enormous damage on Japanese cities, destroying about one-quarter of the country's factories and infrastructure.[2] Many of Japan's research laboratories, too, had suffered bomb damage or had been evacuated to rural areas to escape the air-raids. The economy was in chaos, and food production dropped to levels far too low to feed a population swollen by demobilised soldiers and Japanese migrants returning from the lost colonial empire. Into this wasteland came the Allied Occupation Forces—the great majority of them American—

161

bringing with them the message of liberal democracy, and the material civilisation of the richest nation in the world. US troops rode in powerful Jeeps, and the PX stores on their bases sold chewing gum, Hershey's chocolate, boogie-woogie records and copies of *Readers' Digest*, some of which filtered out through the black market to bemuse a hungry and war-weary Japanese populace.

In a sense, the ideals of the Occupation authorities reiterated but reversed the distinction drawn by wartime technocrats like Miyamoto Takenosuke (see p. 147): there was technology designed to serve the aims of liberal democracy, and there was technology designed to serve totalitarianism. Now, however, it was the first which was to be nurtured, while the second was to be remorselessly eradicated. SCAP (Supreme Commander of the Allied Powers, the name commonly applied to the Occupation authorities as a whole) moved swiftly to dismantle Japan's technological capacity to wage war, and by the end of 1945 atomic and aircraft research had been banned.[3] At the same time, a scientific survey was established, under which all research bodies had to submit regular reports of their activities to the authorities.

Meanwhile, SCAP was also unravelling the organisational structures which had supported Japanese militarism. In the first year of the Occupation they abolished the Technology Agency, rescinded most of the wartime measures to encourage scientific and technological research, and stripped the Institute for Physical and Chemical Research (Riken) of all its commercial activities.[4] (A few of the enterprises which the Institute had founded, though, were to survive and flourish in the postwar period, among them Riken Optics, which became the camera and electronics giant RICOH.) The dismantling of the Riken empire was part of a policy designed to split up the prewar conglomerates (*zaibatsu*), regarded by many people in Japan and abroad as a cornerstone of the authoritarian structure of prewar society. The holding companies which had stood at the apex of the conglomerates were to be abolished, and SCAP began examining the assets of the *zaibatsu* and state armaments factories, with the idea of confiscating their machinery as reparations for Japan's wartime aggression.

In this uncertain atmosphere, production was slow to revive, and efforts by the Japanese authorities to resuscitate key industries like steel production only added to spiralling inflation. In 1947 official prices rose almost fourfold, and the black market remained the only thriving sector of the economy.[5] The very chaos of the early Occupation period, however, created a blank canvas on which it was possible to sketch many visions of the future. To some, like the new head of the Institute for Physical and Chemical Research, Nishina Yoshio, it seemed that the revolutionary technologies emerging from the Second World War contained the hope of an entirely new path for Japanese development. Japanese scientists, he suggested, should focus their efforts on developing fundamental breakthroughs—as radical as the splitting of the atom—which might provide the basis for a transformation of the nation's agriculture and industry.[6]

Others saw an opportunity to convert technology from an instrument of military might into a servant of the people. This hope, which had great popular appeal in the Occupation period, was most powerfully expressed by a report on economic reconstruction commissioned by the Japanese Foreign Ministry in 1946. The report's authors, who included several of the nation's leading left-wing and liberal economists, presented democratisation and technological progress as parallel paths to a better future: 'without democratisation it will be difficult to achieve technological advance, and at the same time without technological advance we will be unable to achieve true economic democratisation'. Government planning, they suggested, would be necessary to stimulate innovation, but this planning should be designed to promote only those technologies which would 'improve the living environment and raise the quality of life'.[7]

As the debates revealed, the 'democratisation' of science and technology could mean different things to different people. In mainstream SCAP philosophy, 'democratic' technology was something rather simple: it implied, on the one hand, technology used to sustain a mass consumer society and, on the other, the military technology used to protect that society from the outside threat of 'totalitarianism' in all its forms. To a few of the more radical SCAP officials, however, as well as to certain Japanese intellectuals, 'democratisation' meant something more utopian and far-reaching: a fundamental change in the way in which technology was created and controlled. These differences of interpretation were not just a matter of rhetoric. In some laboratories researchers, inspired by the upsurge of radical unionism which followed Japan's defeat, were to put the utopian vision of 'democratised' technology into very practical action. At Toshiba, the scene of one of the fiercest postwar labour confrontations, scientists and technicians took over control of the former Tokyo Electric research laboratories, and called for 'laboratory democracy' to replace the traditional hierarchical structures of corporate research and development.[8]

In academia too the relationship between science, technology and society became a topic of impassioned argument. These arguments were fuelled by SCAP's plans to dissolve the prewar institutions for the promotion of science in favour of a more open and accountable body. After much debate the reform movement eventually gave birth to the

Japan Science Council (Nihon Gakujutsu Kaigi), whose constitution allowed for direct election of the council by the entire research community. The Science Council was to serve throughout the postwar period as the main representative body of scientists, and to offer advice to governments on a wide range of scientific and technical issues. Meanwhile more routine scientific and technical advice came from the Scientific and Technical Administration Committee (STAC, Kagaku Gijutsu Gyôsei Kyôgikai), a small committee of official appointees which was set up, like the Science Council, in 1948 and survived until the establishment of a much larger and more formal Science and Technology Agency in 1956.[9]

Back to the Future: Technological and Industrial Recovery

In practice, though, the dreams of a new technological order soon proved to be circumscribed by wider economic and political realities. For, while the Allied Occupation brought with it fundamental changes to many areas of Japanese life, there were also strong strands of social and economic continuity. The democratisation of the Occupation period certainly helped to create a new economic climate for technological change, but this was hardly the environment envisaged by the advocates of 'laboratory democracy'. The more radical elements of the postwar labour movement—who had hoped to shift control of production out of the hands of traditional management—were firmly crushed. Instead, the conflicts of the Occupation period resulted in improvements in wages and working conditions within the conventional corporate system. This meant that, as economic recovery gathered momentum, Japanese firms had an incentive to invest in labour-saving machinery. Higher wages also created the basis for a more prosperous consumer market in the postwar years. Rather than laying the foundations for a radically new approach to technology, then, the Occupation reforms served to remove the obstacles which had slowed down the spread of modern mass-production techniques, so opening the doors to the profusion of refrigerators, radios, televisions and cars which transfigured the face of Japanese society in the postwar decades.

The dissolution of the *zaibatsu* helped to speed the process. Most of the major conglomerates quickly regrouped into more loosely coordinated alliances (known as 'business groups', *kigyô shûdan*), which retained the advantages of being able to share financial and technical resources, while shedding the rigidities of the old hierarchical industrial combines. The more open postwar competitive climate also created room for technically inventive newcomers (like the Honda

Motor Company and Tokyo Communication Industries, later renamed Sony) to push their way up between the cracks.

The postwar restructuring of the Japanese education system, too, had a lasting influence on Japan's technological development. On SCAP's initiative, compulsory education was extended to nine years, and the mass expansion of higher education was encouraged in an effort to undermine the elitism of the old Imperial University system. In practice, the prewar universities retained much of their traditional prestige, but a host of new public and private universities greatly increased the opportunities for tertiary education. By the late 1960s almost 20 per cent of high school graduates were going on to university or junior college, and by the mid-1970s the figure was over 35 per cent.[10] The system established by the postwar reforms can be described as a sort of educational equivalent to the mass-production system: highly standardised, strong on basic education, but generally lacking the resources to support extensive graduate and research programs.[11]

Meanwhile the Occupation reforms had left much of Japan's bureaucratic structure untouched. A few leading officials were purged, but the large number who remained were able to draw on prewar and wartime experience in devising policies for Japan's recovery. By 1948 the Japanese authorities were beginning to reconstruct the basis of technology policy, and in that year, an Agency of Industrial Science and Technology (Kôgyô Gijutsuchô, renamed the Kôgyô Gijutsuin in 1952) was set up under the Ministry of International Trade and Industry (MITI), the postwar replacement for the old Ministry of Commerce and Industry. The agency took over control of the various central research laboratories, and was to play a central role in the development of MITI's postwar policies on industrial technology.

In private business, the technical and managerial skills accumulated over earlier decades remained intact, and as reconstruction gathered momentum, enterprises naturally chose to build on existing technological foundations. Low levels of military spending in postwar Japan resulted in a radical reorientation of production to civilian industries, but the skills in mechanical and electrical engineering accumulated during the war years proved as valuable to consumer production as they had been to the building of Japan's military might. The producer associations which had played such a central role in the life of Japanese industry also survived the war, though in somewhat altered form. In the chaos following Japan's surrender, many of the existing industrial associations simply continued to function on their own initiative. In Iwate Prefecture, for example, officials of the local metal-working industrial association, with the support of the prefectural government, took it upon themselves to tackle the problems of resource shortages by removing unused metal from the Kamaishi Steelworks and nearby arsenals and distributing it to their members.[12] By 1947 the old industrial associations with their coercive powers had been abolished, but two years later the government introduced measures to encourage the setting up of new cooperative associations (*kyôdô kumiai*) by small businesses.[13] These groups were voluntary and much more loosely structured than the prewar Industrial Associations, but in many areas there was a good deal of continuity from one organisation to the next in terms both of membership and of office-bearers, and the new bodies continued to act as channels for the circulation of technical information to small firms in their region.

As far as big business was concerned, the wartime control associations were abolished and never officially replaced. In many industries, though, private firms, taking advantage of personal connections established through the old control associations, set up their own voluntary bodies to lobby for their particular interests.[14] These big business associations formed the core of that ubiquitous but ill-defined creature, the *gyôkai*—best translated, perhaps, as 'industry operating as a community'—and, as we shall see, they were to play a vital role in the development of Japan's postwar innovation network.

In the effort to understand Japan's phenomenal industrial growth during the years which followed the Occupation, two factors are often singled out for attention. The first is Japan's ready access to foreign (particularly US) technology; the second is the guiding hand of the government (and especially the controversial role of the Ministry of International Trade and Industry, MITI). These factors, as we shall see, certainly played a crucial role in Japan's postwar technological transformation. But foreign technology and government guidance worked as they did only because they interacted with organisational structures which had been moulded by prewar and wartime developments, and refined by the paradoxical consequences of postwar reform.

Imported Technology and Indigenous Innovation

At the beginning of 1949, the US administration of Harry S. Truman found itself facing a dilemma. With the impending communist victory in China, the US, already committed to large aid programs in Europe, was forced to direct increased attention to the strategic balance in Asia. Its former enemy, Japan, was now a potential ally in a volatile part of the world, and there was growing pressure for the US to expand its support for the reconstruction of the Japanese economy, as well as providing development aid to the newly independent countries of East and

Southeast Asia. But not even the US had unlimited financial resources. Its aid budget was already stretched by existing assistance programs to defeated enemies and impoverished allies. The solution, it seemed, lay in opening up the treasure-house of US technological know-how. As Truman put it in his inaugural address of January 1949,

> the United States is preeminent among nations in the development of industrial and scientific techniques. The material resources which we can afford to use for the assistance of other peoples are limited. But our imponderable resources in technical knowledge are constantly growing and are inexhaustible. I believe that we should make available to peace-loving peoples the benefits of our store of technical knowledge in order to help them realize their aspirations for a better life.[15]

The recipients of this technological generosity were to be the developing countries, rather than the industrialised nations of Europe; but, as Clyde Prestowitz observes, 'in the rubble of postwar Japan, the West somehow came to regard Japan as a developing country'.[16] The US transfer of knowledge would not be limited to manufacturing technologies. Presidential exhortations to private industry,[17] as well as considerable sums of US aid, were devoted to encouraging the transfer to Japan of know-how in areas like labour management, training and quality control: fields in which the US was internationally recognised as a world leader. An important element in the shift in US policy was a reversal of the approach to Japan's military industries, and particularly towards the aircraft industry, which had earlier been earmarked for destruction. By the early 1950s the United States was channelling large amounts of aid to Japan's aircraft manufacturers, helping to lay the basis, not only for Japan's acquisition of jet propulsion technology, but also for its later entry into the space race.[18]

Looking back on this policy from an end-of-century perspective, the ironies are obvious. Within three decades, the recipient of this largesse would have turned into a formidable competitor, and US managers would be making regular pilgrimages to Japan to learn the secrets of Japanese industrial efficiency and quality control. It is easy to conclude that the United States, in 'guiding Japan into the world' (as one prominent US official put it)[19] had single-handedly created its own nemesis.

The story, however, is not quite as simple as that. US willingness to make technology accessible to Cold War allies extended not only to Japan but also to many other nations. The effects of that technology transfer, however, varied widely according to the social, political and economic structures of the recipients. In Japan's case, several factors helped to smooth the reception of foreign technology. During the final years of the Allied Occupation, Japanese industry experienced rapid recovery, and growth created opportunities to incorporate new techniques into expanding or newly built factories. A vital stimulant to this growth was the Korean War, which broke out in 1950. As a major base for forces involved in the fighting, and as the only industrialised nation in the region, Japan became a source of supply for parts and equipment used in the war. Special war-related procurements (in the form of both goods and services) amounted to some $US 2 billion, and for industries like vehicles manufacture, electronics and communications equipment the Korean conflict was quite simply 'a gift from heaven'.[20]

After the end of the Occupation in 1952, the Japanese government made special efforts to maintain the inflow of industrial know-how. Under Japan's Foreign Exchange Control Law of 1949, all importers— whether of goods or technology—had to apply to the Ministry of International Trade and Industry for foreign exchange to complete their transaction.[21] This system, which remained in force throughout the 1950s, gave the Ministry great power to favour certain types of technology import, as well as to protect local industries from foreign competition. It also enabled MITI to intervene in the process in other ways. As we shall see, the Ministry frequently used its powers to bring Japanese importers of a particular piece of know-how together, so that they could strengthen their bargaining position in relation to the foreign owner of the patent rights.

Other circumstances also helped Japanese companies to acquire foreign technology on unusually favourable terms. The period of the late 1930s and 1940s had been one of extremely rapid technological advance in the United States and Western Europe, making it possible for postwar Japanese firms to draw on a large pool of foreign invention. In many cases, too, several foreign firms held rights to closely related techniques, so Japanese companies were able to pick and choose, and to play one patent-holder off against another. Since few western enterprises were seriously concerned about the threat of Japanese competition, many were willing to license their know-how to Japan without restrictive conditions. As late as 1968 over one-third of technology licences had no conditions attached, and most of those with conditions allowed Japan to export the products of the technology to the expanding East and Southeast Asian markets.[22]

As the world economy entered a boom in the late 1950s, therefore, Japanese firms were able to combine imported techniques and abundant labour to achieve extraordinarily high growth rates. Figure 7.1 shows Japan's soaring imports of technology in the 1950s and 1960s.[23] The apparent sharp rise in long-term technology contracts after 1966 needs some explanation: the figures cover both new technology

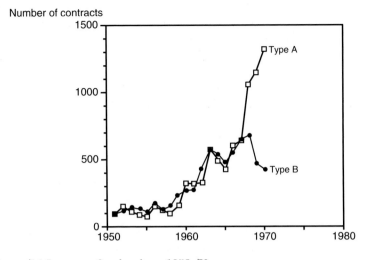

Figure 7.1 Imports of technology, 1952–70
Source: Kagaku Gijutsuchô, *Gaikoku gijutsu dônyû nenji hôkoku, 1970.*
Type A = Contracts lasting more than one year (licences for the use of patents, etc.). Type B = Contracts lasting less than one year (short-term visits by technical advisers, access to blueprints, etc.).

contracts and the renewal of existing contracts; in fact the number of new licence agreements remained roughly steady in the late 1960s.[24] Patterns of new technology imports follow fluctuations in the growth of the Japanese economy as a whole, which reached an annual rate of 13.3 per cent in 1960, and suffered a short but sharp recession in 1961–62 before climbing again to 13.4 per cent in 1968. The largest imports of technology occurred in the rapidly growing machinery, electrical and chemical sectors, and the major source of imported know-how was, predictably, the United States, with Germany coming a distant second (see Figure 7.2).

The most important point to recognise about Japan's import of technology was that it was translated into industrial strength only because it was combined with domestic innovation. As in the prewar period, imported technology was a complement to, not a substitute for, local research and development. Between 1952 and 1958, the number of researchers employed by private companies more than doubled, and between 1959 and 1975 it increased 3.4 times.[25] In the early years particularly this reflected, not so much the growth of very large research laboratories, but the fact that many companies were establishing small laboratories or research divisions to acquire and adapt technology. The pattern of the interwar years, in other words, was being

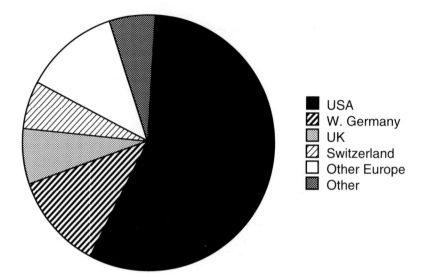

■ USA
▨ W. Germany
▨ UK
▨ Switzerland
☐ Other Europe
▨ Other

Figure 7.2 Imports of technology by country of origin, 1951–70
Source: Kagaku Gijutsuchô, *Gaikoku gijutsu dônyû nenji hôkoku, 1970.*

Table 7.1 *Research investment and the import of technology,
by industry, 1960–1961*

Industry	A Research investment (¥m)		B Import of technology (¥m)		A/B(%)	
	1960	1961	1960	1961	1960	1961
Mining	4,681	10,217	280	368	15	8
Manufacturing	83,408	104,686	33,348	42,441	40	41
Machinery	40,306	54,012	14,174	19,098	35	35
General	3,399	5,028	2,273	5,781	67	115
Electrical	22,885	28,639	7,551	8,007	33	28
Automobiles	8,256	12,581	669	835	8	7
Shipbuilding	3,524	3,945	3,277	3,840	93	97
Other	2,242	3,819	404	635	18	17
Chemicals	15,553	18,191	11,190	9,419	72	52
Textiles	9,166	10,995	3,330	6,132	36	24
Oil refining	1,385	1,461	1,429	2,693	103	184
Iron and steel	7,919	9,810	1,860	2,876	23	29
Other manufacturing	9,079	10,217	1,365	2,223	15	56
Electricity and gas	1,781	2,988	114	462	6	15
Nuclear industry	535	928	10	120	2	13
Other	1,004	1,420	45	37	4	3

Source: A. Hino, *Nihon no kenkyû tôshi,* p. 157.

replicated on a much wider scale, with many relatively small centres of developmental research appearing throughout the country.

A study conducted in the early 1960s showed that, in 1960–61, there was only one industry in which spending on technology imports substantially exceeded investment in research and development. That industry, interestingly enough, was oil refining, which was also the only important branch of Japanese manufacturing to be dominated by affiliates of foreign multinationals (see Table 7.1). Of course, since Japanese firms were often able to purchase foreign technology on very favourable terms, these figures do not tell us anything about the real relative *value* of imported and domestically created techniques. They do, however, emphasise the crucial interdependence of foreign and indigenous innovation.

In some instances, Japanese companies bought licences for technologies on which they had already conducted substantial independent research. A case in point is Sumitomo Chemicals' acquisition of polyethelene technology from ICI in 1955. In the last chapter we saw how Sumitomo made use of the wartime system of 'research neighbourhood groups' to conduct joint research on polyethelene with scientists at Kyoto University (see p. 151). After the war, Sumitomo maintained its association with leading academic chemists and continued work on the chemical. The licensing agreement with ICI, however, enabled Sumitomo both to avoid the risk of legal disputes over ownership of the technology, and to use ICI's experience in overcoming problems involved in the large-scale production of polyethelene. On the other hand, without its experience of independent research in the area, Sumitomo would undoubtedly have had much greater difficulty obtaining the licence from ICI and putting the imported know-how into practical use.[26] The same story was repeated in the synthetic textile industry, where Tôyô Rayon, which had been engaged in research on nylon production since the late 1930s, reached a licensing agreement with Dupont to speed its entry into the rapidly expanding commercial nylon market.[27]

In other cases, the import of technology and the creation of local research capacity went hand in hand. Here the classic example is the story of Tokyo Communication Industries, the innovative new company which was soon to rename itself Sony. The company had been set up in 1946 by two recently demobilised military engineers, Ibuka Masaru and Morita Akio, with the explicit purpose of entering those new areas of technology where 'large firms cannot progress precisely because they are large firms'.[28] Just eight years later they acquired a patent to produce the newly invented transistor (developed by the US Bell Laboratories in 1948), and by 1955 Sony had launched its first transistor radio.[29] Sony's rapid conquest of the transistor radio market is often seen as a triumph of bold imagination, as though all that was necessary was to take the transistor and implant it into the existing technology of the radio. In fact, however, early transistors could not deal with the high frequencies necessary to broadcast the human voice, and it was only because Sony possessed the research capacity to solve these technical problems that it was able to move so quickly into the production of transistor radios.[30] The company's skill at picking technical talent is indicated by its recruitment in 1956 of the physicist Esaki Reona, whose work on the tunnel diode (begun at Sony and continued in the United States) was later to win him a Nobel Prize.[31]

Rationalisation and the Productivity Movement

The US role in Japan's postwar technological history, however, did not just involve encouraging the export of American technology to Japan. It also took the rather unusual form of allowing Japanese industry to pay war reparations to itself. To understand how this came about, we need to consider the wider context of industrial policy in the final stages of the Allied Occupation. By the beginning of the 1950s a consensus was emerging between SCAP and the Japanese authorities over the desirable direction of Japan's technological development. The key to that consensus was the notion of 'rationalisation' (*gôrika*): a term which had been popular both in Japan and the US during the 1930s. In the context of 1950s Japan it meant, above all, promoting the intro-duction of mass-production techniques throughout Japanese industry. This process, which of course involved the large-scale import of machinery and technology from the US, was felt to be the only means by which Japan could raise its productivity sufficiently to survive in postwar world markets.

In 1949 the Ministry of International Trade and Industry set up the Industry Rationalisation Commission (Sangyô Gôrika Shingikai) to examine the state of key industries like steel and coalmining, and in 1952 the Law for the Promotion of Rationalisation (Kigyô Gôrika Sokushin Hô) was passed, providing special tax exemptions and depreciation rates for companies which bought new manufacturing equipment.[32] The law also offered government subsidies for corporate research, and expanded assistance for infrastructure projects like the building of roads and harbours. At the same time, individual rational-isation schemes were being drawn up for several important industries. In the case of steel, for example, the industry's First Rationalisation Plan, produced by MITI in 1951, called for massive investment in new plant and equipment, to be supported by loans from the newly created

Japan Development Bank. The plan was mainly aimed at encouraging the introduction of modern strip mills to produce thin steel sheeting of the sort needed by Japan's new consumer industries such as car manufacturing.[33]

In the car industry itself, the response to the rationalisation drive was particularly swift. Toyota's five-year modernisation plan, devised by senior management in 1951, aimed to double output without increasing the workforce.[34] The early stages of the plan concentrated upon improving the production of trucks, but from 1953 onwards Toyota turned its attention to passenger cars, importing large amounts of semi-specialised machine tools, mainly from the US (Figure 7.3). By 1959 the company had established a massive new factory equipped with the latest transfer machinery and high-speed presses.[35] (Toyota's main rival, Nissan, was somewhat slower to modernise its production system, and it was not until the early 1960s that it too built a series of new factories in which it installed sophisticated forging, stamping and transfer machinery, most of it specially designed for the company by US engineering firms.)[36]

In the wave of rationalisation, however, there was a real danger that the small subcontractors, on whom firms like Toyota so heavily relied,

Figure 7.3 Advertisement for the Toyopet, mid-1950s. Toyota's rapid recovery and growth was fuelled by its success in tapping expanding demand for small family cars like the Toyopet.
Source: Yamazaki H., ed., *Shôwa kôkoku 60-nenshi,* p. 240.

would be left behind: and it was here that the reparations program came to play its part. During the early stages of the Occupation, SCAP had envisaged exacting harsh reparations from Japan by confiscating large amounts of Japanese manufacturing equipment, mainly from armaments factories and the major *zaibatsu*. As the focus of US policy shifted from the destruction of Japan's military machine to the reconstruction of its industries, however, the policy was quietly revised, and in the end, only about one-quarter of the material originally earmarked for reparations was appropriated. This raised the problem of what to do with the remaining equipment: a problem which was ultimately resolved by authorising its release for sale to Japanese companies. From 1953 onwards the Japanese government introduced special arrangements to allow small and medium-sized enterprises to trade in their existing machinery for unclaimed equipment from the reparations program. Prefectural governments and cooperative associations played a central role in the process, helping to match the needs of local firms with the available machinery.[37]

Needless to say, this redistribution of machinery caused serious problems for Japan's own machine-tool producers, whose position became rather like that of an ice merchant at the North Pole.[38] On the other hand, the machinery exchange program played an important part in helping smaller firms, many of them subcontractors, to keep pace with the technological changes of the 1950s. Although the equipment which they obtained was seldom the latest or most efficient model, it provided a stepping stone between the obsolete techniques of the prewar period and the rapid automation of the late 1960s and after. This modernisation program had immensely important implications for the postwar structure of Japanese industry: it was one of the reasons why the subcontracting system survived and developed during the high-growth years, rather than giving way to the creation of large-scale integrated production systems. The 'reparations' scheme also indirectly benefited many large Japanese firms, who were able to match their own capital investment programs to the improved productivity of their subcontractors. A 1959 study of thirty major subcontractors to the Toyota Motor Company, for example, found seventeen of them using equipment released under the machinery exchange program.[39]

The idea of rationalisation was not confined to the introduction of new machinery. There was also a human aspect, which involved the fitting of the worker to the demands of the mass production system. As in the 1920s and 1930s, so too in the postwar world, technological change implied new systems of training, disciplining and motivating the workforce. In response to the upsurge of postwar labour activism, many large Japanese companies introduced systems of lifetime employment, with regular pay rises based on length of service. But this by itself was not enough to ensure the wholehearted commitment of the workforce in the increasingly impersonal and mechanised environment of the modern factory.

The problems of worker motivation were of particular interest to the US government. Both in Europe and in Japan, the US saw its mission as being to prevent the spread of communism by encouraging economic growth and promoting harmony between labour and management. An important part of this mission involved the worldwide dissemination of US managerial techniques. During the late 1940s and early 1950s, the US government used the European Marshall Plan as a vehicle to encourage the spread of the new managerial ideas, and the approach was extended to Japan in the late Occupation period, when officials from the US embassy contacted a newly established group of 'progressive' Japanese executives (the Keizai Dôyûkai, the Japan Committee for Economic Development) to suggest the creation of a productivity movement in Japan. The discussions were gradually widened to bring in other business organisations and the Japanese government (organised labour remained wary, although some individual unionists took part in the discussions), and the eventual result was the setting up in 1953 of the Japan Productivity Center (Nihon Seisansei Honbu), whose aim was to act as a channel for the dissemination of new technology and managerial ideas throughout Japanese industry.[40] The centre was to be financed jointly by the Japanese government, private industry, and (in the initial stages) US aid, with US funding being specifically used to support study visits to the US by Japanese managers and technicians, and lecture tours of Japan by prominent US experts.[41] These exchanges of ideas were to prove crucial to Japan's import of technical and managerial ideas in the 1950s. In 1955, for example, fifteen missions with a total of 174 members visited the United States to study industries such as steel and automobiles. Their effect was magnified by the fact that, on their return, mission members conducted seminars in various parts of Japan to report on their findings.[42] The study tours not only provided a window for Japan on US technology and production systems, but also established the personal connections through which later company-to-company technology agreements could be negotiated.

Like other importers of technology, the Japan Productivity Center 'succeeded' above all because it was an active and adaptive recipient of foreign ideas. It is worth recalling that other productivity centres created on US initiative, including a British centre which attracted much admiring attention in Japan, had far less of a lasting impact on the course of history.[43] The ideas which the Japan Productivity Center introduced through its publications, seminars and overseas study trips were, again like other postwar innovations, an interesting blend of imported and domestically developed techniques. An important influence on the centre's thinking came from the western managerial theories which had become popular during the Second World War. Perhaps the most important of these was the 'human relations' school of management theorists like Elton Mayo who, in reaction to the cold rationalism of Taylor's scientific management, had emphasised the need for companies to foster a sense of community, replacing the lost communal values of rural society.[44] Ideas like these were discussed by Japanese managers and academics in the top management forums which the Japan Productivity Center ran in the mountain resort of Karuizawa from 1958 onwards, and in the process of discussion imported concepts became domesticated, moulded and shaped to the circumstances of Japanese industry.[45]

Another foreign idea which struck a receptive chord in Japan was the notion of quality control (QC), which had been developed in the US largely in response to the wartime need for sophisticated and reliable weaponry.[46] The concept of quality control in itself was not new to Japan: after all, this is what Japanese trade associations had been trying to achieve ever since the Meiji period. US experts like W. Edwards Deming, however, had brought a new scientific rigour to the process by introducing the idea of statistical sampling to check the quality of the finished product. Statistical quality control was introduced to Japan with the encouragement of the Occupation authorities, and was enthusiastically propagated by organisations like the Japan Union of Scientists and Engineers (Nihon Kagaku Gijutsu Renmei) and the Japan Management Association (Nihon Nôritsu Kyôkai). The Korean War procurements program, which forced Japanese producers to meet the demanding specifications of the US military, played an important role in the spread of statistical quality control within Japan.[47]

By the 1950s, however, it was becoming clear to managers in Japan and the US that the complex industries of the postwar era needed more than *post facto* quality control. What was necessary was to involve workers in checking and improving the quality of products *as they were manufactured*. This notion of enlisting the workforce in the process of technological improvement contained echoes of the prewar theories of men like Ôkôchi Masatoshi (see p. 128), and it found a ready audience amongst Japanese managers, particularly as they endeavoured to break into the lucrative markets of Europe and North America. As was the case with other imported technologies, the technique of quality control was refined and adapted to Japanese conditions, most notably by the engineer Ishikawa Kaoru, who in 1960 devised the concept of quality-control circles—small groups of shopfloor workers responsible for monitoring and improving their own productivity. Ishikawa's innovation was particularly attractive to companies because it provided a means of fostering a sense of group identity amongst employees at the very time when the high demand for skilled labour was threatening to weaken the power of management over workers.[48] Quality-control circles, which were set up in many large companies during the 1960s and 1970s, almost certainly contributed to the rising levels of productivity in Japanese industry, and to Japan's success in overcoming its image as a producer of 'cheap but shoddy' goods. But these achievements were accomplished at the cost of considerable demands on the workforce, not least because the meetings of the circles generally occurred outside normal working hours. As management researcher Komai Hiroshi puts it, 'under the guise of voluntary activities, they [the QC circles] represented an effort to get more work out of employees for the same money'.[49]

From Rationalisation to Automation: Postwar Technology Policies

Popular mythology has it that Japan's technological development has been guided by some skilfully formulated, brilliantly executed, long-term master plan. 'Japan's MITI', according to a recent US book, 'has a twenty-year plan for critical technologies and a fifty-year plan for industrial growth.'[50] 'As defined by the Japanese,' we are told, 'industrial policy is not trade policy or tax policy but a strategic plan that affects every facet of the nation's economic system.'[51] The problem for historians of Japanese technology, on the contrary, is that they are confronted by a labyrinthine confusion of coexisting, overlapping and sometimes conflicting policies implemented by a host of different ministries and agencies, many of whom seemed bent on competition rather than cooperation. It is not that there was no plan, but rather that there were any number of plans, most of them endowed with grandiose titles (if they were not Grand Strategies they were usually at least Long Term-visions or Fundamental Outlines) which belied their fairly speculative contents. All of this suggests that the role of the plans was not so much to chart an immutable course for Japanese industry, but rather to disseminate information, stir up debate, enhance the reputation of the ministry concerned and (as often as not) strengthen its case for a larger share of budget funding.

The Role of the Science and Technology Agency

Many Japanese observers identify two main diverging strands in the development of postwar technology policy, and trace the origins of the dichotomy to the second half of the 1950s.[52] By this stage most of the goals of the first phase of rationalisation had been achieved. Japanese industries had replaced their obsolete wartime equipment, and as economic growth accelerated from 1957 onwards, their products began to make rapid inroads into the expanding markets of the industrialised world. But the technology of Japan's more industrialised rivals was not standing still. The postwar boom was the age of large-scale technologies—jet transport, nuclear power, the exploration of space: technologies often supported by national-level projects and massive government funding. A portent of the times was the launch of the Soviet Sputnik in 1957, an event which caused almost as much consternation in Japan as it did in the USA.

Already in the year before the 'Sputnik shock' the Japanese parliament had approved the creation of a Science and Technology Agency (STA, Kagaku Gijutsuchô), whose brief was to promote large-scale innovation in Japan itself. Following the Sputnik launch, in 1959, the government made renewed efforts to promote and coordinate technology policy, setting up a small advisory group, the Council for Science and Technology (Kagaku Gijutsu Kaigi), which was supposed to harmonise the activities of individual ministries with research interests, and to draw up long-range plans for future development.[53]

In practice, however, the council failed to bridge the gap between the differing philosophies espoused by the new Science and Technology Agency and the older and more powerful Ministry of International Trade and Industry, and the bureaucratic rivalries which had plagued Japan's wartime technology policy persisted into the high-growth era. The STA saw its role as being the creation of an indigenous basic research capacity, often involving the setting up of large-scale projects implemented through public corporations like the Power Reactor and Nuclear Fuel Development Corporation (Dôryoku Ro Kaku Nenryô Kaihatsu Jigyôdan). Nuclear energy, indeed, was an area of particular interest to the agency. The late 1950s and early 1960s, of course, were an era of cheap and abundant oil, and Japan made the most of the favourable circumstances by shifting from the development of hydro-electric power projects to the expansion of thermal power stations run on imported oil. The government, however, remained acutely conscious of the vulnerability created by reliance on imported energy, and looked to nuclear power as a long-term solution to Japan's expanding energy needs.

The agency's first *White Paper on Science and Technology*, published in 1958, pointed out that Japan's energy consumption was expected to increase very rapidly over the next two decades. Energy problems, according to the *White Paper*, were likely to become 'the greatest impediment to economic development', and the use of nuclear power was seen as 'a major technological issue' for future energy supply.[54] The agency's strategy for tackling this issue was to launch an ambitious program to develop advanced nuclear technology locally, including advanced thermal reactors and fast breeder reactors. These schemes, however, were plagued by delays and cost overruns (see below, p. 230), while most of the practical advances in Japan's nuclear technology during the 1960s and 1970s came from MITI's alternative strategy of encouraging the import of foreign nuclear know-how.[55]

Another area of particular interest to the Science and Technology Agency was space research. The destruction of Japan's aeronautics research during the Occupation had, of course, placed Japan well back in the field for the space race. In 1955, however, Tokyo University scientists, drawing on the traditions of the university's prewar Institute of Aeronautics, launched the country's first miniature rocket, and in 1960 the STA introduced its first measures to support space science, offering substantial financial assistance to space research and sending groups of researchers overseas to study the latest developments in the field.[56]

MITI's Industry Policies and Technological Innovation

MITI, on the contrary, was more interested in industrial growth than in the originality of domestic research projects. The Ministry's approach was one of providing encouragement and guidance to the initiatives of private business: creating a suitably un-level playing field which would give that critical advantage to industries identified by government as having potential for long-term success. In terms of research and development, therefore, MITI tended to focus more on coordinating and encouraging the efforts of private corporations than on initiating large government-funded projects.

Throughout most of the 1950s and 1960s, the main targets were heavy industries like steel, shipbuilding, chemicals and machinery, identified by MITI as having large and rapidly growing world markets. These industries were supported by generous packages of financial assistance and protection: packages which emulated but refined the systems of industry incentive developed by the Ministry's predecessors in the immediate prewar years. In most cases, a rather brief enabling act was drawn up allowing MITI (on its own or through the Japan Development Bank) to provide subsidies and tax incentives to target industries. During the 1950s the Ministry was able to reinforce these policies with high protective tariffs and with preferential allocations of foreign exchange, but the liberalisation of Japan's foreign trade during the 1960s weakened these powers, forcing it to rely more heavily on other types of incentive. Through individual industry schemes, MITI's support for research and innovation became firmly embedded in a wider system of industry policy, which aimed not only to upgrade technology but also to increase technologies of scale and prevent what the Ministry called 'excess competition'. The Machine Industry Law of 1956 and the Electronics Industry Law of 1958, for example, offered government subsidies for research and development, as well as low-interest loans and depreciation measures to encourage investment, while a series of Measures to Foster the Petrochemicals Industry (1957) provided protection and cheap finance to assist the establishment of huge petrochemicals complexes (*kombinâto*) in coastal towns like Yokkaichi and Niihama.

MITI's most important role in relation to technology, however, was probably its ability to create channels through which new technological ideas could be rapidly disseminated between rival Japanese firms. As we shall see when we turn to specific case studies, this was often done in a quite ad hoc and informal way. By the 1960s, however, MITI was starting to strengthen and formalise this side of its activities, and in 1961 it introduced a policy of encouraging private firms to set up cooperative research associations, which would then receive special tax concessions. Unlike the British research associations, on which they were loosely modelled, the Japanese versions were not permanent institutions covering one particular industry, but were temporary groups—often crossing industrial boundaries—whose aim was to tackle a particular research topic.[57] This group approach to research was taken one step further in 1966, when the Ministry introduced the National Research and Development Program, offering financial support for group research on major projects in key areas of advanced technology.[58]

Although MITI and the STA generally pursued their own diverging courses throughout the high-growth era, cooperation between them was not entirely unknown. One of the most famous inter-ministry projects was the plan, first mooted in 1962, to develop a new 'science city' where academics and researchers from the major government technology institutes could work side by side. The aim of the scheme was to reduce the concentration of research in the overcrowded Tokyo metropolitan area and at the same time to create a critical mass of research activities, so encouraging 'the improvement of the research environment, the common use of facilities, harmonious research cooperation, increased human interchange etc.'.[59] In practice, the new city at Tsukuba, some fifty kilometres northwest of Tokyo, did not begin to take shape until the mid-1970s, and the rather sterile research environment which it created was to be the target of much criticism.

The Tsukuba concept, however, was the forerunner of a host of schemes for 'science' or 'technology' cities which would excite great interest in Japan and abroad in the 1980s and 1990s.

Small Firms and Local Technology Initiatives

Debates on postwar Japan, like debates on the Meiji Era, tend to identify the role of the 'state' with the role of central government. Yet the fact is that, during the 1950s and 1960s, as in the 1870s and 1880s, an intermediate stratum of local institutions—prefectural and city governments—had active industry policies of their own, and exerted great influence on the technological development of Japanese private industry.

The new postwar constitution strengthened the powers of the prefectures, specifically giving them the right to enact ordinances 'within the limits of the law'.[60] Local government's share in total government spending also increased: by 1980, 32.7 per cent of total government revenue was under the control of local, rather than national, government. (This is an unusually high figure for a country which does not have a federal system of government. The comparable percentages for France and Britain were 12.3 and 11.7.)[61] Besides, the nature of the relationship between local and central government helped to ensure that the prefectures would use their enhanced powers to encourage industrial development rather than (for example) to expand welfare services: the central government placed a limit on the maximum level of local taxes, but did not prevent prefectures from *reducing* taxes selectively to foster chosen industries.[62]

One of the first signs of the revitalisation of local industrial policy was the rush to establish new regional research laboratories, many of them focusing on promising postwar industries like machinery. Between 1945 and 1960 twenty-three new prefectural research laboratories were set up.[63] The case of Nagano Prefecture was typical. As we have seen, the local authorities had already begun, in the immediate prewar years, to attract precision machinery firms into the region, in the hope of absorbing labour cast adrift by the collapsing silk industry. The war gave an ironical boost to these hopes. A number of Japanese machinery firms evacuated their factories from Tokyo to avoid Allied air-raids, and by the time of Japan's surrender the old silk towns of Suwa and Okaya had small but thriving communities of machine-makers. In the early postwar years the prefecture tried to maintain the momentum, helping local factories to shift from military to civilian production. In 1951 it introduced a range of incentives to attract manufacturing firms (particularly in the machinery industry) and in 1957 it established a

Precision Machinery Research Laboratory in Okaya. These policies were soon mimicked at the municipal level. By the early 1960s towns like Suwa, Okaya and Sakaki had introduced their own sets of measures—including improved infrastructure and reduced municipal taxes—in a competitive effort to attract firms to their particular part of the prefecture.[64]

The policies were, in a way, local versions of MITI's strategy of 'picking winners'. While Nagano—with its abundance of labour, mountainous terrain and reasonably easy access to Tokyo—chose to focus on precision machinery, other regions with flat coastal landscapes competed to attract oil refineries, steel mills or petrochemical plants. At times, competition between prefectures and cities became a process of beggar-your-neighbour: each tried to offer the greatest concessions in the scramble to attract its share of the 'miracle'. The results may have been a mixed blessing for the local community, but they certainly provided substantial benefits to the select group of industries which local authorities vied to attract.

Although these postwar local industrialisation policies were often aimed at enticing an inflow of investment from large enterprises, prefectural governments were also particularly concerned to help the technological upgrading of local small firms. One popular approach was to encourage small firms to cluster together into specially created industrial estates where they could share infrastructure and where, it was hoped, physical proximity would promote the spread of new technologies. The *kôgyô danchi* (as they were called) were pioneered by Toyama Prefecture in 1960; they made such an impression on MITI bureaucrats that the Ministry took up the scheme and encouraged other regions to follow Toyama's example.[65]

The postwar relationship between central and local technology policy seems in some ways to have retraced the path mapped out in the Meiji period. Economist Saitô Masaru observes that, until the second half of the 1960s, local government tended to chart its own course; as time went on, the coordination of national and local policies increased.[66] An important link between centre and locality was the Small and Medium Enterprise Agency (Chûshô Kigyô Shô), set up in 1963, which created funding to support the technology initiatives of local government and pioneered a range of programs to develop closer ties between public research laboratories and small manufacturers.

The Social Network of Innovation in Postwar Japan

Throughout this book a recurring theme has been the importance of Japan's social network of innovation: the network through which new ideas were transmitted to the workplace. Nowhere does the role of this network seem more clearly evident than in the high-growth era of the 1950s and 1960s. Easy access to foreign technology and vigorous state intervention created a favourable climate for the rapid introduction of new techniques, but neither of these factors would have produced such dramatic results had it not been for an existing system of institutions which allowed new ideas to be readily communicated between companies and put to work in their factories and offices. In this context what matters is not so much the role of the state as a source of financial incentives for technological change, but rather its role in creating nodes in the network, through which knowledge of new techniques could flow to many parts of the industrial system.

It is often pointed out that the research system in postwar Japan was very different from that of other leading industrial nations like the US, Britain and France. While the major share of research in the US and Britain was financed by the state, in Japan the great surge in postwar research spending came from private industry: by 1972 only 27 per cent of the nation's total research budget was funded by government (see Table 7.2). These figures deserve a little further discussion. If we look at the proportion of research performed in universities and other government laboratories, we find that there is relatively little difference between Japan and its main industrial competitors (see Table 7.3). The difference comes from the fact that, particularly in the US, very large sums of money were paid by the government to finance research by private firms, most of this being military research, and most of it being performed by a small number of giant corporations.

A point which is seldom noticed, though, is that the internal structure of Japan's public and private research systems was also very different from that of earlier industrial leaders. In Japan, both public

Table 7.2 *Government research expenditure as a percentage of all research expenditure, various countries, 1972*

Country	Percentage
Japan	27.2
USA	55.5
W. Germany	49.2*
France	62.7
UK	49.5

* = 1973
Source: Kagaku gijutsu hakusho, 1991.

Table 7.3   *Research expenditure by sector of performance,*
various countries, 1972

	Industry %	Government Research Labs %	Universities %	Private Research Labs %	Total %	 ¥m
Japan	65.9	14.7	18.2	1.2	100	1586.7
USA	68.7	16.1	11.9	3.3	100	8634.2
W. Germany	61.3	16.6	21.5	0.5	100	1731.6
France	57.8	25.3	15.7	1.1	100	1097.4
UK	61.3	25.2	11.0	2.5	100	1027.5

Source: Kagaku gijutsu hakusho, 1991.

and private research was divided between a mass of relatively small and often quite poorly funded research bodies. By 1961, in addition to 783 colleges and universities (the vast majority of them established since 1945) Japan had 159 government-controlled *industrial* research laboratories (121 of them run by local government) as well as several hundred government laboratories specialising in agriculture and medicine.[67] Nearly all of the industrial laboratories conducted research of direct relevance to private enterprise. In Britain, by way of comparison, a 1971 survey lists some eighty government-run institutions focusing on research in industrial and engineering areas. The vast majority of these were concerned with military research or with topics related to public services (such as transport research and nuclear power generation). Only five (the Birniehill Institute, the National Physical Laboratory, the National Engineering Laboratory, Warren Spring and the Atlas Computer Laboratory) can be indentified as being directly relevant to the needs of civilian private industry.[68]

The pattern of private industrial research was similar. In 1960 there were over 6500 Japanese companies performing research activities. The scale of research spending of course varied widely: 89 per cent of all spending came from some 2900 relatively large companies, while the remaining 11 per cent was divided amongst more than 3600 small firms.[69] The dispersed structure of Japanese research, though, is striking, particularly when we compare Japan with a country like France. In France, with a total corporate research budget similar to Japan's, 98.5 per cent of all corporate research spending for the year 1964 came from just 440 firms. Even in the United States, with its far greater industrial research spending, 98.9 per cent of all research spending was accounted for by just 2130 companies.[70] (Directly comparable figures for Britain are not available, although the evidence suggests that British research, too, was highly concentrated in relatively large companies.)

The dispersed pattern of Japanese research was partly the legacy of history. Government laboratories followed the model created from the Meiji period onwards, with central government setting up specialist research institutes to serve particular industries, while local authorities established their own laboratories to meet regional technological needs. For private industry, research (as in the prewar years) was not seen as a path to revolutionary breakthroughs, but as an essential part of the process of importing, adapting and improving existing techniques. Hence the general preference for small-scale research closely linked to the workplace. Even when companies were large enough to invest substantially in technological research, many preferred to divide their efforts among several small laboratories rather than concentrating it in one large research centre. The rapidly growing Matsushita Electric Company, for example, set up a central research laboratory which served the general needs of the enterprise as a whole, but also established a whole series of specialised laboratories (eleven in all by 1968), each closely linked to particular factories.[71]

This galaxy of small research centres made the Japanese system particularly efficient at generating certain sorts of innovation. It was, for example, a very flexible system. Research laboratories could co-operate in a range of different combinations to produce differing types of hybrid techniques. This proved to be a great advantage in the development of techniques like mechatronics and optoelectronics, which required particular combinations of technical expertise. The Japanese system was well suited, too, to areas of innovation in which there was scope for competition between several slightly differing models of the same basic technology (as was the case in the television and computer industries).

The wide dispersal of research activities was also important for another reason. Most modern innovations have, as it were, ripple effects which spread out to engulf many surrounding industries. Improvements in shipbuilding technology, for example, required changes in steel production; the introduction of new steelmaking techniques involved changes in the design and construction of furnaces, and so on. Because research capacity was not confined to a few giant firms, it was possible for related industries, parts suppliers and subcontractors to move more or less in step as new technologies were introduced.

None of this would have been possible without an effective flow of information between individual research bodies. It is here that the role of government (both central and local) was crucial, as were the activities of the multilayered system of industrial associations. Japanese corporations, of course, were no more eager to share technical know-how with their competitors than corporations elsewhere. Besides, the legacy of the war years created particular barriers to cooperation between academia and industrial research. Many university researchers had troubled memories of the 'research neighbourhood groups' and their role in the promotion of military technology, and formal links between universities and private corporations were often looked at with some suspicion (although personal, informal contacts between academic and corporate researchers remained relatively common). A vital part of the role of the state, in cooperation with industrial associations, was to overcome these barriers to the flow of ideas.

In some cases, ministries like MITI stepped in directly, setting up committees, think-tanks or research groups to spread technological know-how. The government also made use of public corporations like NHK (Nippon Hôsô Kyôkai, the Japan Broadcasting Corporation) and NTT (Nippon Telegraph and Telephone, Nihon Denden Kôsha) to act as intermediaries in the transmission of technological ideas from one private enterprise to another. In many instances, the government worked in tandem with the voluntary but influential industrial associations which exist throughout the Japanese economy, helping to shape each industry into a *gyôkai*, a body with a consciousness of its own identity. The public research laboratories also made their technical know-how available to private firms, and sometimes organised informal discussion groups with corporate technicians to exchange ideas on leading-edge technologies. In the early 1950s, for example, the Electrical Research Laboratory (later to be renamed the Electro-Technical Research Institute) set up a committee including leading corporate and university scientists to promote Japanese work on the new technology of transistors.[72] Meanwhile, local government and local research laboratories, together with regional industrial cooperatives and the Small and Medium Enterprise Agency, were helping to disseminate new technological ideas amongst the mass of small-scale manufacturing firms throughout Japan.

Two important points need to be made about this exchange of ideas amongst government agencies and Japanese companies. The first is that it only occasionally involved the 'transfer of technology' in the normal sense of the word: that is the transmission of the entire complement of know-how necessary to make a new product. Much more often, think-tanks and discussion groups provided a forum for exchanging views on the general direction of technological change, while allowing individual companies to maintain their own corporate secrets.

This helped individual companies to keep in touch with the latest developments in their field, and to keep a close eye on the technological strategies of their competitors, while at the same time promoting fierce technological competition between participating firms.

The second point is that the exchange of technological ideas took place within certain clearly defined social circles. Central and local government and industry associations encouraged the flow of technological knowledge between the bureaucracy, public research laboratories and private enterprise, but had no interest in involving outsiders such as consumer groups or trade unions in the process. As a result, the exchange of technological ideas came to be bounded by a particular mind-set: one which saw innovation as a source of rapid economic growth and of increasing competitive strength on world markets. It took the environmental disasters and protest movements of the late 1960s to force government and enterprise to take a wider view of the social implications of technological change.

It should also be said that the very factors which explain Japan's success in some technological fields also seem to account for its relative weakness in others. The dispersed, flexible structure of the innovation network, which proved such an advantage in areas like electronics, was a considerable liability in those high-technology areas (like nuclear energy and space research) which demanded single, nationwide development projects and large, centralised research institutions. This will become evident in the next chapter, when we go on to look in detail at 'national projects' like Japan's fast breeder reactor and space programs (see pp. 229-39).

These strengths and weaknesses in Japan's social network of innovation can best be understood by looking at the system in action. A few case studies of particular areas of technological change will help to evoke the dynamics of the system and put flesh on the bones of the analysis which we have just outlined.

Shipbuilding

Shipbuilding was the quintessential heavy industry of the high-growth era. During the 1950s and 1960s Japan's growing stature as an industrial power was marked, not just by the upward curve on the graph of GNP, but also by periodic celebrations surrounding the launch of ever larger and larger ships: 20,000-ton tankers in the early 1950s, 45,000-ton tankers in the late 50s, and the 132,000-ton *Nissho Maru* (among the largest vessels in the world at that time) in 1962.[73]

The industry was one of the key areas singled out for government attention from the early postwar period onwards. Wartime destruction had left Japan with an acute shortage of merchant shipping, and the building up of a new fleet was essential to the country's re-entry into the world economy. Government assistance to shipbuilders took the form of preferential access to foreign exchange, cheap loans and a range of financial subsidies, many of them designed to see the industry through its periodic recessions. By the 1960s, rapidly growing world trade had made shipbuilding a major growth industry, and the state's main concern was to increase economies of scale by encouraging mergers between leading shipyards. By 1976 this had resulted in the emergence of seven very large shipbuilders, alongside sixteen medium-sized firms and more than one hundred small firms.[74] In 1965 Japan was producing over 65 per cent of the world's shipping tonnage.[75]

The rapid rise of the postwar Japanese shipbuilding industry was supported by several important innovations. In terms of design, scientific analysis enabled larger vessels to be constructed and production planning to be streamlined. In terms of the production process itself, structural welding replaced the use of rivets, and the introduction of the 'block' construction system led to great increases in productivity.[76] Under the 'block' system, ships were not built as a whole from the keel up, but were constructed in separate sections which were then fitted together. This allowed work to proceed much more quickly, and prevented delays in one part of the production system from bringing the entire project to a halt.

As in most postwar industries, the key innovations came from overseas, though in shipbuilding they arrived by a somewhat unusual route. When shipping began to revive in the immediate postwar years, a number of US shipbuilders started to look overseas for shipyards with excess capacity which would allow rapid expansion. Among them was the National Bulk Carrier company (NBC), which in 1951 took out a lease on the former Japanese navy dockyard at Kure. In granting the lease, however, the Japanese government insisted that Japanese engineers were to be given unrestricted access to the shipyards to study the techniques in use.[77] In a process reminiscent of the building of Putiatin's sailing ship in 1855, the foreign venture therefore provided the basis for a technical leap forward in Japanese shipbuilding technology.

The acquisition of welding and block construction know-how from NBC, however, was only the beginning of the story. Japanese engineers used the imported innovations as the basis for a series of domestic modifications and improvements, including the development of one-sided automatic welding (replacing the traditional welding method in which the seam had to be welded from both sides) and Electro Print Marking (which allowed design markings to be photographically printed on sheet metal). Productivity was also increased by the widespread introduction of numerically controlled (NC) machinery into shipbuilding in the late 1960s.[78]

A key factor in the development and spread of these innovations was the role of a number of powerful industry associations, particularly the Nihon Zôsen Kenkyû Kyôkai (Japan Shipbuilding Research Association) which, from 1952 onwards, brought company technicians, university researchers and government research laboratories together to study a range of key issues in shipbuilding technology. Between 1952 and 1971, the association set up nine separate research projects, with the results of each project being made freely available to member companies.[79] These projects did not supplant research by individual shipbuilders, but aimed to chart the course of major long-term innovations, while allowing member companies to compete in refining and applying the fruits of joint research.

The association, together with the Japanese Ministry of Transport (Unyu Shô) also served as a go-between in creating technical links between shipbuilding and other industries. One of the greatest early barriers to the spread of the new welding techniques was that, to be reliable, they needed new forms of sheet steel. In 1950 therefore, the association and the Transport Ministry established a steel research group to tackle the problem. This involved researchers from universities and state research laboratories, as well as from the leading steel and shipbuilding companies. The result was the development of a low-carbon steel with a high manganese content, excellently suited to the needs of the shipyards.[80]

The dispersed structure of the Japanese research system made it relatively easy for steel companies to set up similar short-term research programs with a wide range of other industries in order to solve specific technical problems. The Electro Print Marking process, for example, was the result of a joint research project between Mitsubishi Heavy Industries, Fuji Film, and the Kônan Camera Research Laboratory.[81] Less formal technical cooperation was also encouraged by the fact that almost all of Japan's shipbuilding technicians had graduated from one of the eight universities offering major courses in marine engineering. Old-boy networks therefore served as links both between private companies and the universities, and between engineers in the various shipyards.[82]

Steel

In the history of technology, as in economics, everything is connected to everything else. The development of shipbuilding technology encouraged innovations in steel production, but developments in steel technology in turn supported the process of innovation in a wide range of other industries, including shipbuilding and car production. The reconstruction of Japan's war-damaged steel furnaces, and the rapid expansion of the late 1950s and 1960s, occurred at a period of particularly radical change in the steel technology, enabling Japan to incorporate the latest techniques into its postwar production system. The result was a remarkably rapid rise in productivity. In 1960 the Japanese steel industry was only half as productive (in terms of hours of labour per ton of steel) as its European counterpart, and one-third as productive as the US steel industry; by the early 1980s, Japan's productivity had increased more than fivefold, overtaking both Europe and the United States.[83]

The technological changes underlying this surge in productivity can be divided into three groups. First, there were changes in the smelting process itself. Here the key innovation was the basic oxygen process, developed in Austria in the early 1950s. This process used pure oxygen rather than air to convert molten iron into steel. Its advantage was that it was economical, highly productive, and could handle a wide range of raw materials and produce a wide range of different types of steel.[84] Its main disadvantage, on the other hand, was that it produced large amounts of smoke and dust pollution.[85] The second area of change concerned the conversion of molten steel into saleable products. Important developments in this field were the introduction of strip mills, which produced thin sheet steel suitable for postwar civilian industries, and the continuous casting process, which greatly reduced the consumption of energy in the making of cast steel products.[86] Thirdly, the growth of the postwar steel industry was accompanied by the development of new forms of special steel for purposes like shipbuilding and aircraft manufacture, and by improvements in the testing and preparation of raw materials (resulting in higher-quality and more reliable steel).[87]

Leonard Lynn, in his careful study of the introduction of the basic oxygen process, argues that the rapid spread of this new technology in Japan was not just a result of a happy coincidence: not just, in other words, a consequence of the fact that the technology appeared at a time when the Japanese industry was expanding rapidly. Instead, he suggests that there were several aspects of the Japanese industrial structure which made Japanese firms quick to seize on the new technique. For one thing, the Japanese steel industry was made up of a number of firms of roughly equal size and structure, so that technology suitable to one firm could readily be adopted by another. This contrasted with the situation in the United States, where a couple of very large firms coexisted with numerous smaller or medium-sized companies. Lynn also emphasises the importance of the Japanese business groups (*kigyô shûdan*) in the spread of new techniques. The postwar groups, like their prewar ancestors the *zaibatsu*, generally included a large trading company (*sôgô shôsha*) which often handled the sales of goods produced by member companies. The trading firms, with their excellent international networks, played an important part in scouting out promising foreign technologies, and in establishing the connections which enabled manufacturing firms to negotiate for the import of those technologies.[88]

The case of the basic oxygen steel process also illustrates the importance of the flow of information, both within the steel industry itself and between the steel producers and other related industries. Lynn suggests that, in the early days, Japanese steel firms had *less* ready access to information about the new technology than their US counterparts. In the United States, widely read technical journals published by the professional associations quickly brought news of innovations to the attention of the leading steel firms. The flow of information between Japanese engineers was at first more uncertain. In 1955, however, two Japanese companies, Nippon Kôkan and Yawata Steel, began to show interest in obtaining licences for the basic oxygen process. The Ministry of International Trade and Industry, which was approached by the companies for the necessary foreign exchange clearance, chose to broker an arrangement whereby one firm, Nippon Kôkan, would be the principal licensee, but would also be able to sublicense the technology to all other Japanese steel producers. As part of the arrangement a special body, the Basic Oxygen Technique Committee, was set up in 1956, and from then on acted with missionary zeal to spread knowledge of the new technology throughout the steel industry. The committee, which was later absorbed into the Iron and Steel Institute of Japan (Nihon Tekkô Kyôkai), held regular meetings to exchange information on the implementation of the basic oxygen process, and provided the basis for a network of more informal personal contacts between engineers involved in the introduction of the technology.[89]

While the committee acted as a node for the diffusion and exchange of basic information on the innovation, individual companies competed to refine and improve the imported technique. One of the main problems with the basic oxygen process, for example, was that the bricks used to line the converters wore out very quickly. In Japan, this problem was overcome by a cooperative research project between Yawata Steel and a relatively small refractory brick-making company, Kurosaki, which developed a new form of brick specially suited to the new converters.[90] This sort of cooperation was nothing new. In 1951, for example, MITI, together with two industrial associations—the Japan Iron and Steel Federation (Nippon Tekkô Renmei) and the Refractory Brick Association (Taika Renga Kyôkai)—had set up a research association to develop locally made substitutes for the high-quality bricks imported from overseas.[91]

In steel as in shipbuilding, therefore, the key to rapid technological change was a system which allowed the ready exchange of information between companies on the overall directions of development, while at the same time allowing firms to conduct their own competitive research into methods of improving the basic innovations. Because research capacity was widely dispersed across many industries, it was possible for steel firms to work with technicians in other industries in areas where a combination of different skills was necessary. These links, both between the steel firms themselves and between the steel producers and ancillary industries, were nurtured by central government, industry associations, and a variety of semi-official, semi-private organisations set up with their help.

From Television to Video

Japan's striking successes in the development of television and videos depended on a pattern of communication and competition very similar to that of the shipbuilding and steel industries. As far as the communication of ideas was concerned, a key role in the early stages of both technologies was played by the state-owned broadcaster, NHK. Basic technologies pioneered by NHK's research laboratories were passed on to private firms, who competed vigorously in developing them. We have already seen that Japanese interest in the development of television dated back to the 1920s (see p. 113). Immediately after the war, the original pioneer of the field, Toshiba, became the only private company permitted by the Occupation authorities to continue television research (presumably as a reward for its long-standing links with powerful US enterprises). During the late 1940s Toshiba and NHK began joint research into basic television technology, and a number of experimental transmissions were staged to test and demonstrate the potential of TV broadcasting.[92]

By the time that full-scale public broadcasting began in 1953, corporate interest in television manufacture was so great that more than fifty companies applied for the necessary government clearance to import television technology from the United States or Britain, a number which MITI eventually cut down to thirty-five.[93] These included relatively small, specialised newcomers like Sony and Akai, as well as established electrical firms like Hitachi, Toshiba and Matsushita.

Interestingly enough, in some of the older giants such as Hitachi there was considerable reluctance amongst top management to enter this new field, and the cause of television was pushed by individual researchers, who initiated unauthorised research projects and used their results to lobby management on behalf of the new technology. This bottom-up form of development seems to have been repeated across a number of industries in postwar Japan. Lynn, for example, describes a similar process in the adoption of basic oxygen steelmaking by Nippon Kôkan.[94]

For many companies, the development of television production involved a step-by-step process of domesticating imported technology. At first, most parts were imported from the US and merely assembled in Japan, but gradually local production took over from import. As this happened, indigenous modifications were incorporated into the imported technology. One exception to the general rule was Sony, which from the first concentrated on developing its own, more fundamental variations of imported technology. In 1960 it launched the world's first fully transistorised television set. Although this was more expensive than conventional valve-operated sets, its small size made it a best-seller in Japan (where space in living-rooms was at a premium) and the Sony TV set came to be one of the first products to establish the notion of miniaturisation (rather than large size) as a status symbol in home electronics.

In the mid-1960s, as the technology of colour television reached Japan, Sony's strategy again diverged from that of other Japanese manufacturers, most of whom chose to rely on techniques licensed from RCA. Sony's more risky goal was to commercialise an alternative technique (known as 'Chromatron') developed by a subsidiary of Paramount, which produced very high-quality pictures but was technically extremely complex. After several years' research, it became evident that the Chromatron technology was unsuitable for mass-produced televisions. By this time, however, Sony had fallen far behind rivals like Toshiba and Matsushita in the race to market colour televisions. The Sony management therefore decided to gamble on pursuing an independent line, attempting to develop its own technology to replicate the best features of the Chromatron system. The result was Trinitron, a distinctive technique in which the three basic colour beams were emitted from a single source, rather than from three separate sources, producing a brighter and sharper picture.[95]

As the industry began to move into the production of colour televisions in the 1960s, the question of parts production became a particularly crucial one. A colour television set contains about 1000 parts, whose cost and reliability are crucial to the success of the finished products. Although most television-makers set up their own factories making television tubes, transistors, and later integrated circuits, many also nurtured the development of a mass of small subcontracting companies specialising in particular electronic components. Hitachi's Shibahara factory, for example, soon gathered around it a collection of little 'satellite companies', most concentrating on a narrow range of electronic parts and components.[96] The parent companies provided technical assistance to their more important suppliers, and sometimes took part in joint research projects with them.

At the same time, many of these subcontracting companies also had access to technical advice and ideas through the regional networks created by local industrial associations and local government research laboratories. Nagano Prefecture's Precision Machinery Research Laboratory was just one of a host of regional organisations which offered contract research, technical training and consultancy services to electronic parts producers.[97] Among the numerous beneficiaries was Sankyô Precision Works, a little local firm which started up in 1946 with a staff of ten. During the late 1940s and the 1950s, Sankyô developed a flourishing business manufacturing musical boxes, using the delicate manual dexterity of woman workers from the vanishing silk industry, and by the early 1970s it had extended its skills in miniaturisation into the more technically complex field of precision machine parts and miniature motors.[98] Although Sankyô achieved an unusually rapid rate of growth, its humble origins were typical of the 6000-odd component producers whose existence was to prove vital to new developments in the electronics industry during the 1970s and 1980s.[99]

The success of television was not, of course, simply a matter of hardware. The mass domestic market for television sets reflected both the growing prosperity of Japanese consumers and the ability of Japanese television companies to devise programs which attracted huge audiences. Like other areas of technological development, this was the product of trial and error, of import and adaptation. Protected by the language barrier, Japanese television was not swamped by US or European programs. Although shows like *Rawhide* and *Laramie* were among the popular favourites in the early 1960s,[1] there was plenty of scope for the creation of distinctively Japanese programs. Semi-realistic soap operas, which appeared during the early days of television, became a vehicle for interpreting social change. The drama series *Mukô sanken ryôtonari* (*Our Neighbourhood*), first shown in 1957, deliberately set out to explore the 'democratisation of the Japanese family'.[2] On the other hand, popular costume dramas, and the brief segments on traditional seasonal festivals which have become a regular feature of Japanese news broadcasts, created a carefully crafted window through which millions of urban Japanese saw their own past. The success of the public and commercial broadcasters in creating at least a partial substitute for vanishing communal forms of entertainment turned Japan into the ultimate TV culture. By the early 1980s there were more than 150 television sets for every 100 Japanese households.[3]

The innovation to benefit most directly from this legacy of television was the video recorder. Work on the development of video tape recorders (VTRs) was begun in the 1950s by (amongst others) the American television manufacturer RCA and the British Broadcasting Corporation, but the first commercial success was a video recorder designed for use by television broadcasters, which was launched onto the market in 1956 by the US firm Ampex.[4] By this time a few Japanese pioneers such as Sony had already begun their own research into VTRs, but they were still a long way from producing a marketable version.

Soon after the launch of the Ampex video, however, the national broadcaster NHK began applying to MITI for foreign exchange to buy equipment from Ampex, and this alerted the Japanese government to the potential importance of video. In 1958, on MITI's initiative, the VTR Discussion Group (VTR Kondankai) was set up, bringing together technicians from NHK, the leading makers of electrical appliances, the private broadcasting companies and other research centres. The discussion group served to coordinate negotiations for the import of foreign technology, and to define the main directions for basic VTR research within Japan, laying the foundations for the successful commercialisation of video from the late 1960s onwards.[5] Meanwhile, NHK's research laboratory was also carrying out its own research into video technology, and providing technical assistance and conducting joint projects with selected private firms (including Sony, Matsushita, Canon and Mitsubishi Electric).[6]

The existence of the VTR Discussion Group helped Japanese firms to coordinate their basic research strategies (for example, to focus on producing small, light video recorders for domestic use), but at the same time it made individual companies acutely aware of their rivals' interest in the technology, so encouraging intense competition between firms in developing and marketing their own VTR models. The fiercest competition came to be between the group of companies (led by Sony) which opted to develop Beta format machines, and the group (including most notably Matsushita) which chose the VHS format: a battle which was ultimately won by the VHS producers, as much because of successful marketing tactics as for any technical reasons.

The speed with which Japanese companies gained control of the world VTR market reflected, not only the effective flow of information between the main producers, but also the ability of the video-makers to draw on their experience in several distinct technological areas. Video technology was essentially a composite technology, requiring know-how both in the fields of magnetic recording and of image transmission. Many of the Japanese video producers already had experience as manufacturers of television and tape-recorders, and were successful in putting together video research teams which made use of their expertise in both areas.[7] Matsushita, for example, could create a team which included researchers from its electronics laboratory, its wireless research laboratory and its materials laboratory, as well as from the Matsushita Central Research Laboratory.[8] Equally important was the existence of that multitude of specialist parts producers which had evolved in response to the needs of television manufacture. Sankyô, the maker of musical boxes, was by now a large electronics firm with over 2000 employees and numerous subcontractors of its own; it provided the necessary expertise in the production of miniature motors, which it supplied to Sony, Hitachi, Matsushita and other leading VTR producers.[9] Other television subcontractors contributed know-how in the making of condensers and cylinder heads, or in producing specialised machine tools to manufacture VTR parts.[10] The combination of energetic competition between individual VTR makers and rapid flows of information amongst competitors (together with the exchange of information between manufacturers and their subcontractors) helped the Japanese industry to acquire a dominant position in foreign, as well as home, markets. By 1985, over 80 per cent of all video recorders were produced by Japanese companies or their overseas affiliates.[11]

Computers

The more scientifically complex the technology, the more important was the flow of information between universities, government research laboratories and private industry. In areas like computing, a particularly crucial role was played by those semi-official industry groups which formed the nodes in the social network of innovation.

Japan had been isolated from the crucial wartime developments which had laid the foundations of computer technology in Europe and the United States. For many Japanese scientists, therefore, news of the advent of the computer age arrived in the form of a *Newsweek* article of February 1946, announcing the completion of ENIAC (the first US computer, constructed by engineers at the University of Pennsylvania in 1945). Computing excited considerable interest in Japan, and by 1952 three Japanese computers had been designed: one at Osaka University, one by an engineer from the Fuji Film company, and one by a research team from Toshiba and the University of Tokyo.[12] Japan's expertise in the field, however, remained far behind that of the United States and Britain. After all, most early US and European computers were created to serve the needs of the military for complex ballistic calculations. In the immediate postwar period, however, Japan, with its peace constitution, had little need for such high-level military mathematics, and Japan's early computers were built either from scientific curiosity or to serve other industrial purposes. (For example, FUJIC, the Fuji Film computer, was designed to automate the complex calculations involved in the making of lenses.[13])

During the 1950s the government-run Electro-Technical Laboratory played an important role in promoting computer research, but Japanese technology was still far too weak to have any real hope of competing commercially with emerging US computer companies like the giant IBM. This company controlled many of the key computer patents, and its Japanese subsidiary, established in 1950, was already making rapid inroads into the Japanese market.[14] Besides, the development of computing in Japan was affected by an interesting but ultimately unsuccessful attempt to commercialise a truly original indigenous innovation. In 1954 Gôtô Eiichi, a young researcher at Tokyo University, had combined a ferrite magnetic core with a condenser to create an electronic device which he called the 'parametron'. This could be used in place of valves in electronic equipment such as computers, and since valve failure was the main source of computer breakdowns, Gôtô's invention attracted considerable interest from Japanese computer researchers. Public research bodies like the laboratories of Nippon Telegraph and Telephone, as well as private companies like Hitachi, devoted substantial resources to developing parametron-based computers, which were indeed more reliable than their valve-based counterparts. Meanwhile, however, the parametron was being overtaken by the development of transistors, whose high speed made them better suited to the large-scale computers of the 1960s.[15]

By the mid-1950s, both government and business were becoming seriously concerned that, without active support, the Japanese computer industry might never get off the ground. As a result, an Electronic Computer Investigation Committee (Denshi Keisanki Chôsa Iinkai), bringing together representatives of industry, academia and public research laboratories, was set up in 1956 to examine the state of the industry in Japan and the USA.[16] With funding from MITI and the Japanese car industry, the committee conducted a two-year study of worldwide computing trends, and its findings helped to set a pattern which was to characterise the development of Japanese computer technology for the next two decades. One element in this pattern was a series of cooperative projects, organised either by industry associations or by MITI, which enabled the major computer firms to share know-how and define the directions of future research. A second element—coexisting rather than conflicting with the first—was an intense rivalry between the commercial programs of individual firms: a rivalry sustained by technical tie-ups with western (mostly US) companies. All of this activity took place within the nurturing environment which MITI created through its policies of support and protection for the computer and electronics industry.

The first major cooperative research program was set up on the initiative of the Japan Electronics Industry Promotion Association (Nihon Denshi Kôgyô Shinkô Kyôkai), an industry body established in 1958. Their plan, a little reminiscent of the much later Fifth-generation Computer Project (see p. 215) involved joint research by Tokyo University and leading electronics companies (including NEC, Toshiba, Oki Electric and Fuji Communications), with each company being responsible for particular areas of research. The project received financial support under MITI's newly introduced Electronics Industry Law, but its economic and technical resources were always too small to have much prospect of success. Although it laid a basis for further developments by the private firms involved, it failed to produce a commercially usable system.[17]

Other aspects of the association's work, however, had greater results. Its Electronic Computer Centre (Denshi Keisanki Sentâ), opened in the autumn of 1958, provided a showcase for the latest in Japanese computer technology, as well as a maintaining a library of software and running training courses for programmers. The association's Patent Investigation Committee also became involved in examining and collecting data on foreign computer patents, and its careful scrutiny revealed a number of anomalies which enabled Japanese firms to challenge some crucial patents in the US courts.[18]

MITI, too, played a direct and active role in securing access to foreign patents and in establishing joint research programs by Japanese companies. In 1960 it used its foreign exchange control powers as a bargaining lever to persuade IBM to license its major patents to Japanese firms and (as in the case of the steel industry) ensured that this know-how was distributed to all the major Japanese computer makers.[19] During the 1960s and 1970s a series of MITI-sponsored research projects endeavoured to force the pace of innovation in Japanese computing. Few of these achieved their stated objectives, but they did serve to create a shared pool of know-how on which individual firms were later able to build their own, much more successful, development programs. The FONTAC project of 1962, for example, was an unsuccessful joint effort by a team of researchers from Fujitsu,

NEC and Oki to create a Japanese rival to IBM's 1401 computer series,[20] while the Super High-Performance Computer Project—one of the first schemes to be launched under the new National Research and Development Program—involved collaborative research by Japan's six main computer companies (Hitachi, Fujitsu, NEC, Toshiba, Mitsubishi Electric and Oki) with support from the Electro-Technical Laboratory. As one US scholar notes, although this project produced no commercial computer system, it 'spurred the industry to make technological headway in integrated circuits and high-speed memory',[21] so paving the way for later commercial successes in the 1970s and 1980s.

From the point of view of the computer manufacturers, cooperative research projects provided expertise which enabled them to make better use of the foreign know-how which they obtained through tie-ups with US firms. During the early 1960s each of the major Japanese players formed technological links with one or more foreign companies: Hitachi, for example, signed licensing arrangements with RCA, Oki with Sperry Rand, and Toshiba with General Electric.[22] The joint projects sponsored by MITI and the Electronics Industry Promotion Association gave these companies an improved capacity to absorb this foreign know-how and adapt it to the demands of the Japanese market. By the end of the decade, the major Japanese computer makers were competing to market their own mainframe systems, in which imported know-how had been adapted to deal with problems like the high-speed handling of Japanese phonetic script (*katakana*).[23]

MITI's role in relation to computer technology was not limited to supporting joint research. The Ministry was also keen to encourage all sectors of Japanese industry to adopt the use of computers, so at once promoting 'rationalisation' and expanding the market for domestic computer makers. In 1961, it acted as midwife to the birth of the Japan Electronic Computer Company (JECC, Nihon Denshi Keisanki), an enterprise jointly formed by the main computer manufacturers to lease Japanese-made computers to customers at low cost. With the help of government subsidies, JECC was to play a vital role in seizing back control of the Japanese market from IBM and other foreign competitors.[24] In 1960 Japanese companies had produced only 27 per cent of the computers sold or leased within Japan itself, but by 1970 their share had soared to 60 per cent.[25]

NC Machinery

Japan's growing strength in computer technology was important not only in its own right, but also because computers held the key to other emerging techniques: most notably the techniques of factory

automation, which combined the use of computers with the automation of machine tools. Numerical control—allowing the full
automation of machine tools—was originally invented by a subcontrac-
tor to the US Airforce and developed during the early 1950s by the
Airforce in cooperation with the Massachusetts Institute of Technology
(MIT). The MIT system allowed programs to be encoded onto tape and
used to control the movements of milling machines and other tools.[26]
Knowledge of the technique, in the form of an MIT report, was brought
to Japan by Takahashi Yasuhito, a Japanese professor then employed at
the University of California, and was publicised through an industry
research group, the Automatic Control Research Association (Jidô
Seigyo Kenkyûkai). Like the Japan Shipping Research Association and
the Electronics Industry Promotion Association, this body was an
important channel for the diffusion of information on new technology.
The concept of NC was then quickly picked up by a number of public
research bodies, including Tokyo Institute of Technology, Tokyo
University and the government's Mechanical Technology Research
Laboratory (Kikai Gijutsu Kenkyûjo), which conducted their own
research programs as well as running joint study groups with interested
private companies.[27]

The first company to undertake serious research on the technology
was Fujitsu, which was looking for ways to extend its existing base in the
communications industry. A research team led by one of the company's
most talented engineers began a process of absorbing and experimenting with the information contained in the MIT report, and by
1956 Fujitsu had produced its very first prototype NC machine tool (a
turret punch press) which it proudly exhibited to potential customers
and academic researchers.[28]

The Fujitsu machine was still far too unreliable to be put to practical
use, but the company's work on NC technology attracted the interest of
one of Japan's more innovative machine tool companies, Makino, who
invited them to join a research project combining Fujitsu's electronics
expertise with Makino's specialised skills in the production of milling
machinery. The result was an NC milling machine which was first
displayed at a major industrial exhibition held in Osaka in April 1958
(though faults in its electronic system meant that it had to be whisked
away to a backroom for repairs half way through its first public
appearance).[29] Despite its embarrassing breakdowns, the Fujitsu–
Makino machine aroused great curiosity amongst other Japanese
companies, and was the forerunner to Japan's first commercially usable
NC machine, which was developed jointly by Fujitsu, Hitachi and
Mitsubishi Heavy Industry for use in Mitsubishi's Nagoya aircraft
factory.[30]

By this time Japanese companies were beginning to go beyond the mere replication of ideas from MIT. In the construction of their milling machine, Fujitsu and Makino had already confronted design problems not dealt with by the original MIT report. In the late 1950s Fanuc, the new company which Fujitsu had set up to develop NC machinery, began to work on more fundamental variations to the US design. One of these (developed jointly with Hitachi) was an open loop system which greatly simplified the control mechanism of the machinery.[31] Another was the incorporation of the latest electronic developments into the equipment.[32] As Japanese companies such as Fujitsu, Matsushita and Sony absorbed new technological developments, first in transistors and then in integrated circuits from the United States, so it became possible for NC machinery to become less cumbersome and more reliable. Just as Sony had been quick to spot the commercial potential of the transistor, so now in the 1960s Fujitsu recognised the potential of the integrated circuit, first produced in the United States in 1959.

By 1966 Fanuc had become the first company in the world to market an NC machine tool using integrated circuits, and this was to prove crucial, because it was the cost reductions resulting from the use of the new microelectronic circuits which made NC machinery cheap enough to reach a wide range of companies.[33] Fanuc's own research program was accompanied and strengthened by an active program of technology import, including the acquisition, in the early 1970s, of servomotor technology from the US specialist Getty.[34]

When we compare the history of NC technology in Japan and the United States, a number of clear contrasts stand out. In the US, NC machinery was first produced in response to the needs of the military. This meant that emphasis was placed on the development of highly sophisticated hardware and software, and designers had (in David Noble's words) 'little concern with cost effectiveness and absolutely no incentive to produce less expensive machinery for the commercial market'.[35] Although the US was the pioneer in the field, ordinary manufacturers were therefore slow to make use of NC machinery, and the impact of the innovation was less dramatic than it was in Japan.

In the Japanese case, on the other hand, companies like Fujitsu and Makino worked from the start with the commercial market in mind. The development of NC technology was supported, not by outstanding leading-edge know-how of the sort supplied by the Massachusetts Institute of Technology, but by the steady though less spectacular parallel progress of the various technologies needed for NC production: machine tool technology, microelectronics and computing. By the late 1960s the technology was beginning to enter a new phase: the era of direct numerical control (DNC), where several machines would be linked directly to computers rather than being operated by paper tape or other prerecorded programs. At this point MITI started to play an active part in bringing the relevant know-how together, setting up a research group including leading machine tool and computer companies and the government-controlled Mechanical Technology Research Laboratory. With funding support from the Ministry, the group worked on a series of DNC machine tools, accumulating know-how which was to provide the basis for the factory automation of the 1970s and 1980s.[36]

The flow of technological information in Japan was important, not only in terms of production but also in terms of consumption. Bodies like the Small and Medium Enterprise Agency and the Machine Tool Industrial Association spread the word about the new technique, encouraging even quite small manufacturers to introduce NC machinery. During the 1970s prefectural research laboratories and local industrial associations began to run seminars and publish information on the technology, while organisations like local chambers of commerce, local government, or the central government's technical assistance schemes for small firms (initiated in 1967) often provided financial support for the purchase or loan of NC machines.[37]

At the same time, parent companies frequently encouraged subcontractors to adopt automated equipment, and the spread of the new machine tools was also helped by trends in the wider economy. The rapid growth of the 1960s had exhausted the pool of underemployed labour which had once existed in Japanese agriculture, and labour costs rose sharply throughout the late 1960s and early 70s. For small firms, who now found that they could no longer pay wages which were significantly lower than those of their larger counterparts, automation provided a logical solution. By 1970, Japanese companies had invested some ¥2 billion in NC machinery, less than a third of that investment coming from small firms: by 1974 the figure had risen to almost ¥5 billion, and about half of the investment was accounted for by small firms.[38] The foundations, in short, had already been laid for Japan's emergence as a world leader in the age of robotics and the automated factory.

Technology, Society and the Environment

The new age, however, would also be one in which technological progress itself became a topic of new questioning. For, at the very moment when Japanese industry seemed in sight of its long-held ambition—catching up with 'the west'—aspects of industrial technology which had long been ignored began to force themselves on the attention of managers and technicians.

When Ôshima Takatô constructed Japan's first blast furnace in 1858, the little town of Kamaishi, where the furnace was built, was famous for its fisheries. Its offshore waters teamed with tuna and bonito and its rivers with salmon which swam upstream every year to spawn in the clear mountain headwaters above Kamaishi Bay. In 1882 local fishermen recorded catches which included 19,530 tuna and 141,000 river salmon. As the steelworks expanded under private ownership from the 1880s onwards, however, the environment of Kamaishi began to change. Timber was cut from the surrounding mountains to fuel the early charcoal-fired furnaces, causing soil erosion and siltation of the river. Later, as the furnaces shifted to coal, increasing amounts of effluent were released into the waterways, adding to their burden of pollution. By the early 1930s, the effects on the fish stocks were severe enough to arouse protests from the local community, but these were easily contained by the managers of the steelworks, who were not only the major local employers but also a powerful force in municipal politics. By the late 1960s the annual migration of the salmon had ceased, and river fishing was only maintained with the help of tons of fish fry shipped in from Lake Biwa on the other side of Japan.[39]

The same story was repeated in steel towns throughout Japan. In Yawata, where the great state-owned steelworks had been opened in 1901, signs of serious water pollution had appeared by the time of the First World War. As pollution and land reclamation gradually devoured the local fishing industry, the steelworks was repeatedly persuaded to pay compensation to fishing families, but the modest sums of compensation were small recompense to people who had lost their livelihood, their skills and their traditions. By the 1960s the seas surrounding Yawata were virtually lifeless, and the fishing industry had vanished. One old fisherman who, as a schoolboy, had stood amongst the crowds celebrating the ceremonial opening of Yawata Steel, observed that the growth and development of the steelworks had served the interests of the nation well, but that 'with the development of the Japanese nation, and the development of this region, it is us fishermen who have become the victims'.[40]

As the stories of Kamaishi and Yawata show, the heavy costs of rapid technological change were apparent throughout Japan's industrial history. From the Meiji period onward, industrialisation had imposed massive burdens on the human workforce and the natural environment, and had provoked repeated protests, large and small, from those who bore a disproportionate share of the burden. The environmental crisis of the late 1960s, then, was not something new or unforeseen. Rather, it was a consequence of the whole way in which technology had come to be understood and controlled in Japanese society. The postwar network of technology was underpinned by a social vision which was, for the most part, so pervasive as to be taken for granted. According to this vision, the aim of the game was to assimilate existing technological know-how as quickly as possible, and use that know-how to produce highly competitive commercial products as cheaply as possible. Because the network of groups involved in the shaping of technology was relatively narrow, there was little opportunity for this underlying vision to be questioned or challenged. The channels which so effectively conveyed technological information between the bureaucracy, public research bodies and private companies provided no scope for the exchange of ideas between enterprises and the local residents most severely affected by environmental damage; and although quality-control circles gave the workforce a voice in the process of technical change, their scope was severely limited. They encouraged workers to offer suggestions on increasing productivity, but had no concern with suggestions which might have improved the working or living environment unless these also translated into tangible increases in profit.

The challenge to the prevailing vision of technological change therefore came, not from within the social network of innovation itself, but from outsiders: small groups of farmers, fishermen, shopkeepers or factory-workers, with women often playing a prominent role as organisers and activists. These groups were supported by a handful of dissident technicians and engineers who were disillusioned by their own experiences in conventional research.

The case of Yawata was a typical one. Water pollution was not the only problem facing the local residents. The steelworks, like many other large industrial enterprises, also darkened the skies with their noxious smoke and gases. One elderly resident, interviewed in the 1970s, recalled the prewar summers when she had eaten her lunch out of doors, and soon found her rice covered with speckles of black soot from the steelworks.[41] Postwar expansion and technological changes only intensified the problems of air pollution, while the establishment of new chemical factories and the coming of the motor car added to the brew of poisonous emissions. In 1961, four years after it had introduced the new basic oxygen technology, Yawata steel was depositing 27 tons of particulate matter per day on the surrounding districts.[42] Surveys conducted around this time showed exceptionally high levels of respiratory disease amongst the local schoolchildren. However, in a town where the steelworks not only provided most of the jobs but also financed the hospital, several schools, the fire station and the community hall, few were prepared to take a stand. In the end it was a group of local women, many of them mothers of young children, who became the spearhead of the Yawata anti-pollution movement, educating themselves about the technical causes of pollution, making films and conducting surveys which pressured officialdom into taking action.[43]

As this story suggests, anti-pollution movements were often the products of a long gestation. They reflected a gradual recognition by local people that the costs of rapid technological change were not just temporary inconveniences. High growth and rapid industrialisation had, of course, brought many improvements to the lives of ordinary people. Health standards and education had improved dramatically, and new consumer industries had filled the average Japanese house with a mass of cheap, good-quality electrical appliances: washing machines, refrigerators, televisions and vacuum cleaners (see Figure 7.4). The stories of rapidly industrialising areas like Yawata need to be balanced against those of more remote rural areas, where the coming of electricity, telephone, television, piped water and sealed roads had reduced the burden of farm work and widened social horizons. British sociologist Ronald Dore, who conducted research in a small Japanese village in the 1950s, returned in the 1970s to find it transformed almost beyond recognition:

> When I left in 1956 I sold my somewhat decrepit motor-scooter to my host. That made him, apart from two or three young men who commuted to jobs outside the village on motor-bikes, the most mobile farmer in the hamlet ... Now, nearly every house in the village, except those where there is only a single old couple left, have a car and either a small 500-cc truck or a 9–12 horsepower two-wheeled multi-purpose unit which can be used as a walkbehind tiller for the rice fields or hitched to a trailer with seats on ... Overhead, the single low-power line of 1955 has given place to a mass of wires—a new power system on tall concrete posts to feed the hamlet's profusion of electrical appliances, the wires of the Co-op telephone system and the hamlet broadcasting system leading to every house.[44]

It is surely true, as Dore observes, that most of those who can remember prewar poverty 'revel in their new-found comforts',[45] and yet there has been, since the early 1960s, a growing popular sense of unease with the fruits of growth. By that time, Japan was the third-richest country in the world, and there began to be a feeling that the lives of ordinary people did not adequately reflect that wealth. Investment in new factories and machinery had not been balanced by investment in social capital. Housing in the rapidly growing cities was often cramped and of poor quality, and recreational space was minimal. Worse still, it was becoming obvious that industrial pollution was causing real physical harm to some people.

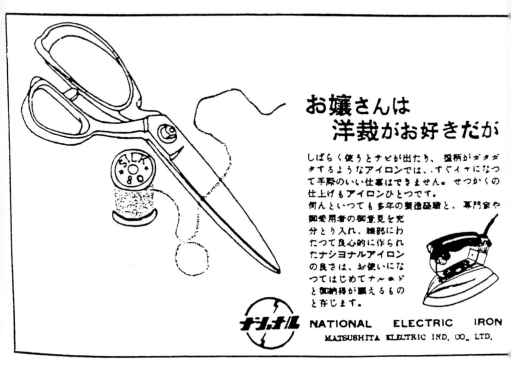

Figure 7.4 Consumer goods in postwar Japan: advertisements for an electric iron (1950) and electric rice-cooker (1958)
Source: Yamazaki H., ed., *Shôwa kôkoku 60-nenshi,* pp. 202 and 263.

Often it was the invisible problems which had the greatest destructive potential. In Nagano Prefecture, where precision machinery producers had replaced the old silk factories, a study of fish taken from Lake Suwa in 1969 found that they contained significant levels of cadmium, chrome, copper, nickel and lead.[46] The most potent symbol of this insidious side of modern technology came to be the town of Minamata, where Noguchi Jun had set up his chemical works before the First World War. By the 1950s Nippon Chisso, the company which Noguchi had founded, was a giant enterprise engaged in the production of a range of chemicals, including acetaldehyde and polyvinyl chloride. For years, however, it had been quietly and invisibly polluting the seas around Minamata with mercury effluent. This was absorbed into the food chain, and eventually into the fish eaten by local people, who began, during the 1950s, to suffer from strange neurological disorders. By the 1970s dozens of people had died as a result of mercury poisoning and many, probably several thousand more, had suffered some effects, ranging from relatively mild symptoms to devastating physical and mental disabilities. After years of protest, negotiation and court cases, Chisso was forced in 1972 to accept liability and pay compensation to the sufferers of 'Minamata disease', although controversy has continued over the official recognition of victims.

The costs of the single-minded pursuit of productivity are perhaps most vividly conveyed by Ishimure Michiko's account of Minamata, with its abandoned fishing boats and its desolate damaged children:

> Most of these children cannot call for help, even if they fall into the fireplace. Some of them have lost their fathers or their older brothers or sisters to Minamata disease. They are totally unaware that they are victims of congenital Minamata disease, to say nothing of their ignorance of the fate which has befallen their families. At any rate, even if their brothers and sisters are still alive and off at school, and their parents are out fishing or in the fields, it is not their own idea to be forced to live lashed to a pillar in an empty house. The gaze of these children left lying around for years at a time shows more than mere wonderment; it looks clairvoyant.[47]

The eminent sociologist Hidaka Rokuro has written, 'to know Minamata is to know Japan. From Minamata, Japan becomes visible.'[48] Certainly, without Minamata, no understanding of Japan's technological transformation is complete.

Japan's postwar technological strength was built in part on the legacies of war and in part on the reforms of the Occupation years. Prewar and wartime technology policies had helped to forge strong links amongst individual private enterprises, and between government and industry. These created a basis for ongoing exchanges of ideas in the postwar period. Now, however, the rigid structures of wartime industrial associations and 'research neighbourhood groups' were replaced by a much more flexible system relying on voluntary cooperation and incentive, rather than on compulsion and coercion.

The spread of education and, above all, easy access to foreign technology created an exceptionally favourable environment for innovation. Japanese companies took advantage of this by following a pattern pioneered by a few adventurous firms in the interwar years. In other words, they combined the import of technology with their own research programs, in which they tried (by and large) to maintain close links between the laboratory and the shop floor. The result was the appearance of many small centres of corporate research throughout the country, creating an innovation network which was exceptionally well suited to the development of commercial, consumer-oriented technologies.

Between 1945 and the oil crisis of 1973, technological innovation helped Japan to achieve rates of economic growth far higher than anything experienced before or since. But by the end of the high-growth era the experience of rapid technological change was raising serious questions about the social and environmental implications of modern technology. The idealists of the Occupation period had believed that formal political democracy would ensure the responsible use of technology, and that technological development would strengthen the foundations of democracy. A quarter of a century later, both of those propositions looked doubtful. Technology, it was clear, was a double-edged sword, which could produce economic wealth and cheap consumer goods while at the same time impoverishing the natural environment and creating costs which fell disproportionately on the least powerful sections of society.

Meanwhile, new problems were beginning to cloud the horizon: threats of protectionism from other industrialised countries; growing competition from neighbouring industrial newcomers; rising prices of raw materials and a diminishing stock of foreign technology to be imported and adapted. These concerns were to create new controversy about the directions of technological change in the last decades of the twentieth century.

CHAPTER 8

High-tech Japan

Tanegashima, the island to which a storm-driven Portuguese man-of-war brought the first firearms in 1542, lies about thirty kilometres off the southern coast of Kyûshû. It is a long thin stretch of land, running north to south. Its thickly forested interior is surrounded by white sand beaches, interspersed here and there with reddish cliffs pitted with caves. If you travel by boat along the coastline, northeast from the point where the Portuguese landed, your attention will probably be caught, not so much by the natural beauty of the landscape, as by a series of curious structures which rise abruptly from the green canopy of semi-tropical vegetation. The most striking of these is a collection of tall square towers, clad in a complex mesh of steel scaffolding. The towers are the most conspicuous part of the complex of high-tech structures, 8.6 million square metres in area, which makes up Tanegashima Space Centre, the main launch site for Japan's entry into the exploration of space.

Tanegashima was chosen as a launch site because of its southerly location and remoteness from major cities, but the Japanese space agency, in making its choice, was also clearly conscious of a certain historical symbolism; and the symbolism is indeed appropriate. The coming of western technology to Tanegashima marked the beginning of a long process of transformation which was eventually to make Japan one of the richest nations in the world. But the new techniques, particularly those represented by European firearms, also brought with them profound and continuing dilemmas about the social and political implications of technological change. In the same way, Japan's embarkation on its first voyages into space marks the beginning of an era in which Japan is increasingly seen as a technological leader by other nations. This position of leadership provides enormous opportunities for technological creativity, but simultaneously raises a new set of political and social dilemmas for Japan's political leaders and citizens: dilemmas well illustrated by the problems which have surrounded the development of the Japanese space program.

The Collapse of High Growth and the Birth of the 'Information Society'

A convenient starting point for examining Japan's new role in world technology is the year 1973. In October of that year the fourth Middle Eastern War broke out, and the Arab oil producers announced massive increases in the price of oil, while at the same time suspending oil exports to countries which they regarded as supporting Israel. Japan was now dependent on imports (mostly from the Middle East) for 86 per cent of its energy needs, and the crisis worsened an already alarming inflation rate. Government efforts to rein in price rises caused a sharp slump, and economic growth, which had been running at over 9 per cent in 1972–73, plummeted to –1.3 per cent in 1974. Although the figures recovered to a more respectable average level of 3–4 per cent per annum in the late 1970s and 1980s, the era of 'miraculous' growth rates was over.

But the oil crisis of 1973 was no more than the superficial stimulus to a process of change whose roots lay deeply embedded in the structure of the Japanese economy. Rising wages and land prices, growing domestic opposition to pollution, increasing protectionism in Japan's foreign markets: all these contributed to the collapse of high growth. In terms of technology, three challenges faced Japan's future development. The first was growing competition in relatively standardised areas of technology from newly industrialising countries like South Korea, Taiwan and Singapore. Secondly, Japan's own inroads into world markets had made western companies very wary of licensing their technical know-how to Japan. In the advanced industries of the 1970s and 1980s, secrecy would become an increasingly essential part of competitive strategy. Lastly, Japan was suffering the ultimate cost of success: by the early 1970s, Japanese industry had reached a level which was in many respects equal to that of other advanced industrialised countries. Even when foreign firms were prepared to sell their technology, there was little left to buy. From now on, Japan would need more than ever to generate its own fundamental scientific and technological research.

The government response to the crisis was to endeavour to shift Japan's industrial structure away from reliance on traditional heavy industries and towards so-called 'knowledge-intensive' industries.

Japan, having successfully transformed itself into an industrial society, was now to become an 'information society'. What this meant in practice was, firstly, that reliance on traditional heavy industries would give way to the development of high-tech industries in which research (rather than materials and labour) was the most important input; secondly, that computer and microelectronics technology would be applied to make surviving heavy industries more 'knowledge-intensive'; and thirdly, that government and industry would pay greater attention to developing basic original technology within Japan itself.

The ultimate aim, as a MITI report of 1980 put it, was to transform Japan from being 'a nation built on trade' to being 'a nation built on technology'. The phrase used—*gijutsu rikkoku*, 'technological nation-building'—was sometimes translated as 'techno-nationalism', and caused such alarm amongst Japan's industrial competitors that it was quickly abandoned.[1] But the vision underlying this phrase, far from being new, was one which had reappeared in different guises at many times throughout Japan's modern technological history. The essence of this vision was that Japan, as a small, overcrowded, resource-poor nation, had only one means to assure its place in the modern world economy—by developing the technological knowledge and creativity of its people. As early as 1917, the establishment of the Institute for Physical and Chemical Research had been supported on the grounds that 'our country, with its dense population and shortage of industrial materials, has no alternative but to rely upon the power of learning [*gakumon*] to develop industry and promote the fortunes of the nation'.[2] In the war years too, science and technology had been seen as a potential substitute for the material resources which Japan lacked.

Now, once again, knowledge was the ultimate resource which, it was hoped, would enable Japan to overcome impending crisis:

> Technological innovation is the fountainhead of social progress. As far as our country is concerned, there are great possibilities for overcoming resource limitations by ... promoting creative technological development (in the fields both of hardware and software) and thus striving to become a nation built on technology.[3]

The context of this 'technological nation-building' in the late twentieth century was, however, very different from that of the First and Second World Wars. Japan had, by this time, accumulated a wealth of expertise which placed it in a position to play a really active role at the forefront of technological research, and the processes of postwar technological change had created a new institutional basis on which to develop the government's plans for a 'knowledge-intensive' economy.

Next Generation Technologies

The official vision of technological change operated at several different levels. Throughout the 1970s and much of the 1980s a succession of committees (often jointly staffed by bureaucrats, business people and academics) produced a stream of reports on the desirable directions of technological change. The reports themselves were often repetitive, and, in their enthusiasm for their cause, tended to overstate the division between the 'old' Japan with its reliance on foreign ideas and the 'new' creative Japan which they sought to construct. They did, however, serve a significant purpose in providing channels for the exchange of ideas about high technology between government, business and academia, and in publicising the importance of research in certain key areas of technology—so, as one report puts it, helping to create a 'technological development mind [*gijutsu kaihatsu maindo*] within the private sector'.[4] By the end of the 1970s the process had produced a widely accepted image which equated 'knowledge-intensive' industry with electronics, computing, robotics, new materials and biotechnology.

At first, the promotion of these industries relied on fairly conventional tools of industry policy. In 1978, for example, the Ministry of International Trade and Industry introduced a law to encourage the 'integration of machinery, electronics and information' through the new technologies of robotics and factory automation. This was closely modelled on the laws which had earlier been used to encourage the growth of the automobile and electrical machinery industries: in other words, it offered a range of low-interest loans, credit guarantees and tax concessions to help companies develop new automation technologies, and to encourage those in existing industries to install automated production equipment.

By the late 1970s, though, official attention was turning away from direct incentives to investment and towards the promotion of invention itself. Here the government drew inspiration from its experiences in promoting technologies like computers and numerical control under the National Research and Development Program of 1966. Its aim, in other words, was to strengthen and formalise the exchange of ideas between rival firms in key areas of technology, while at the same time encouraging the firms to compete with one another in the marketplace for newly emerging high-tech products; or, to put it another way, the government was starting to take a more active and interventionist role in creating those nodes in the social network of innovation which, during the 1950s and 1960s, had been allowed to develop in a relatively haphazard and informal way.

The Very Large Scale Integration Project

One of the earliest and most successful of these efforts to stimulate corporate creativity was the Very Large Scale Integration (VLSI) Project, set up under the auspices of MITI's National Research and Development Program in 1976. The VLSI scheme was in part a response to rumours that US companies were on the brink of developing new and much more powerful integrated circuits (ICs).[5] Since the integrated circuit itself is the key to the development of microelectronic technology—the rice of high-tech industry, it is often called—the Japanese government viewed US dominance of IC technology with almost as much alarm as it viewed OPEC's control of oil.

By the mid-1970s, Large Scale Integration (LSI) had created microchips capable of storing up to 64,000 bits of memory: the next step was to multiply the capacity of the chip to 256,000 or even to 1 million bits, greatly reducing the size and cost of complex electronic equipment such as video recorders and computers. MITI's VLSI project was to lay the foundations of general technological know-how for the manufacture of these very powerful chips, and to develop the necessary production techniques, while leaving individual producers free to use the technology in creating their own particular brands of commercial VLSI technology.[6] The pattern, in other words, was that mixture of technological communication and competition which we observed in the development of shipbuilding, video and other technologies. In the case of the VLSI Project, though, the joint development of new technology was greatly strengthened by the formation of the VLSI Technology Research Association—consisting of researchers from Fujitsu, Hitachi, Mitsubishi, NEC, Toshiba, MITI's Electro-Technical Laboratory and the public communications company NTT. Also of assistance was generous government funding: ¥30 billion of the ¥72 billion spent by the research association between 1976 and 1979 came from the state.[7] Under an agreement worked out with the participating companies, income from patents was at first used to repay government subsidies, but the long-term rights to each patent were assigned to the company responsible for developing it.[8]

The VLSI Project ran for four years and produced impressive results. About one thousand innovations were patented, and the scheme helped Japanese companies to obtain an early foothold in the rapidly expanding market for VLSI chips.[9] Its success attracted lively interest overseas, giving a substantial boost to the international prestige of MITI's technology policies. But the VLSI scheme operated in unusually favourable circumstances. The companies involved already had a wealth of experience in the development of integrated circuits and a strong interest in the development of the next generation of more powerful ICs. Besides, the logical 'next step' in the evolution of ICs was self-evident to all involved in the industry: the only challenge was to find the most effective and reliable way of achieving that step. In this sense the VLSI Project was very different from some of the later MITI technology schemes, whose goals were both more ambitious and much less clearly defined.

The Next Generation Basic Technology Project

The Next Generation Basic Technology Project illustrates MITI's increasingly adventurous approach to the promotion of innovation. Devised in the late 1970s through a process of consultation between business people, scientists and the Agency of Industrial Science and Technology, the scheme set out, not to encourage research in one specific area of technology, but to identify the areas of innovation which would open doors to technological success over the next decade. Eventually three core fields of research—new materials, biotechnology and new forms of microelectronic technology—were chosen, and were in turn subdivided into twelve specific research topics (including fine ceramics, recombinant DNA technology and three-dimensional circuit technology).[10] Each topic would be pursued by a team of researchers drawn from private industry, state laboratories and academia, and the government agreed to support the research with a budget of some $US500 million over the life of the project (from 1981 to 1990).[11]

By the middle of the 1980s, however, it was already clear that the scheme was running into trouble. Faced with mounting government budget deficits, the Ministry of Finance imposed severe cutbacks on the project's spending, while some of Japan's leading high-tech companies proved reluctant to involve themselves in the joint research program. One reason for this reluctance seems to have been the fact that the Next Generation Basic Technology Project (unlike the VLSI Project) did not offer ownership of patented know-how to individual firms. Instead, all patents were to be placed under the control of MITI, which planned to make the newly created technologies available to all interested companies at low cost.[12] The research programs developed under the Next Generation Basic Technology Project did produce some worthwhile innovations, particularly in the field of micro-electronics, but they failed to yield much in the way of major break-throughs, or even to support visible commercial successes of the sort associated with the VLSI scheme. By the second half of the 1980s, therefore, even MITI itself was losing interest in the project, and was turning its attention to new schemes for promoting innovation, such as the Key Technology Promotion Center (see below).

The Fifth-generation Computer

By far the most famous and controversial of the joint research projects was undoubtedly the Fifth-generation Computer Project, announced with considerable fanfare in October 1981. According to the publicity which surrounded its launch, this project would design the 'computers of the 1990s' and propel Japan into a position of technological leadership in the world computer industry.[13] Specifically, it set out to create the foundations of a new generation of computers, the successors not only to the already existing first three generations (based respectively on valves, transistors and integrated circuits) but also to the emerging fourth generation (based on very large scale integration). The fifth-generation computer would embody radically new architecture involving large-scale parallel processing, would be capable of inference and problem solving (allowing it to handle complex expert systems) and would understand speech and visual images.[14]

This visionary project was to run for ten years, and was given a budget of some $US450 million. Specific parts of the scheme were contracted to the major Japanese computer companies (Mitsubishi Electric, Oki Electric, NEC, Toshiba, Hitachi and Fujitsu) and to Tokyo University, while the overall project was coordinated by an Institute for New Generation Computer Technology (ICOT), established in 1982.[15] The announcement of the program caused immediate consternation around the world. Other industrialised nations saw Japan stealing a march on them in computing as it had done in automobiles, television, video and microchips, and a number of hastily organised advanced computing projects (such as the British Alvey project and the European Esprit program) were established to counter the 'Japanese threat'. But while some western observers waxed lyrical about the computer's potential—US writers Edward Feigenbaum and Pamela McCorduck, for example, compared it to the best elements of Roosevelt's New Deal[16]— others were more sceptical. J. Marshall Unger's study *The Fifth Generation Fallacy* argued that the project was little more than an ill-conceived scheme to develop computers which were capable of accepting instructions in Japan's cumbersome semi-phonetic, semi-ideographic script.[17] As the years passed, and it became evident that the project was not going to deliver most of its more ambitious promises, comments on it began to emphasise that the initial excitement had been misplaced. The real goals, it was argued, had always been to raise the quality of basic and applied computing research in Japan and to train a cohort of advanced computer researchers, rather than to produce a marketable product. There were also suggestions of somewhat Machiavellian attempts by Japan to inflate the goals of the project, so encouraging leading western researchers to take part in ICOT conferences and giving Japanese firms greater access to the latest US and European research.

In all of these assessments there has been a tendency to exaggerate the foresight and single-mindedness of the Japanese government. In fact it seems clear that, from the first, the planners of the Fifth-generation Project had differing, and sometimes conflicting, views about their aims. Some (including ICOT's director Fuchi Kazuhiro) seem to have had a genuine vision of a revolutionary breakthrough in computing. Others (including some MITI bureaucrats) were more cautious about the prospects for the scheme. An even stronger voice of caution came from the Ministry of Finance, which was very reluctant to see large sums of money committed to such a speculative project. It was, indeed, the Finance Ministry's opposition which forced the project to reduce its budget and abandon some key aspects, such as the development of voice and visual recognition systems. Perhaps the most telling observation came from the head of MITI's Electronics Policy Section, who observed that, while most of the Ministry's projects were 'goal fulfilling' (*mokuhyô tassei kei*), this one was 'goal investigating' (*mokuhyô tansaku kei*): in other words, it made up its own objectives as it went along.[18]

That being the case, one can hardly say that the project failed, but its results, revealed at a final conference in June 1992, were certainly less dramatic than many people had expected. As in the case of earlier, lesser-known efforts to encourage 'great leaps forward' in Japanese computer technology (see p. 198), the outcome was not a radically new, commercially usable system, but more modest improvements in the basic technological capacity of participating firms. Fifth-generation research, for example, has stimulated Japanese innovation in the area of parallel processing (a technique enabling computers to speed the solution of complex problems by breaking them down into separate parts and processing the various parts simultaneously), and trained a large number of Japanese engineers in advanced computing.[19] Another important stimulus to corporate research in these areas came from the less publicised Supercomputer Project, wholly funded by the government through MITI's Agency of Industrial Science and Technology. This ran concurrently with the Fifth-generation Project but concentrated, not on futuristic visions, but on improving existing know-how in areas like parallel processing and the production of high-speed logic and memory chips.[20]

Controversy over the Fifth-generation Project does not seem to have deterred MITI from pursuing its long-standing tradition of projects to create the great computer of the future. It is noticeable that the aims of the new Real World Computing Project, announced by MITI the month after the conclusion of the Fifth-generation Project, sounded suspiciously like the original aims of its predecessor (including the ability to recognise images, operate intuitively and process incomplete or 'fuzzy' information). The main difference was that the new scheme involved greater overseas participation, including the use of two large-scale parallel-processing computers from the US.[21]

The Key Technology Promotion Center

Government innovation projects proliferated in the 1980s, as ministries competed for influence in leading areas of high technology. Schemes which ran into difficulties were seldom abandoned, but were rather allowed to simmer quietly while the focus of attention was diverted to new projects built upon the experience of previous successes and failures. The problems of the Next Generation Basic Technology Project, for example, encouraged MITI to consider innovation policies which would rely more on the initiatives of private enterprise, and less on the dubious munificence of the Ministry of Finance. The outcome was the establishment of the Key Technology Promotion Center (Key-TEC, Kiban Gijutsu Kenkyû Sokushin Sentâ), set up jointly by MITI and the Ministry of Posts and Telecommunications in 1985. Key-TEC was to be financed from a variety of special funds outside the control of the Ministry of Finance (including profits from the privatisation of the Nippon Telephone and Telegraph Company and the Japan Tobacco Corporation), and its resources would help groups of private companies to set up special joint research subsidiaries. The companies themselves would bear 30 per cent of the research costs, while the remaining 70 per cent would come from the Key Technology Center.[22]

By the early 1990s the Key Technology Promotion Center had supported several hundred research projects, most relatively small and virtually all concentrated in the areas of microelectronics, new materials and biotechnology. The Centre had also come to play an important part in government efforts to satisfy the growing chorus of foreign critics who accused Japan of unwillingness to share information with overseas researchers: several of its research projects involved foreign companies, providing non-Japanese researchers (mostly from the US and Europe) with an opportunity to spend periods of time at work in Japanese laboratories.[23]

The ERATO Project

A slightly different approach to the promotion of innovation has been developed by the Japan Research and Development Corporation, a body set up and loosely controlled by the Science and Technology Agency.[24] It identifies a crucial barrier to Japanese creativity as the weak links between private enterprise and academia in postwar Japan. The main plank in its solution to this problem is the Exploratory Research for Advanced Technology or ERATO program, initiated in 1981: a program which has attracted enthusiastic comments from outside observers.[25]

ERATO tries to circumvent the normal bureaucratic and restrictive system of academic research funding by offering generous financial support to selected projects, whose leaders then have considerable power to decide how money should be spent. Project leaders are generally prominent researchers from universities or private industry, and each is allowed to choose a team of research workers from a range of different public or private research institutions.[26] The ERATO programs cross intellectual as well as institutional frontiers, often combining knowledge from a range of different scientific disciplines. A good example is the Nagayama Protein Array Project, which seeks to turn proteins into the engineering materials of the future. One result of this research may eventually be the development of protein-based microelectronic devices which are extremely small and fast.[27] By the end of 1991 twelve ERATO projects had been completed, while a further seventeen were still in operation.[28] Like the Key Technology Center, ERATO has recently turned its attention to promoting cooperation between Japanese and overseas researchers. After some unsuccessful efforts to establish joint projects with US universities, a series of international research exchange programs was set up under the ERATO umbrella, offering (amongst other things) language training and fellowships for foreign researchers in Japan.[29]

Projects like ERATO, though, raise complex issues about access to scientific and technological information. As academic and corporate research become more closely intertwined, the need for commercial secrecy is limiting the conventional academic concept of the free flow of information. In Japan, as in other industrialised countries, efforts to cultivate high-tech innovation seem to be reshaping the ways in which advanced scientific knowledge is created and diffused. The classical model of science and technology was one in which fundamental scientific research occurred within the universities, and was freely exchanged between researchers, while individual firms competed to apply appropriate new scientific ideas to practical production. Of course, in the real world, the processes of innovation often failed to fit this model: in Japan, for example, prewar bodies like the Research Institute for Physics and Chemistry were already blurring the boundaries between pure science and corporate technology. Since the 1970s, however, model and reality seem to have diverged more sharply than before. Group research projects, of the sort encouraged by the Key Technology Promotion Center and the ERATO program, smooth the flow of knowledge between academia and business, and between Japan and other industrialised countries. At the same time, though, crucial parts of this knowledge tend to be contained within the small and select team of researchers until the private enterprises involved in the project have begun to reap the benefits of commercialisation. This system enables high-tech companies to tap the best possible sources of advanced scientific know-how. On the other hand, though, there are fears that it may stifle the free circulation of scientific knowledge beyond the elite circle of well-funded high-tech projects, and inhibit the non-commercial, curiosity-driven scientific research which has often yielded the most original intellectual discoveries.[30]

The Changing Shape of Corporate Research

The Japanese government's schemes to encourage technological creativity tend to be regarded with a mixture of awe and anxiety by outside observers, who envisage their results in terms of momentous technological breakthroughs and massive increases in Japan's competitive capacity. The evidence so far suggests that their real role has been rather different. Perhaps their most important function has been to ensure that, in an age of growing corporate technological secrecy, the flow of ideas between firms is sufficient to sustain the momentum of innovation. In other words, they have continued and strengthened the pattern of developing strong communication links between separate public and private research institutions: links which will both allow an exchange of basic technological know-how and encourage competition in the commercial development of that know-how. So, while government-supported technology schemes have helped to define the overall directions of technological development, the main commercial successes have come from individual enterprises, in fierce competition with one another, building upon the basis of this shared pool of knowledge.

In computing, for example, while the Fifth-generation Computer Project produced nothing in the way of commercially viable new computing systems, it helped open the way to the rapid advance of Japanese companies into the expanding realms of the very large, high-speed computer system. In 1988 a major US survey of Japanese technology was already acknowledging Japanese advances in super-computing research,[31] and by the first three years of the 1990s the leading Japanese computer makers were vying with one another to launch ever larger and more sophisticated machines onto the market. NEC's 3S-X, unveiled in 1990, was the first Japanese supercomputer to incorporate parallel processing. Although its US rivals (like Cray Research's Y-MP series) contained a greater number of processors, the very high speed of the processors used in the NEC machine enabled it to reach peak speeds which exceeded those achieved by US machines.[32] By early 1992 NEC's local rival Hitachi had struck back, launching its S13800 series, which it claimed as the fastest supercomputer in the world.[33] In September of the same year Fujitsu introduced its VPP500 parallel-processing supercomputers which, predictably, were also heralded as achieving record processing speeds.[34]

In general, the mass of research schemes created under the Key Technology Center, ERATO and other programs have served, less to generate dramatic breakthroughs, than to ensure that Japanese firms have access to leading-edge ideas in a wide range of separate but related technological areas. Though a few of the Key Technology Center projects (such as the optoelectronics research program) have produced genuinely original results, technology observer Bob Johnstone comments that most consortia are simply forums for the exchange of information, with usable findings being 'whisked back into the develop-ment labs of the participating companies'.[35] A good example is the Giantelectronics Technology Corporation—a Key Technology project which aims to develop large-scale liquid crystal display (LCD) panels necessary for the next generation of high-definition televisions. LCD technology is an area of research where Japanese firms have already achieved world leadership: Sharp and Seiko, drawing on their expertise in calculator and watch displays, control a large share of the booming international market for LCD computer screens.[36] Schemes like Giant-electronics, then, have less to do with initiating entirely new branches of research than they do with creating an exchange of ideas which will whet the competitive appetite to produce bigger and better products.

The government may have developed a more intrusive and formal role in encouraging the exchange of ideas on advanced technologies, but unofficial bodies like industry associations continue to play a crucial part behind the scenes. The technology of high-definition television (HDTV) itself was originally developed—like earlier forms of television and video technology—under the leadership of the national broadcaster NHK. NHK's Hi-Vision system was created through a process which has been described as 'coordinated competition', with particular research tasks being allocated to one or more electronics firms: 'fierce competition emerged among manufacturers in performing these tasks, while NHK sought to orchestrate the effort to avoid needless duplication'.[37] Hi-Vision technology expands the number of lines on a TV screen from about 500 to over 1000, producing a clear and sharp picture even on very large screens, but the complexity and expense of the system puts Hi-Vision sets out of the reach of normal household consumers. In response, Japanese firms have developed their own cheaper modifications: improved-definition television (IDTV) and extended-definition television (EDTV), which are in effect stepping stones between existing TV technology and full-scale HDTV. In 1992 Sharp launched a home Hi-Vision system, which uses modifications to the television's decoder to reduce the cost of the technology.[38] In all of these developments a key role has been played, not just by NHK and the Ministry of Posts and Telecommunications, but also by industry groups like the Broadcasting Technology Association (Hôsô Gijutsu Kyôkai) and the Japan Electronics Machinery Industry Association (Nihon Denshi Kikai Kôgyôkai), which act as clearing-houses for general information on the new technology, ensuring that individual companies develop compatible standards and enforcing uniform definitions of the new technology on their sometimes reluctant members.[39]

In fact some of the most successful commercial applications of high technology have come, not from government-sponsored research projects, but from joint initiatives by private firms which have caught even government planners by surprise. Both bureaucrats and technological experts tended to interpret the 'information society' in terms of grandiose projects like the Fifth-generation Computer Project. But, while these schemes may help to accumulate knowledge for future purposes, out in the real world Japan's greatest inroads into foreign markets have continued to come, less from breakthroughs in high technology than from imaginative projects which combine and use new techniques in unexpected ways. In the end, the most tangible symbol of Japan's success in the information age so far has surely been, not the Fifth-generation Computer nor the VLSI chip nor yet the advanced application of biotechnology, but the game computers produced by Nintendo, a maker of playing cards and arcade games whose origins go back to the 1880s.

In the immediate postwar era, Nintendo grew rapidly, sustained by its flair for popular designs: its 'Disney playing cards', in which Mickey Mouse and other cartoon characters replaced the conventional playing card kings and queens, became national best-sellers. When its traditional markets approached saturation point in the mid-1960s, the company added new technical skills to its repertoire, creating a development division which it staffed with young electrical engineers. This enabled Nintendo to branch out successfully into the making of electronic arcade games.[40] The company's move into the more complex world of game computers came about through a tie-up with Mitsubishi Electric, whose strength in television and microchip technology helped Nintendo produce a low-cost game system with visual effects to compete with those of US rivals like Atari.[41] Nintendo's Famicon (Family Computer) succeeded because it harnessed high-level expertise in microelectronics to the accumulated know-how of Japan's huge entertainment industry. Card games, mahjong, pinball and comic books (*manga*) had all had massive sales in prewar Japan, creating a large stratum of skills in the design of commercial games. Nintendo's best-selling games like *Donkey-Kong* and *Super Mario Brothers* tapped those skills, while the hardware it designed fitted neatly into the existing household technological system (using televisions, for example, as video monitors). It was also shrewd enough to create a system which would support only its own selected software. As a result, the company, and rivals like Sega and Sony, have succeeded in sweeping the world with their products. By the end of 1992 Nintendo had sold some 60 million family game computers worldwide, and corporate Japan, through the computer game industry, was exerting an influence on worldwide culture comparable to influence once wielded by Mickey Mouse and Donald Duck. As in the case of Walt Disney, the cultural influence of Nintendo and its rivals was also becoming an issue of growing concern. A video game launched by Sony in 1992, for example, offered players a nightmare journey through a post–nuclear holocaust world, with successful survivors being rewarded with a trip to Solar City, a playground full of 'beaches, babes and fun' [sic].[42]

If the real commercial successes came from less exalted spheres of technology, however, the much-publicised Key Technology Center, ERATO and other schemes certainly helped to make Japanese firms acutely aware of their rivals' interest in specific areas of technology, so encouraging individual companies to expand their own in-house research programs. Other features of the economic and social environment have helped to push Japanese firms in the same direction. The dramatic revaluation of the yen in 1985, for example, made it more difficult for Japan to compete in world markets for conventional industrial products, forcing them to rely on innovation rather than price competition. The share and property price crash of 1991, although it reduced the funds available for research and development, may also have directed companies' attention away from the alluring world of *zaitech* (electronic financial speculation) and towards longer-term investment in the development of new ideas. As Kodama Fumio of the National Institute of Science and Technology Policy points out, the research and development expenditure of Japan's manufacturing companies more than doubled between 1980 and 1987, and by 1986–87 had actually exceeded expenditure on capital investment.[43]

The passion to promote inventiveness has produced qualitative changes in management style as well as a quantitative expansion of research budgets. Japanese companies have pioneered a variety of schemes to open up space for creativity within the hierarchical world of business management. The well-known 'amoeba system' used by the fine ceramics maker Kyocera, for example, involves semi-independent work teams who are responsible for the management and development of their own particular stage of the production process.[44] At the optics giant RICOH (one of the private companies which grew out of the postwar dismemberment of the Riken industrial empire) researchers are encouraged to devise their own topics for exploratory research. To cut through the normal red-tape of corporate bureaucracy, a system has been created where research managers can approve imaginative programs by individual researchers on the basis of a simple one-page proposal. Annual research symposia and strategic research plans are used as a means of involving all researchers in forward planning, and of tapping their imaginations for visions of future development.[45]

The growing strength in corporate research has been accompanied by significant though subtle changes in the structure of Japan's social network of innovation. In the high-growth era, as we saw, technological change was supported by a diffuse research and development system, where research spending was evenly distributed throughout a large number of institutions (both private companies and government laboratories). This helped to create a flexible structure, in which outside ideas could easily be absorbed and adapted, and various firms, both small and large, could combine in different ways to generate innovation. As Japanese firms have moved towards frontier technology and developed larger and more sophisticated research programs, though, the system has begun to change. Research is gradually becoming concentrated in specific high-tech areas and in a few leading high-tech firms. For example, the percentage of research workers employed by the five manufacturing companies with the largest research programs increased from 10.6 per cent in 1970 to 14.9 per cent in 1990 (see Table 8.1).

The widening gap is particularly evident when we turn our attention to small firms. In terms of the *number* of firms conducting research,

Table 8.1 *The concentration of research and development (R&D) in Japan, 1970 and 1990*

PERSONNEL
(Percentage of R&D personnel employed by manufacturers with largest research programs)

	1970	1990
Top 5 companies	10.6	14.9
Top 10 companies	10.4	21.6
Top 20 companies	27.2	29.3

SPENDING
(Percentage of intramural R&D spending accounted for by manufacturers with largest research programs)

	1970	1990
Top 5 companies	16.4	19.0
Top 10 companies	24.7	28.4
Top 20 companies	34.3	37.3

Source: Sômu Chô Takei Kyoku, *Kagaku gijutsu kenkyû chôsa hôkoku*, 1970, pp. 146–7, and 1990, pp. 164–5.

small firms experienced more rapid growth than large firms during the 1970s, though the trend was reversed in the 1980s. When we look at research expenditure and employment, the figures appear very different. For example (excluding companies which performed no research at all) small manufacturing firms in 1970 were on average spending as high a proportion of their sales turnover on research as their large-firm counterparts. By 1990, however, their ratio of research expenditure was only about half that of large manufacturers. The ratio of researchers to other employees was also growing much more slowly in small firms than it was in large companies (see Table 8.2).

Perhaps the growing concentration of research and development in large firms and large projects is an inescapable consequence of technological leadership. Leading-edge research is, on the whole, a costly and speculative business which relatively few enterprises can afford. The changing structure of Japan's research system in this sense reflects a maturing of Japan's industrial structure. Whether the maturing will involve (as it has in the US and elsewhere) a certain loss of flexibility—a hardening of the technological arteries—is a question which remains to be answered.

Table 8.2 *Small firms' share in Japanese research and development—manufacturing industry*

	1970		1980		1990	
	Small firms	Large firms	Small firms	Large firms	Small firms	Large firms
% of firms conducting research[a]	7.2	60.5	16.7	74.5	9.3	64.2
(Index)	(12.7)	(100)	(22.6)	(100)	(14.5)	(100)
Research spending per firm (¥m)[b]	6.7	229.2	18.6	857.0	46.6	2701.9
(Index)	(2.9)	(100)	(2.2)	(100)	(1.7)	(100)
Researchers per firm[c]	1.6	32.2	1.9	52.7	3.3	100.1
(Index)	(5.0)	(100)	(3.6)	(100)	(3.3)	(100)
Research spending as % of sales[d]	1.4	1.4	1.2	1.8	1.8	3.5
(Index)	(100)	(100)	(66.7)	(100)	(51.4)	(100)
Researchers per 10,000 employees[e]	199.6	178.3	241.2	348.0	378.1	623.2
(Index)	(111.9)	(100)	(69.3)	(100)	(60.6)	(100)

Notes: Small firms: firms with fewer than 300 employees.
Index: ratio for small firms where large firms = 100.
Figures in lines b–e exclude firms which conduct no research.
'Researchers' excludes assistant research workers, technicians and clerical support staff.
Sources: Chûshô Kigyô Chô, ed., *Gijutsu kakushin to chûshô kigyô—chûshô kigyô kindaika shingikai hôkoku*, 1985, p. 95; Sômu Chô Tôkei Kyoku, ed., *Kagaku gijutsu kenkyû chôsa hôkoku*, 1990, pp. 112–13.

Small-scale Manufacturing and the Technopolis Vision

The Japanese government is, of course, not unaware of the special problems faced by small firms in the 'information society', and has introduced a variety of schemes to help these firms adapt to the changing technological environment. With government help, small companies can lease computers and robots at low cost and, as a result, automation has spread quickly amongst small-scale manufacturers: by 1988 some 57 per cent of small manufacturers were using numerically controlled machinery and 39 per cent were using computer-aided design (CAD) equipment.[46] The system of grants to support research and development by small firms (which had been in existence since the 1950s) was strengthened and expanded, and new loan schemes were introduced to encourage these companies to enter emerging high-tech industries such as new materials and biotechnology.[47]

The 'small firm problem' was also a key concern of the famous Technopolis scheme, which attracted widespread overseas attention (and some efforts at emulation) during the 1980s. The goals of the scheme were both to speed the pace of technological change and to ensure that its benefits were evenly distributed throughout the country. A number of regional cities (twenty-five in all by the end of the 1980s) were designated by MITI as Technopolises, and were to be the targets of increased infrastructure spending and special grants to make them attractive sites for advanced industries and research centres (see Figure 8.1). The original Technopolis plan, published in 1980, reflected the strong strand of utopianism apparent in much official Japanese writing about new technology. Technopolises were not just to be centres of advanced technology; they also aimed to

> infuse the energy of high technology industry into the culture, traditions and natural abundance of the regions, and to achieve the creation of urban communities by harmonising industry (advanced technological production), learning (academic and experimental research institutions) and lifestyle (a rich and comfortable living environment).[48]

An important part of this infusion of energy was to be the transfer of new technological knowledge to existing small-scale, local companies, enabling them to adapt to the rapidly changing environment of the 1980s and 1990s.

By the end of the 1980s, however, it was becoming obvious that these projects had failed to fulfil their original promise. Few of the Technopolises had met their targets for high-tech job creation, and in many cases the infrastructure spending connected with the scheme had left local governments saddled with large debt burdens.[49] An unforeseen problem was the sharp revaluation of the yen in the mid-1980s, which encouraged many Japanese companies to set up factories off-shore— particularly in the burgeoning economies of East and Southeast Asia— rather than in the Japanese Technopolises. Though some Technopolises, such as the city of Kumamoto in Kyûshû, had managed to create advanced technological research centres, these often served the needs of Tokyo-based firms rather than performing research relevant to local small enterprises.[50]

MITI's own reassessments of the Technopolis scheme have emphasised the need in future to encourage locally planned projects, rather

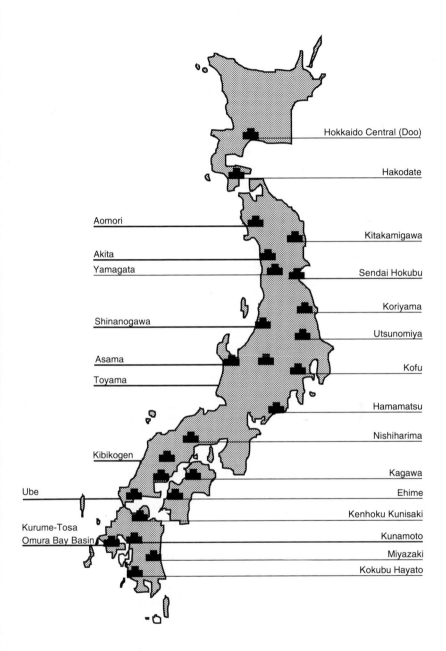

Figure 8.1 Designated technopolises (as of March 1990)
Source: M. Sasaki, 'Japan, Australia and the Multifunctionpolis', p. 143.

than imposing grand strategies from above. In other words, as economist Sasaki Masayuki puts it,

> the real achievements of the technopolis project are seen to be in the reconfirmation by the people of the regions of the importance of relying on their own efforts to raise the local technological levels and local enterprises, not in reliance on the central government, or MITI, or large-scale hi-tech enterprises.[51]

Some of the most important initiatives, in fact, have come from small firms themselves, who have confronted the problems of technological change and foreign competition by readjusting their relationship with large-scale customers or parent companies. For small subcontractors making parts and components, this often means increasing their level of specialisation: concentrating on the production of small batches of technologically complex parts, while allowing the manufacture of more routine components to be shifted overseas.[52]

Traditional small companies, meanwhile, have continued to discover ways of combining old skills with new technologies. In Arita, for example, larger potteries such as Kôransha have begun to apply their experience in the moulding of ceramics to the production of fine ceramic products like turbine blades.[53] A similar coming-together of tradition and high technology is taking place in saké-brewing, where some small producers of the *kôji* mould used in fermentation (see p. 50) have begun to use biotechnology to increase the efficiency of production (though the quality of their product is a matter of debate amongst connoisseurs). These developments generally receive the most effective support, not from grand national schemes like the Technopolis project, but from the much simpler and older network of local research establishments created since the late nineteenth century.

By the 1990s almost every prefectural government had its own particular support scheme to help local enterprises acquire new technology, and prefectural research laboratories were involved in dozens of research projects to apply developments in microelectronics, new materials and biotechnology to small firms. In Niigata, relatively advanced work on robot vision was being developed side by side with projects to apply computer control to weaving looms;[54] in Mie Prefecture research was being carried out on (amongst other things) the application of computer control to brewing systems;[55] in Kanazawa (whose research centre is the descendant of the Industrial Museum established in 1876) projects ranged from work on improved computer numerical control of lathes to the compilation of a database of raw materials for lacquer-making.[56] These in-house research projects were often combined with commissioned research carried out on behalf of small firms, and with training courses for local technicians on topics like computer design and genetic engineering.

National Technology Projects: Nuclear Power and Space

Small-scale firms have not been left out of the wave of technological change sweeping Japan, but the most striking feature of Japan's emergence as a technological leader is surely the growing visibility of national projects: that is, of projects which aim to produce a single, large-scale technological complex, and whose main sponsor and assessor is the state. In Europe and the United States, national technology programs have been particularly associated with the military, although they have also included various non-military (or semi-military) space projects and ventures like the Apollo missions and the Anglo-French Concorde. In Japan, too, rising military expenditure is associated with the development of increasingly ambitious military technology projects, the most famous example being the controversial FSX fighter project.[57] The character and implications of Japan's recent national technology projects, though, are perhaps best understood by considering the examples of nuclear power and space exploration.

There are a number of features which make Japan's nuclear power and space programs very different in character even from large projects like the Fifth-generation Computer Project. That scheme was essentially a generic technology project. In other words, it set out to lay the foundations of the next stage in the development of computer technology, but the intention was always that ideas from the project would be taken up and incorporated into a variety of different commercial computers produced by rival firms. The major nuclear power and space projects, on the other hand, set out to produce a single product: a particular design of fast breeder reactor or rocket which will meet standards laid down by the government agencies concerned. Projects like these may have technological spin-offs—ideas generated in the process of research may be applied by private companies to a wide range of quite different products—but the scale and nature of the nuclear power and space industries leaves no room for genuine technological competition. Not even the Japanese market is big enough to sustain more than one domestic design of fast breeder reactor or large-scale rocket system.

The chronicle of the typical national technology project, as told by historians of technology in Europe and the United States, often seems to go as follows. A government agency commissions a group of large corporations to develop a new piece of technology. Considerable amounts of public money, and of political credibility, are invested in the project. The companies involved in the research scheme have substantial bargaining power vis-à-vis their sponsor (the state), and this fact, together with the inherent uncertainties of large-scale technological innovation, frequently results in big cost overruns. The more public money is committed to the project, the harder it is for the government to abandon it in midstream. Instead, politicians and government agencies feel obliged to see the research program through to its conclusion, and attempt to recover its costs by pressing the completed technology on domestic users, even if it is less than optimally efficient.[58]

If this has been the case in other industrialised countries, have Japan's national technology projects followed the same path? Japan's plans for the development of domestically designed nuclear generators and space launch systems are not yet complete, so it is perhaps too early to answer the question. Their history so far, however, may give some pointers towards a conclusion.

Nuclear Power: The Search for Resource Security

Japan's nuclear power program is deeply bound up with the question of resource security. The pattern of Japanese industrialisation is one which has made the country heavily dependent on imported raw materials. Ever since the early twentieth century Japan's political and business leaders have been acutely aware of the nation's vulnerability, particularly to restrictions on its access to strategic energy sources such as oil. As we have already seen, Japan's nuclear power program began to take shape in the late 1950s (see p. 178). At this time, it should be remembered, there was great worldwide optimism about the potential of nuclear energy. The slogan 'atoms for peace' (popularised by the US Eisenhower administration) expressed a widely felt hope that the technology which had wrought such massive wartime destruction could, as it were, redeem itself through its application to peaceful, productive uses. In Japan, this hope was articulated even by radical scientists such as Taketani Mitsuo, who argued strongly for the development of independent Japanese nuclear power technology, and for the involvement of scientists in decision-making on nuclear issues.[59]

The destruction of Japan's atomic research during the Occupation, however, had left the country with a weak basis for developing nuclear technology. In the early stages, therefore, Japan's nuclear power program was almost entirely reliant on imported technology. The original foreign model was Britain, seen by many Japanese experts as being the most advanced nuclear generating nation. Japan's first nuclear power plant, opened at Tôkai Mura in Ibaragi Prefecture in 1965, relied on Calder Hall gas-cooled technology imported from the

UK. But the Tôkai Mura project quickly showed problems which were already becoming evident in other British gas-cooled reactors. Repeated breakdowns meant that two years of adjustments were necessary before the reactor operated normally, and as a result of this experience, later Japanese nuclear power projects chose boiling-water or pressurised-water technology imported from the United States.[60]

Through agreements with leading US firms like Westinghouse, Japanese companies began to accumulate an expanding pool of expertise in nuclear technology, but even in the early years of the nuclear power program there was concern in the Japanese bureaucracy about the country's dependence on foreign technology. While MITI generally supported the gradual acquisition of nuclear technology from the US, some officials (particularly within the Science and Technology Agency) were worried that the strengthening of nuclear non-proliferation treaties might restrict Japan's access to crucial advances in reactor technology.[61] They argued instead for the development of independent nuclear generating technology which would be specially designed to meet Japan's needs.[62]

From Japan's point of view, the most important variable in nuclear technology was the efficient use of uranium. Since Japan is wholly dependent on imported uranium, the aim of domestic research was to design a reactor which would use this scarce resource as sparingly as possible. In conventional nuclear power technology, as much as 99.3 per cent of natural uranium (the part consisting of uranium 238) goes to waste. It is only the remaining 0.7 per cent (consisting of uranium 235) which is used as fuel. Enrichment can increase the fuel content of uranium to about 3 per cent, but even this suggests massive waste of a limited and expensive raw material.[63] In 1967, therefore, Japan's Nuclear Reactor and Fuel Development Agency (Dôryoku Ro Kaku Nenryô Kaihatsu Jigyôdan, or Dônen for short) put forward a proposal to develop a new Advanced Thermal Converter Reactor which would make more efficient use of imported uranium. Dônen—the largest research institution in Japan, employing several thousand scientists—contracted various parts of the project to five leading heavy industrial corporations: Hitachi, Toshiba, Mitsubishi Heavy Industries, Fuji Electric and Sumitomo Heavy Industries. The experimental reactor—known as the Fugen—was built in Fukui Prefecture on the Japan Sea coast, at a cost of ¥23 billion (about $US64 million). By mixing enriched uranium with plutonium—which could be obtained from the waste of other nuclear power plants—Fugen would reduce the waste of raw materials and lessen Japan's external resource dependence, and it was expected to pave the way for a new generation of power plants by the late 1980s.[64]

The Fugen reactor began operation in 1979, but was temporarily closed soon after to deal with unexpected technical problems. Meanwhile, the cost of construction had blown out to more than ¥50 billion,[65] while falling oil prices in the 1980s were reducing the attractions of this very costly form of electricity generation. By the early 1990s no commercial generators of the Fugen type were yet in operation. At the same time, though, the Japanese government was pressing towards a more ambitious goal, to which Fugen was merely the stepping stone. This was the development of indigenously designed fast breeder reactor (FBR) technology. Fast breeder reactors differ from conventional reactors in that they consist of a core of plutonium, around which is packed a layer of uranium 238. As the nuclear reaction occurs, the uranium 238 is converted into plutonium. Depending on the efficiency of the reactor, the amount of plutonium produced may be as much as 1.4 times as great as the amount of plutonium consumed (though in practice it is more often in the region of 1.2 times). Fast breeder reactors have, for this reason come to be seen by some as 'reactors which create their own fuel'. FBR technology, it is said, will convert the noxious wastes of existing nuclear power plants into a valuable source of energy, and thus Japan, by the miracle of technology, will be turned into a resource-rich country.

The official enthusiasm for fast breeder reactors is therefore readily understandable. By 1966 the government's basic plan for nuclear energy was already arguing that

> to ensure the secure supply and efficient use of nuclear fuel, we should aim to establish a reliable nuclear fuel cycle. It is also necessary, in order to raise our country's technological level and strengthen its industrial basis, to undertake the autonomous development of nuclear reactors. For these reasons we should rapidly embark on the independent development of a Fast Breeder Reactor program.[66]

As this statement suggests, a great attraction of fast breeder reactors was their potential to create 'a reliable nuclear fuel cycle': that is, to ensure that the entire process of fuel use, recycling and re-use occurred within Japan, thus freeing the country from external sources of raw materials as well as technology.

Japan's first small-scale experimental FBR began operation in 1977, and the project (carried out by Dônen in cooperation with Hitachi, Toshiba, Fuji Electric and Mitsubishi Heavy Industries) was also plagued by cost overruns and technical difficulties. Nevertheless, work proceeded on the much larger, developmental fast breeder reactor, Monju, which was completed in 1991. The commissioning of the Monju reactor attracted worldwide attention to Japan's nuclear power program, because it involved the shipment of plutonium fuel from a

French reprocessing plant to Japan. This aroused international fears of an accident or hijacking, and evoked protests from several countries through whose waters the ship was expected to pass. (It also gave currency to the peculiarly Japanese neologism *kakujakku*, an amalgam of the words *kaku*, nuclear and *haijakku*, hijack.)

The shipment was completed without incident, but the development of Japan's independent FBR program raises controversies which will not so easily be resolved. In the first place, as many critics within Japan have pointed out, nuclear power generation, and particularly the use of fast breeder reactors, is an extremely expensive process which cannot readily be justified in economic terms.[67] (The high cost of this technology helps to explain why it has been abandoned by most other industrialised countries.) Although the FBR program is enthusiastically supported by prominent bureaucrats and technicians, Japan's power-generating companies (as well as many electricity consumers) view it with greater caution.[68]

Secondly, there are still serious and unresolved questions about the safety of fast breeder reactors and about the disposal of their toxic wastes (see Figure 8.2). Although Japan's nuclear power program so far has not yet created any disasters on the scale of Chernobyl or even Three Mile Island, there have been enough minor incidents to warn against complacency. Official statistics list 424 notified 'faults and problems' at nuclear power stations between 1968 and 1990.[69] While most were minor, they include some serious incidents, like the accident at Tsuruga Power Station in March 1981, which resulted in the release of contaminated water into a nearby bay.[70] Even when power stations are operating 'normally', there are serious concerns about the safety of workers—particularly of those casual labourers, 'nuclear gypsies', who are employed in many Japanese plants to perform routine jobs in the most heavily contaminated areas.[71] A number of Japanese workers have been exposed to dangerous levels of nuclear radiation, and in May 1993 the Ministry of Labour acknowledged for the first time that the death of a former power plant worker had been caused by radiation.[72]

Perhaps the most important concern, however, relates to the very nature of fast breeder technology itself. One argument in support of these reactors is that they consume plutonium waste produced by conventional nuclear power stations. Since plutonium is also the raw material of nuclear weapons, fast breeders can be seen as making productive use of a doubly dangerous waste product. On the other hand, because it uses plutonium as fuel and creates more plutonium than it consumes, the fast breeder reactor encourages the production of this extremely dangerous material. The logic of the FBR is one of perpetual growth, with more and more reactors being constructed in order to

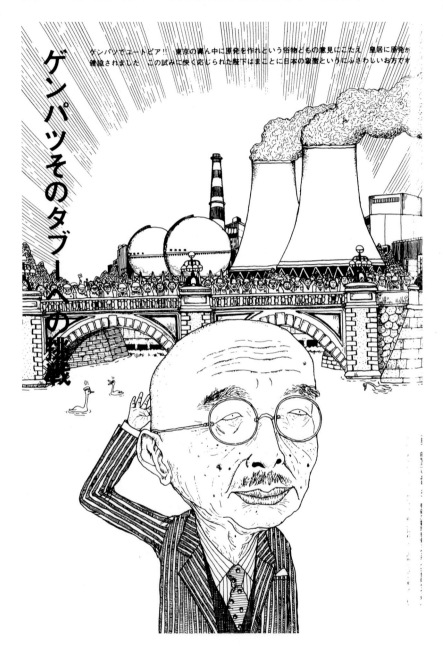

Figure 8.2 Nuclear power as a social issue. This Japanese cartoon from the 1970s challenges official assurances about the safety of nuclear power by depicting a nuclear power-station built on the site of the Imperial Palace in central Tokyo with Emperor Hirohito in the foreground
Source: Han Gempatsu Jiten Hensan Iinkai, ed., *Han Gempatsu Jiten,* vol. 1, p. 75. Illustrated by Hashimoto Masaru, © Gendai Shokan.

consume the ever-expanding world stock of plutonium. This means that, once an FBR program has been started, it becomes very difficult to abandon it and switch to other generating technologies. Besides, as plutonium becomes a valuable fuel, it will be more widely traded and transported from one power plant to another. In short there is a danger (as one observer puts it) of creating a world 'swimming in plutonium'.[73] Concerns about this aspect of the technology are so great that the director of Dônen has even spoken of the need to control the pluto-nium-generating capacity of Japan's FBRs: thus, in effect, contradicting the original purpose of the expensive and controversial program.[74]

The greatest risk is that the Japanese, having staked so much on this self-replicating technology, may feel a need to recover the costs of development and dispose of surplus plutonium by selling the technique to other parts of world: particularly to those neighbouring Asian coun-tries whose industrial expansion is creating a rapidly growing demand for energy. At least one Japanese government report has pointed out that the expansion of electricity generation by conventional means in East and Southeast Asia would seriously aggravate the greenhouse effect, and argued that the developed nations should provide leadership in creating an 'appropriate' mix of electricity-generating technologies— including nuclear power—for newly industrialising countries.[75] It would be ironic if Japan's search for resource security were to lead to the spread of technology which posed such potential threats to the wider political and military security of the region.

The Industrialisation of Space

In 1988 the Society of Japanese Aeronautics Companies issued a blueprint for the 'Cosmopia Concept', outlining an idealised picture of a Japanese space program to be in place by the year 2015. Cosmopia envisages, not only improved satellites and space transportation, but also permanent space stations and colonies, orbiting factories and moon bases to explore the untapped wealth of lunar resources. This is not the fantasy of an eccentric fringe group. The society represents some of Japan's leading corporations, and a similar future is depicted in a recent publication by the major Japanese space agency NASDA (the National Space Development Agency, Uchû Kaihatsu Jigyôdan), which looks to space for a solution to the terrestrial mistakes of the twentieth century. In NASDA's opinion,

> We can help to solve resource problems by using observations from space to discover new resources on earth, and by developing the resources of the moon. If we could create self-sufficient cities on the moon, this would also help to relieve population problems.

Indeed, with the development of space colonies, NASDA points out, 'even if life on spaceship earth were to come to an end, humans would probably be able to find new worlds somewhere in space'.[76] Meanwhile, two leading private construction companies, Ohbayashi Gumi and Shimizu Corporation, have also been devising and publicising their own schemes for the lunar cities of the twenty-first century.[77]

These dreams of cosmic construction are, of course, just part of the popular Japanese practice of devising long-term grand strategies: visions splendid which (like the Technopolis schemes) may have relatively little bearing on how things turn out in practice. They do, however, help to draw attention to Japan's growing, but so far rather neglected, role as a space nation. At the same time, they also serve to emphasise the changing nature of the space race itself. While the Soviet and US space programs of the 1950s and 1960s were all about military supremacy and the search for national glory, space rivalries today are driven by more overtly commercial concerns, including competition for market shares in the lucrative business of launching satellites and (in the longer term) the prospect of using the microgravity of space for the manufacture of new materials and biotechnological products. They are part, in other words, of the industrialisation of space.

Until recently, Japan's space program tended to be regarded with considerable scepticism by foreign observers. In the early 1980s, the *Economist* magazine was still arguing that 'Japan's rocket program is too little, too late. They should scrap the tin-pot rocket system and use Ariane or the Shuttle instead.'[78] This scepticism was partly based on Japan's lack of experience as a space nation. As in the case of nuclear power, defeat in the Pacific War resulted in the dismantling of much of the technological basis necessary for entry into the space race. While the US and USSR were developing their manned space programs in the 1950s and 1960s, Japan was still at the stage of testing miniature rockets designed by small teams from Tokyo University. NASDA itself was not created until 1969, and it was only in 1978 that the first specific long-term plan for the development of space policy was drawn up.[79] From the late 1970s, however, Japan's space budget grew rapidly. By the end of the 1980s, although it was still far behind the US space program in terms of size, it had exceeded the space expenditure of leading European nations such as Britain, France and Germany.

Japan's growing role as a space nation is particularly apparent in its expanding participation in large international space projects. The most important of these is the international space station 'Freedom', planned for the latter part of the 1990s. The station—consisting of living quarters, two experimental modules and a mass of complex monitoring equipment—will be put together from components

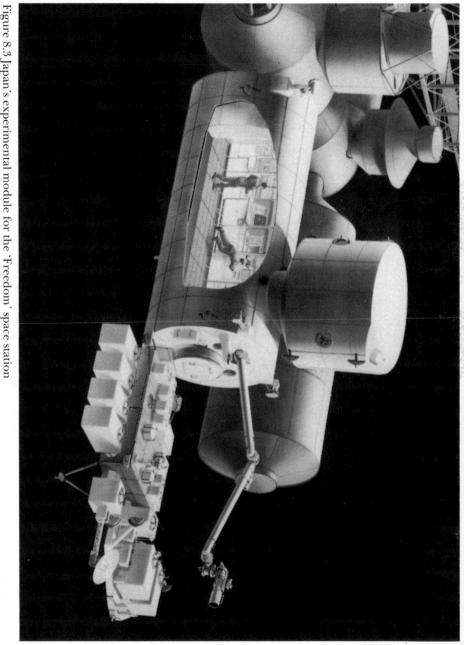

Figure 8.3 Japan's experimental module for the 'Freedom' space station
Source: National Space Development Agency of Japan (NASDA)

supplied by the United States, Canada, Japan and the European space program. It is expected to serve as a permanent experimental centre for teams of seven or eight astronauts from the participating countries, to pave the way for the development of orbiting factories. NASDA's contribution, emphasising its interest in the implications of the project for industrial technology, will be the Japanese Experimental Module (JEM), one of the space laboratories which form twin centres for the station's research activities (Figure 8.3).[80]

Cooperation on ventures like 'Freedom', however, goes hand in hand with intense competitive rivalry between the leading space nations. So while Japan prepares for its role in the international space station, it is also developing rocket technology which will bring it into direct competition with the US Shuttle and European Ariane programs. In the early years of the 1990s, the morning calm of Tanegashima was regularly shattered by the roar of engines as NASDA test-fired its H-II rocket—the first major rocket to be wholly made in Japan. Often the roar was short-lived, as the rocket motors yet again closed down because of faults in the system. The development of the H-II was plagued by problems, including a serious accident when an engine exploded during testing at a Mitsubishi Heavy Industry factory, killing one technician.[81] The launch, originally planned for 1990, was repeatedly postponed, and it was not until February 1994 that the rocket finally got off the ground.

However, as one commentator put it 'the development of H-II has crossed the Rubicon'.[82] By the early 1990s both NASDA and the consortium of contracting companies (which includes Mitsubishi Heavy Industries, Mitsubishi Electric, NEC and Kawasaki Heavy Industries) were too deeply committed to the project to withdraw, and research was increasingly being directed towards methods, not simply of achieving a successful launch, but also of reducing the costs of its construction so that they could eventually recoup the large development expenses.[83]

The stories of nuclear and space technology emphasise Japan's emergence as a leading player in the development of complex, large-scale technologies, but also illustrate some of the dilemmas created by this new role. The exploration of space, like the development of nuclear power, raises issues of environmental ethics and of international friction. Rocket and satellite systems, though they may be used to help us monitor the earth's environment more effectively, consume scarce resources and disrupt the environment of areas (like Tanegashima) which are used as launch bases. Japan's rapid advances in space technology are also ruffling feathers in the United States, where space was seen, until recently, as a realm in which the US enjoyed unchallenged dominance. Referring to Japan's satellite and rocket programs, one NASA report observed with consternation that 'a single $100 million launch contract is the equivalent in economic terms to the import of 10,000 Toyotas'.[84]

As far as the theme of this book is concerned, however, the most important issue raised by the national technology projects is the issue of 'technological lock-in'. Very large projects based on complex advanced technology in areas like nuclear power or space almost inescapably require single, risky, expensive projects like the Fugen, Monju and H-II rocket schemes. These monopolistic, state-supported national technology schemes, however, have tended, in Japan as elsewhere, to be characterised by delays and cost overruns. This suggests that the high levels of efficiency and technological competitiveness found in other areas of the Japanese economy are not the product of some immutable national culture, but are rather a reflection of organisational structures. If a flexible system of dispersed, small-scale research activities was a key to Japan's rapid technological change in consumer industries, how will the growing importance of large national projects affect the country's technological future? Is it possible, indeed, for a country in a position of world technological leadership to maintain the institutional flexibility through which that leadership was won? Or is it inevitable that Japan, as its industrial system matures, will find itself committed to research institutions too large to adapt readily to a changing social environment, and burdened with technological systems whose internal self-expansionary momentum moves ever further away from economic or social rationality?

Japan as an Exporter of Technology

These questions are ones whose answers will affect, not just Japan itself, but also the rest of the world; for as Japan has become a world leader in more and more technological fields, so it has also acquired a huge influence on the technological development of other nations. Studies of Japan's role in the 'export' or 'transfer' of technology often look at three main sets of figures. The first is foreign direct investment—the overseas establishment of factories or offices by Japanese companies— which commonly involves some export of productive machinery, skilled technicians etc. As countless books and news reports have pointed out, Japan's role as a foreign investor expanded enormously during the 1980s. Between 1980 and 1989 Japanese direct overseas investment in manufacturing rose from $US2.3 billion to $16.3 billion, before falling back slightly to $15.5 billion in 1990.[85] A second measure is provided by statistics for 'technology exports' in the strict sense of the licensing of know-how or sales of blueprints to foreign customers. This type of technology export is very closely linked to direct investment: a large share of licensing agreements are made between Japanese based firms and their foreign subsidiaries or affiliates. It is not surprising, then, to find that here too the lines on the graph curve sharply upwards. During the 1980s, while Japan's imports of technology almost trebled, its exports more than quadrupled (see Figure 8.5) and by the end of the decade had exceeded the technology exports of Germany and France. The largest share of Japan's exports of technology went to the Asian region, but a substantial and rapidly growing proportion was directed to North America (Figure 8.6). Thirdly, technology is also 'exported' through technical aid programs, which in Japan's case are mainly operated by the Japan International Cooperation Agency. Between 1986 and 1990 Japan's technical aid, most of which goes to other Asian countries, rose from about $US32 million to about $66 million.[86]

The figures alone, however, tell a dry and often misleading story. Foreign investment projects, even when they involve some licensing of technology to overseas subsidiaries, may not necessarily bring about a real international communication of ideas. They may simply result in Japanese firms using Japanese technology to produce something in a foreign country. To illustrate the point we might consider a United Nations study of two enterprises manufacturing monosodium gluta-mate in Thailand. One firm was the subsidiary of a major Japanese producer. Although this company had signed several licensing agreements with its Japanese parent, and in the early 1980s (after twenty years of operation) was transferring 4 per cent of its sales earnings to Japan as royalty payments, 'foreign experts generally controlled the more critical areas of production'.[87] The second company was established by a Thai firm which, on its own initiative, had become interested in acquiring technology to produce MSG. This firm entered into a joint venture with the largest Taiwanese producer of MSG, which had in turn originally obtained its technical know-how from a Japanese company. Under the joint venture agreement, the Taiwanese partner provided the core technology free of charge, while the Thai partner, which had considerable experience in related industries, was able to play an active role in the choice of equipment for the factory. Although parts of the key fermentation process were still foreign-controlled, local technicians were operating the main produc-tion systems, performing performance analysis and receiving regular training overseas.[88]

In terms of the official statistics, the first of the two Thai ventures involved a substantial 'transfer of technology' from Japan, while the second involved none at all. In practice, though, the flow of knowledge from Japan to Thai technicians and managers was surely greater in the

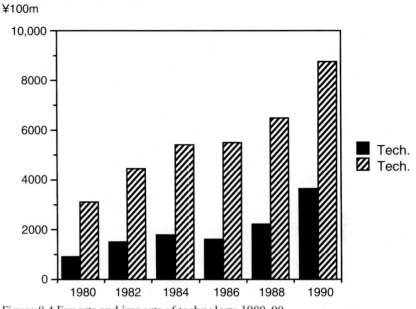

Figure 8.4 Exports and imports of technology, 1980–90
Source: Kagaku gijutsu hakusho, 1991.

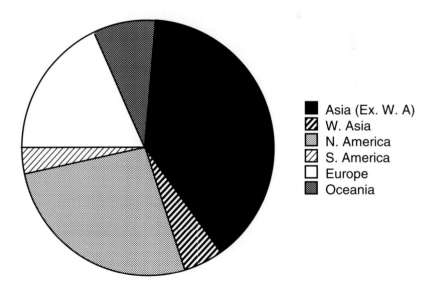

Figure 8.5 Exports of technology by region, 1980–89
Source: Kagaku gijutsu hakusho, 1991.

second case than in the first. These contrasting stories draw attention to two particularly important features of Japan's technological influence on its Asian neighbours. The first is the fact that the influence is now very often an indirect one. Technological know-how from Japan reaches Southeast Asia and other parts of the world not only through the direct presence of Japanese companies, researchers or aid programs, but also circuitously, as a consequence of the enormous Japanese influence on the technological development of neighbouring countries like Taiwan and South Korea. The second is the fact that the impact of Japanese technical know-how on other countries depends very much upon the responses of the recipient. As in the case of Japan's own acquisition of foreign technology, knowledge is never passively 'transferred', but is acquired and adapted by an active process of learning at the receiving end.[89]

Even careful case studies of investment projects and technology licensing, however, reveal only the tip of the iceberg. Japan's technological influence reaches other countries not only consciously, through deliberate efforts at 'technology acquisition', but also subtly and indistinctly, embedded in a mass of visible and invisible exports. Japanese pocket calculators are used in street markets throughout Asia; Japanese photocopiers and portable phones are transforming the way in which small firms throughout the region do business; Japanese cars and televisions sets have become part of the landscape of everyday life from Manila to Mexico City. Less tangible products of high-tech Japan are also leaving their mark on the evolving shape of societies all over the world. The Japanese TV soap opera *Oshin*, which tells the story of Japan's postwar miracle through the struggles of a tenacious and courageous businesswoman, was seen by millions of viewers worldwide. For one of the program's countless fans in the People's Republic of China, the moral of the program was as follows:

> Right now we are in a period of super development in economics and technology. From TV we need programs to stimulate people's attitudes and spirit to work for economic development and technological improvement to make China strong. We can look to Japan for an example ... They learnt about modern technology from the West. Take automobiles for example. Now the Japanese occupy a strong position in the American car market ... Japan focuses on practical science. From *Oshin* we learn that in hard times you must work hard and develop your career. Only if people adopt this attitude can we realise the four modernisations.[90]

As this statement implies, Japan's technological impact on the region is not just a material one—not just a matter of the transmission of value-free industrial know-how. The influx of Japanese gadgetry and investment carries with it a particular set of ideas about the nature of prosperity, and about the political means to achieve that prosperity. In East and Southeast Asian countries particularly, the Japanese model of technological development is carefully studied and eagerly copied. The lessons derived from Japan's development, however, have tended to rely heavily on a limited vision of Japan's industrial and technological history. The role of MITI, for example, has been much discussed, and has inspired attempts at imitation in Singapore, Malaysia and elsewhere.[91] Japan's high-tech research projects (like the Fifth-generation Computer Project) and its science parks and technopolises have also been popular models for emulation. This book has tried to show, though, that these conspicuous examples of Japanese technology policy are only a small part of the explanation for rapid technological change in modern Japan. Other aspects of Japan's experience, such as the existence of many small-scale centres of private and local government research, may contain equally useful lessons, particularly for the later industrialising countries of Southeast Asia. At the same time, the environmental costs of technology highlighted by Japan's experience suggest important lessons in what to avoid.

Discussions of Japan's technological impact on the rest of the world bring us back to a question which we first encountered in the introduction: how 'Japanese' is Japanese technology? Is Japan's growing international influence imposing a distinctively Japanese model of technological development on the rest of the world, or is it merely the instrument by which the 'East' is becoming westernised? There is an important sense, of course, in which Japanese technology is part of a universal, international modern technology. The characteristic of this technology, as Martin Heidegger first observed, is that it turns all of nature into a resource for human use. The analytical power of modern science is used to 'pursue and entrap nature as a calculable coherence of forces',[92] to draw the natural environment into systems which maximise usable material output and economic growth.

At the same time, within this overarching system of modern technology, there is room for differences of emphasis and style. The nature of Japanese technology, as we have seen, has been influenced by an obsessive concern about issues of resource security. The managerial systems developed in response to the problems of mass production have helped to create the high standards of reliability which are often seen as a hallmark of Japanese products. Meanwhile, the structure of the innovation system—in which basic technological ideas were swiftly transmitted between enterprises but the refinement of those ideas was the result of fierce competition—has also given a distinctive flavour to Japanese innovation. Rather as in the Edo period (though for very different reasons) there tends to be an endless reproduction of variants on basic themes (whether the themes themselves are imported, like radio, or indigenously developed, like high-definition television). It is this tireless improvement, refinement and modulation which has produced more energy-efficient cars, sharper television pictures, more accurate machine tools, faster computers, watches with a dozen different functions, and automatic-flush lavatories with heated seats.

The story of Japan's modern technological development has been one, not only of astonishingly rapid learning, but also (from the start) one of continuous innovation. It has enormously increased the human store of consumer goods, and made available to many people a whole range of commodities which, fifty years ago, would have been beyond their wildest dreams. For other newly industrialising countries, however, the Japanese model is one which cannot be closely imitated. Global pollution problems and resource shortages have closed off that particular path. Already, in cities like Bangkok, while the streets are full of reliable Japanese-designed cars, the pressure of traffic makes it quicker to travel by motorised trishaw or by bicycle.

Dealing with these future technological challenges will require something more than the social network of innovation which has sustained Japan's technological innovation so far, and something more than efforts to promote high-tech-creativity in areas like super-computers and space stations. Technological research projects in Japan, as in other industrialised countries, have tended to focus on indi-vidual end products. They have looked for ways to produce a new commodity—a more versatile engineering material, a faster computer, a more efficient car engine, or whatever—and for ways to produce this commodity more economically. But in the process (as the Bangkok example illustrates) they often fail to grasp the relationship between the individual product and the wider industrial and social system. What is increasingly necessary, in the face of environmental challenges, is the ability to take a fresh look at whole systems—be they chemical factories or cities—and to consider a wide variety of ways to make the system better serve the material and social needs of the people who use it. These ways may be organisational as well as 'technological' in the narrow sense of the word: they will require a crossing of intellectual boundaries, not just between one field of science and another, but also between 'technology' itself and other human and social sciences. Japan—with its educated population, its experience of innovation in traditional as well as high-tech industries—has the skills to contribute to the task. How its corporate and political institutions will respond to the challenge remains to be seen.

Notes

Chapter 1: Introduction

1 A number of economic studies have identified technological change as a major factor in Japan's rapid growth since the Second World War: see E.F. Denison, and W.K. Chung, 'Economic Growth and its Sources', in H. Patrick, and H. Rosovsky, eds, *Asia's New Giant: How the Japanese Economy Works*, Washington DC, Brookings Institution, 1976, pp. 63–151; R. Minami, *The Economic Development of Japan: A Quantitative Study*, London, Macmillan, 1986, pp. 107–8. Fagerberg and others have argued that a major reason for the rapid growth of Japan and other 'late industrialisers' since the Second World War has been a combination of the large technology gap which existed between these countries and older industrialised nations, and the substantial effort which some late industrialisers have invested in acquiring technology from overseas. See J. Fagerberg, 'A Technology Gap Approach to Why Growth Rates Differ', *Research Policy*, vol. 16, nos 2–4, 1987, pp. 87–99.

2 Kagaku Gijutsuchô, *Kagaku gijutsu hakusho 1990*, Tokyo, Ôkurashô Insatsu Kyoku, 1990, p. 4.

3 Taniura T., *Ajia no kôgyôka to gijutsu iten*, Tokyo, Ajia Keizai Kenkyûjo, 1990.

4 J. Mokyr, *The Lever of Riches*, Oxford, Oxford University Press, 1990, p. 304.

5 See, for example, A. Pacey, *Technology in World Civilization: A Thousand-year History*, Oxford, Basil Blackwell, 1990; I. Inkster, *Science and Technology in History: An Approach to Industrial Development*, London, Macmillan, 1991.

6 Morishima M., *Why Has Japan 'Succeeded'? Western Technology and the Japanese Ethos*, Cambridge University Press, Cambridge, 1982, pp. 176–7 .

7 See Murakami Y., 'Ie Society as a Pattern of Civilization', *Journal of Japanese Studies*, vol. 10, no. 2, 1984, pp. 279–363.

8 Murakami Y., 'Technology in Transition: Two Perspectives on Industrial Policy', in H. Patrick and L. Meissner, eds, *Japan's High Technology Industries: Lessons and Limitations of Industrial Policy*, Seattle and Tokyo, University of Washington Press/University of Tokyo Press, 1986, pp. 211–41.

9 For example, A. Fabayo and L. G. Gatugata, *Technology Transfer and Industrialisation in the Developing Countries: Some Lessons from Japan*, Tokyo, International Development Centre of Japan, 1984, pp. 19–20; Inkster, op. cit.,

245

ch. 7; T.C. Smith, *Political Change and Industrial Development in Japan, 1868–1880,* Stanford, Stanford University Press, 1965.

10 C. Johnson, *MITI and the Japanese Miracle: the Growth of Industrial Policy 1925–75,* Stanford Cal., Stanford University Press, 1982.

11 D.I. Okimoto, *Between MITI and the Market: Japanese Industrial Policy for High Technology,* Stanford, Stanford University Press, 1989, p. 49.

12 Fabayo and Gatugata, op. cit., pp. 17–20; C. Freeman, *Technology Policy and Economy Performance: Lessons from Japan,* London and New York, Pinter Publishers, op cit., pp. 32–49; P. Kevenhörster et al., *Forschungs- und Technologiepolitik, Forschungs– und Entwicklungssystem in Japan, Untersuchungsteil 4,* Basel, Prognos AG, 1983; Hayashi T., *The Japanese Experience in Technology: From Transfer to Self–Reliance,* Tokyo, United Nations University, 1990; P. Sörbom, 'The Reception of Western Technology in China and Japan', in E. Baark and A. Jamison, eds, *Technological Development in China, India and Japan* London, Macmillan, 1986, pp. 35–56, (esp. pp. 46–8).

13 The exception to this generalisation is Hayashi, op. cit., which provides an overview of the Japanese experience since the Meiji period. This, however, is not a single historical overview but essentially a collection of reports on various aspects of the Japanese experience.

14 Keizai Kikakuchô Chôsakyoku, *Keizai Yôran 1990,* Tokyo, Ôkurashô Insatsu Kyoku, 1990.

15 D. Friedman, ed, *The Misunderstood Miracle: Industrial Development and Political Change in Japan,* Ithaca NY, Cornell University Press, 1988, esp. ch. 5; on the role of small firms, see also Hayashi, op. cit., ch. 11.

16 Iida K., 'Nihon ni okeru kindai kagaku gijutsu shisô no keisei', in *NKST,* vol. 14, p. 433.

17 For example T.C. Smith, *The Agrarian Origins of Modern Japan,* Stanford, Stanford University Press, 1959; P. Francks, *Technology and Agricultural Development in Pre–War Japan,* Yale, Yale University Press, 1984.

Chapter 2: Society and Technology in Tokugawa Japan

1 Although the word 'technology' existed in the previous century, David Noble points out that it was introduced into popular usage in its modern sense by Jacob Bigelow in a series of lectures published in the 1820s. See D. Noble, *America By Design: Science, Technoloy and the Rise of Corporate Capitalism,* Oxford and New York, Oxford University Press, 1977, p. 3.

2 C. Lamarre, and F. de Fontpertuis, 'Le Japon', in C. Lamarre, and F. de Fontpertuis, eds, *Les Pays Etrangers et l'Exposition de 1878: La Chine et le Japon,* Paris, Librarie Ch. Delagrave, 1878, p. 6.

3 Ishii T., *Tekunorando: Nihon no gijutsu ga saikô ni omoshiroi,* Tokyo, Purejidentosha, 1983, p. 120.

4 J. Mokyr, *The Lever of Riches: Technological Creativity and Economic Progress,* Oxford, Oxford University Press, 1990, p. 13.

5 See Tashiro K., 'Tokugawa jidai no bôeki', in Hayami A. and Miyamoto, M., eds, Nihon keizai shi 1: Keizai shakai no seiritsu, Tokyo, Iwanami Shoten, 1988, pp. 129–70.

6 R. Storry, *A History of Modern Japan,* London, Penguin Books, 1972, p. 66.

7 Higuchi K., 'Seikatsu no shashika to Nanban fûyô no ryûkô', in *Zusetsu Nihon bunka no rekishi,* vol. 7, Tokyo, Shôgakukan, 1980, p. 146.

8 See M. Sugimoto, and D.L. Swain, *Science and Culture in Traditional Japan,*

Rutland Vt and Tokyo, Charles E. Tuttle, 1989, p. 183; Iida K., 'Kinzoku', in Itô et al., eds, *Nihonjin no gijutsu*, Tokyo, Kenkyûsha Shuppan, 1977, pp. 128, 133.

9 Okumura S., *Hinawajû kara kurofune made*, Tokyo, Iwanami Shinsho, 1970, pp. 34–5; Hayama T., 'Teppô no dentô to sono hamon', in Hayama T., ed., *Nihon no kinsei 4: Seisan no gijutsu*, Tokyo, Chûô Kôronsha, 1992, pp. 77–106.

10 J.C. Covell, and A. Covell, *Korean Impact on Japanese Culture: Japan's Hidden History*, N.J. Elizabeth, Hollym International Corp., 1984; Sumita Y., *Arita: hakuji no machi*, Tokyo, Nihon Hôsô Shuppan Kyôkai, 1974, p. 51.

11 Yabuuchi K., *Chûgoku no kagaku to Nihon*, Tokyo, Asahi Shinbunsha, 1972, pp. 50–1.

12 See Yabuuchi K., ed., *Tenkô kaibutsu*, Tokyo, Heibonsha, 1969. For an English translation of this work see Sun E.-T.Z. and Sun S.-C., *T'ien–Kung K'ai–Wu: Chinese Technology in the Seventeenth Century*, University Park and London, Pennsylvania State University Press, 1966.

13 Tashiro, op. cit., p. 136.

14 Sugimoto and Swain, op. cit., p. 225.

15 J. Merson, *Roads to Xanadu: East and West in the Making of the Modern World*, Sydney, Child and Associates/ABC Books, 1989, p. 116; Sumita, op. cit., p. 68.

16 Higuchi K., 'Shinkô toshi Edo no seikatsu', in *Zusetsu Nihon bunka no rekishi*, vol. 8, Tokyo, Shôgakukan, 1980, pp. 136–52; esp. p. 144.

17 Sugimoto and Swain, op. cit., pp. 117–19, 241–2; it should be noted that although the 'House Learning' of the court nobility lost its intellectual influence in the early Tokugawa period, family learning continued to play an important part in areas such as medicine during the eighteenth and early nineteenth centuries.

18 Endô M., *Kinsei shokunin no seikatsu*, Tokyo, Yûsankaku, 1985, pp. 69–72.

19 Ibid., p. 68.

20 Ibid., p. 77.

21 See, for example, J.G. Roberts, *Mitsui: Three Centuries of Japanese Business*, New York and Tokyo, Weatherhill, 1973, p. 30.

22 Ichikawa K., 'Kiryû no orimono', in Chihôshi Kenkyû Kyôgikai, ed., *Nihon sangyôshi taikei: Kantô chihô hen*, Tokyo, Tokyo Daigaku Shuppankai, 1959, p. 300.

23 Endô, op. cit., p. 80.

24 See Nôsan Gyoson Bunka Kyôkai, ed., *Meiji nôsho zenshû*, vol. 5, Tokyo, Nôsan Gyoson Bunka Kyôkai, 1983, pp. 4–5; Unno F. and Abe M., 'Kaikoku to nôgyô no henyô', in *Zusetsu Nihon bunka no rekishi* vol. 10, Tokyo, Shôgakukan, 1980, pp. 68–9; the cocoon samples, which were collected from 1818 to 1884, are still kept in the Tajima family storehouse.

25 See Nakayama S., *Characteristics of Scientific Development in Japan*, New Delhi, Centre for the Study of Science, Technology and Development, 1977, pp. 9–10.

26 Jôfuku I., *Hiraga Gennai*, Tokyo, Yoshikawa Kôbunkan, 1971, pp. 18–19; H. Maës, *Hiraga Gennai et son Temps*, Paris, Ecole Française d'Extrême Orient, 1970, pp. 17–19.

27 Sugimoto and Swain, op. cit., p. 315.

28 G.K. Goodman, *Japan: the Dutch Experience*, London, Athlone Press, 1986, chs 11, 13.

29 Jôfuku, op. cit., pp. 42–9, 68–70.
30 Ibid., pp. 129–37; S. Jones, 'Scholar, Scientist, Popular Author: Hiraga Gennai, 1728–1780', Columbia University, unpublished PhD thesis, 1968, pp. 74–8.
31 Jôfuku, op. cit., pp. 137–41.
32 See for example Jones, op. cit., p. 56.
33 Jôfuku op. cit., pp. 104–28.
34 Ibid., pp. 106–12; Jones, op. cit., p.52
35 Maës, op. cit., pp. 172–3; Jôfuku, op. cit., pp. 185–92.
36 Kikuchi T., 'Kaisetsu', in *EKKS*, vol. 11, p. 60.
37 See F.L. Schodt, *Inside the Robot Kingdom: Japan, Mechatronics, and the Coming Robotopia*, Tokyo and New York, Kodansha International, 1988, pp. 60–7.
38 On the Tekitekisai Juku (so called after a pen–name of Ogata's), see Goodman, op. cit., pp. 180–4; a lively fictionalised account of the school is given in Shiba Ryôtarô's *Kashin*, vols. 1–3, Tokyo, Shinchôsha, 1976.
39 See Fukuzawa Y., *The Autobiography of Fukuzawa Yukichi*, trans. E. Kiyooka, New York and London, Columbia University Press, 1966, pp. 58–92.
40 The vast majority of students of Dutch learning were men, but there were exceptions. The first officially recognised woman doctor in Japan was a daughter of the German physician, Philipp Franz von Siebold, and a Japanese geisha, who set up as a practitioner of western medicine in the last decades of the Tokugawa period.
41 Nakayama, op. cit., pp. 22–3.
42 Sugimoto and Swain, op. cit., p. 289.
43 See Goodman, op. cit., p. 133; Kikuchi, op. cit., pp. 61–6.
44 For example, R. Wuthnow, 'The Emergence of Modern Science and World System Theory', *Theory and Society*, vol. 8, 1979: pp. 215–43; Rosenberg and Birdzell also suggest that the plurality of power centres in Japan and Europe may have contributed to the emergence of capitalism in these regions. See N. Rosenberg, and L.E. Birdzell, *How the West Grew Rich: The Economic Transformation of the Industrial World*, New York, Basic Books, 1986, pp. 61–2.
45 Fujino T., *Bakusei to hansei*, Tokyo, Furukawa Kôbunkan, 1979, pp. 122–3.
46 Ibid., pp. 124–5.
47 Izuta C., *Uzen chihôshi no kenkyû*, Tokyo, Ikubundô Shoten, 1979, pp. 17–18; Yamamoto S., *Seishigyô Kindaika no kenkyû*, Maebashi, Gumma Ken Bunka Jigyô Shinkôkai, 1975, p. 4.
48 Narita J., *Sanshi kinuburui taisei*, (1813) in *NNZ*, vol. 35, pp. 319.
49 Akita Ken, *Akita Ken shi*, vols 2 and 3, Akita, Akita Ken, 1964.
50 Doi S., 'Kinsei tatara seitetsu no gijutsu', in Nagahara K. and Yamaguchi K. eds, *Nihon gijutsu no shakaishi*, vol. 5, Tokyo, Nihon Hyôronsha, 1983, pp. 101–2.
51 The export porcelain produced in Arita was commonly known as Imari ware, after the nearby port of Imari, from which it was shipped to Nagasaki. Information on the export of Imari ware is derived from Saga Prefecture's Kyûshû Ceramic Museum in Arita.
52 Saga Ken Shi Hensan Iinkai, *Saga Ken shi*, vol. 2, Saga, Saga Ken, 1968, p. 388.
53 Ibid., pp. 378–83; Ikeda S., 'Saga Han no tôjikigyô', in Chihôshi Kenkyû Kyôgikai, ed., *Nihon sangyôshi taikei: Kyûshû chihô hen*, Tokyo, Tokyo Daigaku Shuppankai, 1960, pp. 231–50.
54 Saga Ken Shi Hensan Iinkai, op. cit., pp. 377–8.

55 Suzuta Y., 'Kindai ni okeru Arita yôgyô gijutsu no hensen', *Gijutsu to bunmei* vol. 2, no. 1, 1985, p. 7.
56 Sumita, op. cit., pp. 102–3.
57 Ibid., pp. 121, 124–5.
58 Ibid., pp. 121–2; Suzuta, op. cit., p. 7.
59 Saga Ken Shi Hensan Iinkai, op. cit., p. 384.
60 Ishii K., *Taikei nihon no rekishi 12: Kaikoku to ishin*, Tokyo, Shôgakukan, 1989, pp. 54–6.
61 Narita, op. cit., p. 368.
62 Ishii K., *Nihon keizai shi*, Tokyo, Tokyo Daigaku Shuppankai, 1991, p. 70.
63 Okumura, *Hinawajû kara kurofune made*, pp. 100–9.
64 Maruyama Y., *Nihon no kinsei 6: Jôhô to kôtsû*, Tokyo, Chûô Kôronsha, 1992, pp. 22–3.
65 Sugimoto and Swain, op. cit., p. 186.
66 Hayashi H., 'Chiiki bunka to shisho no ikizama', in *Zusetsu Nihon bunka no rekishi*, vol. 10, Tokyo, Shôgakukan, 1980, p. 50; Nagatomo C., *Kinsei kashihonya no kenkyû*, Tokyo, Tôkyôdô Shuppan, 1982.
67 See W.H. Coaldrake, *The Way of the Carpenter*, New York and Tokyo, Weatherhill, 1990, p. 140.
68 H.J. Graff, *The Legacies of Literacy: Continuities and Contradictions in Western Culture and Society*, Bloomington and Indianapolis, Indiana University Press, 1987.
69 Whether the changes involved were large enough to warrant the term 'revolution' is, of course, open to debate. See Hayami A., 'Kindai Nihon no keizai hatten to Industrious Revolution', in Hayami A. et al., eds, *Tokugawa shakai kara no tembô*, Tokyo, Dôbunkan Shuppan, 1989.
70 See F. Bray, *The Rice Economies: Technology and Development in Asian Societies*, Oxford, Basil Blackwell, 1986, esp. pp. 113–16.
71 Muraoka K. and Okamura K., *Folk Arts and Crafts of Japan*, New York and Tokyo, Weatherhill/Heibonsha, 1973, pp. 79–89.
72 B. Jacomy, *Une Histoire des Techniques*, Paris, Editions du Seuil, 1990, pp. 247–8.
73 Ichikawa, op. cit., p. 294.
74 Negishi H., 'Bakumatsu kaikôki ni okeru seishi sôshi gijutsu tenkan no igi ni tsuite', *Shakai keizaishi gaku*, vol. 53, no. 1, 1989, pp. 1–28.
75 Quoted in Sasaki J., *Endogenous Technology in Japan*, Tokyo, United Nations University, 1981, p. 23.
76 Ibid., p. 20.
77 Takahashi K. and Furushima T., *Yôsangyô no hattatsu to jinushi seido*, Tokyo, Ochanomizu Shobô, 1958, pp. 39–40.
78 Yoshimura J., 'Bakuhansei shakai to hatasaku gijutsu', in Sasaki J., ed., *Gijutsu no shakaishi*,vol. 2, Tokyo, Yûhikaku, 1983, p. 136.
79 Kudô K., Negishi H. and Kimura H., 'Kinsei no yôsan, seishigyô', in Nagahara K. et al., eds, *Kôza: Nihon gijutsu no shakaishi 3: Bôseki*, Tokyo, Nihon Hyôronsha, 1983, p. 120.
80 N. Rondot, *L'Art de la Soie: Les Soies* (2nd edn), Paris, Imprimerie National, 1885, p. 296.
81 Narita, op. cit., p. 345.
82 See Nakamura Z., 'San tôkei hiketsu' (1849),' in *NNZ*, vol. 35, pp. 425–39.
83 Yoshimura, op. cit., p. 134.
84 Kudô, Negishi and Kimura, op. cit., pp. 111–12; Takahashi and Furushima, op. cit., p. 40.

85 L. de Rosny, *Traité de l'Education des Vers à Soie au Japon par Sirakawa*, Paris, Maisonneuve et Cie, 1868, p. 118.
86 Uekaki M., *Yôsan hiroku* (1803), in *EKKS*, vol. 13, p. 90.
87 L. Pasteur, *Etudes sur la Maladie des Vers a Soie*, vol. 1, Paris, 1870, p. 294.
88 De Rosny, op. cit., p. 117.
89 Ibid., p. xliii.
90 Tomita T., *Gijutsu ni kokkyô wa aru ka: Gijutsu iten to kikô fûdo shakai*, Tokyo, Daiyamondo Sha, 1991, p. 54.
91 Hayashi R., 'Kinsei shakai no mensaku to mengyô', in Nakahara K. and Yamaguchi K., eds, *Kôza: Nihon gijutsu no shakaishi 3: Bôseki*, Tokyo, Nihon Hyôronsha, 1983, pp. 199–200; Kodama K., *Taikei nihonshi sôsho 11: Sangyôshi*, vol. 2, Tokyo, Yamakawa Shuppan, 1965, pp. 281–2.
92 Hayashi, op. cit., p. 190.
93 See Tsunoyama Y., 'Inoue Den, Kagiya Kana: momen gasuri no joseitachi', in Nagahara K. et al., eds, *Kôza: Nihon gijutsu no shakaishi*, annex vol. 1, Tokyo, Nihon Hyôronsha, 1986, pp. 247–62.
94 Muraoka and Okamura, op. cit., p. 56.
95 Tashiro, op. cit., 1988, p. 137.
96 Quoted in C. MacFarlane, *Japan: An Account, Geographical and Historical*, London, George Routledge and Co., 1852, p. 12.
97 Sasaki J., 'Kôgyô ni okeru gijutsu no hatten', in Sasaki J., ed., *Gijutsu no shakaishi*, vol. 2, Tokyo, Yûhikaku, 1983, pp. 179–81.
98 Ibid., pp. 189–90.
99 Iida, op. cit., p. 136.
1 See *Sado kingin saisei zenzu* (late 18th–early 19th c.), reproduced in *EKKS*, vol. 1; also Sasaki J., *Endogenous Technology*, p. 16.
2 Sasaki, *Endogenous Technology*, p. 16.
3 Yoshiki F., *How Japan's Metal Mining Industries Modernised*, Tokyo, United Nations University, 1980, pp. 3–4.
4 Sasaki, 'Kôgyô ni okeru gijutsu no hatten', pp. 187–9; *Akita han shi*, Akita, Akita Ken, 1964, vol. 1, p. 302.
5 Anon., *Kodô zuroku* (1801), reproduced in *EKKS*, vol. 1.
6 See Iida, op. cit., pp. 127–8.
7 Quoted in Doi, op. cit., p. 71.
8 Ibid., p. 92.
9 Ibid., pp. 88–9; see also Iida K., *Nihon tekkô gijutsu shi*, Tokyo, Tôyô Keizai Shinpôsha, 1979, pp. 39–40.
10 Doi, op. cit., pp. 77–9; Iida, 'Kinzoku', p. 143.
11 Doi, op. cit., p. 81; see also Okumura S., *Koban, seishi, watetsu*, Tokyo, Iwanami Shinsho, 1973, pp. 139–40.
12 On iron smelting in the Nambu region, see Iida, *Nihon tekkô*, pp. 54–7. Also Nakaoka Tetsurô, 'Gijutsushi no shiten kara mita Nihon no keiken', in Nakaoka Tetsurô et al., eds, *Kindai Nihon no gijutsu to gijutsu seisaku*, Tokyo, Kokusai Rengô Daigaku/Tokyo Daigaku Shuppankai, 1986, p. 23.
13 Uemura M., 'Nada shuzôgyô no hatten', *Shakai keizaishi gaku*, vol. 55, no. 2, 1991, pp. 14–15.
14 Ibid., pp. 18–19; Katô B., *Nihon no sake no rekishi*, Tokyo, Kenseisha, 1977, pp. 239–55.
15 Katô, op. cit. pp. 243–4; see also Yunoki M., *Nihon no gijutsu 3: nihonshu*, Tokyo, Daiichi Hôki Shuppan, 1988, p. 93.
16 See Katô, op. cit., pp. 227–8.

17 Ibid., pp. 213–14.
18 Ibid., p. 213; see also Yunoki M., 'Nihon ni okeru shuzôgyô no tenkai', *Shakai keizai shigaku*, vol. 55, no. 2, 1991, pp. 2–3.
19 Hino E., *Nihon no gijutsu 7: mokkôgu no rekishi*, Tokyo, Daiichi Hôki Shuppan, 1989, p. 105.
20 Coaldrake, op. cit., pp. 148–9.
21 Hino, op. cit., p. 104.
22 Okumura S., *Hinawajû kara kurofune made*, pp. 189–91.
23 Ibid., pp. 191–3; Hosokawa's text on automata, the *Karakurizui* is reprinted in *EKKS* vol. 3.
24 Okumura, *Hinawajû kara kurofune made*, p.193.
25 On Vaucanson, see Jacomy, op. cit., pp. 139–50.
26 Information on Benkichi is derived from the Ishikawa Prefectural Museum of History, Kanazawa; see also Tachikawa Shôji, *Karakuri*, Tokyo, Kawade Shobô, 1987, pp. 103–8.
27 For further information on Tanaka Hisashige, see Schodt, op. cit., pp. 68–72; Imazu K., *Kindai gijutsu no senkusha: Tôshiba sôritsusha Tanaka Hisashige no shôgai*, Tokyo, Kadokawa Shinsho, 1962; Imazu K., *Kindai Nihon no gijutsuteki jôken*, Tokyo, Yanagihara Shoten, 1989.
28 See T. Morris–Suzuki, *A History of Japanese Economic Thought*, London and New York, Routledge, 1989, ch. 1.

Chapter 3: Opening the Doors

1 For an account of the incident, see C. MacFarlane *Japan: An Account, Geographical and Historical*, London, George Routledge and Co., 1852, pp. 89–93.
2 Ibid., ch. 1.
3 Sumita Y., *Arita: hakuji no machi*, Tokyo, Nihon Hôsô Shuppan Kyôkai, 1974, p. 130.
4 See *NKGST*, vol. 1, pp. 29–30.
5 Okumura S., *Koban, kiito, watetsu*, Tokyo, Iwanami Shinsho, 1973, pp. 180–1; see also G.K. Goodman *Japan: the Dutch Experience*, London, Athlone Press, 1986, pp. 145–55.
6 *NKGST*, vol. 1, pp. 29–31.
7 Iida K., *Nihon tekkô gijutsu shi*, Tokyo, Tôyô Keizai Shimpôsha, 1979, p. 72.
8 Ibid., pp. 72–3.
9 E. Pauer 'The Years Economic Historians Lost: Japan, 1850–1890', *Japan Forum*, vol. 3, no. 1, 1991, p. 2.
10 Iida, op. cit., p. 74.
11 Ôshima T., 'Tetsujû seizô goyô chûshinkan no gairyaku', (1889) in *NKST*, vol. 14, pp. 47–52.
12 See Okumura, op. cit., pp. 187–9.
13 Ibid., pp. 193–6; Iida, op. cit., pp. 75–7.
14 Ôshima, op. cit., p. 52.
15 See Iida, op. cit., p. 77.
16 Pauer, op. cit., p. 3.
17 Nakaoka T., 'Gijutsushi no shiten kara mita Nihon no keiken', in Nakaoka T. et al, eds, *Kindai Nihon no gijutsu to gijutsu seisaku*, Tokyo, Kokusai Rengô Daigaku/Tokyo Daigaku Shuppankai, 1986, p. 23.

18 Ibid., p. 24.
19 Sugiyama S., 'Thomas B. Glover: A British Merchant in Japan, 1861–70', *Business History*, vol. 26, no. 2, 1984, p. 119.
20 Okumura S., *Hinawajû kara kurofune made*, Tokyo, Iwanami Shinsho, 1970, p. 126.
21 Muramatsu T., Iida K. and Kikuchi T., 'Kurofune no shôgeki to gijutsu no shintenkai', in their work, *Zusetsu Nihon bunka no rekishi*, vol. 10, Tokyo, Shôgakukan, 1980, pp. 132–4.
22 Yamazaki T., *Gijutsu shi*, Tokyo, Tôyô Keizai Shimpôsha, 1961, pp. 6–8; Okumura, *Hinawajû kara kurofune made*, p. 125.
23 Okumura, *Hinawajû kara kurofune made*, pp. 125–6.
24 Kaneko E., *Gendai Nihon sangyô hattatsu shi*, vol. 10, Tokyo, Gendai Nihon Sangyô Hattatsushi Kenkyûkai, 1960, pp. 23–4.
25 Ibid., pp. 126–7.
26 Ibid., p. 123.
27 W.G. Beasley *The Rise of Modern Japan*, London, Weidenfeld and Nicolson, 1990, p. 31.
28 Sugiyama S., 'Kokusai kankyô to gaikoku bôeki', in Umemura M. and Yamamoto Y., eds, *Nihon keizaishi 3: Kaikô to ishin*, Tokyo, Iwanami Shoten, 1989, p. 184.
29 See *NKGST*, vol. 1, pp. 33–4.
30 See O. and S. Checkland, 'British and Japanese Economic Interaction under the Early Meiji: The Takashima Coal Mine 1868–88', *Business History*, vol. 26, no. 2, 1984, pp. 139–55; J. McMaster, 'The Takashima Mine: British Capital and Japanese Industrialisation', *Business History Review*, vol. 37, no. 3, 1963, pp. 217–39; Sugiyama S., 'Thomas B. Glover', pp. 126–7.
31 Katô K., 'G. Wagener to shokusan kôgyô seisaku no ninaitetachi', in Nagahara K. and Yamaguchi K., eds, *Kôza: Nihon gijutsu no shakaishi*, annex vol. 2, Tokyo, Nihon Hyôronsha, 1986, p. 68; Sumita, op. cit., pp. 138–43.
32 Gumma Ken, *Gumma Ken hyakunen shi*, vol. 1, Maebashi, Gumma Ken, 1971, pp. 304–5; Miyamoto M., *Onogumi no kenkyû*, vol. 3, Tokyo, Shinseisha, 1970, pp. 178–9.
33 Yamazaki, op. cit., pp. 12–13; Muramatsu et al., op. cit., p. 136; Nakaoka T., 'The Transfer of Cotton Manufacturing Technology from Britain to Japan', in J.D. Jeremy, *International Technology Transfer: Europe, Japan and the USA, 1700–1914*, London, Edward Elgar, 1991, pp. 181–3.
34 This memorandum, by Ishikawa Masatatsu (1826–95), is reproduced in Saigusa H., 'Gijutsu shi' (1940), in *Saegusa Hiroto chosakushû*, Tokyo, Chûô Kôronsha, 1973, pp. 131–4.
35 Umetani N., *Oyatoi gaikokujin 1: Gaisetsu*, Tokyo, Kashima Kenkyûjo Shuppansha, 1968, p. 227; the figures are for 1872.
36 In addition to the groups sent by Satsuma and Chôshû, certain students, e.g. Kusakabe Tarô of Echizen, went overseas on an individual basis; see Ishizuki M., 'Overseas Study by Japanese in the Early Meiji Period', in A.W. Burks, ed., *The Modernizers: Overseas Students, Foreign Employees, and Meiji Japan*, Boulder and London, Westview Press, 1985, pp. 162–5.
37 Some Japanese exhibits, collected by British Consul Rutherford Alcock, had been included in the London Exhibition of 1862. See Yoshida M., *Bankoku hakurankai: gijutsu bunmeishiteki ni*, Tokyo, Nihon Hôsô Shuppan Kyôkai, 1970, pp. 7–13.
38 Sumita, op. cit., pp. 132–3.

39 For example, Hattori Kyôsuke, a potter sent to the Paris Exhibition, studied oil-painting and photographic techniques, and later set up a studio in Edo where he taught these techniques to others: ibid., p. 137.

40 See Kamijô H., 'Paul Brunat: Kikai seishi gijutsu no dokusôteki ishokusha', in Nagahara K. and Yamaguchi K., eds, *Kôza: Nihon gijutsu no shakaishi*, annex vol. 2, Tokyo, Nihon Hyôronsha, 1986, pp. 13–14.

41 Fukuzawa Y., *The Autobiography of Fukuzawa Yukichi*, trans. E. Kiyooka, New York and London, Columbia University Press, 1966, pp. 115–16.

Chapter 4: Technology and the Meiji State, 1868–1912

1 Mori Ô. (trans. Ivan Morris), 'Under Reconstruction', in I. Morris, ed., *Modern Japanese Stories*, London, Eyre and Spottiswood, 1961, pp. 37–8.

2 Nôshômushô Tôkeika, *Kôjô tôkei fukenbetsu hyô* (1911), reprinted in *MZSHSS*, annex vol. 92–2, Tokyo, 1971.

3 Nishikawa S. and Abe T., 'Gaisetsu: 1885–1914', in Nishikawa S. and Abe T., eds, *Nihon keizaishi 4: Sangyôka no jidai 1*, Tokyo, Iwanami Shoten, 1990, pp. 12, 16.

4 Minami R., *The Economic Development of Japan: A Quantitative Study*, London, Macmillan, 1986, p. 117.

5 See, for example, A. Fabayo and L. G. Gatugata, *Technology Transfer and Industrialisation in the Developing Countries: Some Lessons from Japan*, Tokyo, International Development Centre of Japan, 1984, pp. 17–20; Okita S., *The Developing Countries and Japan: Lessons in Growth*, Tokyo, Tokyo University Press, 1980; K. Ohkawa and G. Ranis, *Japan and the Developing Countries: A Comparative Analysis*, London, Basil Blackwell, 1985, esp. chs 7–11.

6 I. Inkster, *Science and Technology in History: An Approach to Industrial Development*, London, Macmillan, 1991, see esp. p. 203.

7 See *NKGST*, vol. 1, p. 186.

8 Ibid., p. 181.

9 Information about samurai attacks on telegraph poles is contained in the memoirs of Richard Henry Brunton, a British engineer who came to Japan to supervise the construction of lighthouses, and was also responsible for the development of the Tokyo–Yokohama telegraph link. See R.H. Brunton, *Oyatoi gaikokujin no mita kindai Nihon*, trans. S. Tokuriki, Tokyo, Kôdansha, 1986, p. 31. The original version of Brunton's memoirs is published as *Building Japan 1868–1876*, Folkstone, Sandgate, 1991.

10 Yuzawa T., 'The Transfer of Railway Technologies from Britain to Japan, with Special Reference to Locomotive Manufacture', in D.J. Jeremy, ed., *International Technology Transfer: Europe, Japan and the USA, 1700–1914*, London, Edward Elgar, 1991, p. 204.

11 Harada K. 'Tetsudô no dônyû to kensetsu', in Unno F., ed., *Gijutsu no shakaishi*, vol. 3, Tokyo, Yûhikaku, 1982, pp. 119–20.

12 See Kôransha, *Arita tôgyô no nagare to sono ashiato*, Arita, Kôransha, 1980, pp. 20–1.

13 See Yoshiki F., *How Japan's Metal Mining Industries Modernised*, Tokyo, United Nations University, 1980, pp. 25–6; Yoshida M., *Nihon gijutsushi kenkyû*, Tokyo, Gakugei Shuppansha, 1961, pp. 8–20.

14 See Iida K., *Nihon tekkô gijutsushi*, Tokyo, Tôyô Keizai Shimpôsha, 1979, pp. 91–100, 113–21.

15 See Suzuki T., *Aru machi no kôgai monogatari*, Tokyo, Tôyô Keizai Shimpôsha,

1973; also Shoji K. and Sugai M., 'The Ashio Copper Mine Pollution Case: The Origins of Environmental Destruction', in Ui J., ed., *Industrial Pollution in Japan*, Tokyo, United Nations University, 1992, pp. 18–63.

16 Yamazaki T., *Gijutsushi*, Tokyo, Tôyô Keizai Shimpôsha, 1961, pp. 23–4; see also Smith, *Political Change*, p. 48.

17 Ibid., p. 184.

18 Kandachi H., 'Kindai bôsekigyô no ishoku to "ringukei kôjô" no seiritsu', in Unno, op. cit., pp. 139–41.

19 Miyamoto M., *Onogumi no kenkyû*, vol. 3, Tokyo, Shinseisha, 1970, pp. 179–80.

20 Gumma Ken, *Gumma Ken hyakunen shi*, vol. 1, Maebashi, Gumma Ken, 1971, p. 309.

21 Quoted in Yoshida M., *Gijutsu to Nihon kindaika*, Tokyo, Nihon Hôsô Shuppan Kyôkai, 1977, p. 78.

22 See, for example, Hoshino Y., *Gendai Nihon gijutsushi gaisetsu*, Tokyo, Dai–Nihon Tosho, 1956, pp. 27–33; Yoshida, *Nihon gijutsushi kenkyû*, pp. 7–20; Nakayama S., 'Science and Technology in Modern Japanese Development', in W. Beranek and G. Ranis, eds, *Science, Technology and Economic Development: A Historical and Comparative Study*, New York and London, Praeger Publishers, 1978; F.B. Tipton, 'Government Policy and Economic Development in Germany and Japan: a Skeptical Revaluation', *Journal of Economic History*, vol. 16, no. 1, 1981.

23 Andô Y., *Kindai Nihon keizaishi yôran*, (2nd edn), Tokyo, Tokyo Daigaku Shuppankai, 1979, pp. 56–7; slightly different figures for investment in some state enterprises are given in Smith, *Political Change*, pp. 90–1.

24 Yamamura K., 'Success Illgotten? The Role of Meiji Militarism in Japan's Technological Progress', *Journal of Economic History*, 1977, vol. 37, no. 1, 1977, p. 124.

25 T. Chida and P.N. Davies, *The Japanese Shipping and Shipbuilding Industries: A History of their Modern Growth*, London, Athlone Press, 1990, pp. 16–19.

26 Ibid., pp. 121–4.

27 Ibid., p. 119.

28 See Hoshino, op. cit., pp. 118–19; Yamazaki, op. cit., pp. 81–3.

29 Yamamura, op. cit., pp. 126–7; Yamazaki, op. cit., pp. 81–2.

30 Andô, op. cit., p. 87.

31 This, for example, is generally true of Hoshino's analysis of Meiji Japan, although his study does include some brief discussion of educational reforms on pp. 21–2; see Hoshino op. cit.; a similar emphasis is evident in Unno, op. cit.

32 For example, Inkster, op. cit.

33 See Saigusa, op. cit., pp. 250–8.

34 See Fukuzawa Y., 'Kunmô kyûri zukai' (1868), chs 1–2, in *NKST*, vol. 14, pp. 101–12.

35 H. Dyer, *The Evolution of Industry*, London, Macmillan, 1895, p. 191.

36 See Takahashi Y., *Ayrton to sono shûhen—Kôbu Daigakukô oyatoi gaikokujin kyôshi ni tsuite no shiten*, Tokyo, Tokyo Nôkô Daigaku, 1989.

37 Ôkubo T., 'Hakubutsukan no gi' (1875), in *NKST*, vol. 6, pp. 358.

38 See Katô K., 'G. Wagener to shokusan kôgyô seisaku no ninaitetachi', in Nagahara K. and Yamaguchi K., eds, *Kôza: Nihon gijutsu no shakaishi*, annex vol. 2, Tokyo, Nihon Hyôronsha, 1986, pp. 63–90; Yoshida M., *Bankoku hakurankai: gijutsu bunmeishiteki ni*, Tokyo, Nihon Hôsô Shuppan Kyôkai, 1970, pp. 128–9.

39 See the Exhibition catalogue, reproduced in *MZSHSS*, vol. 7, part 3.
40 Yoshida, *Bankoku hakurankai*, pp. 130–42.
41 *NKGST*, vol. 2, pp. 15–22; Musée National des Techniques, *L'Aventure du Mètre*, Paris, Musée National des Techniques, 1989, p. 67.
42 See M. Hane., *Peasants, Rebels and Outcastes: the Underside of Modern Japan*, New York, Pantheon Books, 1982, p. 63.
43 *NKGST*, vol. 2, p. 15.
44 Smith, *Political Change*, p. v.
45 Yoshida, *Gijutsu to Nihon kindaika*, p. 59; see also *NKGST*, vol. 1,pp. 179–86.
46 See Nakaoka T., 'On Technological Leaps of Japan as a Developing Country—1900–1940', *Osaka City University Economic Review*, no. 22, 1987, p. 3.
47 Nakaoka T., 'The Role of Domestic Technical Innovation in Foreign Technology Transfer', *Osaka City University Economic Review*, no. 18, 1982, p. 54.
48 Nakaoka T., 'Gijutsushi no shiten kara mita Nihon no keiken', in Nakaoka T. et al., eds, *Kindai Nihon no gijutsu to gijutsu seisaku*, Tokyo, Kokusai Rengô Daigaku/Tokyo Daigaku Shuppankai, 1986, pp. 27–45.
49 See, for example, ibid., pp. 101–2.
50 Nakaoka T., 'The transfer of Cotton Manufacturing Technology from Britain to Japan', in J.D. Jeremy, ed., *International Technology Transfer: Europe, Japan and the USA, 1700–1914*, London, Edward Elgar, 1991, p. 195.
51 See, for example, G. Saxonhouse, 'A Tale of Technological Diffusion in the Meiji Period', *Journal of Economic History*, vol. 34, 1974, pp. 149–65; K. Otsuka, G. Ranis and G. Saxonhouse, *Comparative Technology Choice in Development: the Indian and Japanese Cotton Textile Industries*, London, Macmillan, 1988, pp. 21–52.
52 Otsuka, Ranis and Saxonhouse, op. cit., pp. 23–4.
53 E.P. Tsurumi, *Factory Girls: Women in the Thread Mills of Meiji Japan*, Princeton University Press, Princeton NJ, 1990, pp. 141–2.
54 Otsuka, Ranis, and Saxonhouse, op. cit., p. 204.
55 Ibid., pp. 87–91.
56 Umegaki M., 'From Domain to Prefecture', in M.B. Jansen and G. Rozman, eds, *Japan in Transition: From Tokugawa to Meiji*, Princeton NJ, Princeton University Press, 1986, pp. 91–110.
57 See Kano M., 'Josetsu: Tôji taisei no keisei to chiiki', in Kano M. and Yui M., eds, *Kindai Nihon no tôgo to teikô*, Tokyo, Nihon Hyôronsha, 1982, pp. 1–40.
58 See R.W. Bowen, *Rebellion and Democracy in Meiji Japan*, Berkeley, University of California Press, 1980.
59 On the Lake Biwa scheme, see Homma H., 'Suiryoku kaihatsu to denki kikai no kokusanka', in Uchida H., ed., *Gijutsu no shakaishi*, vol. 5, Tokyo, Yûhikaku, 1983, pp. 102–6; *NKGST*, vol. 1, pp. 254–7.
60 This account of the rattling spindle and its inventor is derived from Ishikawa K., 'Gaun Tokimune: Garabô no hatsumei', in Nagahara K. and Yamaguchi K., eds, *Kôza: Nihon gijutsu no shakaishi*, annex vol. 2, Tokyo, Nihon Hyôronsha, 1986, pp. 157–87.
61 Ibid., p. 160.
62 Nakaoka, 'Domestic Technical Innovation', p. 54.
63 Ibid., p. 59; Nakaoka, 'Gijutsushi', p. 82.
64 Nagano Ken, *Nagano Ken shi: Kindai shiryô hen*, vol. 5, part 1, Nagano, Nagano Ken, 1991, p. 5.
65 Ibid., p. 10.
66 Ishikawa, op. cit., p. 161.

67 Hamamatsu Shiyakusho, *Hamamatsu Shi shi*, Hamamatsu, Hamamatsu Shiyakusho, 1980, pp. 69–93.

68 Iwate Ken Kôgyô Shidôsho, *Iwate Ken Kôgyô Shidôsho no rekishi to genjô*, Iwate, Iwate Ken Kôgyô Shidôsho, 1962, pp. 1–2.

69 Waseda Daigaku Keizaishi Gakkai, *Ashikaga orimono shi*, vol. 1, Ashikaga, Ashikaga Seni Dôgyôkai, 1960, p. 567.

70 Ibid., pp. 567–8.

71 Ibid., p. 569.

72 Ibid., p. 574.

73 Yoshida, *Gijutsu to Nihon kindaika*, pp. 96–101; Kamatani C., *Gijutsu taikoku hyakunen no kei*, Tokyo, Heibonsha, 1988, pp. 150–3.

74 Nagano Ken, op. cit., pp. 17–21.

75 Ishikawa, op. cit., p. 168; Waseda Daigaku Keizaishi Gakkai, op. cit., p. 568.

76 Ishikawa Ken, *Ishikawa Ken*, vol. 4, Kanazawa, Ishikawa Ken, 1931, pp. 717–23.

77 See *MZSHSS*, vol. 10, part 6, pp. 1–5.

78 Ibid., p. 720.

79 Waseda Daigaku Keizaishi Gakkai, op. cit., pp. 572–5.

80 *MZSHSS*, vol. 61, part 1, pp. 2–13.

81 Ibid., p. 13.

82 Ichikawa K., 'Kiryû no orimono', in Chihô Kenkyû Kyôgikai, ed., *Nihon sangyôshi taikei: Kantô chihô hen*, Tokyo, Tokyo Daigaku Shuppankai, 1959, pp. 309–10; Kyôto Shi Senshoku Shikenjô, *Gojûnen no ayumi*, Kyoto, Kyôto Shi Senshoku Shikenjô, 1966, p. 8.

83 Shiritsu Okaya Sanshi Hakubutsukan, *Okaya Sanshi Hakubutsukan*, Okaya, Shiritsu Okaya Sanshi Hankubutsukan, 1970, pp. 26–7.

84 Ishii K., *Nihon sanshigyôshi bunseki*, Tokyo, Tokyo Daigaku Shuppankai, 1972, p. 67.

85 See, for example, Gumma Ken, *Gumma Ken hyakunen shi*, Maebashi, Gumma Ken, 1971, pp. 299–304.

86 Aichi Ken, *Aichi Ken shi*, vol. 3, Nagoya, Aichi Ken, 1939, pp. 431.

87 Ishikawa, op. cit., pp. 179–80.

88 Nakayama, op. cit., pp. 213–26.

89 A. Pacey, *Technology in World Civilization: A Thousand-year History*, Oxford, Basil Blackwell, 1990, p. vii.

90 The orgins of the rikisha are a topic of much controversy, but it appears that the vehicle was a Japanese modification of earlier forms of wheeled transport which was developed simultaneously by three Tokyo craftsmen around the time of the Meiji Restoration. See Saitô T., *Jinrikisha*, Tokyo, Kuori, 1979, pp. 48–74; although rikisha receive scant attention in most Japanese studies of technology, their development has been discussed elsewhere; see for example P. Rimmer, *Rikisha to Rapid Transit: Urban Public Transport Systems and Policy in Southeast Asia*, Sydney, Pergamon Press, 1986, ch. 2.

91 Saitô, op. cit., p.172.

92 Ibid., pp. 195–203.

93 Ibid., pp. 108–9.

94 For details of the report, see I. Inukai and A.R. Tussing, '*Kôgyô Iken*: Japan's Ten Year Plan, 1884', *Economic Development and Cultural Change*, 1967, vol. 16, no. 1, pp. 51–71.

95 Ibid., p. 53.

96 *NKGST*, vol. 1, p. 253.
97 Uchida H., 'Gijutsu iten', in Nishikawa S. and Abe T., eds, *Nihon keizaishi 4: Sangyô no jidai 2*, Tokyo, Iwanami Shoten, 1990, p. 291.
98 For details of the Katakura enterprise, see Ishii K., 'Meiji chûki ni okeru seishi keiei: Katakura to Gunze', *Keieishi gaku*, vol. 3, no. 1, 1968, pp. 9–32.
99 *NKGST*, vol. 1, pp. 248–52.
 1 Ibid., p. 67; *NKGST*, vol. 1, pp. 248–52.
 2 Miyamoto M., Nakagawa K. and Hazama H., *Nihon no kigyô to shakai*, Tokyo, Nihon Keizai Shimbunsha, 1977, p. 149.
 3 See Hayashi T., *The Japanese Experience in Technology: From Transfer to Self-Reliance*, Tokyo, United Nations University, 1990, pp. 160–3.
 4 Sumita Y., *Arita: hakuji no machi*, Tokyo, Nihon Hôsô Shuppan Kyôkai, 1974, pp. 165–6.
 5 Ibid., pp. 133–4.
 6 Industrial Research Laboratory, *The Industrial Laboratory*, Tokyo, Industrial Research Laboratory, 1909, pp. 2–7, 14.
 7 Ishii, *Nihon sanshigyôshi*, p. 84.
 8 Quoted in J.R. Bartholomew, *The Formation of Science in Japan*, New Haven and London, Yale University Press, 1989, p. 100.
 9 J. Bolle, *Der Seidenbau in Japan*, Budapest, A. Hartleben's Verlag, 1898, p. 5.
10 Industrial Research Laboratory, op. cit., pp. 15–16, 22.
11 Ibid., pp. 7–8.
12 Yunoki M., *Nihon no gijutsu 3: Nihonshu*, Tokyo, Daiichi Hôki Shuppan, 1988, p. 137.
13 For example, Jôzô Shikenjo, *Hiroshima Ken shuzô chôsa hôkoku*, Tokyo, Jôzô Shikenjo, 1909.
14 Industrial Research Laboratory, op. cit., pp. 28–9.

Chapter 5: Systems-building and Science-based Industry, 1912–1937

1 Hitachi Seisakusho, *Hitachi Seisakusho shi*, vol. 1, Tokyo, Hitachi Seisakusho, 1960, pp. 29–32.
 2 Uchida H., 'Kigyô nai gijutsusha soshiki no keiseiki: 1900–1910 nen gijutsushasû no tôkeiteki kenkyû kara', *Tokyo Keidaigakkai shi*, nos 109–10, 1978, pp. 53–74.
 3 Hitachi Seisakusho, op. cit., p. 16.
 4 Tokyo Shibaura Denki KK Tsurumi Kenkyûjo, *Kenkyû 55–nen no ayumi*, Tokyo, Tokyo Shibaura Denki, 1961, pp. 11–68.
 5 Kamatani C., 'Kigyô o chûshin toshite kenkyû taisei no suii—sono rekishiteki hatten no tokuchô', in Hiroshige T., ed., *Nihon shihonshugi to kagaku gijutsu*, Tokyo, San-Ichi Shobô, 1962, p. 94; Kôgyô Gijutsu Chô, *Kenkyû hakusho*, Tokyo, Kôgyô Gijutsu Chô, 1951, p. 43.
 6 D.F. Noble, *America By Design: Science, Technology and the Rise of Corporate Capitalism*, Oxford and New York, Oxford University Press, 1977, p. 116; Tokyo Shibaura Denki KK Tsurumi Kenkyûjo, op. cit., p. 757.
 7 Tokyo Shibaura Denki Tsurumi Kenkyûjo, op. cit., p. 27.
 8 Ibid., p. 22.
 9 Hitachi Seisakusho, op. cit., p. 120.
10 Minami R., 'The Introduction of Electric Power and Its Impact on the Manufacturing Industries: With Special Reference to Smaller Scale Plants', in H. Patrick, ed., *Japanese Industrialisation and its Social Consequences*,

Berkeley, Los Angeles and London, University of California Press, 1976, pp. 299–325.

11 Kurihara T., *Gendai Nihon sangyô hattatsu shi 3: Denryoku*, Tokyo, Kôjunsha Shuppankyoku, 1964, p. 180 and annex p. 21.

12 Uchida H., 'Western Big Business and the Adoption of New Technology in Japan: The Electrical Equipment and Chemical Industries 1890–1920', in Okochi A. and Uchida H., *Development and Diffusion of Technology: Electrical and Chemical Industries*, Tokyo, Toyko University Press, 1980, pp. 152–4.

13 Fujita N., 'Ties Between Foreign Makers and Zaibatsu Enterprises in Prewar Japan: The Case of Mitsubishi Oil Co. and Mitsubishi Electric Manufacturing', in Yuzawa T. and Udagawa M., eds, *Foreign Business in Japan Before World War II*, Tokyo, Tokyo University Press, 1990, p. 133.

14 Mitsubishi Denki KK, *Kengyô kaiko*, Tokyo, Mitsubishi Denki KK, 1951, pp. 68–72; see also Yamamura K., 'Japan's Deus ex Machina: Western Technology in the 1920's', *Journal of Japanese Studies*, vol. 12, no. 1, 1986, pp. 73–5.

15 Tokyo Shibaura Denki KK, *Tokyo Shibaura Denki Kabushiki Kaisha hachijû gonen shi*, Tokyo, Tokyo Shibaura Denki KK, 1963, pp. 795–6.

16 Ibid., pp. 33, 758, 790.

17 Ibid.

18 Moritani M., *Gijutsu kaihatsu no Shôwa shi*, Tokyo, Tôyô Keizai Shimpôsha, 1968, pp. 35–7.

19 Ibid., p. 532.

20 *NKGST*, vol. 21, pp. 267–72.

21 Hoshino Y., *Gendai Nihon gijutsushi gaisetsu*, Tokyo, Dai Nihon Tosho, 1956, p. 109; B. Molony, *Technology and Investment: The Prewar Japanese Chemical Industry*, Cambridge Mass., Harvard University Press, 1990, pp. 63–73.

22 *NKGST*, vol. 21, p. 269.

23 Ibid., p. 271.

24 Kamatani, op. cit., pp. 110–11, 121.

25 Ui J., 'Minamata Disease', in Ui J. ed., *Industrial Pollution in Japan*, Tokyo, United Nations University, 1992, pp. 103–32.

26 Hitachi Seisakusho, op. cit., pp. 125–6, 157–8.

27 Teijin KK, *Teijin no ayumi*, vol. 1, Tokyo, Teijin KK, 1968, pp. 48–83.

28 See Ôkôchi Masayoshi, *Shinkô Nihon no kôgyô to hatsumei*, Tokyo, Nihon Seinenkan, 1937, pp. 102, 120–1.

29 Toyota Jidôsha Kôgyô KK, *Toyota Jidôsha sanjûnen shi*, Toyota City, Toyota Jidôsha Kôgyô KK, 1967, pp. 1–13; Hoshino, op. cit., p. 154.

30 Hoshino, op. cit., pp. 155–6.

31 Quoted in ibid., 156.

32 Ajinomoto KK, *Aji o tagayasu: Ajinomoto hachijû nen shi*, Tokyo, Ajinomoto KK, 1990, pp. 39–41, 46–53.

33 Kanagawa Kenritsu Kawasaki Toshokan, *Keihin kôgyô chitai kôgai shi shiryô shû*, Kawasaki, Kanagawa Kenritsu Kawasaki Toshokan, 1972, pp. 56–9.

34 Tasugi K., *Shitaukesei kôgyô ron*, Tokyo, Yûhikaku, 1941, p. 204.

35 Mori K., *Machi kôjô: mô hitotsu no kindai*, Tokyo, Asahi Shimbunsha, 1979, p. 190.

36 Hitachi Seisakusho, op. cit., pp. 28–9, 167–70.

37 Ibid., p. 169.

38 A. Gordon, *The Evolution of Labour Relations in Japan: Heavy Industry 1853–1955*, Cambridge Mass. and London, Harvard University Press, 1985, p. 200.

39 Hashimoto J., 'Kyodai sangyô no kôryû', in Nakamura T. and Odaka K., *Nihon keizai shi 6: Nijû kôzô*, Tokyo, Iwanami Shoten, 1989, pp. 127–8.
40 Hitachi Seisakusho, op. cit., p. 33.
41 Toyota Jidôsha Kôgyô, op. cit., p. 114.
42 Nihon Keizai Shimbunsha, ed., *Nihon gijutsu jimmyaku*, Tokyo, Nihon Keizai Shimbunsha, 1989.
43 Tokyo Kôgyô Shikenjô, *Tokyo Kôgyô Shikenjô gojûnen shi*, Tokyo, Tokyo Kôgyô Shikenjô, 1951, pp. 5–6.
44 *NKGST*, vol. 21, pp. 265, 279; Mikami, op. cit., pp. 206–7.
45 Teijin KK, op. cit., esp. pp. 82–3.
46 Isuzu Jidôsha KK, op. cit., pp. 24–7.
47 Uchida, 'Gijutsu seisaku', p. 226.
48 J.R. Bartholmew, *The Formation of Science in Japan*, New Haven and London, Yale University Press, 1989, p. 218.
49 Kôri T., *Nihon no kôkû 50–nen*, Tokyo, Kantôsha, 1960, pp. 173, 177–9.
50 Bartholomew, op. cit., pp. 217–23, 243.
51 Kôri, op. cit., p. 182.
52 Moritani, op. cit., p. 21.
53 See L.H. Lynn, *How Japan Innovates: A Comaprison with the US in the Case of Oxygen Steelmaking*, Boulder Col., Westview Press, 1982, pp. 67–8; Hoshino, op. cit., pp. 196–8.
54 Rikagaku Kenkyûjo, *Tokushu Hôjin Riken Sanjûnen Shi*, Tokyo, Rikagaku Kenkyûjo, 1988, p. 5.
55 Saitô S., *Shinkô kontserun Riken no kenkyû*, Tokyo, Jichôsha, 1987, p. 154.
56 Ibid., pp. 170–6.
57 Ôkôchi, op. cit., p. 69.
58 Ibid.
59 Calculated from Saitô, op. cit., pp. 170–6.
60 Ibid., p. 122.
61 See, for example, Ôkôchi M., 'Ichi–kôjô ippin no shôri', *Riken Kontserun Geppô*, vol. 4, no. 8, August 1940, pp. 2–5.
62 Yamazaki T, *Gijutsu shi*, Tokyo, Tôyô Keizai Shimpôsha, 1961, pp. 232–4; on the Industrial Harmony Association, see W.D. Kinzley, *Industrial Harmony in Modern Japan: The Invention of a Tradition*, London and New York, Routledge, 1991.
63 Ibid., p. 84.
64 Nôshômu Daijin Kanbô Tôkeika, *Kôjô tôkei hyô*, Tokyo, Nôshômu Daijin Kanbô Tôkeika, 1921.
65 Kurihara, op. cit., p. 181. The British figure is for 1933.
66 See Kurihara, op. cit., p. 197; R. Schwartz Cowan, *More Work for Mother: The Ironies of Household Technology from the Open Hearth to the Microwave*, New York, Basic Books, 1983, pp. 196–7.
67 R.J. Smith and E.L. Wiswell, *The Women of Suye Mura*, Chicago, University of Chicago, 1982, p. xxix.
68 See Suzuta Y., 'Kindai ni okeru Arita yôgyô gijutsu no hensen', *Gijutsu to bunmei*, vol. 2, no. 1, 1985, pp. 15–29.
69 Oshikawa I. et al., eds, *Chûshô kigyô ni okeru gijutsu shimpo no jittai*, Tokyo, Tôyô Keizai Shimpôsha, 1960, pp. 148–9.
70 Fifty of the prefectural and municipal laboratories still existing in 1989 gave their date of establishment as being between 1914 and 1941. Other local laboratories founded in the period may well have disappeared before the end of the 1980s. See Kagaku Gijutsuchô, *Zenkoku shiken kenkyû kikan meikan*, 1989–90, vol. 1, Tokyo, Rateisu, 1989.

71 R. Clark, *The Japanese Company*, New Haven and London, Yale University Press, 1979, p. 49.
72 Tasugi, op. cit., p. 197.
73 Ibid., p. 228.
74 Toyota Jidôsha Kôgyô, op. cit., p. 123.
75 On this strategy, see M. Cusumano, *The Japanese Automobile Industry: Technology and Management at Nissan and Toyota*, Cambridge Mass. and London, Harvard University Press, 1989, pp. 248–9.
76 Tasugi, op. cit., p. 204.
77 Kôransha, *Arita tôgyô no nagare to sono ashiato*, Arita, Kôransha, 1980, pp. 118–21.
78 Kobayashi, op. cit., p. 181.
79 Oshikawa I., *Chûshô kigyô no hattatsu*, Tokyo, Tôyô Keizai Shimpôsha, 1962, p. 31.
80 Yui T., *Chûshô kigyô seisaku no shiteki kenkyû*, Tokyo, Tôyô Keizai Shimpôsha, 1964, pp. 189–99; Abe T., 'Senkanki ni okeru chihô sangyô no hatten to kumiai, shikenjô—Imabari men orimonogyô no jirei o chûshin ni', *Nempô— Kindai Nihon kenkyû*, no. 13, 1991, p. 226; see also D. Friedman, *The Misunderstood Miracle: Industrial Development and Political Change in Japan*, Ithaca and London, Cornell University Press, 1988, pp. 161–6.
81 See, for example, Abe, op. cit., p. 234.
82 Tasugi, op. cit., pp. 292–3.
83 Yamagata Ken Kôgyô Gijutsu Sentâ, *Yamagata Ken Kôgyô Shikenjô rokujûnen shi*, Yamagata, Yamagata Ken Kôgyô Gijutsu Sentâ, 1977, pp. 43–7.
84 Ibid., p. 49; Tasugi, op. cit., p. 296.
85 Tasugi, op. cit., p. 281.
86 Nagano Ken, ed., *Nagano Ken shi*, section 9, vol. 3, Nagano Shi, Nagano Ken, 1990, p. 119.
87 Ibid., p. 61.
88 Ibid., p. 213.
89 Ibid., p. 214.
90 Ibid., pp. 215, 222; Inui S., *Kagaku gijutsu seisaku: Sono taikeika e no kokoromi*, Tokyo, Tôkai Daigaku Shuppankai, 1982, p. 18.
91 Uchida, 'Gijutsu seisaku', p. 222.
92 Ibid., pp. 223–5.
93 See C. Johnson, *MITI and the Japanese Miracle: The Growth of Industrial Policy 1925–1975*, Stanford, Stanford University Press, 1982, p. 118; Friedman, op. cit., p. 37.
94 Kôgyô Gijutsuchô, *Kenkyû hakusho 1951*, Tokyo, Kôgyô Gijutsuchô, 1951, p. 43.
95 Johnson, op. cit., p. 118.
96 Ibid., pp. 109–10.
97 Occasional awards to outstanding individuals had been given since the 1880s. See Uchida H., 'Gijutsu seisaku no rekishi', in Nakaoka T. et al., eds, *Kindai Nihon no gijutsu to gijutsu seisaku*, Tokyo, Kokusai Rengô Daigaku/ Tokyo Daigaku Shuppankai, 1986, p. 223.
98 Ibid., p. 228.
99 Kôgyô Gijutsuchô, op. cit., p. 43.
1 Nakayama S., *Science, Technology and Society in Postwar Japan*, London and New York, Kegan Paul International, 1991, p. 69.
2 Hiroshige T., 'Kenkyû taisei no kindaika', Hiroshige T., ed., *Nihon*

shihonshugi to kagaku gijutsu, Tokyo, San-Ichi Shobô, 1962, p. 23; Commission on the History of Science and Technology Policy, *Historical Review of Japanese Science and Technology Policy*, Tokyo, Science and Technology Agency, 1991, p. 39.
3 Ibid., pp. 19, 29 and 32–4.
4 See Fujisawa T., *Gijutsu seisaku*, Tokyo, Hakuyôsha, 1943, pp. 28–30.
5 Kuroiwa T., *Nihon no gijutsu ron: Shigen kaihatsu riyô no gijustsushiteki bunseki*, Tokyo, Tôyô Keizai Shimpôsha, 1976, p. 129; Minami Manshû Tetsudô KK, *Minami Manshû Tetsudô KK dainiji jûnen shi*, Dalien, Minami Manshû Tetsudô KK, 1928, pp. 883–4; Moritani, op. cit., 1986, p. 29.
6 Johnson, op. cit., pp. 120–1 and 132–3.
7 Fujisawa, op. cit., p. 15.

Chapter 6: A War of Science and Technology, 1937–1945

1 Aikawa H., *Sangyô gijutsu*, Tokyo, Hakuyôsha, 1942, p. 198.
2 See, for example, Kudo, A., 'The Tripartite Pact and Synthetic Oil: The Ideal and Reality of Economic and Technical Cooperation Between Japan and Germany', *Annals of the Institute of Social Science*, Tokyo University, no. 33, 1992, pp. 29–66.
3 Moritani M., *Gijutsu kaihatsu no Shôwa shi*, Tokyo, Tôyô Keizai Shimpôsha, 1986, pp. 29–30.
4 Fujisawa T., *Gijutsu seisaku*, Tokyo, Hakuyôsha, 1943, p. 28.
5 Ibid., p. 30.
6 C. Johnson, *MITI and the Japanese Miracle: The Growth of Industrial Policy*, Stanford, Stanford University Press, 1982, p. 133.
7 D. Friedman, *The Misunderstood Miracle: Industrial Development and Political Change in Japan*, Ithaca and London, Cornell University Press, 1988, p. 53.
8 Toyota Jidôsha Kôgyô KK, *Toyota Jidôsha sanjûnen shi*, Toyota City, Toyota Jidôsha Kôgyô KK, 1967, p. 132.
9 Kamatani C., 'Kigyô o chûshin toshite kenkyû taisei no suii—sono rekishiteki hatten no tokuchô', in Hiroshige T., ed., *Nihon shihonshugi to kagaku gijutsu*, Tokyo, Sanichi Shobô, 1962, p. 119.
10 Yamazaki T., *Gijutsushi*, Tokyo, Tôyô Keizai Shimpôsha, 1961, p. 227.
11 Kamatani, op. cit., p. 120; *NKGST*, vol. 4, pp. 337–8.
12 Ibid., p. 232.
13 Miyamoto T., 'Gijutsu kokusaku ron' (1940), in *NKGST*, vol. 4, p. 235.
14 See *Kagaku gijutsu shintaisei kakuritsu yôkô*, in *NKGST*, vol. 3, p. 355.
15 Ibid., p. 347.
16 See, for example, Ishihara J., 'Kagaku no tame ni' (1940), in *NKGST*, vol. 3, pp. 347–9.
17 See R. Coombs, et al., *Economics and Technological Change*, London, Macmillan, 1987, p. 220.
18 Yamazaki, op. cit., p. 231.
19 M. Low, 'Japan's Secret War? "Instant" Scientific Manpower and Japan's World War II Atomic Bomb Project', *Annals of Science*, no. 47, 1990, pp. 349–50.
20 Tokyo Shibaura Denki KK, *Tokyo Shibaura Denki Kabushiki Kaisha hachijû gonen shi*, Tokyo, Tokyo Shibaura Denki KK, 1963, pp. 190–2; see also Kamatani, op. cit., pp. 125–6.
21 Kamatani, op. cit., p. 125; Hitachi Seisakusho Chûô Kenkyûjo, *Hitachi*

Seisakusho Chûô Kenkyûjo shi, Tokyo, Hitachi Seisakusho Chûô Kenkyûjo, 1972, pp. 17–18.

22 Toyota Jidôsha Kôgyô KK, p. 20.

23 Tokyo Shibaura Denki KK, op. cit., p. 177.

24 Kodama S., *Kenkyû kaihatsu e no michi*, Tokyo, Tokyo Kagaku Dôjin, 1978, pp. 184–5.

25 See *NKGST*, vol. 3, p. 432; Kôgyô Gijutsu Chô, *Kenkyû hakusho 1951*, Tokyo, Kôgyô Gijutsu Chô, 1951, p. 47.

26 Mori K., 'Senjika no machi kôjô', in Uchida, ed., *Gijutsu no shakai shi*, vol. 5, Tokyo, Yûhikaku, 1983, pp. 223–4.

27 Ibid., pp. 226–8.

28 Ibid., pp. 232–4.

29 Toyoda E., *Toyota: Fifty Years in Motion*, Tokyo and New York, Kodansha International, 1987, p. 58.

30 Kôri T., *Nihon no kôkû 50–nen*, Tokyo, Kantô Sha, 1960, p. 190.

31 *NKGST*, vol. 4, p. 28.

32 M. Low, 'Towards a Gendered Approach to Teaching About the History of Japanese Science and Technology', in V. Mackie, ed., *Gendering Japanese Studies*, Melbourne, Japanese Studies Centre, 1992, p. 80.

33 Low, 'Japan's Secret War?', pp. 354–7.

34 Miyata S., *Doku gasu to kagakushatachi*, Tokyo, Kôjinsha, 1991, pp. 110–13, esp. 113.

35 See Tsuneishi K., 'Kagakusha to sensô: Ishii butai to sono shakaiteki haikei', paper presented at the 5th National Conference of the Japanese Studies Association of Australia, Brisbane, 1987.

36 Prosecution of those involved in the human experiments was not pursued by the Allies after the war, in part, it seems because the US government wished to monopolise access to the information gathered about the experiments and their results. See ibid., pp. 11–12.

37 For a discussion of Astroboy, see F.L. Schodt, *Inside the Robot Kingdom: Japan, Mechatronics and the Coming Robotopia*, Tokyo and New York, Kodansha International, 1988, pp. 77–9. The endearing Astroboy has a disturbing side to him: see John Russell's discussion of racist stereotypes in the work of Tezuka Osamu in 'Narratives of Denial: Racial Chauvinism and the Black Other in Japan', *Japan Quarterly*, vol. 37, no. 4, October–December 1991, pp. 416–28.

Chapter 7: Technology and the 'Economic Miracle', 1945–1973

1 See *NKGST*, vol. 5, p. 44.

2 Nakamura T., *The Postwar Japanese Economy: its Development and Structure*, trans. J. Kaminsky, Tokyo, University of Tokyo Press, 1981, p. 15.

3 *NKGST*, vol. 5, pp. 40–1.

4 *NKGST*, vol. 5, pp. 41, 59–60; Rikagaku Kenkyûjo, *Tokushu Hôjin Riken sanjûnen shi*, Tokyo, Rikagaku Kenkyûjo, 1988, p. 8.

5 See Nakamura, op. cit., pp. 32–4.

6 See Nishina Y., 'Nihon saiken to kagaku' (1946), in *NKGST*, vol. 5, pp. 80–4.

7 Gaimushô Chôsakyoku Tokubetsu Chôsa Iinkai Hôkoku, 'Nihon keizai saiken no kihon mondai', in ibid., vol. 5., pp. 74–7; quotations from pp. 74–5; the committee's members included the liberal economist Nakayama Ichirô and the Marxian economists Arisawa Hiromi, Tsuru Shigeto and Uno Kôzô.

NOTES (CHAPTER 7) 263

8 Nakayama S., *Science, Technology and Society in Postwar Japan*, London and New York, Kegan Paul International, 1991, p. 22.
9 Commission on the History of Science and Technology Policy, ed., *Historical Review of Japanese Science and Technology Policy*, Tokyo, Science and Technology Agency, 1991, pp. 64–7.
10 *Nihon yutakasa dêtabukku*, special edition of the journal Sekai, January 1988, p. 191.
11 Nakayama, op. cit., pp. 46–56.
12 Iwate Ken Kinzoku Kôgyôkai, *Iwate Ken kinzoku kôgyô gojûnen no ayumi*, Morioka, Iwate Ken Kinzoku Kôgyôkai, 1986, p. 12.
13 Denki Shôkô Shimbunsha, ed., *Denki gyôkai 35–nen shi*, Osaka, Denki Shôkô Shimbunsha, 1981, p. 115.
14 On these bodies, see for example D. Friedman, *The Misunderstood Miracle: Industrial Development and Political Change in Japan*, Ithaca NY and London, Cornell University Press, 1988, pp. 74–5.
15 Department of State (USA), *A New Era in World Affairs: Selected Speeches and Statements of President Truman, January 20 to August 29, 1949*, Washington, Office of Public Affairs, 1949, p. 7.
16 C.V. Prestowitz, *Trading Places: How We Allowed Japan to Take the Lead*, New York, Basic Books, 1988, p. 9.
17 Eisenhower, for example, actively encouraged business leaders to increase their imports from, and expand their exports of technology to, Japan. See ibid., pp. 193–4.
18 See J. Weste, 'Salvation from Without: Mutual Security Assistance and the Military–Industrial Lobby in Post-War Japan', *Japan Forum*, vol. 4, no. 2, 1992, esp. pp. 279–80.
19 See *Far Eastern Economic Review*, 5 December 1991, p. 47.
20 Toyoda E., *Toyota: Fifty Years in Motion*, Tokyo and New York, Kodansha International, 1985, p. 114; see also *NKGST*, vol. 5, p. 267; Nakamura, op. cit., p. 41.
21 See T. Ozawa, *Japan's Technological Challenge to the West, 1960–1974: Motivation and Accomplishment*, Cambridge Mass. and London, MIT Press, 1974, p. 18.
22 Kagaku Gijutsuchô, *Gaikoku gijutsu dônyû nenji hôkoku 1970*, Tokyo, Kagaku Gijutsuchô, 1970, pp. 18–19.
23 Ozawa, op. cit., p. 18.
24 Kagaku Gijutsuchô, op. cit., p. 8.
25 Uchino A., *Nihon no kenkyû tôshi*, Tokyo, Jitsugyô Kôhôsha, 1952, p. 118; *Kagaku gijutsu hakusho*, 1991, p. 278.
26 See Kodama S., *Kenkyû kaihatsu e no michi*, Tokyo, Tokyo Kagaku Dôjin, 1978, pp. 190–1; Arakawa K., *Nihon no gijutsu hatten saikô*, Tokyo, Kaimeisha, 1991, p. 22.
27 Arakawa, op. cit., pp. 19–20.
28 Kibi M., *Kiseki o umitsuzukeru takokuseki kigyô Sony*, Tokyo, Asahi Sonorama, 1980, p. 15.
29 Ibid., pp. 27–31.
30 See Kikuchi M., *Nihon no handôtai yonjûnen: Haiteku gijutsu kaihatsu no taiken kara*, Tokyo, Chûkô Shinsho, 1992, pp. 90–3.
31 Arakawa, op. cit., p. 24.
32 Yamazaki T., *Gijutsushi*, Tokyo, Tôyô Keizai Shimpôsha, 1961, pp. 266–7.
33 Nihon Keizai Shimbunsha, ed., *Shôwa no ayumi: Nihon no sangyô*, Tokyo, Nihon Keizai Shimbunsha, 1988, pp. 50–1.

34 M. Cusumano, *The Japanese Automobile Industry: Technology and Management at Nissan and Toyota*, Cambridge Mass. and London, Harvard University Press, 1989, p. 230.
35 Ibid., pp. 231–3.
36 Ibid., pp. 223–5.
37 See Iwate Ken Kinzoku Kôgyôkai, op. cit., pp. 22–3.
38 See Friedman, op. cit., p. 73.
39 Oshikawa I. et al., *Chûshô kigyô ni okeru gijutsu shimpo no jittai*, Tokyo, Tôyô Keizai Shimpôsha, 1960, p. 257.
40 Nihon Seisansei Honbu, *Seisansei undô 30-nen shi*, Tokyo, Nihon Seisansei Honbu, pp. 59–104.
41 Ibid., pp. 102–4.
42 Ibid., pp. 195–201.
43 The British body, officially called the Anglo–American Productivity Council, was set up in 1948 under the Marshall Plan, and was carefully studied by MITI before the establishment of the Japan Productivity Center. See ibid., pp. 44–7.
44 Ibid., pp. 78–80.
45 Ibid., pp. 290–59.
46 See W.E. Deming, *Quality, Productivity and Competitive Position*, Cambridge Mass., Massachusetts Institute of Technology Center for Advanced Engineering Study, 1982, p. 101.
47 See Nakayama, op. cit., pp. 92–4.
48 See Komai H., *Japanese Management Overseas: Experiences in the United States and Thailand*, Tokyo, Asian Productivity Organisation, 1989, p. 23.
49 Ibid., p. 26.
50 M. Tolchin, and S.J. Tolchin, *Selling Our Security: The Erosion of America's Assets*, New York, Alfred A. Knopf, 1992, p. 293.
51 W.S. Dietrich, *In the Shadow of the Rising Sun: The Political Roots of American Economic Decline*, University Park, University of Pennsylvania Press, 1991, p. 98.
52 See for example Nakayama, op. cit., p. 123; Yoshioka H., *Kagaku bunmei no bôsô katei*, Tokyo, Kaimeisha, 1991, pp. 150–1.
53 Inui S., *Kagaku gijutsu seisaku: Sono taikeika e no kokoromi*, Tokyo, Tôkai Daigaku Shuppankai, 1982, pp. 20–1; see also Nakayama, op. cit., p. 107.
54 Kagaku Gijutsuchô, *Kagaku gijutsu hakusho 1958*, p. 10.
55 Nakayama, op. cit., p. 120.
56 Ibid., pp. 238–9.
57 Uchino, op. cit., p. 196.
58 Tamura S. and Urata S., 'Technology Policy in Japan', in H. Soesastro and M. Pangestu, eds, *Technological Challenge in the Asia-Pacific Economy*, Sydney, Allen and Unwin, 1990, pp. 136–9.
59 Ibid., p. 106.
60 S.R. Reed, *Japanese Prefectures and Policymaking*, Pittsburgh, University of Pittsburgh Press, 1986, p. 24.
61 Ibid., p. 28.
62 Ibid., p. 29.
63 Kagaku Gijutsuchô, *Zenkoku shiken kenkyû kikan meikan*, vol. 1, Tokyo, Rateisu, 1989.
64 See Okaya Shi, *Okaya Shi shi*, Okaya, Okaya Shiyakusho, 1982, pp. 216–19; Sakaki Machi, *Tekunohâto Sakaki—Sakaki Machi kôgyô hattatsu shi*, Sakaki, Sakaki Machi, 1988, p. 52; on Sakaki, see also Friedman, op. cit., ch. 5.

65 Toyama Ken, *Toyama Ken shi: Tsūshi hen*, vol. 7, Toyama, Toyama Ken, 1983, pp. 694–5.
66 Saitô M., *Gijutsu kaihatsu ron: Nihon no gijutsu kaihatsu mekanizumu to seisaku*, Tokyo, Bunshindô, 1988, pp. 218–20.
67 Uchino, op. cit., p. 167.
68 S.E. Macreavy, ed., *Guide to Science and Technology in the UK*, London, Francis Hodgson, 1971.
69 Ibid., p. 141.
70 Organisation for Economic Cooperation and Development, *The Overall Level and Structure of R&D Efforts in OECD Member Countries*, Paris, Organisation for Economic Cooperation and Development, 1967, p. 45.
71 Ômori H., *Kenkyū kaihatsu seisaku: Matsushita Denki no jirei kenkyū*, Tokyo, Senzô Shobô, 1974, p. 81.
72 Kikuchi, op. cit., pp. 81–2.
73 Katayama N., *Nihon no zōsen*, Tokyo, Nihon Kôgyô Shuppan, 1970, p. 192.
74 T. Chida, and P.N. Davies, *The Japanese Shipping and Shipbuilding Industries: A History of their Modern Growth*, London, Athlone Press, 1990, p. 163.
75 Nihon Keizai Shimbunsha, op. cit., p. 100; the figure is for ships above 100 deadweight tons.
76 Chida and Davies, pp. 109–11, 132–4.
77 Ibid., pp. 111–13.
78 Itami H., *Nihon no zôsengyô: Sekai no ôza o itsu made mamoreru ka*, Tokyo, NTT Shuppan, 1992, pp. 159–61.
79 Ibid., pp. 172–3.
80 Ibid., p. 176; Chida and Davies, op. cit., p. 110.
81 Itami, op. cit., p. 176.
82 Ibid., p. 175.
83 K. Jones, *Politics vs. Economics in World Steel Trade*, London, Allen and Unwin, 1986, p. 63.
84 L.H. Lynn, *How Japan Innovates: A Comparison with the US in the Case of Oxygen Steelmaking*, Boulder Col., Westview Press, 1982, p. 16.
85 Ibid., p. 18; see also Hoshino Y., 'Japan's Post-Second World War Environmental Pollution', in Ui J., ed., *Industrial Pollution in Japan*, Tokyo, United Nations University, 1992, p. 68.
86 Arakawa, op. cit., pp. 40–1.
87 Nihon Tekkô Renmei, *Sengo tekkô shi*, Tokyo, Nihon Tekkô Renmei, 1959, ch. 7.
88 Lynn, op. cit., pp. 169–70, 173.
89 Ibid., pp. 82–4, 172.
90 Ibid., pp. 86–7.
91 Nihon Tekkô Renmei, op. cit., p. 742.
92 Tokyo Shibaura Denki KK, *Tokyo Shibaura Denki Kabushiki Kaisha hachijū gonen shi*, Tokyo, Tokyo Shibaura Denki KK, 1963, p. 516.
93 Okamoto Y., *Hitachi to Matsushita*, vol. 1, Tokyo, Chûô Kôronsha, 1979, p. 225.
94 Ibid., pp. 226–30; Lynn, op. cit., pp. 72–4.
95 Kibi, op. cit., pp. 96–112.
96 Okamoto, op. cit., vol. 2, p. 287.
97 See Okaya Shi, op. cit., p. 226.
98 Suwa Kyôiku Kai, *Suwa no kingendai shi*, Suwa, Suwa Kyôiku Kai, 1986, pp. 734–5.

99 Itami H., *Nihon no VTR sangyô: Naze sekai o seifuku dekita no ka*, Tokyo, NTT Shuppan, 1989, p. 148.

 1 See Nihon Hôsô Seron Chôsajo, ed., *Terebi shichô no sanjûnen*, Tokyo, Nihon Hôsô Shuppan Kyôkai, 1983, p. 52.

 2 Shiga N., *Terebi o tsukutta hitotachi*, Tokyo, Nihon Kôgyô Shimbunsha, 1979, p. 115.

 3 Keizai Kôhô Center, ed., *Japan: An International Comparison*, 1983, Tokyo, Keizai Kôhô Center, 1983, p. 76.

 4 Itami, *Nihon no VTR sangyô*, p. 87.

 5 Ibid., pp. 168–9.

 6 Ibid., pp. 168–70.

 7 Ibid., pp. 10–12.

 8 Ibid., p. 167.

 9 Ibid., p. 149; Suwa Kyôiku Kai, op. cit., p. 135.

10 Itami, *Nihon no VTR sangyô*, pp. 149, 177.

11 Ibid., p. 37.

12 Jôhô Shori Gakkai Rekishi Tokubetsu Iinkai, ed., *Nihon no kompyûta no rekishi*, Tokyo, Ômu Sha, 1985, pp. 45–8.

13 Ibid., p. 47.

14 Kimoto T., 'Jôhô gijutsu no hattatsu to shakai', in Yamazaki T., ed., *Gijutsu no shakaishi*, vol. 6, Tokyo, Yûhikaku, 1990, p. 214.

15 Jôhô Shori Gakkai Rekishi Tokubetsu Iinkai, op. cit., pp. 57–60.

16 Ibid., p. 177.

17 Ibid., p. 178.

18 Ibid., pp. 185–8.

19 Ibid., p. 188; M. Anchordoguy, *Computers Inc.: Japan's Challenge to IBM*, Cambridge Mass., Harvard University Press, 1989, p. 24.

20 Ibid., pp. 43–4.

21 Ibid., p. 48.

22 Kimoto, op. cit., p. 216.

23 See for example Okamoto, op. cit., pp. 196–8.

24 Jôhô Shori Gakkai Rekishi Tokubetsu Iinkai, op. cit., pp. 188–90; Anchordoguy, op. cit., ch. 3.

25 Anchordoguy, op. cit., pp. 34–5.

26 D. Noble, 'Social Choice in Machine Design: the Case of Automatically Controlled Machine Tools', in D. MacKenzie, and J. Wajcman, eds, *The Social Shaping of Technology: How the Refrigerator Got its Hum*, Milton Keynes, Open University Press, 1983, p. 111.

27 Nukui, *Kiiroi robotto: Fujitsu Fanuc no kiseki*, Tokyo, Yomiuri Shimbunsha, 1982, pp. 48–9, 56.

28 Nikkan Kôgyô Shimbunsha, *Gijutsu o hiraita hitobito*, vol. 1, Tokyo, Nikkan Kôgyô Shimbunsha, 1984, pp. 1–4.

29 Ibid., pp. 5–8.

30 Nikkan Kôgyô Shimbunsha, op. cit., p. 9; Hitachi Seisakusho, *Hitachi Seisakusho shi*, vol. 3, Tokyo, 1971, pp. 280–1.

31 Nukui, op. cit., p. 38.

32 Nikkan Kôgyô Shimbunsha, op. cit., pp. 9–10; Moritani, op. cit., pp. 96–7.

33 Nikkan Kôgyô Shimbunsha, op. cit., p. 11; see also G. Gregory, *Japanese Electronics Technology: Enterprise and Innovation*, Chichester and New York, John Wiley and Sons, 1985, p. 317.

34 Nukui, op. cit., p. 74.

35 Noble, op. cit., p. 113.
36 Nikkan Kôgyô Shimbunsha, op. cit., pp. 11–12.
37 Friedman, op. cit., p. 194.
38 Chûshô Kigyôchô, ed., *Gijutsu kakushin to chûshô kigyô: Chûshô kigyô kindaika shingikai hôkoku*, Tokyo, Chûshô Kigyôchô, 1985, p. 99.
39 Suzuki T., *Aru machi no kôgai monogatari*, Tokyo, Tôyô Keizai Shimpôsha, 1973.
40 Quoted in Kamata S., *Tetsu no machi no kiroku: Yawata, Kamaishi wa ima*, Tokyo, Daiyamondo Sha, 1982, p. 74.
41 Hayashi E., *Yawata no kôgai*, Tokyo, Asahi Shimbunsha, 1971, p. 56.
42 Hoshino, op. cit., p. 68.
43 Hayashi, op. cit.
44 R.P. Dore, *Shinohata: A Portrait of a Japanese Village*, London, Allen Lane, 1978, pp. 66–7.
45 Ibid., p. 313.
46 Kawana H., *Dokyumento Nihon no kôgai*, vol. 1, Tokyo, Rokufû Shuppan, 1987, p. 216.
47 C. Stevens, 'Ishimure Michiko's 'The Boy Yamanaka Kuhei'', in E.P. Tsurumi, ed., *The Other Japan: Postwar Realities*, Armonk NY, M.E. Sharpe, 1988, p. 144.
48 Hidaka R., *The Price of Affluence: Dilemmas of Contemporary Japan*, trans. G. McCormack, Melbourne, Penguin Australia, 1985, p. 161.

Chapter 8: High-tech Japan

1 Yoshioka H., *Kagaku bunmei no bôsô katei*, Tokyo, Kaimeisha, 1991, p. 162.
2 Quoted in Rikagaku Kenkyûjo, ed., *Tokushu Hôjin Riken sanjûnen shi*, Tokyo, Rikagaku Kenkyûjo, 1988, p. 5.
3 Tsûsanshô Kikai Jôhô Sangyô Kyoku, ed., *Yutaka naru jôhôka shakai e no dôhyô: sangyô kôzô shingikai jôhô sangyô bukai tôshin*, Tokyo, Kompyûta Êji Sha, 1981, p. 52.
4 Sangyô Kôzô Shingikai, *Sangyô kôzô no chôki bijion 1978*, Tokyo, Tsûshô Sangyô Chôsakai, 1978, p. 25.
5 Kikuchi M., *Nihon no handôtai yonjûnen: haiteku gijutsu kaihatsu no taiken kara*, Tokyo, Chûkô Shinsho, 1992, p. 136.
6 Imai K., 'Japan's Industrial Policy for High Technology Industry', in H. Patrick, and L. Meissner, eds, *Japan's High Technology Industries: Lessons and Limitations of Industrial Policy*, Seattle and London, University of Washington Press, 1986, p. 144.
7 Ibid., p. 143; Tamura S. and Urata S., 'Technology Policy in Japan', in H. Soesastro, and M. Pangestu, *Technological Challenge in the Asia-Pacific Economy*, Sydney and London, Allen and Unwin, 1990, p. 341.
8 Imai, op. cit., p. 144.
9 Ibid.
10 *Kagaku gijutsu hakusho*, 1983, pp. 220–3.
11 Mori S., 'Sentan gijutsu kaihatsu no nerai', in Watanabe E. and Mori S., eds, *Sentan sangyô shakai no yume to genjitsu*, Tokyo, Rokufû Shuppan, 1984, pp. 24–5.
12 See M.V. Brock, *Biotechnology in Japan*, London and New York, Routledge, 1989, pp. 101–2.
13 See Yokoi T., *Daigo sedai kompyûta: Jinkô chinô e no kakehashi*, Tokyo, Ômu Sha, 1985, p. 78.

14 Ibid., p. 82.
15 E.A. Feigenbaum and P. McCorduck, *The Fifth Generation: Artificial Intelligence and Japan's Computer Challenge to the World*, London, Michael Joseph, 1983, p. 12; Tatsuno S., *Created in Japan: From Imitators to World-Class Innovators*, Grand Rapids, San Francisco and London, Ballinger, 1990, pp. 170–1.
16 Feigenbaum and McCorduck, op. cit., pp. 152–3.
17 J.M. Unger, *The Fifth Generation Fallacy: Why Japan is Betting its Future on Artificial Intelligence*, Oxford and New York, Oxford University Press, 1987.
18 Quoted in Karatsu H., 'Daigo sedai konpyûta', in Shin-Gijutsu Kenkyûkai, ed., *Genkai gijutsu e no chôsen*, Tokyo, Nikkei Saiensu Sha, 1985, pp. 7–8.
19 See *Japan Times*, 11 June 1992; *Straits Times*, 5 June 1992.
20 See M. Anchordoguy, *Computers Inc.: Japan's Challenge to IBM*, Cambridge Mass., Harvard University Press, 1989, pp. 151–3.
21 *Japan Times*, 27 August 1992.
22 For further information on the Key Technology Promotion Center, see Tatsuno, op. cit., pp. 240–2, and Brock, op. cit., pp. 103–5.
23 See for example *Japan Times*, 8 August 1989.
24 A. Anderson, *Science and Technology in Japan*, London, Longman, 1984, pp. 70–1.
25 A 1988 report by JTECH (the US government body which monitors Japanese technology), for example, was full of praise for the scheme's role in promoting Japan's scientific creativity. See G. Gamota and W. Frieman, *Gaining Ground: Japan's Strides in Science and Technology*, Cambridge Mass., Ballinger, 1988.
26 Ibid.
27 *Japan Times*, 31 July 1990.
28 Ibid., 22 December 1991.
29 *Mainichi Daily News*, 28 November 1990.
30 See for example Nakayama S., *Science and Technology in Postwar Japan*, London and New York, Kegan Paul International, 1991, pp. 232–4.
31 See Gamota and Frieman, op. cit., pp. 28–30.
32 *Japan Times*, 14 May 1990.
33 *Asahi Shimbun*, 1 April 1992.
34 Ibid., 11 September 1992.
35 *Asia Technology*, November 1989, p. 54.
36 Ibid.; *Far Eastern Economic Review*, 2 July 1992, pp. 38–40.
37 L.L. Johnson, *Development of High Definition Television*, Washington DC, RAND Corporation, 1990, p. 10; on the HDTV project see also Tatsuno, op. cit., pp. 130–42.
38 Tatsuno, op. cit., pp. 141–2; *Asahi Shimbun*, 8 February 1992.
39 See *Asahi Shimbun*, 8 February, 14 March 1992.
40 Hibi S., *Atarashii asobi o enshutsu suru Nintendô*, Tokyo, Asahi Sonorama, 1980, pp. 90–2.
41 Ibid., pp. 76–80; Nakada *Nintendô senryaku*, Tokyo, JICC Shuppan, 1990, p. 15.
42 *Far Eastern Economic Review*, 24, 31 December 1992, p. 71.
43 Kodama F., *Analyzing Japanese High Technologies*, London and New York, Pinter Publishers, 1991, p. 21.
44 See Kitaya Y., 'The Age of Holonic Management', *Japan Echo*, vol. 13, special issue, 1986, p. 51.
45 Okamoto A., 'Creative and Innovative Research at RICOH', *Long Range Planning*, vol. 24, no. 5, 1991, pp. 9–16.

46 Chûshô Kigyôchô Shidôbu Gijutsuka, *Chûshô kigyôsha no gijutsuryoku kôjô no tebiki*, Tokyo, Tsûshô Sangyô Chôsakai, 1990, p. 33.
47 Ibid., pp. 165–8; see also Chûshô Kigyôchô, ed., *Gijutsu kakushin to chûshô kigyô: chûshô kigyô kindaika shingikai hôkoku*, Tokyo, Chûshô Kigyôchô, 1985, pp. 122–30.
48 Quoted in Segawa H., 'Tekunoporisu kôsô: Genkei to keii', in Miyamoto K., ed., *Kokusaika jidai no toshi to nôson*, Tokyo, Jijitai Kenkyûsha, 1986, p. 48.
49 Kanazawa F., 'Tenki ni tatsu tekunoporisu seisaku to chihô zaisei', in Uehara N., ed., *Sentan gijutsu to chiiki kaihatsu*, Tokyo, Ochinomizu Shobô, 1988.
50 Itô I., 'Kumamoto tekunoporisu no shinchoku jôkyô to shomondai', in Nihon Kagaku Gijutsu Kaigi, ed., *Kyûshû keizai no kokusaika, jôhôka*, Tokyo, Ôtsuki Shoten, 1989, p. 204.
51 Sasaki M., 'Japan, Australia and the Multifunctionpolis', in G. McCormack, ed., *Bonsai Australia Banzai: Multifunctionpolis and the Making of a Special Relationship with Japan*, Sydney, Pluto Press, 1981, p. 145.
52 Seki M. and Ishiro K., eds, *Chûshô kigyô no sentan gijutsu senryaku*, Tokyo, Shin Hyôron, 1991, pp. 92–7.
53 *Nikkan kôgyô shimbun*, 8 November 1990.
54 Niigata Ken Kôgyô Gijutsu Sentâ, *Kôgyô Gijutsu Nempô 1989*, Niigata, Niigata Ken Kôgyô Gijutsu Sentâ, pp. 23–6.
55 *Mie Ken Kôgyô Gijutsu Sentâ*, mimeograph, n.d.
56 Ishikawa Ken Kôgyô Shikenjô, *Nempô 1989*, Kanazawa, Ishikawa Ken Kôgyô Shikenjô, pp. 48, 51.
57 The highly controversial FSX project was a scheme initiated in 1989 for the joint development of a fighter aircraft by Japan and the United States. The project was strongly opposed by some US politicians, who believed that it would give Japan access to advanced and strategic US technology. On the other hand, the alternative—autonomous development by Japan of its own advanced fighter plane—was felt by some to pose even greater problems for the long-term security of the region.
58 This pattern has been outlined, for example, in Mary Kaldor's studies of armaments technology; see M. Kaldor, *The Baroque Arsenal*, London, Deutsch, 1982.
59 See M.F. Low and H. Yoshioka, 'Buying the "Peaceful Atom": The Development of Nuclear Power in Japan', *Historia Scientiarum*, no. 38, 1989, pp. 37–8.
60 Jishu Gijutsu Kenkyûkai, *Nihon no genshiryoku gijutsu: enerugî jiritsu e no michi*, Tokyo, Nikkan Kôgyô Shimbunsha, 1981, pp. 2–4.
61 Ibid., p. 7.
62 Low and Yoshioka, op. cit., pp. 36–40.
63 Murota Takeshi, *Genshiryoku no keizaigaku* (2nd edn), Tokyo, Nihon Hyôronsha, 1986, p. 139.
64 Jishu Gijutsu Kenkyûkai, op. cit., pp. 8, 35–9; Anderson, op. cit., p. 60.
65 Jishu Gijutsu Kenkyûkai, op. cit., pp. 31–5.
66 Quoted in ibid., p. 190.
67 See for example Murota, op. cit., pp. 77–98.
68 See *Asahi Shimbun*, 30 November 1992.
69 Genshi Enerugîchô Kôeki Jigyôbu et al., eds, *Genshiryoku hatsuden kankei shiryô*, Tokyo, Genshi Enerugîchô Kôeki Jigyôbu, March 1992, p. 12.
70 Murota, op. cit., pp. 259–61.
71 Tanaka Y., 'Nuclear Power Plant Gypsies in High-Tech Society', in E.P.

Tsurumi, ed., *The Other Japan: Postwar Realities*, Armonk NY, M. E. Sharpe, 1988, pp. 149–62.

72 *Asahi Shimbun*, 6 May 1993.

73 D. Toke, *Green Energy: A Non–Nuclear Response to the Greenhouse Effect*, London, Greenprint, 1991, p. 25.

74 *Asahi Shimbun*, 28 November 1992.

75 Kankyôchô Kagaku Gijutsu Seisaku Kenkyûjo, ed., *Ajia no enerugî riyô to chikyû kankyô*, Tokyo, Ôkurashô Insatsu Kyoku, 1992, p. 282.

76 Uchû Kaihatsu Jigyôdan, *Jidai wa uchû e*, Tokyo, Uchû Kaihatsu Jigyôdan, 1989, p. 2.

77 J. Johnson-Freese et al., 'Return from Orbit: Economics as a Driver of Japanese Space Policy', *Technology in Society*, no. 14, 1992, pp. 397–8.

78 Quoted in United States Senate, *Japanese Space Industry: An American Challenge*, Hearing before the Subcommittee on Foreign Commerce and Tourism of the Committee on Science and Transportation, Washington DC, US Government Printing Office, 1989, p. 2.

79 Kagaku Gijutsuchô Kenkyû Kyoku Uchû Kikakuka, *Uchû kaihatsu shinjidai*, Tokyo, Nikkan Kôgyô Shimbunsha, 1989, p. 19.

80 Uchû Kaihtasu Jigyôdan, op. cit., pp. 18–19.

81 *Asahi Shimbun*, 10 August 1991; *Far Eastern Economic Review*, 27 February 1992, p. 46.

82 Nashiro T., *Uchû bijinesu*, Tokyo, Tôyô Keizai Shimpôsha, 1991, p. 171.

83 *Asia Technology*, July 1990, p. 37.

84 Quoted in United States Senate, *Japanese Space Industry*, p. 14.

85 Tokunaga S., ed., *Japan's Foreign Investment and Asian Economic Interdependence: Production, Trade and Financial Systems*, Tokyo, University of Tokyo Press, 1992, p. 273.

86 Gaimushô/Kankyôchô, eds, *Kankyô to kaihatsu: Nihon no keiken to torikumi*, Tokyo, Ôkurashô Insatsukyoku, 1992, p. 18. The figures have been converted into $US using the average exchange rates given in *Kagaku gijutsu hakusho 1991*.

87 ESCAP/UNCTC Joint Unit on Transnational Corporations, *Technology Acquisition Under Alternative Arrangements with Transnational Corporations: Selected Industrial Case Studies in Thailand*, New York, United Nations, 1987, pp. 10–11.

88 Ibid., pp. 17–19.

89 The importance of active learning in the transmission of technology is eloquently argued by Richard Nelson; see R.R. Nelson, 'Acquiring Technology', in H. Soesastro and M. Pangestu, *Technological Challenge in the Asia-Pacific Economy*, Sydney, Allen and Unwin, 1990, pp. 38–47.

90 Quoted in J. Lull, *China Turned On: Television*, Reform and Resistance, London and New York, Routledge, 1991, p. 179.

91 See Awanohara, 'Look East: The Japan Model', *Asian-Pacific Economic Literature*, vol. 1, no. 1, 1989, pp. 75–89.

92 M. Heidegger, *The Question Concerning Technology, and Other Essays*, trans. W. Lovitt, New York, Harper and Row, 1977, p. 21.

Chronology

1542 First matchlock muskets introduced through Tanegashima.
1549 Francis Xavier introduces mechanical clock to Japan.
1592–98 Invasion of Korea under Toyotomi Hideyoshi.
1600 Victory of Tokugawa Ieyasu at Battle of Sekigahara.

Tokugawa Period, 1603–1867

1639 'Closed country' policy introduced.
1691 Introduction of first balance bellows (*tenbin fuigo*) at Besshi mines.
1702 Publication of first Japanese text on silkfarming.
c. 1710 Introduction of spinning wheels in cotton-spinning.
1720 Shogunate begins to encourage some 'Dutch learning'.
1738 Introduction of tall looms (*takabata*) to Kiryû district.
1757 First known use of *zaguri* silk-reeling equipment in northern Japan.
1771 Publication of Japanese edition of *Tian Gong Kai Wu*.
1776 Hiraga Gennai produces static electricity machine.
1783 Invention of water-powered silk-throwing machine by Iwase Kichibei.
1796 Hosokawa Yorinao's treatise on automata published.
1838 Establishment of Ogata Kôan's college in Osaka.
1849 Publication of Nakamura Zen'emon's text on the use of thermometers in silk-reeling.
1850 Construction of reverberatory furnace in Saga.
1852 Saga Domain establishes centre for western learning (the Seirenkata).
1853 Arrival of Commodore Perry.
1854 Nirayama reverberatory furnace established.
1855 Technicians in Satsuma Domain complete working model of a steamship.
1856 Shogunate opens Institute for the Study of Barbarian Documents (Bansho Shirabesho).
1858 Kamaishi blast furnace starts operation.
1861 Nagasaki dockyards opened.
1866 Satsuma Domain establishes western-style cotton factory.
1867 Japan takes part in Paris International Exhibition.

271

Meiji Period, 1868–1912

1868 Meiji Restoration.
1870 Kôbushô (Ministry of Industry) established.
1871 Domains abolished.
Kyoto City's Bureau of Chemistry (*Seimikyoku*) established.
Tsukiji silk factory opened.
1872 Tomioka silk factory opened.
Tokyo–Yokohama rail line opened.
1873 Imperial College of Engineering (Kôgakuryô Daigaku) established.
Jacquard loom and Kaye's flying shuttle introduced to Japan.
1877 Tokyo University established.
First National Industrial Promotion Exhibition opened in Tokyo.
1881 Sale of government enterprises begins.
Ministry of Agriculture and Commerce (Nôshômushô) established.
1883 Osaka spinning mill established.
1884 Trade Associations Ordinance (Dôgyô Kumiai Junsoku).
Maeda Masana's 'Opinions on the Promotion of Industry' (*Kôgyô iken*) completed.
1885 Kôbushô abolished.
Japan's first patent law introduced.
1890 Beginning of protest movement against pollution at Ashio copper mine.
1890s First private research laboratories established.
First company training schools established.
1891 Japan's first public hydoelectric power station opened.
Electrical Research Laboratory established.
1900 Tokyo Industrial Research Laboratory established.
1901 Yawata steelworks opened.
Ordinance regulating establishment of technical research laboratories.
1903 Technical Schools Ordinance (Semmon Gakkô Rei).
1904 Breweries Research Laboratory established.
1905 Beginning of government funding for local research laboratories.
1908 Ikeda Kikunae patents process for manufacture of monosodium glutamate.
1909 Calcium cyanamide process introduced at Minamata.

Taisho Period, 1912–1925

1915 Inawashiro power station completed.
1916 Toyoda automatic loom patented.
1917 Institute for Physical and Chemical Research (Rikagaku Kekyûjo) established.
1918 Imperial Artificial Silk Co. (Teijin) begins synthetic silk production.
Institute of Aeronautical Research opened at Tokyo University.
Military Industries Mobilization Law (Gunji Sangyô Dôin Hô).
First government grants for university research.
1923 Navy Central Research Laboratory established.
1925 Army Central Research Laboratory established.
Industrial Associations Law (Kôgyô Kumiai Hô).
Ministry of Commerce and Industry (Shôkô Shô) established.
1926 Government assistance for private research introduced.
First experimental television transmission (of a single still image).

Showa Period, 1926–1989

1927 Bureau of Resources (Shigenkyoku) established.
1928 Physics and Chemistry Industry Promotion Company (Rikagaku Kôgyô established.
1929 First manufacture of chemical weapons at Okunojima.
1931 Japan seizes control of Manchuria.
     Major Industries Control Law (Jûyô Sangyô Tôseihô).
1932 Japan Committee for the Promotion of Science (Nihon Gakujutsu Shinkô Kaigi) established.
1934 Japan Steel established.
1936 Toyota opens first car factory.
1937 Outbreak of war with China.
1938 National Mobilization Law (Kokka Sôdôin Hô).
     First protoype Zero fighter produced.
1941 Outline Plan for Founding a New Order for Science and Technology (Kagaku Gijutsu Shintaisei Kakuritsu Yôkô) announced.
     Pacific War begins.
1942 Technology Agency (Gijutsuin) established.
     First 'research neighbourhood groups' (kenkyû tonarigumi) established.
1943 Tôyô Rayon begins experimental production of nylon.
     First Japanese research on polyethelene.
1945 Atomic bombing of Hiroshima and Nagasaki.
     Japan surrenders to Allies.
     Technology Agency abolished.
1946 Commercial activities of Institute for Physical and Chemical Research abolished.
1948 Agency of Industrial Science and Technology (Kôgyô Gijutsuchô) established.
1949 Japan Science Council (Nihon Gakujutsu Kaigi) established. Ministry of International Trade and Industry (Tsûshô Sangyôshô) established.
1950 Outbreak of Korean War.
1952 Law for the Promotion of Rationalisation (Gôrika Sokushin Hô).
1953 First public TV broadcast by NHK Tokyo.
     Major Japanese firms license TV production technology from RCA.
     Japan Productivity Center (Seisansei Honbu) established.
1955 Sony launches transistor radio.
     Sumitomo licenses polyethelene technology from ICI.
1956 Science and Technology Agency (Kagaku Gijustuchô) established.
     Japanese firms acquire licence for basic oxygen steel process.
     Fujitsu produces prototype numerically controlled machine tool.
     Machine Industry Law passed.
1958 Japanese firms begin research on video technology.
     Electronics Industry Law passed.
1959 Council for Science and Technology (Kagaku Gijutsu Kaigi) established.
1960 Concept of quality control circle introduced by Ishikawa Kaoru.
1961 Japan Electronic Computer Company (Nihon Denshi Keisanki KK) established.
1963 Bullet train (Shinkansen) begins trial operation.
     Small and Medium Business Agency (Chûshô Kigyôchô) established.

1965 First Japanese nuclear power station opened at Tôkai Mura.
1966 National Research and Development Program introduced.
1968 Sony launches Trinitron colour television.
1969 National Space Development Agency (Uchû Kaihatsu Jigyôdan) established.
1970 NHK begins research on high-definition television.
1972 Chisso Corporation admits responsibility for Minamata disease.
1973 First oil crisis.
1976 Very Large Scale Integration Project set up by MITI.
1978 Machine Information Law passed.
1979 Second oil crisis.
      Fugen advanced thermal reactor opened.
1980 Technopolis plan announced.
1981 Next Generation Basic Technology project initiated.
      Fifth-Generation Computer Project begins.
      ERATO project begins.
      Supercomputer project begins.
1985 Key Technology Promotion Center established.

Heisei Period, 1989–

1989 FSX fighter project announced.
1990 First Japanese parallel-processing supercomputer launced by NEC.
1992 Real World Computing Project announced.
      First shipment of plutonium to Monju fast breeder reactor.
1994 Launch of HII rocket.

Bibliography

Collections of Documents

Edo kagaku koten sôsho (*EKKS*), Tokyo, Kôwa Shuppan, 1976-82.
Meiji zenki sangyô hattatsu shi shiryô (*MZSHSS*), Tokyo, Meiji Bunken Shiryô Kankôkai, 1959-1971.
Nihon kagaku gijutsu shi taikei (*NKGST*), Tokyo, Daiichi Hôki Shuppan, 1964–67.
Nihon kindai shisô taikei (*NKST*), Tokyo, Iwanami Shoten, 1988–90.
Nihon nôsho zenshû (*NNZ*), Tokyo, Nôsan Gyoson Bunka Kyôkai, 1977–81.

Newspapers and Weekly Magazines

Asahi Shimbun
Asia Technology
Far Eastern Economic Review
Japan Times
Mainichi Daily News
Nikkan Kôgyô Shimbun

Material in Japanese

Abe T., 'Senkanki ni okeru chihô sangyô no hatten to kumiai, shikenjô: Imabari men orimonogyô no jirei o chûshin ni', *Nempô–Kindai Nihon kenkyû*, no. 13, 1991.
Aichi Ken, *Aichi Ken shi*, vol. 3, Nagoya, Aichi Ken, 1939.
Aikawa H., *Sangyô gijutsu*, Tokyo, Hakuyôsha, 1942.
Aira R, 'Gendai sakezukuri jinbutsu ron', *Nihon hatsugen*, vol. 7, 1979.
Ajinomoto KK, *Aji o tagayasu: Ajinomoto hachijû nen shi*, Tokyo, Ajinomoto KK, 1990.
Akita Ken, *Akita Ken shi*, vols 2 and 3, Akita, Akita Ken, 1964.
Andô Y., *Kindai Nihon keizaishi yôran*, 2nd edn, Tokyo, Tokyo Daigaku Shuppankai, 1979.
Arakawa K., *Nihon no gijutsu hatten saikô*, Tokyo, Kaimeisha, 1991.
Arisawa H., *Nihon sangyô hyakunen shi*, Tokyo, Nihon Keizai Shimbunsha, 1966.

Brunton, R. H., *Oyatoi gaikokujin no mita kindai Nihon*, trans. S. Tokuriki, Tokyo, Kôdansha, 1986.

Chûshô Kigyôchô, ed., *Gijutsu kakushin to chûshô kigyô: Chûshô kigyô kindaika shingikai hôkoku*, Tokyo, Chûshô Kigyôchô, 1985.

Chûshô Kigyôchô Shidôbu Gijustuka, *Chûshô kigyôsha no gijutsuryoku kôjô no tebiki*, Tokyo, Tsûshô Sangyô Chôsakai, 1990.

Denki Shôkô Shimbunsha, *Denki gyôkai 35-nen shi*, Osaka, Denki Shôkô Shimbunsha, 1981.

Doi S., 'Kinsei tatara seitetsu no gijutsu', in Nagahara K. and Yamaguchi K., eds, *Kôza Nihon gijutsu no shakaishi 5: Saikô to yakin*, Tokyo, Nihon Hyôronsha, 1983, pp. 69–103.

Endô M., *Kinsei shokunin no seikatsu*, Tokyo, Yûsankaku, 1985.

Fujino T., *Bakusei to Hansei*, Tokyo, Furukawa Kôbunkan, 1979.

Fujisawa T., *Gijutsu seisaku*, Tokyo, Hakuyôsha, 1943.

Gaimushô/Kankyôchô, eds, *Kankyô to kaihatsu: Nihon no keiken to torikumi*, Tokyo, Ôkurashô Insatsukyoku, 1992.

Genshi Enerugîchô Kôeki Jigyôbu et al., eds, *Genshiryoku hatsuden kankei shiryô*, Tokyo, Genshi Enerugîchô Kôeki Jigyôbu, March 1992.

Gifu Ken Tôjiki Shikenjô, *Sôritsu gojûnen kinenshi*, Tajimi, Gifu Ken Tôjiki Shikenjô, 1961.

Gumma Ken, *Gumma Ken hyakunen shi*, vol. 1, Maebashi, Gumma Ken, 1971.

Hamamatsu Shiyakusho, *Hamamatsu Shi shi*, vol. 3, Hamamatsu, Hamamatsu Shiyakusho, 1980.

Han Gempatsu Jiten Hensan Iinkai, Han Gempatsu Jiten, vols 1–2, Tokyo, Gendai Shokan, 1978.

Harada K., 'Tetsudô no dônyû to kensetsu', in Unno F., ed., *Gijutsu no shakaishi*, vol. 3, Tokyo, Yûhikaku, 1982.

Hashimoto J., 'Kyodai sangyô no kôryû', in Nakamura T. and Odaka K., eds, *Nihon keizai shi 6: Nijû Kôzô*, Tokyo, Iwanami Shoten, 1989.

Hayama T., 'Teppô no denrai to sono hamon', in Hayama T., ed., *Nihon no kinsei 4: Seisan no gijutsu*, Tokyo, Chûô Kôronsha, 1992.

Hayami A., 'Kindai Nihon no keizai hatten to Industrious Revolution', in Hayami A. et al., eds, *Tokugawa shakai kara no tenbô*, Tokyo, Dôbunkan Shuppan, 1989.

Hayashi E., *Yawata no kôgai*, Tokyo, Asahi Shimbunsha, 1971.

Hayashi H., 'Chiiki bunka to shisho no ikizama', in *Zusetsu Nihon bunka no rekishi*, vol. 10, Tokyo, Shôgakukan, 1980.

Hayashi R., 'Kinsei shakai no mensaku to mengyô', in Nagahara K. and Yamaguchi K., eds, *Kôza Nihon gijutsu no shakaishi 3: Bôseki*, Tokyo, Nihon Hyôronsha, 1983.

Hibi S., *Atarashii asobi o enshutsu suru Nintendô*, Tokyo, Asahi Sonorama, 1980.

Higuchi K., 'Seikatsu no shashika to Nanban fûyô no ryûkô', in *Zusetsu Nihon bunka no rekishi*, vol. 7, Tokyo, Shôgakukan, 1980.

———, 'Shinkô toshi Edo no seikatsu', in *Zusetsu Nihon bunka no rekishi*, vol. 8, Tokyo, Shôgakukan, 1980.

Hino E., *Nihon no gijutsu 7: mokkôgu no rekishi*, Tokyo, Daiichi Hôki Shuppan, 1989.

Hiroshige T., 'Kenkyû taisei no kindaika', in Hiroshige T., ed., *Nihon shihonshugi to kagaku gijutsu*, Tokyo, Sanichi Shobô, 1962.

Hirota M., 'Bunmei kaika to minshû', in Emura E. and Nakamura S., eds, *Nihon minshû no rekishi*, vol. 6, Tokyo, Sanseidô, 1974.

Hitachi Seisakusho Chûô Kenkyûjo, *Hitachi Seisakusho Chûô Kenkyûjo shi*, Tokyo, Hitachi Seisakusho Chûô Kenkyûjo, 1972.
Hitachi Seisakusho, *Hitachi Seisakusho shi*, Tokyo, Hitachi Seisakusho, 1960.
Homma H., 'Suiryoku kaihatsu to denki kikai no kokusanka', in Uchida H., ed., *Gijutsu no shakaishi*, vol. 5, Tokyo, Yûhikaku, 1983.
Hoshino Y., *Gendai Nihon gijutsushi gaisetsu*, Tokyo, Dai Nihon Tosho, 1956.
——, 'Kôgyô gijutsu no hatten', in *Hoshino Yoshirô chosakushû*, vol. 5, Tokyo, Keisô Shobô, 1978.
Ichikawa K., 'Kiryû no orimono', in Chihôshi Kenkyû Kyôgikai, ed., *Nihon sangyôshi taikei: Kantô chihô hen*, Tokyo, Tokyo Daigaku Shuppankai, 1959.
——, et al., *Nagano Ken no jiba sangyô*, Nagano, Shinano Kyôiku Kai, 1986.
Iida K., 'Kinzoku', in Itô Shuntarô et al., eds, *Nihonjin no gijutsu*, Tokyo, Kenkyûsha Shuppan, 1977.
——, *Nihon tekkô gijutsu shi*, Tokyo, Tôyô Keizai Shimpôsha, 1979.
Iida T., *Tekunorando: Nihon no gijutsu ge saikô ni omoshiroi*, Tokyo, Purejidento Sha, 1983.
Ikeda S., 'Saga Han no tôjikigyô', in Chihôshi Kenkyû Kyôgikai, ed., *Nihon sangyôshi taikei: Kyûshû chihô hen*, Tokyo, Tokyo Daigaku Shuppankai, 1960.
Imai R., *Kagaku to kokka*, Tokyo, Iwanami Shinsho, 1968.
Imazu, K., *Kindai gijutsu no senkusha: Tôshiba sôritsusha Tanaka Hisashige no shôgai*, Tokyo, Kadokawa Shoten, 1964.
——, *Kindai Nihon no gijutsuteki jôken*, Tokyo, Yanagihara Shoten, 1989.
Inui S., *Kagaku gijutsu seisaku: Sono taikeika e no kokoromi*, Tokyo, Tôkai Daigaku Shuppankai, 1982.
Ishii K., '1910-nen zengo ni okeru Nihon sanshigyô no kôzô', in Otsuka H., ed., *Shihonshugi no keisei to hatten*, Tokyo, Tokyo Daigaku Shuppankai, 1968.
——, 'Meiji chûki ni okeru seishi keiei: Katakura to Gunze', *Keieishi gaku*, vol. 3, no. 1, 1968.
——, *Nihon sanshigyôshi bunseki, 1972*, Tokyo, Tokyo Daigaku Shuppankai, 1972.
——, *Taikei Nihon no rekishi 12: Kaikoku to ishin*, Tokyo, Shôgakukan, 1989.
——, *Nihon keizai shi*, 2nd edn, Tokyo, Tokyo Daigaku Shuppankai, 1991.
Ishikawa Ken Kôgyô Shikenjô, *Nempô 1989*, Kanazawa, Ishikawa Ken Kôgyô Shikenjô, 1990.
Ishikawa K., 'Gaun Tokimune: Garabô no hatsumei', in Nagahara K. and Yamaguchi K., eds, *Kôza Nihon gijutsu no shakaishi*, annex vol. 2, Tokyo, Nihon Hyôronsha, 1986.
Ishikawa Ken, *Ishikawa Ken*, vol. 4, Kanazawa, Ishikawa Ken, 1931.
Isuzu Jidôsha KK, *Isuzu Jidôsha shi*, Tokyo, Isuzu Jidôsha KK, 1957.
Itakura, K., *Nihon kôgyô no chiiki shisutemu*, Tokyo, Daimeidô, 1988.
Itami H., *Nihon no VTR sangyô: Naze sekai o seifuku dekita ka*, Tokyo, NTT Shuppan, 1989.
——, *Nihon no zôsengyô: Sekai no ôza o itsu made mamoreru ka*, Tokyo, NTT Shuppan, 1992.
Itô I., 'Kumamoto tekunoporisu no shinchoku jôkyô to shomondai', in Nihon Kagaku Gijutsu Kaigi, ed., *Kyûshû keizai no kokusaika, jôhôka*, Tokyo, Ôtsuki Shoten, 1989.
Iwate Ken Kinzoku Kôgyôkai, *Iwate Ken kinzoku kôgyô gojûnen no ayumi*, Morioka, Iwate Ken Kinzoku Kôgyôkai, 1986.
Iwate Ken Kôgyô Shidôsho, *Iwate Ken Kôgyô Shidôsho no rekishi to genjô*, Iwate, Iwate Ken Kôgyô Shidôsho, 1962.

Izuta C., *Uzen chihôshi no kenkyû*, Tokyo, Ikubundô Shoten, 1979.

Jishu Gijutsu Kenkyûkai, *Nihon no genshiryoku gijutsu: enerugî jiritsu e no michi*, Tokyo, Nikkan Kôgyô Shimbunsha, 1981.

Jôfuku I., *Hiraga Gennai*, Tokyo, Yoshikawa Kôbunkan, 1971.

Jôhô Shôri Gakkai Rekishi Tokubetsu Iinkai, ed., *Nihon no kompyûta no rekishi*, Tokyo, Ômu Sha, 1985.

Jôzô Shikenjo, *Hiroshima Ken shuzô chôsa hôkoku*, Tokyo, Jôzô Shikenjo, 1909.

Kagaku Gijutsuchô, *Kagaku Gijutsuchô jûnen shi*, Tokyo, Kagaku Gijutsuchô, 1966.

——, *Gaikoku gijutsu dônyû nenji hôkoku 1970*, Tokyo, Kagaku Gijutsuchô, 1970.

——, *Zenkoku shiken kenkyû kikan meikan*, Tokyo, Rateisu, 1989.

——, *Kagaku gijutsu hakusho*, various years, Tokyo, Ôkurashô Insatsukyoku.

Kagaku Gijutsuchô Kenkyûkyoku Uchû Kikakuka, *Uchû kaihatsu shinjidai*, Tokyo, Nikkan Kôgyô Shimbunsha, 1989.

Kamata S., *Tetsu no machi no kiroku: Yawata, Kamaishi wa ima*, Tokyo, Daiyamondo Sha, 1982.

Kamatani C., 'Kigyô o chûshin toshite kenkyû taisei no suii—sono rekishiteki hatten no tokuchô', in Hiroshige T., ed., *Nihon shihonshugi to kagaku gijutsu*, Tokyo, Sanichi Shobô, 1962,

——, *Gijutsu taikoku hyakunen no kei*, Tokyo, Heibonsha, 1988.

Kamijô H., 'Paul Brunat: Kikai seishi gijutsu no dokusôteki ishokusha', in Nagahara K. and Yamaguchi K., eds, *Kôza: Nihon gijutsu no shakaishi*, annex vol. 2, Tokyo, Nihon Hyôronsha, 1986, pp. 9–36.

Kanagawa Kenritsu Kawasaki Toshokan, *Keihin kôgyô chitai kôgai shi shiryô shû*, Kawasaki, Kanagawa Kenritsu Kawasaki Toshokan, 1972.

Kanazawa F., 'Tenki ni tatsu tekunoporisu seisaku to chihô keizai', in Uehara N., ed., *Sentan gijutsu to chiiki kaihatsu*, Tokyo, Ochanomizu Shobô, 1988.

Kandachi H., 'Kindai bôsekigyô no ishoku to "ringukei kôjô" no seiritsu', in Unno F., ed., *Gijutsu no shakaishi*, vol. 3, Tokyo, Yûhikaku, 1982, pp. 139–41.

Kaneko E., *Gendai Nihon sangyô hattatsu shi*, vol. 10. Tokyo, Gendai Nihon Sangyô Hattatsu Shi Kenkyûkai, 1960.

Kankyôchô Kagaku Gijtsu Seisaku Kenkyûjo, ed., *Ajia no enerugî riyô to chikyû kankyô*, Tokyo, Ôkurashô Insatsukyoku, 1992.

Kano M., 'Josetsu: Tôji taisei no keisei to chiiki', in Kano M. and Yûi M., eds, *Kindai Nihon no tôgô to teikô*, Tokyo, Nihon Hyôronsha, 1982.

Karatsu H., 'Daigo sedai kompyûta', in Shin-Gijutsu Kenkyûkai, ed., *Genkai gijutsu e no chôsen*, Tokyo, Nikkei Saiensu Sha, 1985.

Katayama N., *Nihon no zôsen*, Tokyo, Nihon Kôgyô Shuppan, 1970.

Katô B., *Nihon no sake no rekishi*, Tokyo, Kenseisha, 1977.

Katô K., 'G. Wagener to shokusan kôgyô seisaku no ninaitetachi', in Nagahara K. and Yamaguchi K., eds, *Kôza: Nihon gijutsu no shakaishi*, annex vol. 2, Tokyo, Nihon Hyôronsha, 1986, pp. 63–90.

——, 'Yamanobe Takeo to kindaiteki bôsekigyô', in Nagahara K. and Yamamoto K., eds, *Kôza: Nihon gijutsu no shakaishi*, annex vol. 2, Tokyo, Nihon Hyôronsha, 1986, pp. 189–218.

Katô H., *Nihon no sake 5000-nen*, Toyko, Gihôdô Shuppan, 1987.

Kawana H., *Dokyumento Nihon no kôgai*, vol. 1, Tokyo, Rokufû Shuppan, 1987.

Keizai Kikakuchô Chôsakyoku, *Keizai Yôran 1990*, Tokyo, Ôkurashô Insatsukyoku, 1990.

Kenkyû Kaihatsu, Gijutsu Kaihatsu Sôran Henshû Iinkai, *Kenkyû kaihatsu, gijutsu kaihatsu sôran*, Tokyo, Sangyô Chôsakai, 1989.

Kibi M., *Kiseki o umitsuzukeru takokuseki kigyô Sony*, Tokyo, Asahi Sonorama, 1980.

Kikuchi M., *Nihon no handôtai yonjûnen: Haiteku gijutsu kaihatsu no taiken kara*, Tokyo, Chûkô Shinsho, 1992.

Kimoto T., 'Jôhô gijutsu no hattatsu to shakai', in Yamazaki T., ed., *Gijutsu no shakai shi*, vol. 6, Tokyo, Yûhikaku, 1990.

Kobayashi T., *Gijutsu iten: rekishi kara no kôsatsu—Amerika to Nihon*, Tokyo, Bunshindô, 1981.

Kodama K., *Taikei Nihonshi sôsho 11: Sangyôshi*, vol. 2, Tokyo, Yamakawa Shuppan, 1965.

Kodama S., *Kenkyû kaihatsu e no michi*, Tokyo, Tokyo Kagaku Dôjin, 1978.

Kôgyô Gijutsuchô, *Kenkyû hakusho 1951*, Tokyo, Kôgyô Gijutsuchô, 1951.

Kôransha, *Arita tôgyô no nagare to sono ashiato*, Arita, Kôransha, 1980.

Kôri T., *Nihon no kôkû 50-nen*, Tokyo, Kantôsha, 1960.

Kudô K., Negishi H. and Kimura H., 'Kinsei no yôsan, seishigyô', in Nagahara K. and Yamaguchi K., eds, *Kôza Nihon gijutsu no shakaishi: Bôseki*, Tokyo, Nihon Hyôronsha, 1983.

Kurihara T., *Gendai Nihon sangyô hattatsu shi 3: Denryoku*, Tokyo, Kôjunsha Shuppankyoku, 1964.

Kuroiwa T., *Gendai gijutsu shi ron*, Tokyo, Tôyô Keizai Shimpôsha, 1987.

Kyoto Shi Senshoku Shikenjô, *Gojûnen no ayumi*, Kyoto, Kyoto Shi Senshoku Shikenjô, 1966.

Maruyama Y., *Nihon no kinsei 6: Jôhô to kôtsû*, Tokyo, Chûô Kôronsha, 1992.

'Mie Ken Kôgyô Gijutsu Sentâ', mimeograph, n.d.

Minami Manshû Tetsudô KK, *Minami Manshû Tetsudô KK dainiji jûnen shi*, Dalien, Minami Manshû Tetsudô KK, 1928.

——, *Minami Manshû Tetsudô KK daisanji jûnen shi*, vol. 3, Dalien, Minami Manshû Tetsudô KK, 1938.

Mitsubishi Denki KK, *Kengyô kaiko*, Tokyo, Mitsubishi Denki KK, 1951.

Mitsubishi Jûkôgyô KK, *Mitsubishi Jûkôgyô Kabushiki Kaisha shi*, Tokyo, Mitsubishi Jûkôgyô K.K., 1956.

Miyamoto M., *Onogumi no kenkyû*, vols. 1–3. Tokyo, Shinseisha, 1970.

——, Nakagawa K., and Hazama H., *Nihon no kigyô to shakai*, vol. 6, Tokyo, Nihon Keizai Shimbunsha, 1977.

Miyata S., *Doku gasu to kagakushatachi*, Tokyo, Kôjinsha, 1991.

Mori K., *Machi kôjô: mô hitotsu no kindai*, Tokyo, Asahi Shimbunsha, 1979.

——, 'Senjika no machi kôjô', in Uchida H., ed., *Gijutsu no shakai shi*, vol. 5, Tokyo, Yûhikaku, 1983.

Mori S., 'Sentan gijutsu kaihatsu no nerai', in Watanabe E. and Mori S., eds, *Sentan sangyô shakai no yume to genjitsu*, Tokyo, Rokufû Shuppan, 1984.

Moritani M., *Gijutsu kaihatsu no Shôwa shi*, Tokyo, Tôyô Keizai Shimpôsha, 1986.

Muramatsu T., Iida K., and Kikuchi T., 'Kurofune no shôgeki to gijutsu no shintenkai', in *Zusetsu Nihon bunka no rekishi*, vol. 10, Tokyo, Shôgakukan, 1980.

Muramatsu T., Aoki K., and Endô A., 'Kangyô hakurankai to rengazô kenchiku', in *Zusetsu Nihon bunka no rekishi*, 11, Tokyo, Shôgakukan, 1981.

Murota T., *Genshiryoku no keizaigaku*, (2nd edn), Tokyo, Nihon Hyôronsha, 1986.

Nagano Ken, *Nagano Ken shi: Kindai shiryô hen*, section 5, vol. 1, and section 9, vol. 3, Nagano, Nagano Ken, 1991.

Nagatomo C., *Kinsei kashihonya no kenkyû*, Tokyo, Tôkyôdô Shuppan, 1982.

Nakada H., *Nintendô senryaku*, Tokyo, JICC Shuppan, 1980.

Nakamura T., 'Makuro keizai to sengo keiei', in Nishikawa S. and Yamamoto Y., eds, *Nihon keizaishi 5: Sangyôka no jidai 2*, Tokyo, Iwanami Shoten, 1990.

Nakaoka T., 'Gijutsushi no shiten kara mita Nihon no keiken', in Nakaoka T. et al., eds, *Kindai Nihon no gijutsu to gijutsu seisaku*, Tokyo, Kokusai Rengô Daigaku/Tokyo Daigaku Shuppankai, 1986.

——, 'Nihon no kindaika to gijutsu kakushin', Paper presented at the International Conference on Japan and the World, International Center for Japanese Studies, Kyoto, 1991.

Nashiro T., *Uchû bijinesu*, Tokyo, Tôyô Keizai Shimpôsha, 1991.

Negishi H., 'Bakumatsu kaikôki ni okeru seishi sôshi gijutsu tenkan no igi ni tsuite', *Shakai keizaishi gaku*, vol. 53, no. 1, 1989.

Nihon Hôsô Seron Chôsajo, *Terebi shichô no sanjûnen*, Tokyo, Nihon Hôsô Shuppan Kyôkai, 1983.

Nihon Keizai Shimbunsha, ed., *Nihon gijutsu jimmyaku*, Tokyo, Nihon Keizai Shimbunsha, 1989.

——, ed., *Shôwa no ayumi: Nihon no sangyô*, Tokyo, Nihon Keizai Shimbunsha, 1988.

Nihon Seisansei Honbu, *Seisansei undô 30-nen shi*, Tokyo, Nihon Seisansei Honbu, 1985.

Nihon Tekkô Renmei, *Sengo tekkô shi*, Tokyo, Nihon Tekkô Renmei, 1959.

Nihon yutakasa dêtabukku, special edition of the journal *Sekai*, Tokyo, January 1988.

Niigata Ken Kôgyô Gijutsu Sentâ, *Kôgyô gijutsu nempô 1989*, Niigata, Niigata Kôgyô Gijutsu Sentâ, 1990.

Nikkan Kôgyô Shimbunsha, ed., *Gijutsu o hiraita hitobito*, vol. 1, Tokyo, Nikkan Kôgyô Shimbunsha, 1984.

Nishikawa S., 'Zairai sangyô no kindaika', in Nishikawa S. and Abe T., eds, *Nihon keizaishi 4: Sangyôka no jidai 1*, Tokyo, Iwanami shoten, 1990.

—— and Abe T., 'Gaisetsu: 1885-1914', in Nishikawa S. and Abe T., eds, *Nihon keizaishi 4: Sangyôka no jidai 1*, Tokyo, Iwanami shoten, 1990.

Nôshômu Kanbô Daijin Tôkeika, *Kôjô tôkei hyô*, Tokyo, Nôshômu Kanbô Daijin Tôkeika, 1921.

Nukui K., *Kiiroi robotto: Fujitsu Fanuc no kiseki*, Tokyo, Yomiuri Shimbunsha, 1982.

Ôhashi H., 'Kyûshû ni okeru kindai sangyô no hatten', in Chihôshi Kenkyû Kyôgikai, ed., *Nihon sangyôshi taikei: Kyûshû chihô hen*, Tokyo, Tokyo Daigaku Shuppankai, 1960, 350–71.

Okamoto Y., *Hitachi to Matsushita*, vols 1–2, Tokyo, Chûô Kôronsha, 1979.

Okaya Shi, *Okaya Shi shi*, Okaya, Okaya Shiyakusho, 1982.

Ôkôchi M., *Shinkô Nihon no kôgyô to hatsumei*, Tokyo, Nihon Seinenkan, 1937.

——, 'Ichi-kôjô ippin no shôri', in *Riken Kontserun geppô*, vol. 4, no. 8, 1940.

Okumara S., *Hinawajû kara kurofune made*, Tokyo, Iwanami Shinsho, 1970.

——, *Koban, kiito, watetsu*, Tokyo, Iwanami Shinsho, 1973.

Ômori H., *Kenkyû kaihatsu seisaku: Matsushita Denki no jirei kenkyû*, Tokyo, Senzô Shobô, 1974.

Oshikawa I., *Chûshô kigyô ni okeru gijutsu shimpo no jittai*, Tokyo, Tôyô Keizai Shimpôsha, 1960.

——, *Chûshô kigyô no hattatsu*, Tokyo, Tôyô Keizai Shimpôsha, 1962.

Ôyô Kagaku Kenkyûjo, *Ôyô kagaku kenkyûjo gojûnen shi*, Kyoto, Ôyô Kagaku Kenkyûjo, 1972.

Rikagaku Kenkyûjo, *Tokushu Hôjin Riken sanjûnen shi*, Tokyo, Rikagaku Kenkyûjo, 1988.

Saga Ken Shi Hensan Iinkai, *Saga Ken shi*, vol. 2, Saga, Saga Ken Shiryô Kankôkai, 1968.

Saigusa H., 'Nihon no chisei to gijutsu' (1939), in *Saigusa Hiroto chosakushû*, vol. 10, Tokyo, Chûô Kôronsha, 1973.

——, 'Gijutsu shi' (1940), in *Saigusa Hiroto chosakushû*, vol. 10, Tokyo, Chûô Kôronsha, 1973.

——, 'Gijutsu no shisô' (1941), in *Saigusa Hiroto chosakushû*, vol. 7, 1973.

Saitô S., *Shinkô kontserun Riken no kenkyû*, Tokyo, Jichôsha, 1987.

Saitô M., *Gijutsu kaihatsu ron: Nihon no gijutsu kaihatsu mekanizumu to seisaku*, Tokyo, Bunshindô, 1988.

Saitô O. and Tanimoto M., 'Zairai sangyô no saihensei', in Yamamoto Y. and Umemura M., eds, *Nihon keizaishi vol. 3: Kaikô to ishin*, Tokyo, Iwanami Shoten, 1989.

Sakaki Machi, *Tekunohâto Sakaki—Sakaki Machi kôgyô hattatsu shi*, Sakaki, Sakaki Machi, 1988.

Sangyô Kôzô Shingikai, *Sangyô kôzô no chôki bijion*, Tokyo, Tsûshô Sangyô Chôsakai, 1978.

Sasaki J., 'Kôgyô ni okeru gijutsu no hatten', in Sasaki J., ed., *Gijutsu no shakai shi*, vol. 2, Tokyo, Yûhikaku, 1983.

Segawa H., 'Tekunoporisu kôsô: Genkei to keii', in Miyamoto K., ed., *Kokusaika jidai no toshi to nôson*, Tokyo, Jichitai Kenkyû Sha, 1986.

Seki M. and Ishiro K., eds, *Chûshô kigyô no sentan gijutsu senryaku*, Tokyo, Shin Hyôron, 1991.

Sekida H., 'Tosa no kamisuki', in Chihôshi Kenkyû Kyôgikai, ed., *Nihon sangyôshi taikei: Chûgoku Shikoku chihô hen*, Tokyo, Tokyo Daigaku Shuppankai, 1960, 289–307.

Shiba R., *Kashin*, vols 1–3, Tokyo, Shinchôsha, 1976.

Shiga N., *Terebi o tsukutta hitotachi*, Tokyo, Nihon Kôgyô Shimbunsha, 1979.

Shimohirao I., *Gendai dentô sangyô no kenkyû*, Tokyo, Shin Hyôron, 1978.

——, *Gendai jiba sangyô ron*, Tokyo, Shin Hyôron, 1985.

Shiritsu Okaya Sanshi Hakubutsukan, *Okaya Sanshi Hakubutsukan*, Okaya, Shiritsu Okaya Sanshi Hankubutsukan, 1970.

Sugiyama S., 'Kokusai kankyô to gaikoku bôeki', in Yamamoto Y. and Umemura M., eds, *Nihon keizaishi 3: Kaikô to ishin*, Tokyo, Iwanami Shoten, 1989.

Sumita Y., *Arita: hakuji no machi*, Tokyo, Nihon Hôsô Shuppan Kyôkai, 1974.

Suwa Kyôiku Kai, *Suwa no kingendai shi*, Suwa, Suwa Kyôiku Kai, 1986.

Suzuki T., *Aru machi no kôgai monogatari*, Tokyo, Tôyô Keizai Shimpôsha, 1973.

Suzuta Y., 'Kindai ni okeru Arita yôgyô gijutsu no hensen', *Gijutsu to bunmei*, vol. 2, no. 1, 1985.

Tachikawa S., *Karakuri*, Tokyo, Kawade Shobô, 1987.

Takahashi K. and Furushima T., *Yôsangyô no hattatsu to jinushi seido*, Tokyo, Ochanomizu Shobô, 1958.

Takahashi Y., *Ayrton to sono shûhen: Kôbu Daigakkô oyatoi gaikokujin kyôshi ni tsuite no shiten*, Tokyo, Tokyo Nôkô Daigaku, 1989.

Tamura S., 'Gunbi kakuchô to heiki seisan', in Unno F., ed., *Gijutsu no shakaishi*, vol. 3, Tokyo, Yûhikaku, 1982.

Taniura T., *Ajia no kôgyôka to gijutsu iten*, Tokyo, Ajia Keizai Kenkyûjo, 1990.

Tashiro K., 'Tokugawa jidai no bôeki', in Hayami A. and Miyamoto M., eds, *Nihon keizai shi 1: Keizai shakai no seiritsu*, Tokyo, Iwanami Shoten, 1988.

Tasugi K., *Shitaukesei kôgyô ron*, Tokyo, Yûhikaku, 1941.

Teijin KK, *Teijin no ayumi*, vol. 1, Tokyo, Teijin KK, 1968.

Tokyo Kôgyô Shikenjô, *Tokyo Kôgyô Shikenjô gojûnen shi*, Tokyo, Tokyo Kôgyô Shikenjô, 1951.

Tokyo Shibaura Denki KK, *Tokyo Shibaura Denki Kabushiki Kaisha hachijû gonen shi*, Tokyo, Tokyo Shibaura Denki KK, 1963.

Tokyo Shibaura Denki KK Tsurumi Kenkyûjo, *Kenkyû 55-nen no ayumi*, Tokyo, Tokyo Shibaura Denki KK, 1961.

Tomita T., *Gijutsu ni kokkyô wa aru ka: Gijutsu iten to kikô fûdo shakai*, Tokyo, Daiyamondo Sha, 1991.

Toyama Ken, *Toyama Ken shi: Tsûshi hen*, vol. 7, Toyama, Toyama Ken, 1983.

Toyota Jidôsha Kôgyô KK, *Toyota Jidôsha sanjûnen shi*, Toyota City, Toyota Jidôsha Kôgyô KK, 1967.

Tsuneishi K., 'Kagakusha to sensô: Ishii butai to sono shakaiteki haikei', paper presented at the 5th National Conference of the Japanese Studies Association of Australia, Brisbane, 1987.

Tsunoyama Y., 'Inoue Den, Kagiya Kana: momengasuri no joseitachi', in Nagahara K. and Yamaguchi K., eds, *Kôza: Nihon gijutsu no shakaishi*, annex vol. 1, Tokyo, Nihon Hyôronsha, 1986, pp. 247–62.

Tsûsanshô Kikai Jôhô Sangyô Kyoku, ed., *Yutaka naru jôhôka shakai e no dôhyô: Sangyô kôzô shingikai jôhô sangyô bukai tôshin*, Tokyo, Kompyûta Êji Sha, 1981.

Uchida H., 'Kigyô nai gijutsusha soshiki no keiseiki: 1900–1910 nen gijutsushasû no tôkeiteki kenkyû kara', *Tokyo Keidaigakkai shi*, nos 109–110, 1978.

———, 'Gijutsu seisaku no rekishi', in Nakaoka T. et al., eds, *Kindai Nihon no gijutsu to gijutsu seisaku*, Tokyo, Kokusai Rengô Daigaku/Tokyo Daigaku Shuppankai, 1986,

———, 'Gijutsu iten', in Nishikawa S. and Abe T., eds, *Nihon keizaishi 4: Sangyô no jidai 2*, Tokyo, Iwanami Shoten, 1990.

Uchino A., *Nihon no kenkyû tôshi*, Tokyo, Jitsugyô Kôhôsha, 1962.

Uchû Kaihatsu Jigyôdan, *Jidai wa uchû e*, Tokyo, Uchû Kaihatsu Jigyôdan, 1989.

Uemura M., 'Nada shûzôgyô no hatten', *Shakai keizai shigaku*, vol. 55, no. 2, 1991, pp. 12–31.

Ueyama K., 'Kikai seishi no kakuritsu to sanshi gijutsu', in Unno F., ed., *Gijutsu no shakaishi*, vol. 3, Tokyo, Yûhikaku, 1982, p. 198.

Umetani N., *Oyatoi gaikokujin 1: Gaisetsu*, Tokyo, Kashima Kenkyûjo Shuppansha, 1968.

Unno F., 'Gairai to zairai', in Unno F., ed., *Gijutsu no shakaishi*, vol. 3, Tokyo, Yûhikaku, 1982.

——— and Abe M., 'Kaikoku to nôgyô no henyô', in *Zusetsu Nihon bunka no rekishi*, vol. 10, Tokyo, Shôgakukan, 1980.

Urawa S., *Renpô keiei no kokusaika o susumeru Matsushita Denki*, Tokyo, Asahi Sonomrama, 1981.

Waseda Daigaku Keizaishi Gakkai, *Ashikaga orimono shi*, vol. 1, Ashikaga, Ashikaga Seni Dôgyôkai, 1960.

Yabuuchi K., ed., *Tenkô Kaibutsu*, Tokyo, Heibonsha, 1969.

———, *Chûgoku no kagaku to Nihon*, Tokyo, Asahi Shimbunsha, 1972.

———, *Kagaku shi kara mita Chûgoku bunmei*, Tokyo, Nihon Hôsô Shuppan Kyôkai, 1982.

Yamada S., 'Nihonshu no rekishi', *Nihon hatsugen*, vol. 7, 1979.

Yamagata Ken Kôgyô Gijutsu Sentâ, *Yamagata Ken Kôgyô Shikenjô rokujûnen shi*, Yamagata, Yamagata Ken Kôgyô Gijutsu Sentâ, 1977.

Yamamoto S., *Seishigyô kindaika no kenkyû*, Maebashi, Gumma Ken bunka jigyô shinkôkai, 1975.

Yamazaki T., *Gijutsushi*, Tokyo, Tôyô Keizai Shimpôsha, 1961.
Yokoi T., *Daigo sedai kompyûta: Jinkô chinô e no kakehashi*, Tokyo, Ômu Sha, 1985.
Yoshida M., *Nihon gijutsushi kenkyû*, Tokyo, Gakugei Shuppansha, 1961.
——, *Bankoku hakurankai: gijutsu bunmeishiteki ni*, Tokyo, Nihon Hôsô Shuppan Kyôkai, 1970.
——, *Gijutsu to Nihon kindaika*, Tokyo, Nihon Hôsô Shuppan Kyôkai, 1977.
Yoshimura J., 'Bakuhansei shakai to hatasaku gijutsu', in Sasaki J., ed., *Gijutsu no shakaishi*, vol. 2, Tokyo, Yûhikaku, 1983.
Yoshioka H., *Kagaku bunmei no bôsô katei*, Tokyo, Kaimeisha, 1991.
Yui T., *Chûshô kigyô seisaku no shiteki kenkyû*, Tokyo, Tôyô Keizai Shimpôsha, 1964.
Yunoki M., *Nihon no gijutsu 3: Nihonshu*, Tokyo, Daiichi Hôki Shuppan, 1988.
——, 'Nihon ni okeru shûzôgyô no hatten', *Shakai keizai shigaku*, vol. 55, no. 2, 1991.

Material in Western Languages

Anchordoguy, M., *Computers Inc.: Japan's Challenge to IBM*, Cambridge Mass., Harvard University Press, 1989.
Anderson, A., *Science and Technology in Japan*, London, Longman, 1984.
Awanohara, S., 'Look East: The Japan Model', *Asian-Pacific Economic Literature*, vol. 1, no. 1, 1987.
Bartholomew, J. R., *The Formation of Science in Japan*, New Haven and London, Yale University Press, 1989.
Beasley, W.G., *The Rise of Modern Japan*, London, Weidenfeld and Nicolson, 1990.
Bolle, J., *Der Seidenbau in Japan*, Budapest, A. Hartleben's Verlag, 1898.
Bonafous, M., ed., *Yo-San-Fi-Rok: L'Art d'Elever les Vers à Soie au Japon par Ouekaki-Morikouni*, trans. J. Hoffman, Paris, Imprimerie et Librarie de Madame Veuve Bouchard-Huzard, 1848.
Bowen, R., *Rebellion and Democracy in Meiji Japan*, Berkeley, University of California Press, 1986.
Bray, F., *The Rice Economies: Technology and Development in Asian Societies*, Oxford, Basil Blackwell, 1986.
Brock, M.V., *Biotechnology in Japan*, London and New York, Routledge, 1989.
Browa, H., and Wolff, H., *Forschungs- und Technologiepolitik, Forschungs- und Entwicklungssystem in Japan (Abschlussbericht)*, Basel, Prognos AG, 1983.
Burks, A.W., 'The West's Inreach: The Oyatoi Gaikokujin', and 'Japan's Outreach: The Ryûgakusei', in Ardath W. Burks, ed., *The Modernisers: Overseas Students, Foreign Employees and Meiji Japan*, Boulder and London, Westview Press, 1985.
Checkland, O., and Checkland, S., 'British and Japanese Economic Interaction under the Early Meiji: The Takashima Coal Mine 1868–88,' *Business History*, vol. 26, no. 2, 1984.
Chida, T., and Davies, Peter N., *The Japanese Shipping and Shipbuilding Industries: A History of their Modern Growth*, London, Athlone Press, 1990.
Christopher, R., *The Japanese Mind: The Goliath Explained*, New York, Linden Press/Simon and Schuster, 1983.
Clark, R., *The Japanese Company*, New Haven and London, Yale University Press, 1979.
Coaldrake, W.H., *The Way of the Carpenter*, New York and Tokyo, Weatherhill, 1990.

Commission on the History of Science and Technology Policy, ed., *Historical Review of Japanese Science and Technology Policy*, Tokyo, Science and Technology Agency, 1991.

Coombs, R., et al., *Economics and Technological Change*, London, Macmillan, 1987.

Covell, J.C., and Covell, A., *Korean Impact on Japanese Culture: Japan's Hidden History*, Elizabeth NJ, Hollym International Corp., 1984.

Cusumano, M., *The Japanese Automobile Industry: Technology and Management at Nissan and Toyota*, Cambridge Mass. and London, Harvard University Press, 1989.

Deming, W.E., *Quality, Productivity and Competitive Position*, Cambridge Mass., MIT Center for Advanced Engineering Study, 1982.

Denison, E.F., and Chung W. K., 'Economic Growth and its Sources', in H. Patrick and H. Rosovsky, eds., *Asia's New Giant: How the Japanese Economy Works*, Washington DC, Brookings Institution, 1976.

Dietrich, W.S., *In the Shadow of the Rising Sun: The Political Roots of American Economic Decline*, University Park, University of Pennsylvania Press, 1991.

Dore, R.P., *Shinohata: A Portrait of a Japanese Village*, London, Allen Lane, 1978.

Duseigneur, E., *La Maladie des Vers à Soie et le Japon*, Société Imperiale d'Agriculture, d'Histoire Naturelle et des Arts Utiles de Lyon, 1866.

Dyer, H., *The Evolution of Industry*, London, Macmillan, 1895.

Emmanuel, A., *Appropriate or Underdeveloped Technology?*, New York, John Wiley, 1982.

ESCAP/UNCTC Joint Unit on Transnational Corporations, *Technology Acquisition Under Alternative Arrangements with Transnational Corporations: Selected Industrial Case Studies in Thailand*, New York, United Nations, 1987.

Fabayo, A., and Gatugata, L.G., *Technology Transfer and Industrialisation in the Developing Countries: Some Lessons from Japan*, Tokyo, International Development Centre of Japan, 1984.

Fagerberg, J., 'A Technology Gap Approach to Why Growth Rates Differ', *Research Policy*, vol. 16, nos. 2–4, 1987.

Francks, P., *Technology and Agricultural Development in Pre-War Japan*, Yale, Yale University Press, 1984.

Freeman, C., *Technology Policy and Economy Performance: Lessons from Japan*, London and New York, Pinter Publishers, 1987.

—— , ed., *The Economics of Innovation*, London, Edward Elgar Publishing, 1990.

Feigenbaum, E.A., and McCorduck, P., *The Fifth Generation: Artificial Intelligence and Japan's Computer Challenge to the World*, London, Michael Joseph, 1990.

Friedman, D., *The Misunderstood Miracle: Industrial Development and Political Change in Japan*, Ithaca and London, Cornell University Press, 1988.

Fruin, M., *Kikkoman: Company, Clan and Community*, Cambridge Mass. and London, Harvard University Press, 1983.

Fujita N., 'Ties Between Foreign Makers and Zaibatsu Enterprises in Prewar Japan: The Case of Mitsubishi Oil Co. and Mitsubishi Electric Manufacturing', in Yuzawa T. and Udagawa M., eds, *Foreign Business in Japan Before World War II*, Tokyo, Tokyo University Press, 1990.

Fukuzawa Y., *The Autobiography of Fukuzawa Yukichi*, trans. E. Kiyooka, New York and London, Columbia University Press, 1966.

Gamota, G., and Friedman, W., *Gaining Ground: Japan's Strides in Science and Technology*, Cambridge Mass., Ballinger, 1988.

Gille, B., ed., *The History of Techniques*, vol. 1, trans. P. Southgate and T. Williamson, New York, Gordon and Breach, 1986.

Godden, G.A., *Oriental Export Market Porcelain and its Influence on European Wares*, London and New York, Granada, 1979.

Goodman, G.K., *Japan: The Dutch Experience*, London, Athlone Press, 1986.

Gordon, A., *The Evolution of Labour Relations in Japan: Heavy Industry 1853–1955*, Cambridge Mass. and London, Harvard University Press, 1985.

Graff, H., *The Legacies of Literacy: Continuities and Contradictions in Western Culture and Society*, Bloomington and Indianapolis, Indiana University Press, 1987.

Gregory, G., *Japanese Electronics Technology: Enterprise and Innovation*, Chichester and New York, John Wiley and Sons, 1985.

Hane, M., *Peasants, Rebels and Outcastes: the Underside of Modern Japan*, New York, Pantheon Books, 1982.

Hayashi T., *The Japanese Experience in Technology: From Transfer to Self-Reliance*, Tokyo, United Nations University, 1990.

Heidegger, M., *The Question Concerning Technology and Other Essays*, trans. W. Lovitt, New York, Harper and Row, 1977.

Hidaka R., *The Price of Affluence: Dilemmas of Contemporary Japan*, trans. G. McCormack, Melbourne, Penguin Australia, 1985.

Hill, S., *The Tragedy of Technology: Human Liberation Versus Domination in the Late Twentieth Century*, London, Pluto Press, 1988.

Hoshino, Y., 'On Concepts of Technology', in S. Nakayama, D.L. Swain and E. Yagi, eds, *Science and Society in Modern Japan: Selected Historical Sources*, Cambridge Mass., MIT Press, 1974.

——, 'Japan's Post-Second World War Environmental Pollution', in Ui J., ed., *Industrial Pollution in Japan*, Tokyo, United Nations University, 1992,

Ihara S., *The Japanese Family Storehouse*, trans. G. W. Sargent, Cambridge, Cambridge University Press, 1959.

Imai K., 'Japan's Industrial Policy for High Technology Industry', in H. Patrick, and L. Meissner, eds, *Japan's High Technology Industries: Lessons and Limitations of Industrial Policy*, Seattle and Tokyo, University of Washington Press/ University of Tokyo Press, 1986.

Industrial Research Laboratory, *The Industrial Laboratory*, Tokyo, Industrial Research Laboratory, 1909.

Inkster, I., *Science and Technology in History: An Approach to Industrial Development*, London, Macmillan, 1991.

Institute for Future Technology, *Future Technology in Japan*, Tokyo, Institute for Future Technology, 1988.

Inukai, I., and Tussing, A. R., 'Kôgyô Iken: Japan's Ten Year Plan, 1884.' *Economic Development and Cultural Change*, vol. 16, no. 1, 1967.

Ishizuki M., 'Overseas Study by Japanese in the Early Meiji Period', in A.W. Burks, ed., *The Modernisers: Overseas Students, Foreign Employees, and Meiji Japan*, Boulder and London, Westview Press, 1985.

Itakura K., and Yagi E., 'The Japanese Reseach System and the Establishment of the Institute of Physical and Chemical Research', in S. Nakayama, D.L. Swain, and E. Yagi, eds, *Science and Society in Modern Japan: Selected Historical Sources*, Cambridge Mass., MIT Press, 1974.

Jacomy, B., *Une Histoire des Techniques*, Paris, Editions du Seuil, 1990.

Johnson, C., *MITI and the Japanese Miracle: the Growth of Industrial Policy 1925–75*, Stanford Cal., Stanford University Press, 1982.

Johnson, L.L., *Development of High Definition Television*, Washington DC, RAND Corporation, 1990.

Johnson-Freese, J., et al., 'Return from Orbit: Economics as a Driver of Japanese Space Policy', *Technology in Society*, no. 14, 1992.

Jones, S., 'Scholar, Scientist, Popular Author: Hiraga Gennai, 1728–1780', Unpublished Ph.D. thesis, Columbia University, 1968.

Jones, H.J., *Live Machines: Hired Foreigners and Meiji Japan*, Tenterden, Paul Norbury Publications, 1980.

——, 'The Griffis Thesis and Meiji Policy Towards Hired Foreigners', in A.W. Burks, ed., *The Modernisers: Overseas Students, Foreign Employees and Meiji Japan*, Boulder and London, Westview Press, 1985.

Jones, K., *Politics vs. Economics in World Steel Trade*, London, Allen and Unwin, 1986.

Kaldor, M., *The Baroque Arsenal*, London, Deutsch, 1982.

Keizai Kôhô Center, *Japan: An International Comparison*, Tokyo, Keizai Kôhô Center, 1983.

Kevenhörster, P., et al., *Forschungs- und Technologiepolitik, Forschungs- und Entwicklungssystem in Japan*, Untersuchungsteil 4, Basel, Prognos AG, 1983.

Kinzley, W.D., *Industrial Harmony in Modern Japan: The Invention of a Tradition*, London and New York, Routledge, 1991.

Kitaya Y., 'The Age of Holonic Management', *Japan Echo*, vol. 13, special issue, 1986.

Kodama F., *Analysing Japanese High Technologies: the Techno-Paradigm Shift*, London and New York, Pinter Publishers, 1991.

Komai H., *Japanese Management Overseas: Experiences in the United States and Thailand*, Tokyo, Asian Productivity Organisation, 1989.

Kudo A., 'The Tripartite Pact and Synthetic Oil: The Ideal and Reality of Economic and Technical Cooperation Between Japan and Germany', *Annals of the Institute of Social Science*, Tokyo University, no. 33, 1992.

Lamarre, C., and de Fontpertuis, F., 'Le Japon', in C. Lamarre, and F. de Fontpertuis, eds, *Les Pays Etrangers et l'Exposition de 1878: La Chine et le Japon*, Paris, Librarie Ch. Delagrave, 1878.

Lidin, O.G., *The Life of Ogyû Sorai*, Lund, Scandinavian Institute of Asian Studies, 1973.

Low, M., 'Japan's Secret War? "Instant" Scientific Manpower and Japan's World War II Atomic Bomb Project,' *Annals of Science*, no. 47, 1990.

——, 'Towards a Gendered Approach to Teaching About the History of Japanese Science and Technology,' in V. Mackie, ed., *Gendering Japanese Studies*, Melbourne, Japanese Studies Centre, 1992.

——, and Yoshioka, H., 'Buying the "Peaceful Atom": The Development of Nuclear Power in Japan', *Historia Scientiarum*, no. 38, 1989.

Lynn, L.H., *How Japan Innovates: A Comparison with the US in the Case of Oxygen Steelmaking*, Boulder Col., Westview Press, 1982.

Lull, J., *China Turned On: Television, Reform and Resistance*, London and New York, Routledge, 1991.

MacFarlane, C., *Japan: An Account, Geographical and Historical*, London, George Routledge and Co., 1852.

Mackenzie, D., and Wajcman, J., *The Social Shaping of Technology: How the Refrigerator Got its Hum*, Milton Keynes and Philadelphia, Open University Press, 1985.

Macreavy, S.E., *Guide to Science and Technology in the UK*, London, Francis Hodgeson, 1971.

Maës, H., *Hiraga Gennai et son Temps*, Paris, Ecole Française d'Extrême Orient, 1970.

Maruyama M., *Studies in the Intellectual History of Tokugawa Japan*, trans. M. Hane, Tokyo, Tokyo University Press, 1974.

McMaster, J., 'The Takashima Mine: British Capital and Japanese Industrialisation', *Business History Review*, vol. 37, no. 3, 1963.

McMillan, C.J., *The Japanese Industrial System*, Berlin and New York, Walter de Gruyter, 1985.

Merson, J., *Roads to Xanadu: East and West in the Making of the Modern World*, Sydney, Child and Associates/ABC Books, 1989.

Minami R., 'The Introduction of Electric Power and Its Impact on the Manufacturing Industries: With Special Reference to Smaller Scale Plants', in H. Patrick and L. Meissner, eds, *Japanese Industrialisation and its Social Consequences*, Berkeley, Los Angeles and London, University of California Press, 1976.

——, *The Economic Development of Japan: A Quantitative Study*, London, Macmillan, 1986.

Mitcham, Carl, 'Philosophy of Technology', in P.T. Durbin, ed., *A Guide to the Culture of Science, Technology and Medicine*, New York, Free Press, 1980.

Mokyr, J., *The Lever of Riches: Technological Creativity and Economic Progress*, Oxford, Oxford University Press, 1990.

Moloney, B., *Technology and Investment: the Prewar Japanese Chemical Industry*, Cambridge Mass., Harvard University Press, 1990.

Morishima M., *Why Has Japan 'Succeeded'? Western Technology and the Japanese Ethos*, Cambridge, Cambridge University Press, 1982.

Morris, I., ed., *Modern Japanese Stories*, London, Eyre and Spottiswood, 1961.

Morris-Suzuki, T., *A History of Japanese Economic Thought*, London and New York, Routledge, 1989.

Murakami Y., 'Ie Society as a Pattern of Civilization', *Journal of Japanese Studies*, vol. 10, no. 2, 1984.

——, 'Technology in Transition: Two Perspectives on Industrial Policy', in H. Patrick, and L. Meissner, eds. *Japan's High Technology Industries: Lessons and Limitations of Industrial Policy*, Seattle and Tokyo, University of Washington Press/University of Tokyo Press, 1986.

Muraoka K. and Okamura K., *Folk Arts and Crafts of Japan*, New York and Tokyo, Weatherhill/Heibonsha, 1973.

Musée Nationale des Techniques, *L'Aventure du Mètre*, Paris, Musée Nationale des Techniques, 1989.

Nakamura T., *The Postwar Japanese Economy: Its Development and Structure*, trans. J. Kaminsky, Tokyo, University of Tokyo Press, 1981.

——, *Economic Growth in Prewar Japan*, trans. R. A. Feldman, New Haven and London, Yale University Press, 1983.

Nakaoka T., 'The Role of Domestic Technical Innovation in Foreign Technology Transfer', *Osaka City University Economic Review*, vol. 18, 1982.

——, 'On Technological Leaps of Japan as a Developing Country', *Osaka City University Economic Review*, vol. 22, 1987.

——, 'The Transfer of Cotton Manufacturing Technology from Britain to Japan', in D.J. Jeremy, ed., *International Technology Transfer: Europe, Japan and the USA, 1700–1914*, London, Edward Elgar, 1991.

Nakayama, S., *Characteristics of Scientific Development in Japan*, New Delhi, Centre for the Study of Science, Technology and Development, 1977.

——, 'Science and Technology in Modern Japanese Development', in W. Beranek, and G. Ranis, eds, *Science, Technology and Economic Development: A Historical and Comparative Study*, New York and London, Praeger Publishers, 1978.

———, *Science, Technology and Society in Postwar Japan*, London and New York, Kegan Paul International, 1991.

Nelson, R.R., 'Acquiring Technology', in H. Soesastro, and M. Pangestu, eds, *Technological Challenge in the Asia-Pacific Economy*, Sydney and London, Allen and Unwin, 1990,

Noble, D.F., *America By Design: Science, Technology and the Rise of Corporate Capitalism*, Oxford and New York, Oxford University Press, 1977.

Noble, D., 'Social Choice in Machine Design: The Case of Automatically Controlled Machine Tools', in D. MacKenzie, and J. Wajcman, eds, *The Social Shaping of Technology: How the Refrigerator Got its Hum*, Milton Keynes and Philadelphia, Open University Press, 1983,

Ôe K., 'Japan's Dual Identity: A Writer's Dilemma', in M. Miyoshi and H.D. Haroootunian, eds, *Postmodernism and Japan*, Durham NC and London, Duke University Press, 1989.

Ohkawa, K., and Ranis, G., *Japan and the Developing Countries: A Comparative Analysis*, London, Basil Blackwell, 1985.

Oka K., 'Society for the Study of Materialism: Yuiken', in S. Nakayama, D.L. Swain, and E. Yagi, eds, *Science and Society in Modern Japan: Selected Historical Sources*, Cambridge Mass., MIT Press, 1974.

Okamoto A., 'Creative and Innovative Research at RICOH', *Long Range Planning*, vol. 24, no. 5, 1991.

Okimoto D.I., *Between MITI and the Market: Japanese Industrial Policy for High Technology*, Stanford, Stanford University Press, 1989.

Okita S., *The Developing Countries and Japan: Lessons in Growth*, Tokyo, Tokyo University Press, 1980.

Organisation for Economic Cooperation and Development, *The Overall Level and Structure of R&D Efforts in OECD Member Countries*, Paris, Organisation for Economic Cooperation and Development, 1967.

Otsuka, K., Ranis, G., and Saxonhouse, G., *Comparative Technology Choice in Development: the Indian and Japanese Cotton Textile Industries*, London, Macmillan, 1988.

Oya S., 'Reflections on the History of Science in Japan', in S. Nakayama, D.L. Swain, and E. Yagi, ed., *Science and Society in Modern Japan: Selected Historical Sources*, Cambridge Mass., MIT Press, 1974.

Ozawa T., *Japan's Technological Challenge to the West, 1960–1974: Motivation and Accomplishment*, Cambridge Mass. and London, MIT Press, 1974.

Pacey, A., *Technology in World Civilization: A Thousand-year History*, Oxford, Basil Blackwell, 1990.

Pasteur, L., *Etudes sur la Maladie des Vers à Soie*, vols 1–2, Paris, Gauthier-Villars, 1870.

Pauer, E., 'The Years Economic Historians Lost: Japan, 1850–1890', *Japan Forum*, vol. 3, no. 1, 1991.

Peck, M.J. and Tamura, S., 'Technology', in H. Patrick, and H. Rosovsky, eds, *Asia's New Giant: How the Japanese Economy Works*, Washington DC, Brookings Institution, 1976.

Phillips, G.O., and Hughes, M., *Innovation and Technology Transfer in Japan and Europe*, London and New York, Routledge, 1989.

Prestowitz, C., *Trading Places: How We Allowed Japan to Take the Lead*, New York, Basic Books, 1988.

Reed, S.R., *Japanese Prefectures and Policymaking*, Pittsburg, University of Pittsburg Press, 1986.

Rimmer, P., *Rikisha to Rapid Transit: Urban Public Transport Systems and Policy in Southeast Asia*, Sydney, Pergamon Press, 1986.

Roberts, J.G., *Mitsui: Three Centuries of Japanese Business*, New York and Tokyo, Weatherhill, 1973.

Robertson Scott, J.W., *The Foundations of Japan*, London, John Murray, 1922.

Rondot, N., *L'Art de la Soie: Les Soies*, 2nd edn, Paris, Imprimerie National, 1885.

Rosenberg, N., and Birdzell, L. E., *How the West Grew Rich: The Economic Transformation of the Industrial World*, New York, Basic Books, 1986.

de Rosny, L., ed., *Traité de l'Education des Vers à Soie au Japon par Sirakawa*, Paris, Maisonneuve et Cie., 1868.

Russell, J.G., 'Narratives of Denial: Racial Chauvinism and the Black Other in Japan', *Japan Quarterly*, vol. 37, no. 4, 1991.

Sakata Y., 'The Beginning of Modernisation in Japan', in A.W. Burks, ed., *The Modernisers: Overseas Students, Foreign Employees, and Meiji Japan*, Boulder and London, Westview Press, 1985.

Sasaki J., *Endogenous Technology in Japan*, Tokyo, United Nations University, 1981.

Sasaki M., 'Japan, Australia and the Multifunctionpolis', in G. McCormack, ed., *Bonsai Australia Banzai: Multifunctionpolis and the Making of a Special Relationship with Japan*, Sydney, Pluto Press, 1981.

Saxonhouse, G., 'A Tale of Technological Diffusion in the Meiji Period', *Journal of Economic History*, vol. 34, 1974.

Schodt, F.L., *Inside the Robot Kingdom: Japan, Mechatronics and the Coming Robotopia*, Tokyo and New York, Kodansha International, 1988.

Shoji K. and Sugai M., 'The Ashio Copper Mine Pollution Case: The Origins of Environmental Destruction', in Ui J., ed., *Industrial Pollution in Japan*, Tokyo, United Nations University, 1992.

Schwartz Cowan, R., *More Work for Mother: The Ironies of Household Technology from the Open Hearth to the Microwave*, New York, Basic Books, 1983.

Smith, R.J., and Wiswell, E.L., *The Women of Suye Mura*, Chicago, University of Chicago, 1982.

Smith, T.C., *The Agrarian Origins of Modern Japan*, Stanford, Stanford University Press, 1959.

——, *Native Sources of Japanese Industrialisation, 1750–1920*, Berkeley and Los Angeles, University of California Press, 1988.

——, *Political Change and Industrial Development in Japan, 1868–1880*, 2nd edn, Stanford, Stanford University Press, 1965.

Sörbom, P., 'The Reception of Western Technology in China and Japan', in E. Baark, and A. Jamison eds, *Technological Development in China, India and Japan*, London, Macmillan, 1986.

Stevens, C., 'Ishimure Michiko's 'The Boy Yamanaka Kuhei'', in E.P. Tsurumi, ed., *The Other Japan: Postwar Realities*, Armonk NY, M. E. Sharpe, 1988,

Storry, R., *A History of Modern Japan*, London, Penguin Books, 1972.

Sugimoto, M., and Swain, D.L., *Science and Culture in Traditional Japan*, Rutland Vt and Tokyo, Charles E. Tuttle, 1989.

Sugiyama S., 'Thomas B. Glover: A British Merchant in Japan, 1861–70', *Business History*, vol. 26, no. 2, 1984.

Sun E.-T.Z. and Sun S.-C., eds, *T'ien-Kung K'ai-Wu: Chinese Technology in the Seventeenth Century*, University Park and London, Pennsylvania State University Press, 1966.

Taketani, M., 'Methodological Approaches in the Development of the Meson Theory of Yukawa in Japan', in S. Nakayama, D.L. Swain and E. Yagi, eds,

Science and Society in Modern Japan: Selected Historical Sources, Cambridge Mass., MIT Press, 1974.

Tamura S. and Urata S., 'Technology Policy in Japan', in H. Soesastro and M. Pangestu, eds, *Technological Challenge in the Asia-Pacific Economy*, Sydney and London, Allen and Unwin, 1990.

Tanaka Y., 'Nuclear Power Plant Gypsies in High-Tech Society', in E.P. Tsurumi, ed., *The Other Japan: Postwar Realities*, Armonk NY, M. E. Sharpe, 1988.

Tatsuno, S.M., *Created in Japan: From Imitators to World-Class Innovators*, Grand Rapids, San Francisco and London, Ballinger, 1990.

Toke, D., *Green Energy: A Non-Nuclear Response to the Greenhouse Effect*, London, Greenprint, 1991.

Tokunaga S., ed., *Japan's Foreign Investment and Asian Economic Interdependence: Production, Trade and Financial Systems*, Tokyo, University of Tokyo Press, 1992.

Tolchin, M., and Tolchin, S.J., *Selling our Security: The Erosion of America's Assets*, New York, Alfred A. Knopf, 1992.

Toyoda E., *Toyota: Fifty Years in Motion*, Tokyo and New York, Kodansha International, 1985.

Tsurumi, E. P., *Factory Girls: Women in the Thread Mills of Meiji Japan*, Princeton, Princeton University Press, 1990.

Uchida H., 'Western Big Business and the Adoption of New Technology in Japan: The Electrical Equipment and Chemical Industries, 1890–1920', in A. Okochi, and H. Uchida eds, *The Development and Diffusion of Technology: Electrical and Chemical Industries*, Tokyo, Tokyo University Press, 1980.

Ui J., 'A Critique of Industrialisation', *Japan Quarterly*, vol. 23, no. 1, 1976.

——, 'Minamata Disease', in J. Ui, ed., *Industrial Pollution in Japan*, Tokyo, United Nations University, 1992.

Umegaki M., 'From Domain to Prefecture', in M. B. Jansen, and G. Rozman, eds, *Japan in Transition: From Tokugawa to Meiji*, Princeton NJ, Princeton University Press, 1986.

Unger, J.M., *The Fifth Generation Fallacy: Why Japan is Betting its Future on Artificial Intelligence*, Oxford and New York, Oxford University Press, 1987.

United States Department of State, *A New Era in World Affairs: Selected Speeches and Statements of President Truman January 20 to August 29, 1949*, Washington DC, Office of Public Affairs, 1949.

United States Senate, *Japanese Space Industry: An American Challenge*, Hearing before the Subcommittee on Foreign Commerce and Tourism of the Committee on Science and Transportation, Washington DC, US Government Printing Office, 1989.

Weste, J., 'Salvation from Without: Mutual Security Assistance and the Military-Industrial Lobby in Post-War Japan', *Japan Forum*, vol. 4, no. 2, 1992.

Winner, L., *Autonomous Technology: Technics-out-of-Control as a Theme in Political Thought*, Cambridge Mass. and London, MIT Press, 1977.

Wuthnow, R., 'The Emergence of Modern Science and World System Theory', *Theory and Society*, vol. 8, 1979.

Yamamura K., 'Success Illgotten? The Role of Meiji Militarism in Japan's Technological Progress', *Journal of Economic History*, vol. 37, no. 1, 1977.

——, 'Japan's Deus Ex Machina: Western Technology in the 1920s', *Journal of Japanese Studies*, vol. 12, no. 1, 1986.

Yazaki T., *Social Change and the City in Japan*, San Francisco, Japan Publications Inc., 1968.

Yoshiki F., *How Japan's Metal Mining Industries Modernised*, Tokyo, United Nations University, 1980.

Yuzawa T., 'The Transfer of Railway Technologies from Britain to Japan, with Special Reference to Locomotive Manufacture', in D.J. Jeremy, ed., *International Technology Transfer: Europe, Japan and the USA, 1700–1914*, London, Edward Elgar, 1991.

Index

abacus (*soroban*), 17, 20–1
acetaldehyde, 115, 207
Agency of Industrial Science and
    Technology (Kôgyô Gijutsuschô; Kôgyô
    Gijutsuin), 165, 214, 216
agriculture: delegations to China and
    India, 75; development, 14; technology,
    75; tools, 30, 45
aircraft industry, 124–5, 152–3, 167
Ajinomoto, 118–19
Akabane machine works, 75, 88
Akai, 192
Akita, 29–30
'alternate residence' system, 28, 32–3
ammonia manufacture, 123
apprenticeship system, 20, 21, 100–1,
    120–1
Arita, 6–7, 30–1; introduction of chemical
    glazes to, 64–5; porcelain, 30–1, 57;
    produces insulators, 74, 133; technical
    college, 101
arithmetic, *see* mathematics
Army, 125, 135
Army Ministry, 124
arsenals, 79, 125, 134, 166
artificial silk, *see* synthetic textiles
Asano Ôsuke, 82
Ashio, 43, 75
Association for Developing Production
    (Kaisan Sha), 91
automata (*karakuri ningyô*), 14, 26, 52–3
automatic loom, 117–18; *see also* Jacquard
    automatic loom
automation, 200–2, 212, 225
automobile industry, 119, 124, 146, 168,
    197; *see also* rikisha

backstrap loom (*izaribata*), 21
bellows, 47, 48, 61
Benkichi, 53

Bessemer process, 45, 126
Besshi, 43, 44–5, 75
biological weapons, 156
biotechnology, 228
blast furnace, 59, 61
booksellers, 33
borrowing, 2, 5; from Korea and from
    China, 17–18; of suggestion system from
    US firms, 128; *see also* imitation; imports;
    technology
broadcasting, 194–5
Bureau of Resources, 138
'business groups' (*kigyô shûdan*), 164, 191

calendar, 84
cannons, 57–9
carpentry, 51–2; tools, 52
cartels, 88, 134, 139
cash crops, 21, 28–9, 45
centre and periphery, 5–9, 103–4, 182
ceramics industry, 6, 25, 30–1, 74, 228;
    chemical glazes, 65; coal-fired kilns and
    mechanical wheels, 131; experimental
    centre, 92–3; making electrical
    components, 133
chemical industry, 114–15, 116, 123, 147,
    169, 179, 207
chemical weapons, 154, 156
Chikuma, *see* Nagano
China: books from, 17, 33; import of
    cotton from, 42; influence of, 17, 24, 25;
    Japanese ventures in, 117; pottery, 93;
    silkworkers from, 18; technicians from,
    66; techniques from, 16, 50, 66; trade
    with, 18; war with, 147, 156
Chôshû, 66, 71–2
clocks, 14, 26, 52, 83–4; introduction of
    mechanical clock by Francis Xavier, 52
'closed country' (*sakoku*) policy, 15–19,
    32–3, 35, 56

293